Practical Teaching

A Guide to Teaching in the Education and Training Sector

Linda Wilson

Australia • Brazil • Japan • Korea • Mexico • Singapore • Spain • United Kingdom • United States

Practical Teaching: A Guide to Teaching in the Education and Training Sector, Second Edition

Linda Wilson

Publishing Director: Linden Harris

Commissioning Editor: Lucy Mills

Development Editor: Claire Napoli

Development Editor: Lauren Darby

Production Editor: Beverley Copland

Manufacturing Buyer: Elaine Willis

Typesetter: MPS Limited

Cover design: Adam Renvoize

For product information and technology assistance, contact: **emea.info@cengage.com**.

For permission to use material from this text or product, and for permission queries, email emea.permissions@cengage.com.

British Library Cataloguing-in-Publication Data
A catalogue record for this book is available from the British Library.

ISBN: 978-1-4080-7602-6

Cengage Learning EMEA
Cheriton House, North Way, Andover, Hampshire, SP10 5BE, United Kingdom

Cengage Learning products are represented in Canada by Nelson Education Ltd.

For your lifelong learning solutions, visit **www.cengage.co.uk**

Purchase your next print book, e-book or e-chapter at **www.cengagebrain.com**

Printed in China by RR Donnelley
1 2 3 4 5 6 7 8 9 10–16 15 14

Brief contents

Contents

Part Seven Principles and theories

About this book

The book is intended for and written in a style to help those who are embarking on their teaching career, gaining a teaching qualification or working towards Qualified Teacher Learning and Skills (QTLS). It is meant to be informative and user-friendly; it balances the practical aspects of the job, with the reasons why (the theory). Many of the examples are from things I have seen or recommendations I have made to student teachers. The theory relates to current thinking and policy.

Written to coincide with the new teaching qualifications, it will be useful to those completing the Award, Certificate or Diploma in Education and Training, the Cert Ed or PGCE or the former qualifications of PTLLS, CTLLS and DTLLS.

Remember, teaching can be an art or a science; what works in one situation may not work in others. So try things out, go with what feels right and be confident to accept that not every lesson will be brilliant. The important factor must always be the learner's experience.

The book is split into nine main parts relating to core units in the Education and Training qualifications; each part of the book is sub-divided into chapters which relate to topics within the Units of Assessment. A mapping document guides the reader to the links between the parts, chapters and qualification units.

Throughout your qualification you are required to show evidence of how you are meeting the minimum core of literacy, language, numeracy and information communication technologies (ICT). These are collated and presented together in Part 9 with some teaching-related activities to support your development.

The text and activities contained in this publication are to support your studies, but it is intended that attendance of a relevant programme of study is the primary tool to learn your craft.

Terms of reference

Learner refers to the student, trainee, candidate, delegate, apprentice, pupil.

Teacher refers to the lecturer, tutor, trainer, instructor, coach, assessor.

Session refers to the lesson, training activity, class, lecture, tutorial, seminar.

Environment refers to the classroom, workshop, lecture theatre, workplace, shop floor.

Introduction

I came into education in 1984 as a variable hours lecturer, trying to balance a career with being a mum with two toddlers. My previous career as a caterer meant that long and unsociable hours made things like childcare and a social life difficult.

At first, I taught on a Friday afternoon. In those days, full-time staff were not around on a Friday afternoon and following my induction – 'you're in room P55 with the chefs', I learnt quickly to think on my feet and that the only information that I would receive would be that which I acquired for myself.

Anyway, I survived, and despite the endless hours of preparation (nobody told me about that!) I realised that I actually liked teaching. A few more hours appeared and by the end of that first year, I was teaching 12 hours per week. The groups weren't the easiest; I'm sure they were the ones nobody wanted, but that was how it was then.

I did my teaching qualifications over the next few years. That was also a culture shock. I'd done nothing since my own full-time education and so I found studying challenging, sometimes confusing and generally time consuming. I had never had to do anything that academic before, but fortunately the group I studied with were helpful and together we got through. I've since had to do further Master's level qualifications, which I found hard, but looking back now they really helped me to develop myself.

Changes in staff and the way FE was delivered enabled me to secure a full-time position. I still loved the job and was eager to get more responsibility and a better personal profile. Catering was one of the first subjects to go down the NVQ route. This meant that I started getting involved with employers because they needed to become workplace assessors. I'd done a Train the Trainer course when I had a 'real' job, so naturally took up this initiative. As this new curriculum strategy started running through other vocational qualifications my role changed to training employers and staff. I also got involved with initial teacher training and I just became totally absorbed in teaching.

Towards the end of my career I held a number of management posts and became involved in quality and curriculum management, CPD and the management of staff performance.

I have now done my time in Further Education and work as a Training Consultant, supporting staff in the Education and Training Sector.

Teaching is difficult, frustrating, funny, bureaucratic and rewarding. I hope that this book will help new teachers to cope with the skills required of the job, find a user-friendly route through their teaching qualifications and develop into fine professionals.

Linda Wilson

Acknowledgements

This book is dedicated to all of the teacher training students I have tutored and the staff I have coached and mentored through their personal development. I know that at times I have been hard, and sometimes told you things you didn't really want to hear, but, you got there and I am privileged to have been part of that process.

To all the people I have observed as part of my various roles, you have given me some wonderful ideas and made me a better teacher. I've seen some things I wouldn't do, but …

To my former team at South Staffordshire College for their encouragement, opinions and suggestions and for trialling the exercises. To Bradley, for some brilliant ideas and advice.

To Claire Hart for her patience, staff at Cengage Learning and the reviewers for their feedback. To Jon and LSIS staff for sight of the new qualification frameworks.

And finally, to my partner John, for his endless proofreading and commentary – and for borrowing the office!

Credit list

CREDITS

Although every effort has been made to contact copyright holders before publication, this has not always been possible. If notified, the publisher will undertake to rectify any errors or omissions at the earliest opportunity.

Photos

The publishers would like to thank the following sources for permission to reproduce their copyright protected images:

Shutterstock – pp 3 (Sam72), 19 (Monkey Business Images), 28 (Ivelin Radkov), 34 (Lisa F. Young), 43 (Monkey Business Images), 49 (Zurijeta), 60 (auremar), 63 (Goodluz), 78 (Robert Kneschke), 90 (auremar), 113 (Goodluz), 124 (Ermolaev Alexander), 129 (J. Henning Buchholz), 135 (Lisa F. Young), 143 (Monkey Business Images), 148 (wavebreakmedia), 160 (Rikard Stadler), 164 (Goodluz), 187 (Robert Kneschke), 209 (ene), 218 (Constantine Pankin), 226 (wavebreakmedia), 268 (Robert Kneschke), 281 (Monkey Business Images), 287 (Andresr), 305 (Lisa F. Young), 310 (Keith Bell), 317 (Diego Cervo), 323 (auremar), 326 (JHDT Stock Images LLC), 339 (Goodluz), 354 (Tyler Olson), 361 (michaeljung), 374 (auremar), 381 (RyFlip), 399 (AntonioDiaz), 402 (Monkey Business Images), 428 (Monkey Business Images), 447 (Goodluz), 453 (michaeljung), 455 (lightpoet), 466 (Lisa S.), 472 (wavebreakmedia), 477 (Andresr), 482 (Goodluz), 506 (Robert Kneschke), 519 (Monkey Business Images), 528 (Ivelin Radkov), 535 (alexsalo images), 549 (auremar), 555 (StockLite), 583 (Monkey Business Images), 599 (Robert Kneschke), 601 (bikeriderlondon), 612, 624 (William Perugini), 631 (Dusit), 637 (Goodluz), 656 (Paul Vasarhelyi), 675 (Marcin Balcerzak).

Figures

The publishers would like to thank the following sources for permission to reproduce their copyright protected figures:

Figures – pp 62b – adapted from feda.ac.uk; 192 – OfQual, August 2011; 347b – Petty 2004: 47; 434 – Claude Shannon and Warren Weaver 1949/David Berlo (1960); 541 – Race (2005).

Walk through tour

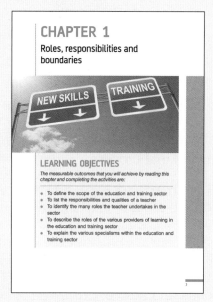

Learning objectives Featured at the beginning of each chapter, you can check at a glance what you are about to learn

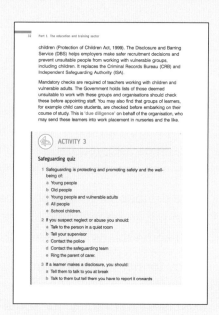

Activity Put your knowledge into action with these practical activities

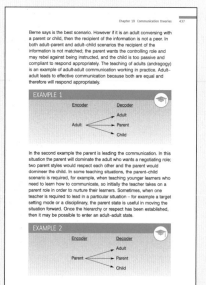

Example Practical, real-world examples illustrate key points and learning objectives in the text

Note box Key information is drawn out in eye-catching boxes

Useful resources Further reading feature offers suggestions for print and online reading material

Revision Revision boxes help you recap on things learned in previous chapters

Glossary of terms Glossary of terms highlighted in the text are listed at the end of each chapter with definitions

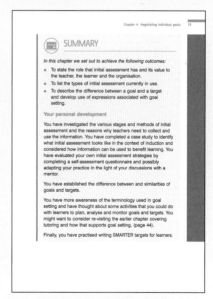

Summary Featured at the end of each chapter, summary boxes help you to consolidate what you have learned

Mapping grid

Relevant Part in Practical Teaching	Unit of Assessment: (arranged in alphabetical order)	L3 Award in Education and Training	L4 Cert in Education and Training	L5 Dip in Education and Training
5	Assessing learners in education and training		✓	
3,6	Delivering education and training		✓	
1, 3, 5, 6, 7	Developing teaching, learning and assessment in education and training			✓
3	Facilitate learning and development for individuals. Level 3 (L&D)	✓		
3	Facilitate learning and development in groups. Level 3 (L&D)	✓		
2	Planning to meet the needs of learners in education and training		✓	
1, 2, 3, 4, 5, 6	Teaching, learning and assessment in education and training			✓ (L4)
7	Theories, principles and models in education and training			✓

Relevant Part in Practical Teaching	Unit of Assessment: (arranged in alphabetical order)	L3 Award in Education and Training	L4 Cert in Education and Training	L5 Dip in Education and Training
6	Understanding and using inclusive approaches in education and training	✓		
5	Understanding assessment in education and training	✓		
1	Understanding roles, responsibilities and relationships in education and training.	✓ (L3)	✓ (L3)	
5	Understanding the principles and practices of assessment. Level 3 (L&D)	✓		
4	Using resources for education and training		✓	
8	Wider professional practice and development in education and training			✓
No link	OPTIONS		15 credits required	45 credits required

Part one

The education and training sector

1 Roles, responsibilities and boundaries

2 Legislation and codes of conduct

3 Support for learners

....

This part and chapters relate to the learning outcomes in the following Units of Assessment:

- Understanding roles, responsibilities and relationships in education and training.
- Teaching, learning and assessment in education and training.
- Developing teaching, learning and assessment in education and training.

The learning outcomes relating to evaluation, reflection and professional/personal development are dealt with in Part 8 and the learning outcomes relating to your development of the minimum core are in Part 9.

CHAPTER 1

Roles, responsibilities and boundaries

LEARNING OBJECTIVES

The measurable outcomes that you will achieve by reading this chapter and completing the activities are:

- To define the scope of the education and training sector
- To list the responsibilities and qualities of a teacher
- To identify the many roles the teacher undertakes in the sector
- To describe the roles of the various providers of learning in the education and training sector
- To explain the various specialisms within the education and training sector

Roles and responsibilities

The role and responsibility of the teacher is a complex one. We are charged with ensuring our learners gain their qualifications in a manner which is favourable to their own learning needs and those of the Awarding Organisations. We have to offer value for money. We have to consider the needs and interests of their parents and employers, as well as the learning institution. Not all learners come into learning to achieve a qualification; some want to gain new skills to help with their employment or simply to cope with the changing world.

The range of provision within the education and training sector is quite broad. It is generally post-compulsory education and covers further education, higher education, work-based training, training for employment, adult and community learning, the voluntary sector, the armed forces and prisons. Learners in the sector may be funded by government bodies, by their employers, by funding councils or by their own finances. Some may be supported by student loans, bursaries or scholarships. In a nutshell, lifelong learning covers everything that is not compulsory education (education and training). Learners can be aged from 14 upwards and learning can occur in any suitable environment.

The demographics (learner/population trends) are ever-changing due to:

● Changes in society
● The need for equality and diversity
● Changes in funding priorities
● Expectations of learners, employers and parents
● Behaviour trends
● Technological developments.

Think, for example, about the typical learners in a Further Education college.

● 14-year-old pupils trying to gain vocational qualifications as an alternative to academic qualifications.
● 16-year-olds embarking upon training and qualifications to meet potential employment needs.

- 19-year-olds developing skills or perhaps catching up on missed opportunities.
- The mature student, returning to learning, maybe thinking about a change in career.
- The unemployed, trying to re-enter the world of work.
- The adult, gaining skills relevant to their work.
- The young mum, returning to a career after a period of time and finding that the workplace has moved on.
- The pensioner, trying to gain skills so that they can communicate in today's electronic era.
- The social learner, learning a skill to provide pleasure and enjoyment.

The teacher will come across many of these examples, each of which has very specific learning goals, in a typical working week. The skills involved will be discussed in detail later in the book, but suffice to say if the learners are all different, so the skills required to teach them will vary. Most people come into teaching because they believe they can make a difference. The amount of energy that a teacher will expend in realising that value will astound the inexperienced teacher. A teacher needs to accept that they will face many challenges in teaching, including risks, but if something goes wrong, it should be seen as more of an opportunity than a threat. In order to succeed, you sometimes need to make mistakes; that's how we learn.

The impact of all of these influences affects the teacher, whose role is far more than just being someone who stands at the front of the class telling people things.

Teaching is not limited to imparting your knowledge, you will also have a responsibility for helping someone to learn. One of the first rules of teaching is:

ASSUME NOTHING

Do not assume that your learners know the most effective way of learning. They will come to you with a variety of experiences, a lot of needs and maybe some misconceptions. If you assume that learners 'already know this', 'can do that' and 'expect this', you are in for a massive learning experience yourself! One of the most influential factors on someone's ability to learn is the teacher. To summarise the breadth of the role:

The role and functions of a teacher:

- Designing programmes of study
- Planning and preparing classes to meet the needs of all learners
- Delivering learning in an inclusive way
- To motivate through enthusiasm and **passion** for the subject
- Developing interesting ways of delivering learning
- Assessing the impact of learning
- Ensuring a safe learning environment
- Marking of work and giving feedback on outcomes
- Keeping records
- Contributing to the development of the programme
- Evaluating the effectiveness of the programme
- Keeping data about retention and **achievement**
- Having a duty of care
- Monitoring the progress of learners and targeting for improvement
- Creating independent learners
- Acting within professional codes
- Monitoring attendance and punctuality
- Contributing to the administration of the programme
- Entering learners for exams and tests
- Contributing to quality assurance requirements
- Acting as a role model
- Pastoral care.

ACTIVITY 1

Let us consider the extent of that responsibility:

Look at each of the headings below and write down what you think you need to consider. It is probably best to focus on your particular subject. You should consider how you might tackle it, who will help you and how you will know if you have got it right.

You will find all the answers within this book, but try not to look yet. Use your existing knowledge and common sense! This will also be a good way of finding out about your own strengths and development needs at this early stage.

Roles and responsibilities	Thoughts and considerations
What will I teach?	
When will I teach it?	
How will I prepare for a session?	
How will I make it interesting?	
What will I do when things go wrong?	
Who else will be involved?	
How will I know when somebody has learnt something?	
Am I getting my topic across?	
What paperwork will I need to complete?	
How will I appear professional?	
Do I know enough to teach my topic?	

You probably now have lots of questions. Using this book and the guidance of your tutor, you can now embark on your own learning journey.

The duties of a teacher will appear on a **job description**. Teaching is far more than just disseminating information to others. It requires many more skills and a lot of balancing of time to ensure everything gets done in a timely manner. The characteristics of a teacher will provide the basis of the '**person specification**' and will include:

Qualities of a teacher:

- Patience
- Team player
- Organised
- Good communicator
- Literate and numerate
- IT literate
- Innovative, creative and resourceful
- Reflective
- Shows empathy and respect
- Fair
- Forgiving/compassionate
- Tactful
- Good sense of humour
- Enthusiastic
- Flexible
- Dedicated/committed
- Hard working
- Aspirational/inspirational
- Friendly
- Autonomous.

This is a tough list to achieve, given that you have to do all of these tasks and be all of these characters to different people constantly during your working day, and probably some of them concurrently!

There are some distinct responsibilities that a teacher may be given. Throughout this publication, the expression 'teacher' is used, but it infers the broader roles of the teacher and is a collective noun for the many different job titles and roles.

The roles a teacher may undertake

Instructor

One who is usually working in a practical session and would work to support and develop technical abilities. An example might be someone working as a Fitness Instructor (or coach) on a Sports programme. The role is usually different from teachers in that their role is more logically defined as a supporting role. This role is important as someone who is expert in the technical skill and works closely with learners to develop those skills. The instructor is perceived as less formal than the teaching role and so may engage well with learners who prefer an informal learning environment.

Trainer/Assessor

One who may be working with individuals in training venues. It is a common role within work-related qualifications where learners are demonstrating competence rather than learning skills. The advantage of this role is the one-to-one strategy that is usually involved. This close working relationship quickly builds trust which creates confidence. If this type of learning is work-based, then the learner is probably more relaxed as they are in familiar surroundings.

Facilitator

This role is similar to an instructor but may differ in that the sessions are usually workshops in which learners are using discovery types of learning techniques, under the support of a subject specialist. This type of learning suits those learners who enjoy the freedom of a more experiential learning mode. Yet they have 'a back up plan' with the expert should they decide they need extra help or the learners need to be re-focused.

Tutor

This is a role in which the teacher is given the responsibility to coach and support a group of learners (maybe a specific cohort or qualification). The class tutor plays an important role in enabling learners to succeed, by ensuring that they stay on their course (**retention**) and achieve their learning goals.

A tutor provides a link between the learner's academic progress and any other concerns or issues they may have. A tutor will have the opportunity to talk – probably on a one-to-one basis about how a learner is doing on the programme. They will review their achievements regularly and aid progress by setting goals and targets for further development. By creating a professional relationship based on trust and openness, the tutor will understand the learner, their motivation and aspirations and engage in discussions with them and others in the teaching team. The relationship should always be based on support towards achievement; a good tutor (and learner) will respect the boundaries of their role and be happy to refer their learners to specialists where appropriate.

The teaching cycle

Teaching and learning should be a structured process. Teaching (and learning) will follow a cycle and the teacher makes use of this to ensure achievement. The teaching cycle (see Figure 1A) is a continuous process, which can be joined at any point, but needs to be followed through to be effective. The process follows the strategy of moving from the known to the unknown.

Figure 1A	The teaching cycle

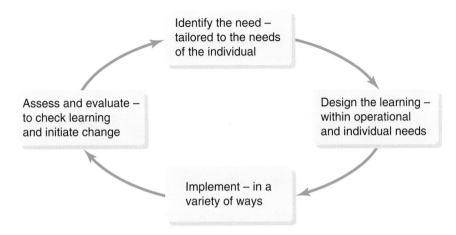

Think of our earlier examples of the types of learners, from both the learner's and the teacher's viewpoint. Let us put them into the teaching cycle using the following case studies.

CASE STUDY EXEMPLAR 1

Sophie is a 16-year-old. She has had her careers interview and wants to be a hairdresser. In this example how a learner wants to learn is reviewed in the context of the teaching cycle.

Stage 1	Sophie has discovered that she doesn't need high grade GCSEs, which is good because she doesn't think she'll get very many. She is artistic in her style and loves chatting to people. She has held a Saturday job in a local hairdressing salon and enjoyed it. She thinks she would like to own her own salon one day. *This is the evaluation stage.*
Stage 2	Sophie wants to go to college, but she also needs to earn some money. She finds out about the courses offered at two local colleges and a large hairdressing chain. *This is the identify need stage.*

Stage 3	She discovers that she has two main choices. She either goes to college full-time and continues with her Saturday job or she can join an apprenticeship programme where she works each day but is released to go to college one day per week. *This is the design stage.*
Stage 4	She decides on the apprenticeship, because she can earn the money she needs and practise skills learnt in college on her clients. *This is the implement stage.*
Stage 5	As she is working she finds that although she is learning skills in college, her employer will only let her do the junior's job. She wants to watch and learn from the stylists. *Sophie is now re-entering the evaluation stage, and so it goes on...*

CASE STUDY EXEMPLAR 2

Julie is a teacher in a college. It is her job to plan and prepare the hairdressing classes to meet learner needs. In this example the teaching cycle is used to show how the curriculum is developed.

Stage 1	Julie knows that she needs to meet the needs of all learners in her class. A few of her learners are employed in local salons and attend part-time. Of the full-time learners, two have done a lower level hairdressing qualification in the same college. One learner has been diagnosed with ADHD and two are dyslexic. Julie has created a profile of her learners. *This is the identify need stage.*

Stage 2	She looks at her scheme of work and plans her sessions to include a wide range of activities. She creates additional resources to upload to a VLE. She contacts the learner support team and arranges for additional learning support in her classes. *This is the design stage.*
Stage 3	Julie delivers to her learners using a wide range of teaching and learning strategies to ensure that all learners engage fully. She uses coloured paper for her dyslexic learners and ensures that the LSA allocated to her class is aware of her lesson preparations so that he can also prepare his support for his nominated learners. *This is the implementation stage.*
Stage 4	Throughout the sessions, Julie checks the progress of her learners. She checks that learners are using the resources she has uploaded to the VLE which is complementing her session delivery. She marks homework regularly and always gives feedback to aid learners' progress. She uses a progress tracker to record and monitor progress. She frequently asks for feedback from her learners. *This is the assess and evaluate stage.*
Stage 5	Julie uses this information and the assessment outcomes to review and amend plans for future sessions. *This re-starts the training cycle.*

The diversity within Education and Training Sector

This initial introduction seeks to help teachers to understand their role within the variety of sectors in the Education and Training Sector.

The Education and Training Sector covers a very diverse area of work. The sector covers community learning, further education, higher education institutions, work-based learning, offender learning and the voluntary sector. Each meets the needs of its clients through education and learning funded either by government bodies – such as the Skills Funding Agency, Education Funding Agency or the Higher Education Funding Council, or through direct government funding, for example offender learning, or through private or charitable funding from individuals and employers.

Community Learning

This responsive sector co-ordinates the work of adult learning, community education, family learning and youth work. It aims to address the demands of several key agendas: widening participation; social inclusion; customised provision; lifelong learning needs; community development; social needs; personal and social development. Much of the learning is unaccredited. The learning is broadly categorised into PCDL (Personal, Community and Development Learning Courses) which are offered widely and delivered in all manner of places, including community centres, schools, day centres and colleges. FLLN learning classes are run in many schools in the UK. They give parents and carers the opportunity to develop their own skills, find out how things are taught in their own child's school, as well as a chance to share ideas with other parents. There are also providers to support Wider Family Learning and Neighbourhood Learning.

Recreational or social learning used to be within the funding responsibility of Local Education Authorities. Then in 1998 the Adult and Community Learning Fund was established with the aim of widening and increasing the participation in learning and improving the standards of basic skills. The fund set out to support those who would not normally participate in education or training and took learning out into the community rather than expecting the community to come to learning establishments. There were clear links between learning and social regeneration. The fund ceased in 2004 when it was taken over by the Learning and Skills Council, with broadly the same mandate. However, in 2006 came a different funding methodology with priorities given to younger learners, with the result that less funding was available to adult community learning. The fund is now (2013) collectively called Community Learning Fund and is managed through Business Innovations and Skills (BIS). Many providers using PCDL money are providing services on behalf of their local education authority. However many courses are provided on a self-financing strategy, which in some areas has resulted in a significant decrease in courses offered for recreational or personal interest outcomes.

Some key contributory factors in the changing view of ACL:

- FE for the New Millennium, DfEE (1998): In a response the Helena Kennedy's Learning Works says, 'The establishment of a learning society in which all people have opportunities to succeed'.
- Success for All (2002): Adult and community learning seeks to provide choice, raise standards and helps to meet skill needs.
- White Paper: twenty-first century skills: Realising our potential (2003), directed focus of learning to those required by employers to meet a skill need.
- Investing in Skills: taking forward the skills strategy (2003). LSC reconsidered the approaches to funding.
- 2010 Skills for Sustainable Growth. Vince Cable.
- In December 2011, BIS announced headline proposals for Community Learning in New Challenges, New Chances Further Education and Skills System Reform Plan.

Voluntary and Community Sector (VCS)

The third sector, which is also sometimes known as 'the charity sector' or 'not-for-profit sector', includes organisations registered with the Charities Commission, housing associations, places of worship, NHS trusts and sport and recreational clubs, etc. The sector works with groups such as those with disabilities or hard to reach groups and under-represented groups. Accredited learning is associated with basic skills and ESOL. Non-accredited learning is concerned with developing relationships and partnerships. This sector is overseen by the Office for Civil Society, part of the Cabinet Office.

The skills of teaching in this sector are broadly similar to teaching related to adults, children and community provision, because the features of the group are similar although venues and social environments may be different. There may be those with specialisms such as working with learners on the autistic spectrum, disabilities, non-English speakers, youth workers. There may be a high focus of working with multiple agencies to support the wider needs of learners.

Further Education (FE)

This sector includes approximately 341 general FE colleges (GFE), tertiary colleges, sixth-form colleges and independent and specialist colleges in England, 36 in Scotland, 19 in Wales and six in Northern Ireland. Many of the colleges work in partnership with other members of the sector and are mainly associated with the delivery of education for 14 to 16-year-old learners. Recent changes in funding have led to a shift from adult learning to the education of younger learners. Colleges are now tasked with supporting adult learning and training through apprenticeships and direct realistic costing of provision. From September 2013, 24+ Advanced Learning Loans will be available to support the cost of courses for over 24-year-olds, very similar to loans for higher education learners. The sector covers a wide variety of subject disciplines and many specialist teaching groups, with many also working in HE, 14 to 16-year-old vocational learning initiatives, community and work-based sectors as well as the more **vocational** and academic subjects. Specialist colleges include Land-based; Art, Design and Performing Arts; Sports provision.

The FE sector is by far the largest provider of post compulsory education; £7.7 billion of funds – public and private, are used to deliver education to over three million people each year. 850 000 of the learners are 16–18, which is more than double the number that stay on to school sixth-forms. Two million adults use the FE sector and 130 000 of them are over 60. 58 000 learners are aged 14–16 and 170 000 study for higher education qualifications at their local FE college. The sector employs 228 000 people, of which 117 000 are teachers.

Source: http://www.aoc.co.uk/en/about_colleges/index.cfm (January 2013)

Higher Education Institutions (HEI)

This sector covers universities, university colleges and colleges of Higher Education (HE). Much of the work in universities is based around graduate and post graduate levels. There are trends to make the sector more diverse and accessible by including programmes which are more vocational and employment related

Recent funding changes (2012) have changed the dynamic of HE delivery. The move to reduce public funding in favour of personal funding supported by student loans and bursaries has impacted on recruitment strategies.

Work Based Learning (WBL)

This sector includes the work around applied vocational training, national training programmes, specialist training programmes and private training. The work is closely linked to the needs of employers and in addressing subject shortages based on employment trends. The work is funded either by government funding councils or by private sources. There are approximately 900 independent training providers and over 2500 sub-contracted training organisations.

WBL is the term used to identify those learners who are on Government sponsored training programmes, as opposed to Work Based Training (WBT), which refers to in-service training and development. There are initiatives to support young people to train for employment as well as schemes to support those who are unemployed or inactive and equip them with the skills they need to re-enter the world of work. There are/

have been Youth Training Schemes (YTS), New Deal, Apprenticeships and Train to Gain as well as work-related Foundation Degrees. Whilst work-based learning schemes are usually associated with 16- to 24-year-olds, they are not limited solely to that age group. The economics of public funding results in regular reviews of funding priorities.

Generally the programmes are a method of gaining employability skills through a combination of work-based practice and training, which is usually day-release type at the premises of a training provider. Training Providers may be private training companies, small or large organisations or FE colleges; the link is the commitment to work with employers to ensure a skilled workforce. The skills are usually measured using qualifications such as National Vocational Qualifications (NVQs), Technical Certificates, and/or Functional Skills, and may be enhanced by training allowances and bursaries. These used to be on a par with other government benefits paid to the trainees, but now employers are encouraged to recruit unqualified staff and pay them fair salaries, whilst receiving sponsored training. This has eliminated a lot of the 'cheap labour' arguments and by offering recognised qualifications has seen value and worth develop into the provision.

Offender learning

This is a key priority and contributor to the Government's Skills for Life strategy and is a way of reducing offending behaviour. Associated with the prison and probation services, offender learning is concerned with improving skills and employability as defined in Making Prisons Work: Skills for Rehabilitation. 2011. http://www.bis.gov.uk/assets/biscore/further-education-skills/docs/m/11-828-making-prisons-work-skills-for-rehabilitation.pdf(accessed March 2012)

The sector is overseen by The Department for Business, Innovation and Skills (BIS). Learners aged between 10 and 18 are held in Young Offender Institutions (YOI), Secure Homes or Secure Training Centres. Those over 18 are held in adult prison establishments. Learning environments in over 140 establishments are overseen by the Skills

Funding Agency; these establishments link to education providers or local authority provision. In addition to the education departments, training is also offered as part of normal work regimes. The sector is now funded and inspected under the auspices of the Skills Funding Agency and Ofsted.

Offenders are often under-achievers (DFES, 2006: 7), particularly in respect of basic skills. These skills need to be improved if the challenge of reducing re-offending is to be achieved. The teaching of offenders is often challenging. Teachers have to balance the requirements of LSC and Ofsted with the additional demands of Home Office policy. Add to this the impact of working safely and securely, and teaching and learning choices are often limited. Where possible, links to employers are seen as advantageous, but teaching therefore should advocate and recognise skills required to gain employment. Some take the opportunity to train or learn new skills either to while away the time or to create purposeful activity. The sector sees many disaffected learners and reluctance to learn is symptomatic of their previous experiences, fears, pressures and in some instances apathy. Teachers frequently have to deal with emotional and behavioural issues; the additional security aspects also constrain activities and movement. An offender's teacher, therefore, must work hard to improve self-esteem and advocate the value of learning in sometimes very difficult conditions. A teacher in this sector frequently works with very minimal resources; ILT teaching strategies such as Internet research are not available to offenders within many prison settings and many community offices do not have the training facilities of other training providers.

Areas of specialism

In the sector, teachers talk about subject disciplines and specialisms. There are many variables here, for instance:

Disciplines – e.g. maths, public services, teacher training, child care, hairdressing. These are the subjects that teachers consider that they are proficient in teaching.

Specialisms – the contexts in which we deliver those disciplines – 14–16, 16–19, adult, offender learning, skills for life, community provision, WBL, etc. These cover the broad type of learner or area of delivery.

Roles – the term 'teacher' has been used as a generic term to cover the name given to one who teaches or initiates learning. It covers facilitator, tutor, instructor, lecturer, trainer, coach, etc.

The skills required to teach within these specialisms are learned through experience, in-service training and development and research. The following is an overview of the main specialisms in which a teacher may find themselves.

Teaching 14 to 16-year-olds

The teaching of younger learners within or in conjunction with the education and training sector, has emerged from changes in government policy resulting from Mike Tomlinson's report – 14–19 Curriculum and Qualification Reform (2004). It set out the following targets:

- Raise participation and achievement
- Improve functional skills
- Strengthen vocational routes
- Provide greater stretch and challenge
- Reduce the assessment burden
- Rationalise the curriculum.

Many organisations work with schools to offer vocational programmes of study as an alternative option to academic study: 'The Increased Flexibility Programme'.

Teachers may teach younger learners within their institution or they may be required to teach in partnership with schools. The strategies of teaching are the same, but younger learners have different needs and the teacher should bear these in mind when preparing their sessions. There are a number of legislations and specialised codes of conduct for working with younger learners: The Children Act, Duty of Care, *In loco parentis*. (See the section on Legislation and codes of conduct in Chapter 2)

The move from school to the education and training sector (FE, WBL, etc.) can be daunting. Some may see it as exciting, but there are differences that a younger learner will see when comparing their learning to their school experiences. These are:

- Sessions are longer in FE timetables.
- Education and training is less teacher dominated.
- Learners are treated as adults – although their immaturity sometimes restricts the development of independence.
- Children are still developing emotionally and may act before thinking.
- Instances of vocational programmes being seen as second to academic routes.
- Shift of teaching from teacher dependent models to learner-centred independent strategies.
- Older learners in classrooms.
- Unsupervised periods (breaks, lunch, etc.).

However well managed the change, young learners will experience a series of emotions arising from this new sense of freedom which may result in:

- Fear
- Lack of confidence
- Noisy outbursts

- Disruptive behaviour
- Transitional problems concerned with school to FE environments
- Apprehension and anxiety.

Many of these emotions could have a negative influence on teaching and learning, although teaching this age group is not always problematic; a teacher just needs to focus on specific skills. In order to ensure teaching and learning is effective the teacher should:

- Increase the importance of analysis of individual learning styles and creating Individual Learning Plans (ILPs) to chart progress.
- Deliver an induction to introduce the differences between school and the education and training sector organisation.
- Create and maintain classroom rules.
- Devise small chunks of activity to maintain interest, promote motivation and increase self-esteem.
- Offer plenty of variety in sessions.
- Initiate relevant support mechanisms.
- Follow recommendations to promote the care of younger learners.
- Prepare learners for the world of work.
- Use rewards and sanctions to control behaviour.
- Be patient; be in control (firm but fair).
- Praise and encourage at every opportunity.
- Use strategies to develop rapport and mutual respect.

Teaching 16 to 18-year-olds

With the changes to the school leaving age, this group of people will form the core of the sector. Those that choose not to remain at school or seek work will probably join a full-time or work-based route to continue their studies. Programmes for this age group are generally either vocationally based or academic subjects. Learners usually come into their programme of study from school and the main providers are the Further Education sector or private training providers. Courses or apprenticeships tend to be full-time and are funded by the Skills Funding Agency. Academic subjects, for example 'A' levels are usually, but not exclusively, delivered within Sixth-Form Colleges, Academies or schools. Priority areas are based on national and local skills needs and funding is allocated accordingly. This leads to colleges having to plan their curriculum offer according to trends. Provision that is not a funding priority is offered on a **self-financing** basis. The needs of the age group are often very similar to those of the 14–16 groups. As they are usually entering directly from school, there has to be a period of personal development towards adulthood, and of course hormones play a big part in influencing behaviour at this age!

This influences the choice of teaching and learning methods. The teacher is responsible for developing autonomy and independence (of learning) in order to prepare the age group for further study or self-development. There is a notional development of **pedagogy** towards **andragogy**.

There is an assumption, although use that assumption cautiously, that learners entering at 16 are following their chosen career path and are eager to learn skills which will prepare them for employment. This group of learners should be seen as 'work in progress', a group in transition from childhood to adulthood. Whilst some have identified their preferred careers, others may need more guidance and direction and will benefit from 'taster' opportunities. Teachers involved with this age group, especially if on a vocational programme, are usually practitioners in the subject and have moved into teaching; this brings a wealth of technical knowledge into the classroom.

 ACTIVITY 2

Can you see what they see?

Imagine you are a 14-year-old … or imagine you are a 16-year-old …

How is the teaching they experience different from school?

Are the rules different? What about the sanctions?

Is the classroom different?

Is the relationship between teacher and learner different?

▶

How do you imagine a 14- or 16-year-old will feel?

You may wish to do this kind of activity at the start of a programme with younger learners and compare this with a repeated activity 6 or 12 months into the programme. Ask your learners for their opinions, compare them with your own views.

Teaching adults

The term given to teaching adults is andragogy (how adults learn) as distinct from how children learn. Theoretically, adult teaching tends to be more learner-centred, however, it is not unusual for adults to comment that they like to be taught – and some feel cheated if they do not go home with an armful of notes and presentations. Adults may come into the environment on work-related training sessions, courses to improve or gain new skills in preparation for a return to work or promotion, or as learners in recreational evening sessions. The teacher should remember that adults come into education with a range of life skills and previous educational experiences. They are generally independent and usually have clear goals for their learning – although there will be some variations (in future chapters we will explore those variations).

Adults expect:

- To be treated as adults
- Their teaching sessions to be relevant to their learning goals
- To be taught in a way that motivates and meets their needs.

There are different beliefs and expectations when it comes to the teacher's role; some adults expect the teacher to teach them via loads of hand-outs and teacher-led sessions – maybe similar to their own learning background. Others are independent and just need the teacher to facilitate their learning (learner-centred). Your role as the teacher is to identify this and reflect it in your choice of teaching strategies and promote a shared responsibility to learning. Teachers may need to coax adults from a 'chalk and talk' style of learning to a more autonomous learner-centred style.

Glossary of terms

Academic relating to education, school or scholarships

Achievement meeting learner goals

Andragogy how adults learn

Apprenticeship a framework or course to learn trade skills

Autonomous learner one who requires minimal guidance from the teacher

Awarding Organisation a body approved by Ofqual to create and certificate qualifications (AO)

Chalk and talk teaching by traditional methods with focus on a chalkboard

Curriculum a programme or model of study

Demographics the structure of the population

Disaffected learners no longer satisfied with the learning environment

Discipline a branch of knowledge

ESOL English for speakers of other languages

ILP Individual Learning Plan

Job description a list of duties typical of the job role

Learning goals what a learner sets out to do

Learning needs things which will help a learner to achieve their goal

Passion a grade one indicator meaning a strong desire to teach

Pedagogy the skill or ability of teaching

Person specification a list of characteristics required in the job role

Post-compulsory education after the age of 16, not mandatory

Qualification a set of specifications (UoA) leading to an award, certificate or diploma of achievement, a skill that makes someone suitable for a job

Retention the number of students who complete their programme

Role a person's position within a function or organisation

Self-financing generating sufficient income to cover costs and profit margins

Specialism a particular focus within the broader meaning of teaching

Teaching to impart knowledge or a skill; what the teacher does during a session

VLE virtual learning environment, e.g. moodle

Vocational relating to learning the skills of an occupation

WBL (work-based learning) learning that takes place predominantly in the workplace

 # SUMMARY

In this chapter we set out to achieve the following outcomes:

- To define the scope of the education and training sector.
- To list the responsibilities and qualities of a teacher.
- To identify the many roles the teacher undertakes in the sector.
- To describe the roles of the various providers of learning in the education and training sector.
- To explain the various specialisms within the education and training sector.

Your personal development

This chapter commenced by reviewing the demographics of the sector and the extent to which the teacher contributes to the sector. In order to contextualise the role of the teacher you were introduced to the Teaching Cycle, as a means to view the role. You developed your investigations into the functions within a job role and explored the many activities a teacher must demonstrate in their 'full' teaching role. Specific reference was made to the role of the tutor and their importance in providing pastoral support to learners. Further you explored how the tutor's role impacts on the learner's enjoyment of the programme and thus is a significant player in the retention and achievement strategies seen in the education and training sector. The discussion then briefly considered other roles a teacher may undertake, or roles performed by others in the learning environment.

You then looked at the breadth of the sector and the main areas of work within the education and training sector, those being: community and voluntary sectors, FE, HE, WBL and offender learning. Each was described in terms of the contribution it makes to the sector, although many areas overlap as they respond to their client market.

In the final section, we reviewed the various specialisms or learner types seen in the sector. Whilst avoiding stereotyping any particular type of learner, the section analysed some of the skills a teacher would need to teach the category of learner.

CHAPTER 2

Legislation and codes of conduct

LEARNING OBJECTIVES

The measurable outcomes that you will achieve by reading this chapter and completing the activities are:

....

- To identify laws, statutes, regulations and codes of practice
- To describe ways in which teachers can establish and maintain safe and supportive learning environments
- To explain your responsibilities for promoting equality and valuing diversity

Law and professional values

As with any area of work, teachers must work within the boundaries of the law and professional values. There are a vast number of laws, directives and professional ethics; they are constantly changing or being updated. Every organisation will have its own policies and procedures relating to these legal aspects and there are some differences in requirements, depending upon the age of learners and the environment. We work within these rules a) to comply with the legal requirements, b) to comply with a regulatory code, ethics and values – to teach with integrity, c) to be safe and support all learners to achieve their goals and d) to provide a framework for maintaining appropriate behaviours and respect.

Whilst this book will endeavour to cover the main aspects, every teacher remains accountable for their own familiarisation with how to remain compliant. Every opportunity should be taken to ensure that you are up to date. Go back to that first rule of teaching – ASSUME NOTHING!

 ACTIVITY 1

How compliance aware are you?

This may be one of your first development points. The following lists the main ways that you will learn about the legislative, regulatory and local codes of practice.

To identify all legislation and codes of practice in relation to teaching (your subject), you are advised to:

- Attend your organisation's induction event.
- Reflect on the rules etc., of the industry or trade you are a specialist in and, how they will be advocated and incorporated into your learning programmes.
- Find out who the health and safety manager or representative is.

- Check out where the policies and procedures are. They may be stored in paper or electronic formats.
- Ask your line manager about particular rules relating to your subject.
- Enquire about the names of key staff to help you.
- Find out about the qualifications and training you need. For example: Health and Safety, First aid, Safeguarding, Equality and Diversity and Sustainable practices.

Prepare a personal action plan to ensure that you understand your responsibilities in relation to your legal duties. Save this information in your folder.

The main acts and rules

Health and Safety at Work Act (1974)

Everyone has a responsibility for the safety of themselves and others. Therefore, rules must be followed and safe practices adhered to, you should demonstrate a model of best practice, lead by example. There are additional rules relating to taking learners on educational visits following a series of tragic accidents. Do not consider taking learners on visits without seeking advice.

 ACTIVITY 2

Safety dilemmas

Question	Your comments:
1. You cut your hand on a staple when unpacking a box. You wrap your handkerchief around it and it soon stops bleeding. Do you report it as an accident?	

2. You notice that several of your colleagues do not wear safety footwear in the workshop. Do you say anything to them or do you tell your supervisor?

3. The fire alarm rings while you are in the middle of a job. It is still ringing after 20 seconds. You feel sure it is a fire evacuation practice as we always have these at the start of term. Do you keep working?

4. As you leave work one day, you notice someone hanging around the car park without an ID badge on. You are on your own. You do not recognise them. Do you approach them to find out what they are doing?

The Management of Health and Safety at Work Regulations (1999)

The legislation seeks to prevent unsafe practices and minimise risk. For example, fire and emergency procedures, first aid at work, safe handling practices, visual display unit codes, risk assessment.

Risk assessment

All activities have an element of risk, some more so than others. It is the teacher's responsibility to assess the level of the risk, establish practices to minimise risk and record such activities.

Child Protection Guidelines

The Children Act 2004, Safeguarding Vulnerable Groups Act 2006.

Recent high-profile cases have brought about the necessity to introduce legislation and guidance on protecting children and vulnerable adults against inappropriate behaviour. Each organisation should exercise their functions with a view to safeguarding and promoting the welfare of children (Protection of Children Act, 1999). The Disclosure and Barring Service (DBS) helps employers make safer recruitment decisions and prevent unsuitable people from working with vulnerable groups, including children. It replaces the Criminal Records Bureau (CRB) and Independent Safeguarding Authority (ISA).

Mandatory checks are required of teachers working with children and vulnerable adults. The Government holds lists of those deemed unsuitable to work with these groups and organisations should check these before appointing staff. You may also find that groups of learners, for example child care students, are checked before embarking on their course of study. This is 'due diligence' on behalf of the organisation, who may send these learners into work placement in nurseries and the like.

 ACTIVITY 3

Safeguarding quiz

1 Safeguarding is protecting and promoting safety and the well-being of:

  a Young people

  b Old people

  c Young people and vulnerable adults

  d All people

  e School children.

2 If you suspect neglect or abuse you should:

  a Talk to the person in a quiet room

  b Tell your supervisor

  c Contact the police

  d Contact the safeguarding team

  e Ring the parent of carer.

3 If a learner makes a disclosure, you should:

  a Tell them to talk to you at break

  b Talk to them but tell them you have to report it onwards

    c Phone Social Services

    d Ask them to talk to their parent/carer.

4 The Data Protection Act will stop me sharing information about a learner:

TRUE   FALSE

5 A person on campus is not wearing any visible identification. Do you:

    a Ignore it, the teacher will know why

    b Tell someone in Learner Services

    c Politely ask them to show their identification

    d Tell them to go to Reception immediately.

6 Ofsted check whether the College is compliant to safeguarding legislation:

TRUE   FALSE

7 A student appears drunk on the college grounds. Do you:

    a Report it to your supervisor

    b Give them a cup of coffee

    c Send them home

    d Start disciplinary processes.

8 A student is throwing a tantrum in the LRC (library). Do you:

    a Report it as a safeguarding issue

    b Ask their friend to have a word

    c Remind them that it is unacceptable behaviour and start disciplinary proceedings

    d Ask them politely to revise their behaviour

    e Ignore the behaviour.

Equality Act 2010

The act replaces previous anti-discrimination laws with a single act to make the law simpler and to remove inconsistencies. This makes the law easier for people to understand and comply with. The act also strengthens protection in some situations.

The act covers nine protected characteristics which cannot be used as a reason to treat people unfairly. Every person has one or more of the protected characteristics, so the act protects everyone against unfair treatment. The protected characteristics are:

- age
- disability
- gender reassignment
- marriage and civil partnership
- pregnancy and maternity
- race
- religion or belief
- sex
- sexual orientation.

The Equality Act sets out the different ways in which it is unlawful to treat someone, such as direct and indirect discrimination, harassment, victimisation and failing to make a reasonable adjustment for a disabled person.

The act prohibits unfair treatment in the workplace, when providing goods, facilities and services, when exercising public functions, in the disposal and management of premises, in education and by associations (such as private clubs).

For the teacher this means delivering learning in an inclusive way to ensure that learning meets all learners' needs. This concept is summarised later and expanded in Part 6.

Data Protection

The Data Protection Act (1998, 2003) requires any organisation that holds any data on individuals, electronic or otherwise, for more than two months, to register as data users. It restricts the sharing of data. Caution should be taken when holding records associated with learners, staff or partner companies. It is common sense that you should never reveal personal information about anyone to another person, however convincing the request!

Duty of care

Common, civil, statute and criminal law all apply to teachers. If you are proven to be negligent, then you may have to compensate the injured party. This applies to individuals as well as a corporate responsibility. Teachers are, in principle, *in loco parentis* to their younger learners. This means they need to offer a safe environment, whilst balancing the need to experiment and develop independence. If you and the organisation have taken all reasonable steps to ensure safety, yet a learner is injured as a result of not following the rules, it is unlikely to be proven that you are in breach of the duty of care. So, if you are using equipment in a workshop, or scissors in a classroom, or taking a group on a visit, you should assess the risk, warn of the safety implications and use protective equipment. Failure to do so is negligence.

Disciplinary policies and sanctions

Keeping order in the classroom will in itself provide a safer learning environment. Corporal punishment is illegal and hitting (teachers hitting learners or learners hitting teachers) is criminal assault. Restraint is a difficult one because it relies on evidence of training and reasonableness. Each organisation will have its own policies on discipline and related issues and what to do if things go wrong, which will include sanctions, use of force, disciplinary hearings and exclusion. Managing behaviour and problems in the classroom and how to deal with them are further discussed in Chapter 17.

Dress codes

There are some vocational areas that require learners to wear particular things in order to meet professional standards, for example trainee chefs wearing 'kitchen whites', motor vehicle learners wearing personal protective clothing and equipment. Dress codes should, wherever practicable, respect safety issues and respect religious beliefs. Guidance on the wearing of uniform, jewellery and other such rules should be shared and advocated throughout the organisation. You should familiarise yourself with the organisation's rules. In terms of the dress code for teachers, one should remember professional values; there is rarely a uniform, but smart, comfortable and practical should prevail.

Terms and conditions of employment

Every teacher will receive a contract of employment which not only details pay and working hours, but defines the rules of the organisation and what would happen if the rules are breached. You should always read everything in your contract and question things that you are unsure about.

Whilst some of these aspects need only an awareness of context, many will impact from your first teaching experience and therefore require a detailed knowledge. You will need to talk this through with your line manager, your mentor or your union representative. The importance of this cannot be over-emphasised.

Useful resources

Useful references for further reading about legislation are Cohen, Manion and Morrison (2004: 85–96)

http://www.hse.gov.uk/services/education/index.htm
http://www.teachers.org.uk/resources/pdf/law-and-you.pdf
http://www.natfhe.org.uk/
http://www.ucu.org.uk/index.cfm?articleid=1738
http://www.rospa.com/safetyeducation/atschool/index.htm
http://www.dfes.gov.uk/

Equality and diversity

Equality and diversity are terms which are expressed quite frequently, yet usually without a clear explanation of what the terms mean. So, here goes …

Equality means more about compliance with the law than diversity. It pre-empts discrimination by adhering to a systematic policy approach to ensure organisations stay within the boundaries of the legislation. It covers the protected characteristics as well as a wider brief to reflect differences in characteristics and preferences.

Whilst equality generally means everyone is treated equally and fairly, it is linked directly to legislation and guidelines, which together drive the initiative. Diversity goes one step further by valuing the differences between individuals, and by ensuring they are participating, you are including everyone (inclusion).

For the organisation, it means setting up a policy and codes of practice which ensure staff are aware of the law and are familiar with how to implement it in their job roles.

Society is diverse. Some people are old, some are young. Some are disabled, some black, some have children, some are male – everyone is different but everyone is valued and respected. Here are some statistics:

In 2010 62 per cent of the population were of working age (16–60 female/16–65 male)

In 2010 approximately 20 per cent of the UK working population were white, male, able-bodied and under 45.

In 2012 70 per cent of the working age population were in employment

In 2011, ethnic minorities made up 17 per cent of the population; in London it was 40 per cent.

Sources:

http://www.ncvo-vol.org.uk (accessed June 2007)
http://www.neighbourhood.statistics.gov.uk (accessed Dec 2012)
http://www.guardian.co.uk (accessed Dec 2012)

Diversity recognises and celebrates differences; it supports equality by respecting rights, valuing individual talents and advocating that everyone's skills are fully utilised. Failing to promote diversity has an expensive outcome; there is a risk of litigation by dissatisfied customers, there is a risk that funding by public bodies will be discontinued and there is the possibility that the organisation's reputation may be harmed.

The equality agenda is more about conformity to laws and policy interpretations. It helps to ensure that the organisation supports equality by advising staff, learners and other stakeholders about its standards. The diversity agenda, in seeking to celebrate the differences in society, looks at the culture of the organisation to check that it promotes equality throughout its business practices.

- Expressed beliefs – that practices do not stereotype or make assumptions.
- Cultural forms – that books and media are appropriate and jokes are not biased.
- Knowledge systems – that learning resources and the curriculum offer is relevant and appropriate.

It will operate at three levels:

1 Individual – checking for verbal, physical abuse and discriminatory acts.
2 Organisational – that practices, policies and procedures are *in situ*.
3 Structural – that buildings support an inclusive regime.

Equality and diversity not only affect teachers' practices, but require the teacher to advocate equality and diversity in their learners. For example, comments of an unfair nature must be challenged rather than ignored and, irrespective of the demography of the learning environment, learners are prepared for the national balance.

 **ACTIVITY 4**

Self-evaluation for practicing teachers

Pre-service teachers should consider the questions in the box and reflect on how they might address similar issues to ensure that their personal skills are able to meet the needs of an inclusive learning environment

How equal and diverse is your practice?

How well do you do in terms of equality and diversity?

Use this evaluation table, but try to avoid yes/no answers by making a comment that discusses how it is and/or how it ought to be.

Question	Evaluative comment
Have you attended equality and diversity training?	
How diverse are your learners?	
Can your learners explain about bullying and harassment?	
Do the placement providers that you use have equality and diversity procedures in place?	
What is the demography of the community you serve?	
Do you monitor applications, retention and achievement in terms of gender, age, ethnicity, etc.?	
Is your course generally taken up by a particular group of people?	
How are complaints dealt with?	
Do social and enrichment events celebrate the diverse society?	

▶

| Are all religious festivals recorded on the business calendar? | |
| Do your resources and teaching methods promote equality and diversity? | |

From your answers, you should now write down ideas about how you can develop your inclusive practice to ensure equality and diversity.

See also Part 6 for an in-depth review of inclusive practice.

Glossary of terms

Demography a study of population trends

Diversity valuing and celebrating the differences in people

Due Diligence proactive investigation to help prevent future incidents occurring

Equality the state of being equal or the same

Inclusion finding opportunities to integrate all learners

Policy a course of action by an organisation; a statement of intent

Sanctions a penalty for disobeying the rules

 SUMMARY

....

In this chapter we set out to achieve the following outcomes:

- To identify laws, statutes, regulations and codes of practice.
- To describe ways in which teachers can establish and maintain safe and supportive learning environments.
- To explain your responsibilities for promoting equality and valuing diversity.

Activity 2 – suggested discussion or self-reflection topics:

1 The use of common sense and when/how to report accidents and incidents

2 The lines of reporting – reporting upwards to line manager especially if not sure which department is responsible

3 Evacuate – no question – role modelling

4 Personal safety, alternative suggestions, e.g. site security.

Answers to Activity 3 – safeguarding quiz

1c; 2d; 3b; 4 false; 5c; 6 true; 7a; 8d.

Your personal development

This chapter commenced with an activity in which you made an initial assessment of how you had/could have been made aware of legislation and rules.

The main body of the chapter summarised the main pieces of legislation, regulation and rules that you need to be aware of as a teacher in the education and training sector:

- Health and Safety at Work Act 1974
- Management of Health and Safety 1999
- Risk assessment
- Child Protection –

  – The Children Act 2004,

  – Safeguarding Vulnerable Groups Act 2006

- Equality Act 2010
- Data Protection Act 1998, 2003
- Duty of care
- Disciplinary policies and sanctions
- Dress codes
- Terms and conditions of employment.

Two activities reviewed your understanding and awareness of two main pieces of legislation which impacts on practice, namely health and safety and safeguarding.

Additional regulatory requirements are also to be found in Part 5 – Assessment (Regulations made by Ofqual, Data Protection 1998, Freedom of Information Act 2000) and in Part 4 – Resources (Copyright, Designs and Patents Act 1988).

The chapter continues to look at your responsibilities as a teacher in respect of equality and diversity. As a conclusion you then engaged with an activity to summarise and evaluate how diverse your teaching style is.

CHAPTER 3
Support for learners

LEARNING OBJECTIVES

The measurable outcomes that you will achieve by reading this chapter and completing the activities are:

....

- To identify own responsibilities and recognise when to refer issues
- To recognise the boundaries between the role of the teacher or other support networks
- To describe ways to use learning support staff to develop learning
- To explain the importance of promoting respect and good behaviour

Supporting learners

Although learners come into education to gain qualifications and experience, they bring with them their lives! The **boundaries** between supporting learners through their academic studies and their **pastoral** (emotional/social) needs are often blurred.

The teacher has an important role in the development of individuals, promoting independence and making learners work-ready. However, they are not the 'be all and end all' required to solve all of the emotional and life problems of their learners. There is a boundary. The boundary is where the teacher's role ends and the specialist counsellor or mentor's role begins. Whilst some teachers find this aspect of their role interesting, specialist support is time consuming and ultimately not their responsibility. The teacher is required to support **independence**, monitor progress and one of the first challenges might be for a learner to seek specialist support for whatever is impacting on their learning. From my experience, if the conversation is becoming too personal and confidential, it is usually time for referral. However, in general the whole **tutorial** process is confidential, but only insofar as it is not appropriate to discuss reasons for absence and hospital appointments within earshot of others.

The role of the class tutor

Further to our earlier definition of the role of tutor, this section focuses on the tutor's role as someone who provides academic and pastoral support.

When operating within an inclusive environment, monitoring progress and providing continuity is paramount. The role of the class tutor and the provision of tutorial time are vital in creating a learning experience that is beneficial to everyone, although respecting boundaries is essential. There is a fine line between a tutor's role and those of a **counsellor**; both tutors and learners must be clear about those boundaries.

The role of the tutor and purpose of tutorials is one of supporting learning which will manifest itself in a variety of ways:

- Preparing for and monitoring learners whilst they learn and study.
- Providing pastoral care – supporting the well-being of the learner, within the boundaries of specialism.
- Making referrals to specialists.
- Initiating introductory and diagnostic support – induction, study skills, ILP, initial assessment, preparing for inclusive learning.
- Completing progress reviews and personal development reviews.
- Addressing retention – looking for and pre-empting cause for concern, offering solutions to issues and monitoring actions.
- Providing opportunities for teacher and learner to communicate on a one-to-one basis.
- Providing individual development in socially accepted values, e.g. behaviour, conduct, language, study skills.
- Providing group development, e.g. citizenship, employability skills.
- Advising other teachers about characteristics of learners which are likely to impact on teaching and learning activities.
- Completing target setting discussions towards achievement.
- Developing communication skills of learners.
- Developing learners' autonomy.
- Addressing individual problems or concerns, including making referrals.
- Showing that you care at individual level.
- Coaching learners to maximise potential.

Tutorials can be costly to operate, especially when delivering one-to-one tutorials. This is due to the time needed to ensure that every learner has a tutorial, thus making tutorials very time-consuming. Seeking accommodation that is appropriate to tutorials can also be problematic; small private rooms are not always available and if trying to do one-to-one interviews at the same time as being responsible for the whole group, it is very challenging – what does the rest of the group do whilst you are chatting to one individual?

Another consideration when tutoring has to be concerned with learners' perceptions of the tutorial; some may consider it puts pressure on them (both staff and learners) or it appears threatening. However, if tutors demonstrate the value of tutorials and always express confidence in the process, it will result in a positive perception, rather than a negative one. This reinforces the need to teach learners about tutoring and its purposes. The benefits of operating a tutorial system significantly outweigh the disadvantages, and are usually a key part of a learning programme. Effective tutoring systems aid retention and achievement, which of course are the key processes measured in education and training.

In carrying out this role it is essential that tutors are selected and trained in the specific skills of being a tutor. It should not be assumed that everyone can tutor. As well as training in the documentation used by an organisation to record the process, a tutor needs many other skills. Walklin (2000: 254) lists functions that can be attributed to the role of the tutor as: catalyst and adviser; fact finder; auditor; technical expert; problem solver; advocate; reflector; solution provider; enabler; facilitator; influencer and implementer. If you consider the tutor as a coach, then the skills required will be:

- Active listening – a tutor should *really* listen; don't interrupt other than to seek clarification or summarising. Look interested but not nosey. Value their opinion – even if it differs from yours and do not voice opinion or inflict your values on the learner, even when asked 'what shall I do?' or 'what would you do?' Respect pauses in the conversation; silence is usually thinking time, especially if your questioning is open and initiates reflection.
- Questioning and explaining – use open questions to encourage learners to reflect on their actions, consider cause and effect. Effective communication is essential; both parties need to be able to talk and understand, listen and hear. Non-verbal communication is also very important. In terms of questioning think about how those questions are asked:

Type of question	Typical example
Open	What do you find difficult?
Closed	Do you find assignments difficult?

Type of question	Typical example
Leading	You are having difficulty with assignments
Hypothetical	What would happen if ...?
Reflective	How will you approach the assignment next time?

 **ACTIVITY 1**

Questioning techniques in tutorials

Think about your own questions in the same style as the example above. The scenario is:

A learner has 75 per cent attendance. You are trying to establish the reasons for this.

Type of question	Your example
Open	
Closed	
Leading	
Hypothetical	
Reflective	

- Record keeping – usually called reviews, plans or similar. The purpose of the document should be to prompt the discussion, record what is said and what the agreed outcomes are. This may be as a paper-based record or more commonly an e-ILP, recorded using a software package.
- Planning – both the tutor and the learner should plan the tutorial. The tutor should have a fairly good idea of progress and pastoral issues relating to their learners and be able to recount them in tutorials;

learners should know the types of discussion topics that will be mentioned so that they can begin to formulate their strategies to develop.

- Time management – ensure that everyone understands how much time is allowed. Manage that period well and if things look like being delayed or over-running take action to control it. If it looks like an issue needs more time, then make another appointment. A learner may also seek guidance on how to plan and use their time effectively.

- Praise, feedback, discipline – commenting about how well things are going, offering constructive feedback on progress and taking responsibility in dealing with problems are required to maintain rapport and the effectiveness of the process.

- Motivational interviewing or discussion – this is a strategy involving techniques to guide the learner into identifying and dealing with their own issues based on intrinsic learning values.

- Anti-discriminatory practice – tutoring without any bias or discrimination.

- Supporting the development of problem-solving skills by encouraging learners to solve their own problems in a supported way.

- Discretion and confidentiality – the tutor may be privy to information which is expressed within a private discussion. You may have to use your discretion about responding to what is said; if what you are told is best shared, then the owner of the information should be the one to share it; exceptions to this may occur if abuse is suspected or if an illegal practice is identified. This emphasises the importance of understanding the boundaries of the role.

- Empathy (not sympathy), non-judgemental – the tutor should try to understand how things make the learners feel and keep opinions to themselves.

- Respect and socially correct – respect should be mutual and aid the development of a good relationship (rapport). There are social parameters to think about when conducting tutorials; respect of personal space, sitting to the side rather than opposite the learner.

- Flexibility – tutoring demands different styles and expectations to meet different learners, yet consistent in methodology and equality.

- Codes of practice and ethics – working within your Duty of Care.

The tutor may or may not teach the group, there are no particular guidelines on this; it may be beneficial to remain independent or be advantageous to get truly involved in both the learner's personal and academic development. You should follow your organisation's methods and remember that the boundaries exist to maintain clarity.

Tutoring, like any other part of teaching, is not without its problems. Tutors who do not prepare for tutorials are likely to end up with unfocused sessions without any meaningful outcomes; crossing the boundaries of tutoring and counselling can lead to ill-informed actions, imprudent use of time and is unprofessional. The tutor should know when to refer the issue to someone more qualified to deal with it. The tutor should balance their approach: not too authoritarian or too nonchalant. If it is found that the support provided is ineffective an evaluation should establish the cause: is it too supportive, meaning that your learner is not challenged to develop their own support mechanisms? You may need to question whether the support is (still) relevant.

Referral

If tutorials are about retention and achievement, then emotional or social problems are beyond the boundary and therefore are better referred to specialists.

Knowing the boundaries of the teacher's role is essential to an effective learning environment. It is also important for the teacher to realise that there are some aspects of the learners' expectations that are beyond the role of the teacher. You may also find that experience plays an important part here; you may not know all the answers because you are new to the role and/or the organisation. The teacher should always consider the interests of the learners as paramount. We might like to help, but are we really the most effective person for the learner to consult? Understanding and respecting professional boundaries is essential.

The boundary between the role the teacher has, in respect of teaching, tutoring and caring for learners, is rarely clear. Each aspect is important and it is equally important for the teacher to learn when their role or help is dealt with more effectively by another trained professional.

Q: *Where does the teacher's role end and the specialist's begin?*

A: If only this were a clear line! The answer really is going to alter given the particular issue the teacher is faced with. The teacher is generally tasked with the front line delivery of learning. Each individual or group of learners will usually be allocated a tutor whose role it is to support learning and academic/ vocational achievement. They may also be involved in a certain amount of personal connection, which means learners may confide in them. However, whether or not the tutor has sufficient time or knowledge to problem solve on behalf of their learners is down to position and experience. You should always remember the implications of legislation and duty of care: thus, if an issue discussed is beyond your knowledge, experience, accountability or responsibility you should refer to your mentor, manager or learner support service department.

There are some rules here:

- Back to the first rule of teaching: assume nothing...
- Remember the first rule of customer service: if you promise to do something – do it.
- And finally, the rule of trust and tutoring – work with integrity and confidentiality.

Q: *Who are the specialists and how do my learners access them?*

A: If you look in the Student Charter or Learner Information sheet, which is usually given to all learners either at enrolment or induction, it will inform them of the support available within the organisation (see Internal Support Services below). In addition to this, there are various external voluntary bodies who will offer information, advice and guidance for all members of the community (see External Support Services from page 54).

Internal support services

Whilst this list is not comprehensive, it will give an idea of the mechanisms usually available within an organisation:

- Learner Services Office
- Crèche
- Counselling
- Tutoring
- Financial support
- Remission of fees for recipients of means-tested benefits
- Learner support for physical and/or educational support needs
- Dyslexia/dyscalculia (words/numbers) support.

Learners who work within companies may not have access to the departments of FE colleges and larger training organisations, however may still need advice and support on these matters.

Using learning support assistants (LSAs)

Generally, there are three types of support workers that you will come across, but there are as many different job titles as there are organisations in which they work. You will need to find out what the titles and associated job roles are within your organisation. The most common titles – as acronyms – are LSA or TA.

Some of the different titles are:

- Classroom Support Assistant
- Classroom Assistant
- Learning Assistant
- Basic Skills Support
- Support Assistant
- Support Tutor
- Support Lecturer
- Care Assistant
- Learner Support Worker
- Teaching Assistant (TA).

Some are there to support the physical needs of learners. They will help learners with personal care needs and at mealtimes: in the classroom they will help by holding things or fetching and carrying to ensure a safe learning experience. Together with the learner they will identify and control what they do. It is likely that the learner has had support throughout their education so will be very comfortable with their support team.

Some are there to support the academic learning needs of an individual or group of individuals – probably functional skills support. They will help learners to make notes, recall facts and comprehend information, write things down, help with literacy and numeracy needs; they help to keep learners on task and may develop resources specifically for their supported group. They are not usually a trained teacher, although they may be trained in supporting the work of teachers or be volunteers or paid employees. They are a group of people that are most valuable in the room, yet very often they are undirected and therefore their value is not fully utilised. The more experienced they are or the longer they work with a particular teacher or group, the more self-sufficient they become.

Some are there to support vocational and academic learning needs or behavioural support. They are probably a trained teacher, perhaps from the same subject specialism and assist the teacher, probably team teaching at times. If they are qualified and from the same subject, they can very much pre-empt what the teacher is trying to achieve and are usually an effective support mechanism. They may team teach, support groups within the main group, develop resources, support the behavioural aspects of the group or promote study skills.

Whatever the type of support worker, communication is the key to the effectiveness of that support. I would suggest that when a teacher plans their session they consider how they want the support worker to work with the learner. If this is annotated onto the learning plan and offered to the support worker then the support worker will be able to see what is going to happen, how you think it will be done and what outcomes you are expecting and use their skills and experience to help you make it happen. Too often I have seen support workers either doing very little, because they do not know what is expected of them or the activities aren't clear so they are unsure of how to support their learner, or in some cases they just do everything for the learner, who forgets to learn how to do things for themselves. The teacher should therefore give clear direction and 'touch-base' throughout the session to monitor what progress is being made. Together the LSA and the teacher can then fine-tune the support in response to the dynamics in the classroom. A support worker cannot support unless they know what you are trying to achieve; telepathy is not yet in their job description! In an ideal world it would be good to have a conversation about what support is required before the session and de-brief on how it went afterwards, but rarely is that feasible. A shared coffee break occasionally is not too demanding though!

Support workers can make valuable contributions:

- in consultations about causes for concern
- when used in an advisory capacity to think about appropriateness of resources and teaching strategies
- in team meetings
- at reporting periods
- as a resource
- when embedding functional skills
- to differentiate teaching.

Who will benefit from support worker assistance?

- learners with mobility, hearing or visual impairments
- learners with special educational needs (SENs)
- learners identified with weak literacy and/or numeracy skills

- teachers with very large or diverse groups
- teachers of learners with behavioural problems.

Research carried out in 1997 found that 'students on learning support were more likely to achieve than those who did not need the support in the first place' (Petty 2004: 513). Accessing learning support and working with support workers must be seen as an opportunity and not as something which categorises learners as different to the rest of the group. This is a cultural shift and is changing positively as teachers, learners and managers see the resulting value. Those of you working in the community or the workplace may not have such staff to support you. However, if you are experiencing situations which regularly need support arrangements you should discuss this with your line manager. Because you work in more isolated situations you may not be familiar with procedures for accessing support or not realise that funding and mechanisms are available. Support, in any circumstance, is not usually systematically employed unless demand or need is assessed. Support can be provided to address diagnostic assessment outcomes (e.g. weak literacy, numeracy standards) or it might be those more formally recognised support needs (e.g. physical, mental or behavioural needs). The assessment of need might be in the form of a previously assessed need, a section 139A: Learning Difficulty Assessment (LDAs), a diagnostic assessment, e.g. BKSB or other identification tool.

Useful information

For more information on LDAs:
   http://www.education.gov.uk/aboutdfe/statutory/g00203393/lda
The Open University provides an extensive list of ideas at:
   http://www.open.ac.uk/inclusiveteaching/pages/inclusive-teaching/learning-environments.php.

External support services

These are the professionals. Offices and telephone lines are staffed by trained personnel and are usually open 24/7 with phone lines normally free or making modest charges to cover costs. Again, this is not comprehensive, but the main ones are listed.

Samaritans	Confidential emotional support
Drugsline	Information about drugs and solvents for those who use them, or are affected by them
Citizens Advice Bureau	Local community help agency, legal advice and general information on a range of issues
Shelter	Legal and housing advice line offering independent information and advice
Childline	Helpline for children and young people up to 18 years old in danger, distress or with a problem
Help the Aged – senior line	Welfare benefits advice for older people
Parent line	Support and information for parents and those in a parenting role
National Debtline	Help for anyone in debt or concerned about falling into debt
Lesbian and gay switchboard	Support and information for lesbians and gay men
Victim Support	Emotional and practical support for anyone affected by crime
National Domestic Violence Helpline	Safe accommodation for those experiencing domestic violence
NHS Direct	Confidential health advice
Crimestoppers	Community service which helps to prevent and solve crimes

Use your local telephone directory for contact information.

It is important when working with learners that you respect their wishes and their confidentiality. You might use statements like 'if I were you...', but they are not you and you should remember that. Advice means that you give someone the benefit of your worldly experience; the nature of advice means that nobody has to accept it.

Issues relating to someone claiming they are being abused or supplied drugs should always be referred – even if only to someone more senior; it is your duty of care.

Glossary of terms

Anti-discriminatory actions taken to prevent discrimination

Boundaries the limits of the field of expertise

Counsellor an advisor or guide specialising in personal, social or psychological matters

Independence free from the influence of others

Pastoral concerned with the well-being of learners

Perceptions to be aware of something through the senses

Referral to send to a specialist

Tutorial a one to one session to support learning

 ## SUMMARY

In this chapter we set out to achieve the following outcomes:

- To identify own responsibilities and recognise when to refer issues.
- To recognise the boundaries between the role of the teacher or other support networks.

- To describe ways to use learning support staff to develop learning.
- To explain the importance of promoting respect and good behaviour.

Your personal development

This chapter looked at the responsibilities of the teacher in respect of supporting their learners. Initially you considered the role and skills of tutoring (as opposed to teaching) and in doing so did a quick exercise on questioning skills to explore the different techniques that can be employed in a tutoring situation.

Questioning as a topic is discussed in detail in Part 5 – Assessment.

In the next section you looked at referral and learned about the importance of understanding where the tutor's role ends and the specialist professional's begins. You reviewed the potential of internal and external support mechanisms and looked in detail about how the teacher can effectively use learning support staff to contribute to learning and development.

Part two

Planning learning

4 Negotiating individual goals

5 Session planning skills

This part and chapters relate to the learning outcomes in the following Units of Assessment:

- Planning to meet the needs of learners in education and training.
- Teaching, learning and assessment in education and training.

The learning outcomes relating to evaluation, reflection and professional/personal development are dealt with in Part 8 and the learning outcomes relating to your development of the minimum core are in Part 9.

CHAPTER 4
Negotiating individual goals

LEARNING OBJECTIVES

The measurable outcomes that you will achieve by reading this chapter and completing the activities are:

....

- To state the role that initial assessment has and its value to the teacher, the learner and the organisation
- To list the types of initial assessment currently in use
- To describe the difference between a goal and a target and develop use of expressions associated with goal setting

The role of initial assessment

Initial assessment is a term given to that part of the learning process that hopes to combine the learner, the teacher and the curriculum. We know (or are learning about) ourselves and what the teacher does, we know what the curriculum sets outs to achieve, but the biggest variable is the learner, and most of us do not meet that variable until day one, week one. We may know their names and maybe their age, address and phone number, but not what they are really like. As we have already discovered (see Part 1), learners are individuals brought together to gain a common goal, but they expect and demand respect and individuality within their group setting. Initial assessment, therefore, is the first stage in a process designed to create an interesting and relevant programme of study for your learners. As well as finding out about personality, character and behaviour, it also measures attainment and potential and identifies skill gaps and aspirations. Initial assessment is used in conjunction with diagnostic assessment to establish starting points. Diagnostic assessment tends to be more formal and is likely to use a recognised assessment strategy to diagnose literacy, numeracy or pre-existing skills, and will identify the support needed and the level of ability of learners. Initial assessment sets out to do quite a lot – but different individuals have come to expect different outcomes from it.

For senior managers it is used to inform strategy and funding, for teachers it identifies the person and informs the scheme of work and resources necessary, and for students it identifies how they will fit in and study. The current Ofsted Common Inspection Framework (CIF) puts significant importance on initial assessment as the vehicle to ensure that teaching and learning is appropriate to needs.

Source: http://www.ofsted.gov.uk/resources/handbook-for-inspection-of-further-education-and-skills-september-2012 Key paragraphs – 161,162. Implications in paragraphs 149, 156, 158, 159, 167, 169.

Figure 2A explains how the various components of initial assessment are linked and how collectively they will create the key ingredients required to make your decisions. The process can occur at any stage of

Figure 2A   Purposes of Initial Assessment

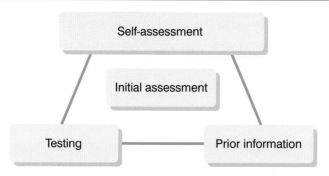

the learner's programme. At pre-enrolment stage it provides the opportunity to make choices, at enrolment it identifies level of study and needs, and on-programme it can inform the type of delivery.

There are many reasons to collect information; there are many uses and equally there are many things which impact on perceived or actual results. In Figure 2B, a spider diagram is used to visualise some of the influencing factors.

Figure 2B   Factors that influence initial assessment

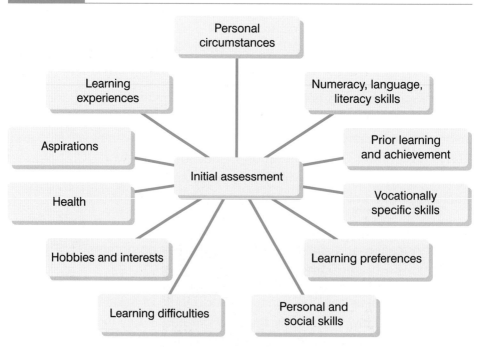

Adapted from feda.ac.uk

These ideas are suggestions about what kind of information to collect. Depending on the answers, and they will be as varied as your learners, the results will impact on learners and the learning environment.

Attitudes

Personal circumstances, personal and social skills, hobbies and interests, health, family attitudes to learning may impact on self-esteem, confidence and motivation (see Figure 2B). Travelling to and from the learning environment will impact on how settled a learner is at the commencement of a session, or if they can arrive on time. Family commitments and personal health may impact on attendance and punctuality or the ability to meet deadlines. Temporary illness may impact on the impression someone gives at their first meeting. If a learner has a long-standing interest in the subject it will improve motivation.

Ability

Numeracy, language and literature skills, prior learning and achievement, vocationally specific skills – a learner's ability in literacy and numeracy (and ICT) will impact on their ability to cope with the course (see Figure 2B). There may be required levels of entry prior to commencing the programme and if learners fail to meet these required levels they may have to choose alternative learning routes. This in turn may affect motivation. A learner's ability to cope on their programme will vary according to their previous qualifications or experience. Work

experience, previous employment or learning experiences will have some impact, as will the learner's reason for studying. Those learners who have experience in the subject may have an advantage on the programme as they may have more confidence; conversely, they may have developed poor habits which need to be modified.

Needs

Learning preferences, learning difficulties, aspirations, learning experiences – discovering how learners prefer to learn and why they are there is an essential part of establishing how to make learning more effective, as is finding out about any other type of support needs. Trying to establish how learners got on in school, training or previous study will help a teacher to understand and overcome any barriers to learning (again see Figure 2B).

Once a teacher understands what is making their learners tick then progress can begin. It is also important that previously unrecognised traits or weaknesses are identified so that appropriate actions can be taken to support the learner.

Methods of initial assessment

The process of initial assessment (IA) can be formal (objective analysis against criteria or standards) or informal (subjective opinions and views). The method of assessment and the way it is administered will influence the formality of the process. The teacher should consider the purpose of the IA and what benefits are sought. In The Chief Inspector's Report (2003), the Adult Learning Inspectorate (ALI) found that 'many providers are using a screening test but not following this up ... the results of the assessment are not being used to inform the ILP', and continued 'different types of learners require different types of initial assessment'. Moving forward to the evaluation of the 2010–11 academic year the Ofsted Chief Inspector's Annual Report (Learning and Skills) cites, 'Errors in initial assessments led to students taking unsuitable courses'. http://www.ofsted.gov.uk/resources/annualreport1011

This research proves that although used, initial assessment is not always effective. Much has improved since those reports, but it nevertheless begs the question of purpose; if you are going to use IA, then use it well with careful consideration of what you are trying to achieve by doing it. Unless this is clear, it becomes another tedious process in induction from which no-one benefits, although it would 'tick a box'. Effective initial assessment is not a one-off activity but the start of an on going informative process.

Initial assessment should:

- Aid direction to the right course
- Help to remove barriers
- Help learners to belong
- Reduce anxiety
- Gather information about learners, their aspirations and abilities
- Identify learning needs
- Inform others about progress
- Ensure legal and moral requirements are identified, planned and implemented
- Aid the planning of an inclusive learning programme
- Inform the structure of the programme.

It may involve:

- The student
- Parents
- School teachers
- Careers Advisors
- Employers
- Former lecturers or trainers
- Carers.

It should take place:

- In comfortable surroundings
- In confidence
- In a familiar place or relaxing atmosphere.

It can be gathered using tools (or methods) which are categorised as:

1 Written tools:
- Paper exercises
- Application forms
- Questionnaires
- References – school, employer, previous course tutor
- Screening tests
- Self-assessment
- Free writing
- Aptitude tests
- Tutorial records.

2 Electronic tools:
- Diagnostic screeners (literacy, numeracy)
- Learning preference questionnaires
- Psychometric tests.

3 Spoken tools:
- Interviews
- Professional discussion
- Informal discussion.

4 Visual tools
- Observation
- Skills tests – mapped to National Occupational Standards.

The initial assessment should result in either an individual learning plan (ILP), the basis of a discussion to negotiate goals and targets or planned differentiated strategies on your scheme of work.

Initial assessment in practice

To put the ideas relating to initial assessment into practice, look at the scenario below and, using a highlighter pen, pick out the many strategies the teacher uses to start the initial assessment of learners.

ACTIVITY 1

Induction case study

- Identify the initial assessment methods.
- List the information gathered before Jamil and Fiona started their course. How does this help to prepare them for learning and college life?
- List the information gathered during their induction to their course. How does this help their tutors to differentiate their learning?

Jamil and Fiona want to go to their local college when they have finished school. They ring up their local college and ask for a list of courses. Jamil wants to do Business Studies and fills out the application card in the prospectus to apply for a place. Fiona is not so sure: she doesn't know whether to do Tourism or Administration. She knows she wants to do something in an office, because that is the advice she got from her parents and her Careers Officer. She may also do Business Studies so that she can stay friends with Jamil. She decides to go to the open day to have a chat with teachers; her Mum comes along to find out about computer courses.

Jamil has now received a letter inviting him for an interview, which he attends, and is offered a place on the BTEC Extended Diploma, subject to his GCSE results. The Admissions Officer applies to the school for a reference. Fiona settles on Administration Level 2 because, following her chats, she decided that it was the most general course and her Mum says they will be good skills for whatever she wants to do.

In September they go along to the induction sessions for their chosen courses. They were surprised that they had to do some tests to check their English and mathematics. Jamil went into a blind panic: he thought he'd finished tests with his GCSEs and was very wary, especially with the English. He thinks he will not be allowed on the course if he fails. Fiona didn't see the point – she got a B in English and a C in maths in her GCSEs so gave the certificates to the teacher; she was told she didn't need to do the tests.

During this first week, they met lots of teachers and some played games to relax them. They also learned each other's names and where they came from. One teacher made them write about what they wanted to gain from going to college. Sometimes the teachers seemed to just listen and watch, at other times they sat down with each of them for little chats. Fiona said 'they tried to find out what we liked and what we wanted to do when we left college'. In some sessions the teacher gave them a programme of what they would do each week, others said that they would give them more details in a few weeks. Jamil said that he preferred some teachers to others, because they were friendlier.

When they bumped into each other on Friday lunchtime, Jamil and Fiona compared notes; they had been asked to complete a questionnaire about their first week in college. They thought that there were bits that were like school, but other bits that were more grown up, they both felt as though most of their teachers were interested in them, but thought that some things weren't explained well – for example why Fiona didn't do the tests and why Jamil did, but was enrolled onto a different Business Studies group. Although Jamil enjoyed the 'getting to know you' sessions, Fiona felt very self-conscious. In general, they felt happy and looked forward to the following week.

Suggested answers to this activity can be found at the end of the chapter.

Some things you should consider. Do you know:

- Why they chose their course?
- What their previous experience of learning is?
- How self-confident they are?
- If they have any previous experience or interests that are relevant?
- If they need any support?
- How they fit into their groups?
- What their preferred learning style is?
- What their expectations are?

How can you use the information to help Jamil and Fiona?

Initial assessment is a complex process involving pre-course assessment, diagnostic assessment and may continue throughout the programme with constant monitoring and reviewing to fine-tune needs. It results in accurate identification of individual needs, i.e. the planning of differentiation.

 **ACTIVITY 2**

Initial assessment in practice

This activity is designed to develop your awareness of initial assessment in practice. How do you make your initial assessment work for you and your learners? How do you modify your teaching following initial assessment?

Evaluating your initial assessment

In order to gain the most from your initial assessment, it makes sense to evaluate the process. Some questions that you may ask yourself to do this are:

- What information or data comes out of the initial assessment?
- Does it impact on the programme or ILP?
- Is the information transmitted to others?
- What does the IA lead to?
- Is it collecting the right information?
- What does the data tell you?
- Who needs the information?
- Does it diagnose existing skills (e.g. basic skills)?
- Does it find out about preferred learning style?
- Does it analyse the person against the skills they require to study, learn, work or progress to higher education?

In summary, initial assessment is aiming to get the best match between your learners and their learning. It should be both backward- and forward-looking.

Planning, negotiating and recording learning goals

A goal is what a learner plans to achieve within a course or period of learning; they are usually based on ambition. A target is a smaller step to help learners achieve their goals; the stepping stones. Small, achievable targets are more easily met than longer-term goals and therefore encourage a feeling of accomplishment. Effective targets are those small, achievable outcomes that enable students to experience early success. They are not vague and they are always in context, relevant and understood by everyone. In this context goals and targets are used to refer to learners' ambitions and aspirations rather than aims and outcomes used by the teacher in sessions. Goals and targets may change over time as factors influence lives and direction, but whatever the goals don't just settle for the basic achievements, strive for challenge by setting aspirational or ambitious goals.

> **'If you don't know where you are going you will probably end up somewhere else.'**
> Laurence J. Peter, 1919–90, Canadian Academic and author of *The Peter Principle* (1969)

Further to our beliefs about the diversity of the education and training sector, we are aware that our learners arrive with many goals:

- Gaining qualifications to prepare for work or further/higher education
- Gaining qualifications to accredit existing skills
- To enhance or update skills
- For personal development or enrichment
- To achieve social integration.

They may also come:

- To meet parental/school targets
- As an alternative to school/work/unemployment benefit.

The motivational aspect of why learners enter the education and training sector (intrinsic or extrinsic) will impact on the provision, the methods and on the relationships that emerge. Goals and targets will improve self-confidence and as goals are achieved the new confidence will raise motivation. In order to exploit or capitalise on the motivational factors, teachers will need to set goals for their learners. However, the better teacher will help their learners to set goals. The learners are then responsible for achieving those goals and therefore accountable. Any lapses in behaviour which might impact on the goal can be corrected using the learner's own goal as the raison d'etre. Goals help learners to become independent and autonomous and, as teachers (or parents) that is our purpose.

Goals are set for achievement over given periods and are usually expressed as:

- Long-term – career plans, ambitions.
- Mid-term – programmes of study, assessment targets, learning outcomes.
- Short-term – what to achieve in each session.

Goals are the building blocks of progression. They aim to move someone (in this instance a learner) forward. Some goals are backwards facing – that is, the learner knows the final outcome and works backwards on how to get there:

Forward goal setting	Backward goal setting
I will attend sessions regularly	I want to run my own business
I will get good grades	I need to save enough money
I will achieve my qualification	I need to get lots of experience
I will get a job	I need to get a job
I will get a better job	I need to achieve my qualification

The size of the goals will vary and good teachers know their learners well enough to know how large or small a target or goal needs to be to ensure achievement. Some like the big picture; some are daunted by too large a goal and are motivated by lots of smaller targets and thus achievements. Whether large or small, a goal needs to be expressed in a statement that the learner understands and the goals need to be stated in the context of the overall ambition.

Expressions you may hear:

- *Goal-oriented* – this means that a learner responds to knowing what can be done now that couldn't be done before.
- *Milestones* – the stepping stones to achieving the overall goal.
- *Negotiated* – this refers to a discussion about how the learner wants to achieve their goals, for example: in what way, by when.
- *Medal/mission* – a method of motivating and praise associated with setting targets and rewarding achievement (Petty 2004: 65).

In order to achieve goals, a learner will need guidance. Generally you will see goals expressed as a series of targets. You will be asked to set your learners SMART targets. You may also hear the extension of the expression SMART as SMARTER which adds interest and monitoring, making it a more complete package. There are several different words associated with the **acronym**; all are correct, but just to clarify the meaning:

S	Specific	Goals that clearly refer to what is expected
M	Measurable	Goals using verbs and phrases that can be judged
A	Achievable Agreed	Goals that can be reached successfully. A more powerful expression because it appears contractual
R	Realistic Relevant	Goals that are reasonable, practical and logical. Goals that are appropriate and important (Avoid using achievable and realistic because they mean broadly the same thing.)

T	Time-bounded	Goals that express when things must be done by
E	Exciting Enjoyable Ethical	Goals that are stimulating Goals that are pleasurable Goals that are fair and decent
R	Reviewed Recorded	Goals that are revisited to check progress Goals that are written down

ACTIVITY 3

Smart

Convert these targets into 'SMARTER targets'

For example 'improve writing skills' could be written as 'always use capital letters for family names when filling in forms'

Hand in assignments on time	
Come to sessions ready to work	
To revise for the exam	
To pass your driving test	

Discuss this activity with your mentor.

Goals and targets, usually recorded on the Individual Learning Plan or ILP, are best negotiated. This will aid ownership of the targets and create useful discussions to inform the most appropriate targets for the learner. An ILP might be a paper-based document or and electronic record. The ILP will be reviewed regularly as a means of checking progress – primarily for the qualification, but to help a learner make decisions about their future. To get ideas for goals and targets and help learners to formulate them you may try mind-mapping or spider diagrams which picture ideas. You could prepare help sheets – 'what I'm good at' and 'what I need to do better' to stimulate the ideas for short term targets, which helps your learners to be realistic about their goals. Then you may display session goals on posters to provide a regular memory aid; this is particularly useful in session rules which appear less autocratic if described as session goals. You may introduce success ladders or thermometers to visualise achievements and are a lot more interesting than a progress tracker!

Glossary of terms

Acronym an abbreviation or series of initial letters which together make a word

Diagnostic assessment assessment occurring early in the learner journey to establish starting points or identify capability or skill level, particularly in relation to functional skills

Extrinsic motivation motivation derived from the outside of the person

Goal an aim or desired result

Induction a formal introduction to a programme/role

Initial assessment assessment occurring very early in the learner journey to establish potential, aspirations, suitability or existing level of learning/experience

Intrinsic motivation motivation from within the person; natural desire

On-programme a term to describe a period of learning

Spider diagram a visual form of note-taking to collect thoughts

Stimulating a grade one indicator meaning to excite or motivate

Target an objective or focused path towards a specified outcome

 SUMMARY

In this chapter we set out to achieve the following outcomes:

- To state the role that initial assessment has and its value to the teacher, the learner and the organisation.
- To list the types of initial assessment currently in use.
- To describe the difference between a goal and a target and develop use of expressions associated with goal setting.

Your personal development

You have investigated the various stages and methods of initial assessment and the reasons why teachers need to collect and use the information. You have completed a case study to identify what initial assessment looks like in the context of induction and considered how information can be used to benefit learning. You have evaluated your own initial assessment strategies by completing a self-assessment questionnaire and possibly adapting your practice in the light of your discussions with a mentor.

You have established the difference between and similarities of goals and targets.

You have more awareness of the terminology used in goal setting and have thought about some activities that you could do with learners to plan, analyse and monitor goals and targets. You might want to consider re-visiting the earlier chapter covering tutoring and how that supports goal setting, (page 44).

Finally, you have practised writing SMARTER targets for learners.

You should be now be confident in the use of initial assessment in your planning of programmes and sessions. In the next chapter you will look at planning your teaching, learning and assessment activities.

Suggested answers to Activity 1 (Induction case study). These are the words that you should have highlighted to demonstrate the information gathered as an initial assessment of Jamil and Fiona:

ring	ask for a list of courses
fills out the application card	prospectus
advice	Careers Officer
stay friends with	open day
a chat with	Mum comes along
letter inviting him for an interview	offered a place
Reference	Mum says
induction sessions	some tests
allowed on the course if he fails	didn't see the point
didn't need to do the tests	they met lots of teachers
played games	learned each other's names
gain from going	listen and watch
sat down with	tried to find out what we liked
programme of what they would do each week	more details in a few weeks

were friendlier	compared notes
questionnaire	were interested in
weren't explained well	getting to know you
felt very self-conscious	happy and looked forward to the following week

CHAPTER 5

Session planning skills

LEARNING OBJECTIVES

The measurable outcomes that you will achieve by reading this chapter and completing the activities are:

....

- To explain the main methods of analysing learning preferences
- To describe the key features and purpose of schemes of work and learning plans
- To list the main parts and how to structure the planning documents
- To state the difference between aims and outcomes
- To write measurable statements
- To explain your choice of appropriate strategies to meet the needs of individuals in your sessions
- To express your planning strategies in the context of learning taxonomies

How do learners learn?

When starting to teach and plan sessions, a teacher should consider the individuals in the session. We have already established that learners will arrive with a variety of learning goals. They will also have had differing experiences of teaching and learning in the past. It is important that you learn how learners – and in particular, your learners, like to learn.

Firstly, this will be completed by talking. In a more formal way it can be accomplished by doing some analysis: together these are the most fundamental tasks of the teacher. A teacher who understands what helps a learner to learn will be a better teacher because they recognise differences and are prepared to alter their teaching to suit those differences. This is one of the ways that you can 'meet learner needs' or plan differentiation.

Learning preferences

There are many theories associated with identifying how learners learn. To complement the learning theories (Part 7) is the notion of learning preferences. The main ones that you may come across are:

Honey and Mumford (1982, 1992) who based their analysis of how people learn on Kolb's (1984) learning cycle (see Part 8). They advocate that people learn best by either doing something (activist), by thinking back on something (reflector), by investigating ideas and concepts (theorist) or by finding relevance or association (pragmatist).

EXAMPLE

Think about learning to play golf.
- A theorist will buy all the books they can find and read up on the best way to do everything, before even going to the practise range.
- An activist will buy all the gear, go down to the first tee and hit balls until they've got round to the 18th.

- A reflector will probably go down to the driving range, hit a few balls and then go to the clubhouse to analyse where and why it went wrong.
- The pragmatist will buy golf sessions, having carefully considered the commitment and then experiment and analyse his or her way around the course.

Another is Gardner's Multiple Intelligence (1983, 1993). He states that understanding intelligence and categorising it will develop learning. The categories are:

- Linguistic – the use of language. Writers and poets are deemed to have a high linguistic intelligence.
- Logical/mathematical – patterns and reasoning. The ability to detect patterns, highly sought in science subjects.
- Musical – appreciation of musical pattern, for example learning the alphabet to song.
- Bodily/kinaesthetic – using body movements, using mental abilities to co-ordinate bodily movements.
- Spatial – using space patterns.
- Interpersonal – working with others. It requires people to understand the intentions, motivations and desires of other people. Teachers need to use this type of intelligence.
- Intrapersonal – understanding oneself; to appreciate one's feelings, fears and motivations in a bid to develop.

Various versions of tests to analyse learners are available on the Internet, although some are adaptions rather than the genuine learning preferences analyses.

Last, and probably the most simple to understand is the VAK *analysis*. This is the suggestion that people learn either through visual senses (sight), auditory senses (hearing) or through kinaesthetic (doing) senses; hence VAK. You may also see the variant VARK – visual, aural, read/write, kinaesthetic. Whichever you decide to advocate, the importance of the senses in learning is prevailing. The Chinese proverb reinforces that learning is about senses:

I hear and I forget;

I see and I remember;

I do and I understand.

Confucius, Chinese philosopher, 551-479BC

Cooper (1996) analysed people's learning preferences, following the assumption that most learning occurs through the left side of the brain (noted for logic and order), yet by using the right side of the brain (noted for creativity), learning could be enhanced. The ideal, therefore, is to create a mixture of visual, auditory and kinaesthetic experiences to meet individual needs, provide variety, promote interest and to stimulate deeper learning. It follows that the teacher will exploit these differences by including teaching methods to meet all sensory needs. This is a major contributory factor to teaching using differentiated strategies.

It is quite common for new teachers to limit their teaching style to that of their own preferred learning style. This will have an impact on the effectiveness of that teaching, in that it does not cater for those with different learning preferences. Sometimes when you finish a session, you think, 'That really went well; I enjoyed that!' The reflective (and effective) teacher will think 'I wonder if everyone enjoyed that as much as I; did all my learners learn?'

Planning sessions

First of all the basics: a scheme of work is the overall programme of study. It may last, for example, one week, ten weeks or two years. It is merely a breakdown of the whole programme into smaller chunks based on the frequency of your meetings with learners. A learning or session plan is a detailed description of one of those chunks in terms of how you will deliver the topic to your learners and what learning development will occur.

Neither the scheme of work nor the learning plan is fixed. They should be considered as 'work in progress' and will alter during their lifetime in response to organisational and learner needs.

Scheme of work

This may be called a scheme of work (SoW), 'a learning programme' or 'a programme of study'. When you start teaching you will probably be asked to take X group in Y room and teach them Z. The first thing you must establish is what 'Z' is. If you are teaching any type of subject that is qualification-based, someone, usually the organisation that issues the certificates, will already have determined what has to be taught. This is usually broken down into smaller components and you will have been employed to deliver one of those components, i.e. Z.

This (Z) may be described to you as a unit, module, subject or even its title. You should always ask to see the official content of the subject. It is usually called the syllabus. Once you have seen the syllabus, then, as a specialist in that subject, you will be able to break it down into smaller chunks. You will include sessions relating to what *must* be known, what *should* be known and what *could* be known (if time allows), thus creating the scheme of work or programme of study. Do not be surprised if this brings on your first panic. New teachers often doubt their knowledge in their specialist area. It is only panic. Just relax and ask yourself 'What is the first thing a new learner must understand before moving to the next?'

Remember:

Always move from the *known* to the *unknown*.

EXAMPLE

For example, when you learnt to drive, what did you do first? Did you go backwards? No! Did you go forwards? Yes – but I bet you learnt about the controls first!

So on this simple scheme of work the first session would include some information about the pedals, switches and steering wheel. Then you would build on that and start moving off and stopping, then gears and turning, etc.

This would be underpinned by the theory – importance of mirrors, what makes the vehicle go and so on, and learning the Highway Code. Can you see how this is starting to build into a 'programme of study?'

However, you may not be working to a subject which is part of a qualification. You may be delivering a recreational programme or addressing a company's training need. In this case, the strategy is the same as above but the goals (the outcomes or the end result) will either be determined by the learners or by the company's training manager. In this case, it is not a syllabus but specified learning outcomes. The same principles will follow. You must breakdown the learning outcomes into small chunks of learning. If you are delivering a one-off training session you would not be expected to complete a scheme of work, they only really apply to multiple sessions.

You will usually be asked to write your scheme of work and present it to your line manager. It is also a good idea to present it to your learners. They are also interested in how they will progress their learning.

The writing of schemes and learning plans is essential to good teaching, yet you can expect this to be a job done outside of the normal working hours. It will take a new teacher as long – if not longer – to plan the session than it will probably take to deliver it! This is normal and it does become easier. I cannot stress enough the value and necessity to complete these documents. However, if you put your detail into your learning plans, there is no need to replicate the information in the scheme of work (or *vice versa*).

Why do a scheme of work?

- To identify the smaller stages of learning
- To prepare for planning of sessions
- To give structure to the learning
- To evenly distribute learning

- To identify resource needs
- To ensure variety
- To monitor progress
- To inform learners of the stages of learning
- To record proposals for learning
- To inform line managers of strategy
- To help colleagues if cover is necessary
- To assist quality processes.

A scheme of work should include:

1 General Information:
   - Who the group is, usually described as a qualification and/or subject. For example: First Year Extended Diploma, Unit 8; Intro to Watercolours, Washes; Functional Skills L1 English; Management Information Group, Intro to Software.
   - Location and Duration of meetings. A record of how often, where and how long sessions are. For example: Monday 9.30 to 11.30 (30 weeks – Room BG004); or Wednesday 7.00 to 9.00 Autumn Term – Apple Centre; or 9.00 till 13.00 in the MIS room.
2 Aims and outcomes of the programme. Detail about what the end result of the programme will be, written from both the teacher's and the learners' viewpoints.
3 Content and structure:
   - Brief detail about the content of each session
   - Details about the teaching and learning methods to be used
   - Links to functional skills
   - Information about assessment of learning.
4 Additional information:
   - Examination or assessment practice
   - Revision periods
   - Assessment planning sessions
   - Progress or tutorial sessions
   - Assignment or catch-up workshops
   - Study skills.

AN EXAMPLE OF A SCHEME OF WORK *PRO FORMA*		
Programme title:		
Programme area:		Module/unit:
Tutor:		Duration:
Aims and outcomes of programme:		
Assessment and qualification:		
Wk	Topic and key learning outcomes	Links to functional skills, criteria, PSD, employability skills
1		
2		
3		
4		
etc.		

The way you break down the syllabus into smaller chunks will depend on how many sessions you have allocated to the topic, the level of the learners, the complexity of the topic and the needs of the learners. The detail is usually recorded on the session/learning plan.

The learning plan

To fail to plan is to plan to fail

(Petty 2004: 422)

The learning plan, usually abbreviated to LP, is the detail that relates to each session/week on your scheme of work. It states the specific expectations (outcomes) of the session, and provides a guide or order of work describing how the teacher will achieve those outcomes. It is the teacher's *aide-memoire*. It will help to provide structure – a beginning, middle and end, remind you of the order you have planned to do things, how you thought to do it and what you have planned and prepared to support you in the session. It will be there in case you forget where you've got to, it will remind you of what is left to do – and provide you with the opportunity to reflect on which bits worked and which bits did not. By timing the activities it will help you to ensure that you have the correct amount of work for the time allowed. This is usually a second period of panic. Have I got enough stuff? Have I got too much? Again, this is perfectly normal – and with practice comes more accuracy in pacing your session. If you want a comfort zone then plan an activity that goes in to the session if time allows or can come out if you run out of time, i.e. give yourself a contingency plan.

Things to consider when planning and preparing sessions:

1 What is the purpose of the session?
2 What do you (the teacher) want out of the session (aim)?
3 What do you want/need your learners to get out of the session (outcome)?
4 Who are your learners?
5 How will you meet the needs of *all* learners in your session?
6 What order will you need to teach things in?
7 How will you keep learners interested?
8 How will you stretch and challenge your more able learners?
9 How will you support and challenge your less able learners?
10 What will be the ratio of teacher- and learner-centred activities?
11 What activities will you include to create an active learning environment
12 How long is the session?
13 How far into the course/programme is this session?
14 What has happened before?
15 How long will each activity last?
16 What accommodation and resources will you want to use?
17 How will you know that learning has occurred?
18 How will you monitor the progress of your learners?
19 How will you promote independent learning (and learners)?
20 What contingency plan do you have?

Let's think about putting all of those answers into your learning plan.
Here is a typical format, but you will probably find that your organisation
has already got a form that is in regular use.

LEARNING PLAN			
Teacher	Date		
Course/level/year of group			
Subject	Time		
Number	Age	14–16 16–18	19+

Previous knowledge

Write here what the learners already know, for example: key words and similar skills/knowledge. How will the session build on the previous session? Always remember to move from the known to the unknown so this section is your starting point

Aim of session

Should be written from the teacher's perspective, for example – understand about..., be aware of... Know about...

Outcomes of session

Should be written from the learners' perspective, for example: By the end of this session, the learner will be able to ...

Describe, write, explain, state, etc., i.e. measurable statements/verbs

Alternative expression is 'objectives' which means the same thing For best practice make the outcomes differentiated to meet the needs of your learners:
e.g. by the end of the session, all learners will be able to... Most learners will be able to... Some learners will be able to...

Outcomes assessed by

How you will know that learning has occurred in this session? Record here how you will measure learner progress – this should be throughout the session and not just at the end. How often will you re-visit the learning outcomes in the session to confirm understanding before moving on?

Content	Method
Firstly – Share learning outcomes with learners Secondly – Introduction (x minutes) Then – Development (x minutes) Next – Conclusion (x minutes) Finally – Summary and bridge to next session (x minutes)	List here the teaching and learning methods you plan to use. Remember variety and links to websites. New learning should commence quite soon into the class to give plenty of opportunities to practise and develop learning.
Resources	Planned differentiation
List the resources you need to deliver the session	How are you going to meet the needs of individuals in your session?

Links to next session
What homework or 'bridging' activities will occur between this & the next session; this might be an exercise, a reading, looking at an Internet site, collecting something, etc.

Session evaluation
This section would be completed soon after the session, and the teacher would talk about what worked and what didn't work. Was there too much, not enough? Which bit was understood well and which bit might have to be revisited? What would be done differently next time? Were the learning outcomes met?

The teaching and learning strategies you choose will ensure that all of your learners receive a positive learning experience and achieve their goals. The strategies will ensure that learners are engaged, participative and actively learning (as opposed to passive compliant behaviours).

Those strategies should not be a random selection or your own preferences. They should directly relate to your learners, i.e. meet their individual (and group) needs supporting, stretching and challenging the differing levels of ability. Varying your teaching and learning strategies will create variety and stimulate interest in learning.

Accelerated learning

A variant on the simple structure recommended above; it relates to the notion of accelerated learning. The idea came about in the late 1990s, when teachers were designing sessions which were time bounded, but needed the depth of learning that longer sessions would favour. In accelerated learning (Smith 1996), learning is fast, deep and promotes a positive learning approach. Learners are aided by their teacher to make links and connect their learning, which they then demonstrate or practise before summarising in preparation for the next stage. It is brilliant in shorter sessions and really encourages a pacey session. In an accelerated learning plan the teacher uses the structure of:

- Connect – to contextualise learning. Recap previous learning to set context, use starter activities to focus learning, explain how the topic fits into the big picture. Express the learning outcomes for the session.
- Activate – to give the underpinning theories and knowledge, exercises. Ensure all learners' needs and preferences are met. Consider sensory learning, creative strategies and movement around the room – even to collect a book or move groups. Offer choices to achieve an outcome: answer questions, write a report, act out a role-play, design an image/graph/poster, read an article and summarise. These could also be stretch activities.
- Demonstrate – what has been learned? Practise the skills and demonstrate progress, maybe role plays or debates, share ideas, posters, presentations, quizzes.
- Consolidate – to summarise and confirm achievement of the learning outcomes. Introduce things to support learning – mnemonics, homework, etc. This could be learner driven – ask the question 'how have you met today's learning outcomes?' or maybe a reflective activity to record /summarise learning.

The 'activate' and 'demonstrate' can be repeated to create chunks of learning of 15-20 minute blocks. This would then create a learning spiral.

Aims, objectives and outcomes

In the previous sections about schemes of work and learning plans, the expression 'aims and outcomes' has been used repeatedly.

The word **aim** is used as a general statement of intent, usually written from the teacher's perspective, for example: 'to raise awareness of the use of filing systems'. As you can see this is really describing the topic: it does not say to what extent a learner should be aware, or the types of filing systems to be included. It is a very broad topic. Other words you may use when writing aims are 'to know about', 'to understand', or 'to appreciate'. These are very general words and can be used to indicate the type of topic or subject that is about to be taught. As it is almost impossible to measure someone's knowledge, understanding or how much they value or appreciate something, these words cannot be used as outcomes. Aims should reflect 'the big picture', not only in what is being learned but why.

The word **objective** is a smaller chunk or more specific statement relating to how the aims will be delivered; they are written as a measurable statement, usually expressed as an outcome. An **outcome** would use words – verbs – to describe what the learner will be able to do. For example 'to list the main types of storage systems used in a legal office'. The statement is an outcome because the word 'list' is measurable. You would be able to do an activity to find out (measure) whether or not the students can 'list' or not.

Other words that can be used when writing outcomes are:

Analyse, bake, compare, demonstrate, explain, fill in, gather, highlight, identify, justify, knit, list, make, note, outline, plan, question, research, state, translate, use, visit, write, xtract, y, z (you can do the last two for yourself!)

 **ACTIVITY 1**

Aims and outcomes

Which of these statements are aims and which are outcomes?

1 To appreciate the works of Mozart
2 To list the main components of blood
3 To label a diagram of the heart.
4 To prepare and bake a Victoria sandwich cake
5 To understand the stages of growth
6 To state Pythagoras' Theorem
7 To replace a tyre
8 To test the effectiveness of…
9 To demonstrate safe working practices
10 To know how to replace a tyre.

1, 5 and 10 are aims, the rest are outcomes

Answers:

Ensuring that the outcomes of learning are clear, explained to learners and meet their varying needs is a fundamental skill and essential to learning. How can you know if your teaching has resulted in learning if you cannot measure the learning that has occurred in the session?

'Learning objectives are not sufficiently challenging'

'The expected learning outcomes for sessions are not always shared with students or expressed using vocabulary they understand'

Cited in Collegenet Update 1, these two quotations are from Ofsted reports (2012), where they are used to describe errors in establishing the purpose of learning.

So, learning outcomes should be:

- Clear
- Shared with learners
- Differentiated to meet their needs
- Able to maximise learner potential
- Able to measure progress.

Some creative ways of expressing outcomes:

- Introduce your learning outcomes as a question:
  'What are we going to find out today?'
  'what do you want to find out about X?'
- Draw your objective and ask 'can you tell me what we're doing today?'
- Why not colour code your learning outcomes to reflect the level of difficulty and stretch learners to achieve the next level.
- 'Here's the answer to today's learning – what is the question?'

Finally, don't just talk about the learning outcomes at the beginning and end of the session, but refer to them throughout the session, measuring progress and if necessary, modifying or re-modelling your plan if progress is less than expected.

Planning to meet individual needs

The way you choose to teach your sessions will depend on a number of factors, but the primary factor should be influenced by your learners. As teachers we need to ensure that as well as us 'doing our stuff' in the classroom, the learners must be 'learning our stuff' too! This is done by meeting their needs. In conjunction with the selection of teaching and learning methods, resources and how previous experiences of learning influence learners, we will be able to devise suitable strategies to deliver and assess learning. In Part 7 we will investigate some useful theories to support the need to meet learners' needs. Strategies are varied according to how learners like to learn and the simplest way of ensuring variety is to remember that learners learn using their senses and will respond to things that they can see (visual learners), hear (auditory learners) or do (kinaesthetic learners). In any session you teach, there will be a mixture of these variations and therefore the choices will go a long way to meeting the needs of all of your learners. Just remember that you must mix and match your teaching and resource selections over a period of time to keep the strategies fresh and interesting.

Things that appeal to learners preferring visual learning techniques are:

- Videos/DVDs/YouTube clips
- Hand-outs
- Demonstrations
- Researching the Internet/journals
- Board work.

Things that appeal to learners preferring auditory learning techniques are:

- Teacher talk (verbal exposition)
- Lectures
- Tape recordings
- Oral questioning
- Group activity feedback.

Things that appeal to learners preferring kinaesthetic learning techniques are:

- Work sheets
- Interactive sessions
- Moving around into different groups
- Discussion
- Workshop (practical) activities.

Further suggestions about teaching and learning methods and resources are in Part 3 and 4 respectively.

Planning for variety (VAK) in your sessions is only part of the way you will 'meet the needs of all learners'. When planning a session, you need to think about your learners and what their needs are. You will need to plan to support your less able learners and stretch your more able learners; all of them will need to be challenged to maximise their potential. You may have a Learning Support Assistant to help you, you may not – that will have been determined by the diagnostic tests done at the start of the course. If you do have support in your session, remember they are not mind-readers and you will need to share your plans with them so that they can offer the support targeted to the learners that require it. Collectively, with your inclusive learning strategies, these will form the differentiation in your classroom. Here are some examples of things you may need to plan when preparing your sessions.

Things to write when planning for differentiated (support, stretch and challenge) strategies on your learning plan:

- Abigail and Sunita need to complete assignment task three.
- Use nominated questioning to challenge learners.
- Support learners struggling with activity by doing 1:1 support.
- Prepare hand-outs for William on A3 paper.
- Extension exercises in case Peter and Sarah finish quickly.
- Give feedback to Iain, Jessica and Faisal on how to improve their assignment grade.
- Two learners require large **font** task sheet.
- B needs to have hand-outs copied onto pale yellow paper.
- Arrange learners into ability groups for task 2.
- Level 3 learners to work with Level 2 learners in salon.
- George, Joseph to library to continue research, Petra away last week needs intro to task, rest continue with task sheet.
- Use screenshot hand-out for Level 1 learners.

As you can see, this will only work if you really know your learners and are methodical about recording their progress. However, it is also important to remember that good teachers have been working in this way for many years and it is only recently that there has been a name for this style of teaching. So, continue 'patrolling' your classroom or workshop, pausing to advise or correct learners and working with mixed levels of ability within the same classroom. Nothing new in this respect, but now you can record it on your learning plan as differentiation.

Devising schemes of work to meet learners' needs

When devising schemes to meet learner needs, the teacher needs to consider the outcome of any initial assessment that has been carried out. In many cases the scheme is devised before the learners commence their course and the specific details to meet learner needs are implemented in the session or learning plans. However, there are some things to think about which mean that you can both forward plan your programme and be proactive in meeting the outcomes of learner needs identified in your initial assessments.

Remember that a scheme of work is a broad outline of the overall programme and should be considered a working document. I would challenge anyone who maintains that it is a final statement, and especially someone who wheels the same document out year after year, to justify how it can possibly be a working, responsive document aimed at creating the best learning opportunity possible. At the very least, technology changes, curriculum content, current practice and legislation are updated, and good teachers take the best of what has happened before and make improvements!

 **ACTIVITY 2**

Basic differentiation

When planning your programme you may want to consider the following questions:

What are you comfortable with?

What are your own strengths?

What do you perceive the difficulties to be?

What do you want your learners to learn?

What resources are available? Can you use them?

Do you know where to get equipment from if it is not already in the room?

Do you know how to prepare the type of resource?

What are the physical surroundings like?

How much material do you need to cover (think about what learners must know, could know, and what would be nice to know)?

Can you negotiate learning or is it already set?

Do you understand the curriculum requirements?

How does it fit with other learning on the course?

The questions in Activity 2 will give you an idea of the way you are able to teach your subject, plus broad ideas about methods and resource needs. By asking a few additional questions (Activity 3) or considering a few other points you will begin to be able to create a more learner-responsive programme.

 ## ACTIVITY 3

Meeting all learners' needs

How will the teaching methods, resources and assessments you have chosen meet individual needs?

Is there something in every session for visual, auditory and kinaesthetic learners?

Is the environment suitable for all types of activities in terms of furnishings, accessibility and mobility?

Is there a balance of teacher- and learner-centred activities?

Is there a blend of traditional and modern teaching styles?

Have you included an introduction to the course, your module or this subject?

How ready are your learners to learn? Do you need to create the rules, set standards and identify boundaries?

How will you promote independence by including activities outside of the classroom?

How will you know that learners are learning? Build in time to do reviews, tutorials, catch-up workshops and revision.

By preparing your scheme in this way, you will have made significant progress in (generally) meeting everyone's needs and hence be able to concentrate on the specific needs of learners, i.e. teaching for learning.

There will always be unforeseen factors, but see them as challenges and face them confidently knowing that your scheme is fluid enough to cope with them, rather than a tablet of stone which cannot be moved.

Devising learning plans to meet learners' needs

In your learning plan you will identify the session outcomes, content, resources and assessment methods. You may also annotate it to justify choices made, for example stating methods against visual, auditory and kinaesthetic (VAK) learning preferences, or teaching/ learning styles (e.g. active (learner-centred) /passive (teacher-centred), listening, note-taking, speaking, etc.). When you are teaching you are using differentiated strategies, but sometimes these just happen, they are not planned. By matching what you know about your learners to the topics being learned, you will be able to improve your teaching and thus the effectiveness of the learning experience.

Teaching for learning

What can you differentiate?
- Learning outcomes
- Tasks and activities

- Teaching methods
- Resources
- Group work
- Assessment
- Support.

These amendments will help to suit the needs and preferences of specific individuals or groups.

These are very broad statements, so let us break them down into actual things that can be done. Some examples of strategies used to differentiate include:

1 Learning outcomes:
   - ILP targets
   - Varying targets – all, most, some style
   - Ability level outcomes (Bloom 1956, 1964, 1967, 2001).
2 Tasks and activities:
   - Balanced VAK/VARK activities
   - Varying complexity of task/s
   - Providing challenges for more and less able learners.
3 Teaching methods:
   - Nominated questioning
   - Language and expression, communication styles
   - Changing seating positions
   - Pre-defined allocation of groups
   - Extension activities and out-of-session study
   - Promoting independent learning
   - Accelerated learning techniques
   - Supporting learner readiness to learn/study/work etc.
4 Resources:
   - Enlarging hand-outs
   - Altering font types and sizes
   - Assistive technology – keyboards, mouse alternatives. etc.
   - Introducing visual images
   - Using modern technology, e.g. the Internet, virtual learning environment (VLE), Intranet.

5 Group work:
- Pyramid group activities
- Buzz groups
- Jigsaw group activities
- Variety in group work choices.

6 Assessment:
- Questioning techniques
- Variety of methods
- Complexity of written questions.

7 Support:
- 1:1 support
- Peer support
- Use of support assistants for reading, writing and comprehension
- Memory aids, recording devices or note frames.

 **ACTIVITY 4**

How do you maximise your learners' potential?

Make a list of some of the things you do in the classroom to meet your learners' needs. Keep this to hand when planning future sessions and prepare to differentiate.

Be proactive and reactive!

Being *proactive* means that you prepare for all eventualities: being *reactive* means that you will listen to your learners and modify accordingly.

Adapting plans and schemes

Effective teaching and learning responds to the individual needs of learners and this is expressed as an idea in the scheme of work, as an intention in a learning plan and demonstrated in the delivery of learning.

Adapting plans and schemes means modifying your teaching and learning activities to meet the needs of those assembled in your group. Teaching 'mixed ability groups' is not new; it is another instance of labelling. Differentiating or adapting is usually modifying or doing something differently, maybe changing the way you (usually) deliver something, or it can be about a specific action you make for an individual or small group. Adaptations in sessions are usually by task, by outcome or by support. Each is responsive to the ability of your learners. The adaptations or differentiation are always about what is in the best interests of the learner. Yes, it does take more time to prepare for everyone in the session, but this will be rewarded when your sessions are interesting, keep everyone occupied and don't let it become a fraught battle of wills. Time will fly because learner-centred activities are more exciting and although they may take longer to achieve the final goal than teacher-centred ones (because they may involve more group exploration and experiential learning), the learners are active so they don't get bored, and you don't become exhausted. Before you know it the session is over and outcomes are achieved successfully. Learner-centred activities are invaluable in creating learner autonomy, developing study skills and the skills of critical analysis and reflective thinking.

To bring in some theory, Benjamin Bloom (1913–1999), created a classification of learning which he called a 'taxonomy'. Additional work by Bloom, David Krathwohl and R. H. Dave extended this work, particularly in respect of the third category (psychomotor domain). Recent revisions in the cognitive aspects of learning (2001) have seen further developments. You will also see variations. For example, Elizabeth Simpson and Anita Harrow have both extended Bloom's original work and devised their own terminology. Each has in common a progression leading from basic actions to standard or habitual practice. The theory can be usefully applied when devising differentiated learning outcomes, because the classifications provide levels of learning. It was originally devised as a means of explaining 'mastery' in tasks, but has been used widely in educational terms in a variety of ways. Although the earlier versions were published nearly 60 years ago, it is timeless and has become one of the classic models of theory.

The first stage of the classification is associated with three skills or **domains**:

- **Cognitive** (intellectual or thinking skills)
- **Affective** (attitudes, beliefs and values)
- **Psychomotor** (physical, practical and co-ordination skills).

Bloom (and others) advocate that all learning can be classified into these three domains. He then subdivides them, which is where it starts to become useful to the teacher.

The low order skills are usually those in the short-term or shallow memory. If you tell your learners a fact or opinion today, they will be able to remember it tomorrow; they won't be able to do anything with the information or transfer its meaning to another context, but they can call to mind the basic fact or recall the skill. This is shallow learning.

With the high order skill, the learner truly understands the fact – the learning is deeper, they can apply it in different situations and argue its worth against other peoples' thinking. It represents second nature. This is deep learning. For the teacher, this theory means that you can develop learning and understanding either in a phased way (using Bloom to structure learning development in your scheme of work) or by ability (using Bloom to provide different levels of task according to the capabilities of your learners). You can stretch learners to meet their full potential by challenging them to work at a higher level. Assessment and questioning can be differentiated using Bloom's theory, either to offer appropriate questions according to ability or to challenge more able learners to think and apply their knowledge. Bloom's Taxonomy, therefore, is a useful tool.

Cognitive domain

Level	Taxonomy	Learners will be able to:
Low order skill	Knowledge	State, list, recognise, draw
	Comprehension	Describe, explain, identify
	Application	Use, apply, construct, solve
	Analysis	List, compare, contrast
	Synthesis	Summarise, argue, explain
High order skill	Evaluation	Judge, evaluate, criticise

Based on Bloom (1956).

Level	Taxonomy	Learners will be able to:
Low order skill	Remember	Tell, find, draw, write, recite
	Understanding	Describe, explain, translate
	Applying	Examine, apply, produce, solve
	Analysing	Analyse, compare, contrast
	Evaluating	Evaluate, judge, debate, argue
High order skill	Creating	Create, invent, propose, devise

Based on Anderson and Krathwohl (2001)

EXAMPLE

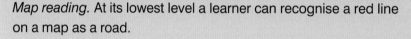

Map reading. At its lowest level a learner can recognise a red line on a map as a road.

At the next level they can identify the red roads and maybe see that other roads are blue and yellow; the next level would be to use a map to work out what road goes from A to B. The next level would have the learner using a map to plot a route between locations, listing alternative options.

At the higher levels learners would be able to plot locations using grid referencing and scale and finally apply their knowledge to other map formats to evaluate the difference between the formats.

Affective domain

Level	Taxonomy	Learners will be able to:
Low order skill	Receiving (being aware)	Choose, describe, use, select
	Responding (reacting)	Answer, discuss, perform, write

Valuing (understanding)	Demonstrate, argue, debate, explain
Organisation and Conceptualisation	Compare, contrast, generalise, modify
High order skill Characterisation (behaviour)	Acts, displays, practises, solves, verifies

Based on Bloom and Krathwohl (1964).

EXAMPLE

Health and safety. At its lowest level, if I say 'don't run' a learner slows down to a walk. At the next level, they usually walk along corridors; in the next level the learner realises why running is not allowed; at organisation level they probably tells others around them about running versus walking in corridors, and finally at the highest level they would probably be putting up notices warning others about running in corridors!

Psychomotor domain

Level	Taxonomy	Learners will be able to:
Low order skill	Imitation	Repeat, copy, follow, replicate
	Manipulation	Re-create, perform, implement
	Precision	Demonstrate, complete, show
	Articulation	Solve, integrate, adapt, modify
High order skill	Naturalisation	Design, specify, invent

Based on Dave (1967).

EXAMPLE

Driving a car. At its lowest level, when the instructor says 'brake and clutch', that's what the learner driver does; at the next level, the learner driver repeats the process without always being told, say at traffic lights; next the learner confidently brakes, probably without stalling the car.

At 'articulation', the learner driver can control the speed of the car using brakes, gears and acceleration and finally, as second nature they drive in any situation without thinking; clutch control in a traffic jam or on a hill are examples of that.

Useful resources

http://www.learningandteaching.info/learning/bloomtax.htm
http://www.nwlink.com/~donclark/hrd/bloom.html
http://www.businessballs.com
http://www.teachers.ash.org.au/researchskills/dalton/htm

 **ACTIVITY 5**

Putting it all together

In order to help you think about differentiating to meet individual needs, look at the following scenarios and decide how you might aid that individual's learning. You may find it advantageous to revise from the previous sections in this chapter before trying this activity.

1 Susan has difficulty in concentrating in group activities
2 Carly struggles with note-taking
3 Shara and Petra were absent last week
4 Matthew has a visual impairment
5 Everyone calls out answers to questions at the same time

6 Barney is dyslexic

7 Four of the group are doing Level 1 within the Level 2 computer session

8 Leroy gets bored but always produces really good pieces of work

9 The transport bus is always late which means learners turn up in dribs and drabs for the first ten minutes of the morning session.

How would you plan to differentiate for these learners? See summary for suggested answers.

Meeting the needs of all learners is one of the keys to outstanding teaching and demonstrates that your teaching is FOR learning.

Glossary of terms

Accelerated learning short, deep learning sessions

Affective concerned with emotions and values

Aim a broad statement of intent

Cognitive domain concerned with thinking skills

Deep learning learning which is memorised and fully understood

Differentiation catering for the needs of all learners to reduce barriers to learning

Domain an area or section of learning; a classification

Font a type or style of lettering in a printed document

High order most thorough level of learning

Learning outcome the result of a learning session

Learning plan a written structure for a session

Low order a superficial level of learning

Objective a specific statement of intended outcome

Outcome the consequence or impact of the learning and assessment strategies

Programme of study a structured list of sessions

Psychomotor concerned with physical, practical and co-ordination skills

Scheme of work a document listing sessions within a programme

Screen shot a visual image from a software programme reproduced into a document to support understanding

Session a period of learning

Shallow learning learning which is retained for a short period

Starter a short activity at the start of sessions to set scene, create learning ethos and engage learners quickly

Syllabus the structure of a qualification

Taxonomy a classification

VAK/VARK visual, auditory (read/write) and kinaesthetic learning preferences – different ways learners like to learn

VLE virtual learning environment

 # SUMMARY

In this chapter we set out to achieve the following outcomes:

- To explain the main methods of analysing learning preferences.
- To describe the key features and purpose of schemes of work and learning plans.
- To list the main parts and how to structure the documents.
- To state the difference between aims and outcomes.
- To write measurable statements.
- To explain your choice of appropriate strategies to meet the needs of individuals in your sessions.
- To express your planning strategies in the context of learning taxonomies.

Your personal development

You can explain the main theories associated with learning preferences and describe how these should inform planning.

You can explain the meaning of the expressions 'scheme of work' and 'learning plan' and describe the key features of the documents. You can explain the difference between an aim (what the teacher hopes the session is about) and an outcome (what the learner gains from the session) and can prepare plans to meet your requirements.

You can state why planning and preparation is important in relation to variety in sessions, and differentiating activities according to the needs of your learners. You should also be aware of some of the expressions used on learning plans.

You should now be able to create documents relating to:

- Producing learning programmes/schemes of work within a specific subject area and to a particular type of learner.
- Devising learning plans which include aims and outcomes, planned differentiation and a range of teaching and learning methods and resources appropriate to the subject being delivered, which prepares you to teach in a teaching session.

You are able to link the theories relating to learning taxonomies and explain how they can be used to promote differentiated learning.

Possible solutions to Activity 5 (these are my offerings, you may have others):

1 Susan – ensure that there are plenty of short activities in the session. Research suggests that even the most highly motivated learner starts to lose concentration after about ten minutes, so that should be the length of these short, snappy activities. When working with others, help her to remain on task by preparing a 'focus sheet' or writing frame giving ideas, with plenty of room to write and some questions or prompts. Maybe she could be the scribe for the group.

2 Carly – you need to find out how she likes to make notes. Does she like everything neatly arranged in a linear format, or does she like bullet points? Does she like themes with brief notes (nuclear) or a thought pattern style e.g. a spider diagram or clouds? Once you've discovered her preferred way of making notes you can help her with pre-prepared note sheets. If she is meticulous and struggles because she really likes you to speak at dictation speed, then I recommend she either uses a tape recorder or other recording device, or you prepare hand-outs from your notes to offer to her at the end of the session. A support assistant could make notes on her behalf. Perhaps during induction you should talk through note-taking styles and make it part of your initial assessment, rather than waiting for it to become a progress problem for one of your learners.

3 Shara and Petra – obviously you can't repeat the session for them, but you do need to get them up to speed. When they arrive, give them a starter type of activity to complete whilst you are setting off the rest of the group in a recap or similar activity. An opener can be a quiz designed to recap previous learning, or a word search, crossword activity or a brain gym activity (http://www.braingym.org). You could ask them to read through your teaching notes or hand-outs from last week (or another learner's notes). Whilst the remainder of the group are completing their activity, you can do a 1:2 session with Shara and Petra to get them to the same level as the rest. You really can see why differentiation should be planned in this scenario; there is no way that you could do this kind of session without preparation.

4 Matthew – this is quite an easy one to deal with, yet Matthew should be respected in terms of which one of the following he is more comfortable with. You can either ask Matthew to move closer to the front so that other learners' heads aren't bobbing about in front of him; however he may prefer to remain where he is. Therefore you would need to copy hand-outs or presentation notes in a font style and size that is legible for him and offer them to him for his use in session. Dependent on the degree of sight impairment you may have specialist support

staff accompanying him, in which case you should brief them at the beginning of the session about what help you need.

5 Questioning – this is about how *you* ask the questions. If you are asking questions generally to the whole group it is not surprising that there is a mass answer. The learners don't know that you only want one person to answer! You need to change your approach to a nominated style, but in doing so you must also teach your learners to use the same style, because again they don't know what you are trying to do. A nominated style is discussed in more detail in the assessment unit, but basically it involves you asking your question, allowing time for all learners to think about the answer and then you nominate one person to share their thoughts with the rest of the group. This is called pose, pause, nominate. I've also heard it called pose, pause, pounce – but that sounds a little aggressive! This is a great way of differentiating because you can pose questions at the level you know your learners can cope with, perhaps using Bloom's theory to devise your questions.

6 Barney – has Barney been officially assessed as dyslexic or is that what he says? If an assessment has been done, the statement will give you clear guidance about what the dyslexia professional considers relevant to aid Barney's learning. You may need to check with another teacher or his tutor to find out what diagnostic assessments have been done. If you suspect dyslexia then seek guidance about how to organise an assessment, again through his tutor if appropriate. If it is Barney's own opinion then you should be a little more suspicious about what is wrong: he may be correct – an assessment will confirm this, but he may be covering another barrier to learning, so that needs investigating. Some of the strategies to support dyslexia might involve use of coloured paper or overlays, font type, reading ability level guidance, specialist support, time allowances, etc.

7 Mixed ability – this involves some compare and contrast research as part of your planning. You must look at the levels of qualifications offered within your session and see where

the similarities are. It could be the level of explanation that is given can be amended, i.e. giving your Level 1 learners info sheets or **screen shot** worksheets to enable them to carry out the tasks. It may be that you have access to a support assistant, in which case brief them on the level of support you want them to offer, which would be enhanced with a subject specialist support (very rare, but maybe possible to organise – if you don't ask …). You may have to structure group work in such a way as to differentiate tasks or use peers to support or integrate learners. In some qualifications it is part of the curriculum that Level 3 learners have to 'supervise' Level 1 or 2 learners in order to prepare them for working within industry.

8 Leroy – he is obviously able if he is submitting good work, unless he is copying from someone else or getting family help. This needs to be checked out. A few questions about the topic in a one-to-one meeting will tell you whether he knows his stuff or whether his work is someone else's. His boredom is probably down to one of two problems; either your session *is* boring, in which case think about alternative teaching and learning methods, or Leroy is very intelligent, grasps things quickly and you are not challenging or stretching him enough, in which case you need to think about alternative teaching and learning methods. A clear case for some reflection about what you are doing here.

9 Transport – the same answer as number 3, using openers to give you some breathing space, but this time everyone does the activities or recaps as they arrive, with the main session topic being introduced when everyone has got there. The danger with this is that those learners that are there on time will gradually get later, so something relevant must happen in the session from the official start time. If transport is late then so be it. You may wish to report this to the group tutor, or the person who organises the transport. If it is public transport, then you could suggest an earlier bus/train! You could always talk about this in a team meeting: does it happen in every morning session? Are the affected learners 'cause for concern'? Should the start time of the session be delayed? (See also Dealing with punctuality in Chapter 17).

Part three

Facilitate learning

6 The purpose of learning

7 Individual and group learning

8 Monitoring and recording progress

This part and chapters relate to the learning outcomes in the following Units of Assessment:

● Facilitate learning and development for individuals.
● Facilitate learning and development in groups.
● Delivering education and training.

- Teaching, learning and assessment in education and training.
- Developing teaching, learning and assessment in education and training.

The learning outcomes relating to evaluation, reflection and professional/personal development are dealt with in Part 8 and the learning outcomes relating to your development of the minimum core are in Part 9.

CHAPTER 6
The purpose of learning

LEARNING OBJECTIVES

The measurable outcomes that you will achieve by reading this chapter and completing the activities are:

....

- To define the purpose of learning and evaluate the constituents of effective delivery of sessions
- To explain the importance of a structured approach to delivering sessions
- To explain the rationale of creating effective group dynamics
- To describe the challenges and barriers to learning
- To analyse strategies to manage poor behaviour and promote good behaviour

Purpose of learning

Firstly, it might be pertinent to establish a definition of the purpose of learning: To develop opportunities to learn new skills and/or prove competence. The benefit of this is a skilled workforce and a literate and numerate society. Learning also has a social purpose, with learners engaging in learning purely as a recreational activity. Whilst most learning is undertaken to realise one or the other of those factors, the level of motivation will vary; as will the experience of the learning in itself. The best learning is led by the learner, designed for the individual learner and maximises potential and opportunities. Teachers no longer just teach; they must teach for learning.

Therefore to provide meaningful learning the teacher needs to employ all of the skills and attributes previously discussed in Part 1. Some of the key factors also discussed in this publication are:

● Knowing your learners

● Modifying learning to suit learner preferences

● Identifying and realising meaningful goals and targets

● Structured and well organised learning environments

● Effective strategies for communication, motivation and managing the learning.

Ofsted reports give an indication of the challenges teachers need to address and overcome:

● 'some learners are not set sufficiently challenging or aspirational targets'

● 'learning objectives are not sufficiently challenging'

● 'questions are not sufficiently probing and are not targeted to provide challenge and extend learning, particularly more able learners'

● 'teachers do not develop learners' independent learning skills sufficiently'

● 'learners tend to be helped too much, rather than making learners think for themselves'

- 'tasks are not always appropriate to reinforce learning'
- 'teachers do not always support the need to make detailed notes and record key learning'
- 'Too little attention is paid to writing skills, including the use of correct spelling, punctuation and grammar'
- 'teachers do not assess how well learners are progressing during lessons'
- 'Few teachers consistently set short-term targets on what they need to do week by week to make better progress'
- 'students are beginning to use the VLE to extend learning as well as supporting interesting delivery…although it must be more than a repository for learning materials'.

Lightbody, B. College Net (2012)

Whilst these quotations refer to the poorer sessions and provide a negative view of the effectiveness of the sector, the expectations of the teacher can easily be identified. This Part reviews the strategies a teacher might consider in developing outstanding individual and group learning opportunities.

 **ACTIVITY 1**

Evaluating teaching and learning

Visit Ofsted's website (http://www.ofsted.gov.uk/inspection-reports/find-inspection-report) and find the latest full inspection report for your place of work or a local adult learning and skills sector provider.

Identify statements within the report which relate to teaching and learning; they will be written throughout the report. List them as either good practice or poor practice.

Now reflect on your teaching and/or learning preferences and analyse it in the same way. Identify at least three actions you will take to improve the experience of learners or implement at the next opportunity.

Structure of learning

References such as 'well planned', 'organised', 'purposeful' are often mentioned in the staffroom and in lesson observations. What this means is that every session should contain some basics, i.e., a beginning, middle and an end.

At the beginning of the session, the teacher should give a clear indication of the purpose of the session (the learning outcomes) and have a 'snazzy starter' to either raise interest in the session topic or establish previous learning.

The 'mighty middle', should contain a range of activities to build and develop skills and knowledge, with frequent opportunities to check where people are before moving forward. Learning can be delivered to individuals or to groups, but in all cases should move from the known to the unknown.

By closing with a 'crisp ending', the learning is summarised, checked and positioned ready to move onwards. Homework or similar out-of-classroom activities are set and the teacher records progress towards the learning outcomes of the session and the objectives of the programme overall.

According to Watkins (2011), a 'Recipe for a successful lesson' is based on the acronym TARGET:

Tasks	– engaging, varied and challenging
Authority	– organised and offering choices
Recognition	– acknowledge effort and contribution
Grouping	– promote collaboration and cooperation
Evaluation	– check progress, feedback and aid improvement
Time	– enables progress and provides pace.

Group dynamics

Dynamics refers to the way teachers, learners and others interact with each other. This includes learners to learner as well as learner to teacher and any other combination possible. The dynamics of the group will be affected by:

- Social aspects
- Behaviour
- Autonomy
- Environment
- Diversity
- Ability
- Self-esteem
- Group size
- Unconscious factors.

How the group interacts, communicates and supports each other; how they respond to their teachers and support workers and how they react to external influences WILL impact on the effectiveness of learning. Therefore there is a direct link between the group dynamic and learning.

Theorists associated with the psychology of group interaction include Freud, Lewin and Tuckman amongst others. Kurt Lewin, in the 1940s and 50s is attributed with initiating the expression 'group dynamics'. Bruce Tuckman is associated with the 'forming, storming, norming and performing' model of group decision making processes (see also Chapter 18) and Sigmund Freud, in the early 1920s considered how groups behave together.

Groups will form an identity and it is not uncommon that if a learner is absent for a session, then the whole dynamic changes. It is the dynamic that affects how effective things are; why an activity will work in one session and not in another. The teacher should therefore never try something only once and 'assume' that if it failed to achieve the expected result, it always will. Try the idea again on a different day, with a different group, at a different time – guaranteed – it will be different. Unfortunately it also works the other way, in that successful ideas sometime go awry. Blame it on the dynamic!

Challenges and barriers to learning

Challenges, barriers and attitudes to learning are general expressions which mean 'things that hold back' learning. Challenges, in this context, usually mean 'making learning difficult'; barriers mean 'things that prevent learning'. Attitudes are feelings and emotions brought into the classroom by learners. As a teacher we want our learners to work to the best of their ability, yet we empathise with factors which from time to time restrict that ability. Some learners may present themselves in our classes with more long-term barriers, challenges and attitudes.

Challenges, barriers and attitudes are often the reason (or occasionally the excuse!) for not learning. 'I can't do this' or 'I've never been any good at …' or 'I hate tests' and any number of similar expressions can be heard in classrooms up and down the country. For teachers, this is our learner's 'cry for help'. When learners say things like this they are demonstrating their lack of motivation or poor self-esteem. We should think, 'how can I make this easier to understand?', 'how can I prepare learners for their future test?', 'is there something else behind that behaviour?' Whatever the cry, whatever the remedy, few people have a phobia of learning (sophophobia); many have challenges, barriers and attitudes which inhibit their learning and so their success.

Remembering some of the challenges, barriers or attitudes to learning can be made easier by using 'DELTA' to classify them:

Disability, Emotional, Language, Technology, Ability (Wilson 2008)

Disability	Chronic pain, Dexterity, Dyscalculia, Dyslexia, Hearing, Long illness, Mental health, Mobility, Visual
Emotional	Behaviour, Child care, Commitments, Concentration, Confidence, Dependents, Discipline, Employer pressure, Fear of unknown, Finance, Hormones, New surroundings, Parental pressure, Peer pressure, Personal problems, Poverty, Previous experience, Returning to education, Stress/worry
Language	Accent, Basic skill needs, Communication, Cultural differences, Foreign language, Pace, Rapport, Terminology
Technology	Car breakdown, Computer skills, Fear of technology, Heating, Lighting, Temperature, Transport
Ability	Absence, Inaccurate advice, Large classes, Motivation, Personal skills, Punctuality, Resources, Short illness, Study support, Support, Teaching styles

Learning to recognise the symptoms of these barriers is essential in attempting to resolve the issues. As many of the barriers arise from emotions, it is difficult to predict how different learners will react, but just recognising that something in the character of your learner is different to their usual behaviour is usually enough. It returns to the idea that we should know our learners. Also, don't forget that people are human before they are teachers or learners and respect, praise and enjoyment are excellent motivators.

Good teachers watch out for behaviour changes that potentially indicate that learners need support or a change of teaching technique is required. Below are some things you might notice that mean it is time to have a 1:1 conversation with your learner or review your learning plan:

- Limited short-term memory
- Carelessness in work
- Lack of eye contact

- Glazed looks
- Repeated and persistent errors
- Time-management difficulties
- Reactions and side-effects to prescribed drugs
- Poor concentration
- Lack of participation or reluctance to participate
- Constantly demanding attention
- Panic or anxiety
- Tiredness or weight variance
- Poor behaviour
- Hyperactivity
- Poor attention span
- Lateness
- Attempts to side-track topic or activity
- Excessive calling out and interruptions
- Loud or demanding behaviour
- Sighing
- Fidgeting
- Putting coats on, or taking layers off.

Before embarking on a one person mission to cure all of your learners' symptoms, you might want to consider using referral agencies such as those discussed in Part 1. What you can do something about are your teaching and learning strategies to ensure an inclusive learning environment. See also Part 6, Delivering Inclusive Learning, for some ideas. Recommendations include:

- Recognise changes in your learner's behaviour and make time to listen to their concerns.
- Include lots of smaller activities to build and develop the topic and praise at each stage of achievement.
- Offer one-to-one support during group activities.
- Use nominated questions, aimed at differentiating to meet learners' individual levels of ability, to increase self-esteem.
- Vary your teaching techniques to ensure a variety of auditory, visual and kinaesthetic activities.

- Know your learners.
- Use signers, note-takers and support workers to aid those with visual and hearing impairments or learning disabilities.
- Allow use of tape recorders; it is difficult to lip read and make notes.
- Offer comfort breaks within longer sessions.
- Provide additional or extended work for less able or quick learners.
- Always start from things that are known before moving to the unknown.
- Experiment with different colours of paper for hand-outs; yellow is good and makes the words easier to read.
- Encourage study skills. Stress key words and when to make notes.
- Use Post-It™ notes for learners to record issues, areas of difficulty, questions, etc., collect them in, read them and act upon the content.
- Ensure writing size on boards is legible: stand at the back of the room before the session and check it out!
- Include images and pictures in hand-outs or PowerPoint presentations.
- Provide moments in the session when learners can ask questions and seek clarification.
- Check learners have adequate fluid intake – and be aware that some may come to their sessions without breakfast.
- Offer rewards for good behaviour or good progress.

Gannon (2012, p14) set out to establish the 'boosters and blockers' that encourage and inhibit learning. He suggests that innovation, creativity and technology encourage learning (the booster) and poor behaviour and passive learning inhibit learning (the blockers).

Following on from the notions of barriers or blockers to learning, we continue with a detailed look at the management of poor behaviours.

Managing behaviour

Successful behaviour management is proactive. By setting clear boundaries, rules and expectations early in the learner's programme, the teacher will set the standard. The standard will then form the respect and values that underpin positive behaviour and promote self-discipline.

Reactive management of poor behaviour is probably too little, too late. The battle lines are drawn and so different strategies are required to remedy situations. The strategies are usually based on punishment and managing conflict as opposed to setting and agreeing standards.

Poor behaviours are more likely in groups than with an individual, although not exclusively. Most poor behaviours are low level, but extremely annoying and tiresome: things such as background chatter, poor concentration span, idleness, minor hindrances, phone misuse, absence, etc. Many of these are preventable through effective teaching and learning strategies and setting of expectations through clear rules and targets.

Why does it happen?

- Classrooms are busy places, so it's easy to lose track of what's going on.
- Classrooms offer an audience for attention seeking behaviours.
- Learners use behaviour to mask other things, such as ability, confidence, etc.
- Learners who are not challenged sufficiently become bored.
- Learner backgrounds are diverse.
- Classrooms link personal, social and academic aspects of life – which sometimes clash.
- Classrooms are not always predictable environments, things happen.

Teachers can influence learners; learners influence other learners and disruptive learners are not acceptable behaviours. So, a reflective question:

Has the poor behaviour in your classroom got anything to do with the way you have or haven't acted? What could you do differently next time?

 ACTIVITY 2

Positive approaches to behaviour management

Consider the two questions below and discuss the interpretation of the positive and negative aspects of the questions. Make suggestions regarding improvements in your approaches to the management of poor behaviour.

How can I create an environment in which learners are focused and productive?

How can I manage the poor behaviour in my classroom?

Some strategies

Preventative strategies

Meet and greet at the door. By welcoming your learners into the room in a calm and quiet manner you set the scene for learning. You can direct them to sit according to your seating plan. Compare that setting with the teacher arriving late and attempting to quieten the conversations that have already begun in the room.

Use seating plans regularly both to facilitate your group work and to manage friendship or influential groups.

Use the organisation's disciplinary code to support behaviours. In many instances a first informal 'chat' rectifies behaviours. If early interventions have not been noted or recorded, it means that unimproved behaviours cannot be escalated in a systematic manner.

Unless someone's life is at risk, count to ten and take a deep breath before doing anything!

Include a thank you in your instruction. 'Thank you for putting your phone onto silent.' Ensure your instructions are clear and understood.

Remove barriers: the teacher sitting behind the desk when teaching is using that desk as a barrier (hiding or protection?). Come out from behind the desk, join table groups during discussion and work alongside learners in practical sessions.

Much poor behaviour occurs in the corridor or social spaces. Learners who have been well behaved in classes need to let off steam (hence playtime in primary schools – but not common in post-compulsory education!). So whilst noise and excitement is inevitable, running, littering, high jinks and the like is not. By teachers being visible in the areas the more disruptive behaviours will either not occur or can be intercepted. Stephen Drew in Educating Essex (Channel 4, 2011) demonstrated this very well and is worth a viewing and subsequent discussion.

Keep learners busy. Plenty of interesting and engaging activities avoid bored or fidgety learners.

Ensure sessions provide a secure and safe environment. This is more than health and safety; this can include structure, routine and organisation.

Use learning mentors, buddy systems and the like to provide support and listening services. Some instances of poor behaviour may result from underlying emotional problems and insecurities.

Protect yourself

Respect the space around a learner. You should make eye contact and work eye-to-eye, so avoid standing over learners as this is a dominant stance. Do not touch learners – even on the arm to encourage. If you need to break the acceptable boundaries of proximity, do so with permission – 'can I show you...' or 'do you mind if I...' Certain subjects require a professional need to touch – for example hairdressers, health subjects, beauty courses. Nevertheless, remember permissions.

Avoid physical contact if comforting upset learners. This is hard as emotionally it is difficult not to want to protect, but unfortunately, your perception of comfort might be misconstrued or misunderstood. So, offer tissues, suggest time out, or ask a friend to accompany them, but don't offer a real shoulder to cry on!

In one-to-one settings there needs to be a balance between public and private contacts. You might try conducting the meetings in semi-open or glass fronted rooms, leaving the door ajar, keeping your hands visible, sitting apart and being careful that actions and conversations are not misinterpreted.

Maintain a teacher/learner relationship. There is a boundary at which point the teacher, whilst being friendly, cannot be the learner's friend. Inexperienced teachers will struggle to find the exact point at which this occurs, but some tips include: not accepting learners as 'friends' on social networking sites (unless it is a dedicated academic site), keep contact information to professional standards – use your work email, give out a work telephone number, don't meet after session.

Remedial strategies

When dealing with disruptive behaviour, there are three ways in which the teacher can respond:

- Telling off
- Remind learners of the session rules
- Promote the values of respect.

When you are at the end of your tether, it is easy to adopt number one, however that is not the best option. Option 2 is a better reminder of preferred behaviour and option 3 has a longer lasting effect. Here are some ideas to consider:

Maintain your dignity. Avoid confrontation and arguments, which only serve to show that you have lost control. Offer a warning, suggest the improvement required and leave the learner to make the choice about how they continue to act. Revisit the learner after a few minutes of reflection time and praise the modified behaviour. If the behaviour has not improved, then remind the learner of the warning and the consequences of continuing without modification. Leave the learner to reflect. If no improvement you need to carry out the consequence. If a secondary behaviour appears – door slamming, falling chairs, this is the learner adopting a psychological distractor – trying to get you to confront the secondary behaviour, thus ignoring the first which hadn't received the correct (in the learner's view) reaction. Again, ignore this. Note it but don't bite. This confrontational behaviour is aimed at control – and you as the teacher must remain in control. Take a deep breath…

Try 'yellow card, red card' warnings or a 'three strike' system. Conversely, name and praise the good behaviours and offer a reward: i.e., earlier break by three minutes, five minutes of Facebook/Hotmail time, reward points (e.g. Vivo Miles).

Countdown from five. To gain attention after an activity or if the noise level has risen, tell your learners 'in a count of five I need you to …' (complete the question you are on, finish the paragraph, summarise the discussion, etc.). Then count five, four, three, (at this point offer a reminder and praise those whose attention you have), two, one. Silence.

Be consistent; follow the team's agreed methods.

Avoid the 'wait until I tell your group tutor' approach. Bad behaviour needs to be dealt with immediately, not deferred.

To summarise, the behaviours in your classroom will influence the learning. In the next chapter we will look at teaching and learning methods applicable to individuals and groups

Further reading

Further reading topics and research on group interactions:
Asch Experiment (conformity) http://www.youtube.com/watch?v=iRh5qy09nNw
Milgram Experiment (obedience) http://www.youtube.com/watch?
    v=BcvSNg0HZwk
Belbin (team roles) http://www.mindtools.com/pages/article/newLDR_83.htm
Tuckman (group decision making) http://www.businessballs.com/
    tuckmanformingstormingnormingperforming.htm

Glossary of terms

Behaviour the way someone conducts themselves

Conflict a disagreement or argument

Dynamics the understandings, sensitivities and interactions within the group

Dyscalculia associated with difficulties in making sense of numbers and calculations

Dyslexia associated with a difficulty in reading or interpreting words and symbols

Inhibit to hinder, prevent or limit

Interact to have an effect on

Potential the opportunity to develop or impact on future success

Proactive creating rather than reacting to a situation

Reactive responding to a stimulus rather than controlling it

Strategies systematic processes

 # SUMMARY

In this chapter we set out to achieve the following outcomes:

- To define the purpose of learning and evaluate the constituents of effective delivery of sessions.
- To explain the importance of a structured approach to delivering sessions.
- To explain the rationale of creating effective group dynamics.
- To describe the challenges and barriers to learning.
- To analyse strategies to manage poor behaviour and promote good behaviour.

Your personal development

You are able to define the purpose of learning in readiness for reviewing the methods explained in the next chapter. You understand the concept of teaching for learning. By reviewing Ofsted reports and quotations you have an idea of what the requirements are of effective sessions and have engaged in an activity to identify at least three modifications or improvements to current beliefs or practice.

You have considered how to structure sessions (in conjunction with suggestions in Chapter 17) and can describe a basic structure to encompass snazzy starters, mighty middles and crisp endings which lead to effective learning development.

You are able to explain how the dynamics of a group will impact on learning and have an idea of who the main exponents of theoretical study are.

You can use DELTA to categorise barriers and challenges to learning and think about ways to overcome the main issues.

Finally, you have analysed the causes of poor behaviour and can make suggestions to overcome poor behaviour. You have considered the importance of preventing poor behaviour rather than responding to the behaviour and can describe many strategies to prevent, protect and remedy unacceptable behaviours.

CHAPTER 7

Individual and group learning

LEARNING OBJECTIVES

The measurable outcomes that you will achieve by reading this chapter and completing the activities are:

....

- To identify the main methods of delivering one-to-one learning
- To identify the main methods of delivering group learning
- To explore and analyse different strategies of creating groups.

Individual learning

Individual learning is teaching and training which is personalised specifically for the individual. It is mostly used in one-to-one sessions or work-based learning environments. It is also possible to personalise learning within a group setting.

Individual learning is advantageous in that it enables teachers to design study to suit learning preferences, ability, pace, motivation and interests of a learner. However, it can be expensive to deliver in this way and may isolate learners. In the workplace, learning can be individualised by creating job swaps or shadowing opportunities to broaden the skills of the workforce.

Learning can be delivered through a variety of styles: distance learning; private study; resource-based; computer-based learning. Each would require an Individual Learning Plan – ILP (as opposed to a learning plan which is usually more focused on group sessions). An ILP records the targets and the progress of the learner and will include actions which enable the targets to be met (see also Chapter 4). The learning, where facilitated by a teacher, is delivered using coaching or mentoring techniques.

INDIVIDUAL LEARNING PLAN				
Name		Start Date		
Qualification		Planned End Date		
Long term goal:				
Short term goal:				
TARGET	ACTION		BY WHEN	PROGRESS
To complete Unit 1.2	● Research four different communication strategies		Next visit Nov 201*	Attended group session and participated well. It was good to see

	• Write up comparisons • Arrange suitable opportunity to observe in the office • Make list of incoming and outgoing communications • Photocopy visitor book • Attend the group session next Wednesday.		how you used your work experiences to scaffold the theories. Research notes made but needs to prepare more detailed compare and contrast analysis. Suggest tabular format. Observation completed at visit – add this to your portfolio. Revisit the list of communications as they are limited to telephone – think about face to face and emails.
Continue with unit 1.2	• Prepare compare and contrast exercise. • Develop list of comms strategies to include face to face and emails. • Look at the notes of barriers to communication and write an explanation of your findings • Analyse one of your own conversations using Berne's Transactional Analysis theory.	Next visit Dec 201*	

ACTIVITY 1

Personalised learning plan

Using either the example or the document in use in your organisation, prepare an ILP for a small chunk of learning. If you are not working with learners who learn in this way, write an ILP for your own learning.

Choose a Unit of Assessment in a qualification and create a list of actions to achieve a specified target. Monitor progress over the next month, completing and adding actions as necessary. This activity can be completed for an individual's learning or for an individual within a group setting.

In this section we review the different ways to engage in individual activities.

Activity	Description
Workshops	An opportunity to work independently, either as an individual or an individual within a group. Workshops are ideal opportunities for catch-up activities or for developing work to achieve higher grades or deeper understanding. Outstanding workshops contain learners who have negotiated their own targets (or are clear about those set for them) and are working confidently and purposefully to achieve them. Teachers facilitate learning and become a resource to their independent learners. In inadequate workshops learners are told to 'get on with your work' and rarely understand and achieve their goals.
Tutorials	Tutorials are one-to-one settings to provide a coaching environment and opportunity to discuss academic and pastoral issues. Tutorials contribute to the success of learner achievement by setting clear targets and monitoring progress, with further opportunity to discuss issues which may hinder that process.

Activity	Description
Virtual Learning Environments (VLE)	Educational computer-based learning platforms which use, for example, Moodle or Blackboard software to host learning programmes. Learners log onto the relevant site and participate in courses online. The sites host support material and can support chat forums to exchange ideas. Learners can submit work for marking electronically. Suited to distance learning courses or for supplementary study opportunities.

Group learning

Group learning is where a group of individuals meet face-to-face or online to learn collaboratively. This is discussed further in Chapter 18. Collaborative strategies involve learners sharing the learning with each other in order to meet the learning outcomes. The learning can be:

- **cooperative**, in which the learners take a greater responsibility for each other's learning whilst in the group.
- **integrated**, which means that the learning is comprised of a number of different learning methods and styles.
- **holistic**, in which the learning covers a wide spectrum of the syllabus.
- facilitated, in which the learning is supervised by the teacher and, dependent on the level of autonomy of the learner, learners are empowered to manage their own learning.
- **self-directed**, in which the learners take responsibility for their own learning though advanced skills in target setting and high levels of self-motivation.

Groups can be large or small. Unfortunately, there is not a definitive number for a group size, and it is very often driven by economics. If one is an individual and two is a pair, then anything from three upwards could be construed as a group. For some a large group might be considered as twelve or more, but for others it might be over fifty. Large conferences might have audiences of hundreds. It therefore follows that the number in the group will inform the teaching methods selected and the efficiency in which the learning is achieved. However big or small the group, there is one key performance indicator – every individual in that group must be able to learn and the teacher is required to know and ensure that they have. That is a challenge, but in reading the types of group activities explained later in the chapter, you will be able to make some informed choices. In its broadest sense, group learning makes the assumption that everyone needs/wants to learn the same topic, in the same way and in the same duration. Reality is proven that this is not the case and so the teacher will need to devise strategies to differentiate learning to meet individual learning needs and preferences (see also Part 6 – delivering inclusive learning).

Key benefits to group learning

- Encourages peer learning
- Promotes a supportive learning environment
- Develops wider generic skills of team building and social interaction
- Cost effective
- Effective differentiation enables individuals to work in their own way whilst interacting with others
- Specialist speakers can be invited to deliver topics to a large number of learners.

Key challenges to group learning

- Confirming individual progress
- Ensuring equal participation
- Promoting variety to differentiate
- Setting targets for individuals to develop learning
- Avoiding delivering learning at the pace of the slowest learner.

Things to consider when devising activities for group learning

- Number of learners
- Time available
- Learning outcomes
- Environment.

Organising group learning

The first thing to do in any group learning event is to organise the group. There are a few different ways of devising groups and the teacher must consider the dynamics, the desired outcomes, the method of delivering learning and the methods of assessing that learning. These factors will influence the teacher's choice.

The simplest way of grouping is to do nothing – allow the learners to group themselves according to where they are sitting. This will usually realise a *friendship* group, i.e., the learners are familiar with each other and usually work with their friend. All the teacher needs to do is arrange tables of the group size they require, or if in a line, tell the learners to work in pairs, threes, fours, etc. The disadvantage of this is that the friendship might restrict learners to the shared views already existing in the group or friends might influence (negatively) on the behaviour or communication of the group – informal chatter about their friendship and social life as opposed to the specified discussion.

Alternatively, the teacher can use predesigned seating plans.

Learners can be assembled in *ability* groups. Using the profiles or known characteristics of the group, the teacher will seat learners with others of the same ability. This allows the teacher to focus support where needed or limit the interactions to suit the ability or independence of the learners in the group. The disadvantage is that teachers may not provide sufficient challenge, and unless differentiated, whole groups will achieve the outcome/s in different times.

The teacher can use a variety of methods to split the group into *mixed ability* groups. This avoids the overfriendliness of the former and enables the groups to mix with others they might not normally work with. Learners can be seated according to a pre-decided seating plan; they might be given a number, letter or colour and at a given prompt, the matching numbers, letters or colour change seats accordingly. The disadvantage of a random alpha-numeric split is that you may get people working together who don't get on and in that case may open up other problems, but generally you would know this and manipulate your allocations accordingly. The advantage of this type of split is that views can be shared and exchanged and 'if all the ones move to the next clockwise group' you can cross-fertilise ideas and regularly change the group dynamic within the larger group.

Finally, you can create *competitive* groups. Think about the groups in the Harry Potter books: Gryffindor, Slytherin, Ravenclaw and Hufflepuff. By creating the groups at the start of the school year and awarding points, the groups became competitive. You could try this within your subject, so that group activities remain constant teams. You might arrange the groups to include a mixture of team players (for example, as described by Belbin 1993) or create 'buddy' groups to exploit the supportive nature of this type of grouping. When creating groups, especially those that you perceive will be long lasting, you should be mindful that it is not instantaneous; according to Tuckman (1965), groups go through stages in their development: forming, storming, norming and performing. This infers that it will take a while before your group is collaborating at its best.

Methods of group work

At the most basic, the teacher will deliver the topic using a range of (differentiated) strategies, but the learning remains predominantly teacher led. At worst, the teacher will show a PowerPoint and talk to (or recite) the slides. Sessions may include some video clips, worksheets and questions to initiate a discussion. By incorporating group learning techniques, the learners become the focus of the learning and thus participate more fully. Yes, it does take longer, but the learning is much deeper than a passive learning scenario. Teachers can structure their sessions into a spiral of learning, i.e. input, activity, consolidate, input, activity, consolidate, etc. and thus chunking learning in a progressive manner. Each round of learning builds on the previous learning and supports/scaffolds the next, with plenty of opportunity to check learner progress and understanding.

Activity	Description
Workshops	An opportunity to work independently, either as an individual or an individual within a group. Workshops are ideal opportunities for catch-up activities or for developing work to achieve higher grades or deeper understanding. Outstanding workshops contain learners who have negotiated their own targets (or are clear about those set for them) and are working confidently and purposefully to achieve them. Teachers facilitate learning and become a resource to their independent learners. In inadequate workshops learners are told to 'get on with your work' and rarely understand and achieve their goals.
Think, pair, share	The topic is introduced to every learner who 'thinks' about the answer or their views. After a period of thought or reflection, the learner shares those thoughts with a peer. It is then subsequently shared with the whole group. The activity is effective in ensuring that everyone has an opinion (which could be noted) and can't hide in a larger group. It is used to generate ideas and improves confidence. It enables learners to understand their own views and compare them with others' opinions.
Buzz group	This is a short informal discussion in which smaller groups discuss a topic and provide the teacher/peer group with a summary of ideas to share. There should be low level noise during the activity. It is used to generate ideas and stimulate interest in the subject. It can be used as an opener or assessment activity to gauge understanding of the topic. It is a very flexible method which can provide quick answers. It suits most environments. The teacher should consider how they are going to stop the discussion, for example with e-timers, music, lights or countdowns. As well as sharing outcomes with the group through verbal participation, the teacher can ask learners to write their ideas onto a 'graffiti wall' or directly onto the

Activity	Description
	board themselves (then photograph it for their notes or print from the iWB). Learners can 'play or pass' as they offer ideas. They can 'ask a friend' or Google an idea to contribute on their Smart phone or tablet.
Circles	Small groups take turns in talking following a period of thinking time. Others must listen without interruption. After everyone has had their say then open discussion can follow, but no new ideas. This is used to generate ideas whilst developing listening skills. It allows everyone to participate equally and so is very inclusive. It can be extended (stretch and challenge) to requiring the speaker to paraphrase the previous speaker's views before adding their own. Ideally suited to environments without the barrier of tables as circles of chairs are the preferred layout. However, the activity can make learners feel under the spotlight and will need careful timing to ensure equal pace in thinking and talking time.
Triads	Groups of three discuss or role play topics. The presence of a third person provides opportunity for an observer, note taker or timer. It can be modified by giving each person a number (1,2,3) and following the first round of discussion all the ones move clockwise to the next group, the number twos move anticlockwise and three remains, thus creating new triads. This type of activity generates ideas and provides 'private role plays' – slightly less intimidating than role play to a larger group. The activity requires a desk free environment and helps to split friendship groups. However the logistics has to work – i.e. groups with a multiple of three and close timing is essential. It is difficult to manage in large groups although not impossible. Monitoring learning is challenging, as would be keeping learners on task.
Snowball/ pyramid activity	Similar to think, pair, share activity, but in this type the groups keep doubling until a single large group emerges to pool ideas. To provide a challenge for more able learners, teachers can add a new dimension, a caveat, a hypothesis or controversial complexity to the discussion. For less able learners the teacher can provide tip cards to stimulate ideas. Adding to the discussion broadens interest

Activity	Description
	and will avoid repetition as the groups get bigger. The activity, however, can take a while to reach a consensus and individual opinion can be lost in the process.
Jigsaw activity	Create small groups of two – five people and assign a topic to the group. They then discuss, research or investigate the subject. Groups can be re-created to share ideas or groups can present their findings to the remaining groups. The aim is to share the learning, whilst providing an opportunity for all learners to receive an overview of the broader topics. This requires cooperative learners who enjoy peer learning. By creating ability groups teachers can differentiate the complexity of the topic. This activity allows learners to get mastery in a topic and aids teamwork. Learners can use their expertise to support learning forums. Groups can create posters to display their findings, which can then become more permanent resources on classroom walls, thus reducing the need for extended (and tedious) feedback sessions. The activity can be used as a bridge between sessions requiring learners to prepare independent research to contribute to the jigsaw group. However, the teacher should be mindful that findings can be biased or limited by the group's knowledge and experience.
Round-robin Flips	This is a mutation of a pyramid and jigsaw activity. Small groups are created and the teacher prepares some flipcharts with a topic or keyword – ideally one topic/keyword for each group present. The teacher may also use 'how, why, what, where and when' prompts to stimulate thought. Each group writes down what they know about the topic/keyword and after a timed period, the flipchart is passed to the next group who then add their thoughts. As the group receives a partially completed flipchart they read the comments already written and add their own. More able or confident learners should be encouraged to record any questions or challenges to previously written comments. Eventually the flipchart will find its way back to the original group who then have a period of reading time and are required to present the findings. In this way, unlike jigsaw activities different views are shared, however, after a while it may be difficult to

Activity	Description
	think of anything new to add. The activity therefore needs to be managed by a very perceptive teacher who can 'read' their group. As a by-product, if groups have different colour marker pens, the poster created is visually very colourful and stimulating.
Fishbowl	Learners sit in two circles – one inside the other. The inner group discusses the topic, role-plays or presents the topic to the out group, who looks for themes, consolidates ideas, reviews style, mannerisms etc. Each group has a separate de-brief and can feedback to their inner/outer circle. This provides opportunities for analysis and evaluation and the teacher can observe the interaction. Several fishbowls can occur in the same room to facilitate larger groups. However, the topics must be stimulating or the activity can lack purpose or be boring.
Problem solving groups – e.g. Six Thinking Hats	In Six Thinking Hats (1999), devised by Edward DeBono, groups of learners work to solve a dilemma from different perspectives. The teacher wears the blue hat (in charge of the process) and coordinates the views of the sub-groups, those wearing the white hat consider the problems from the available facts, past trends, history and find gaps to the facts. The wearers of the red hat consider people's emotions and feelings and why an idea may or may not work based on opinions and attitudes. The black hat belongs to the pessimists and the yellow the optimists, each looks at the problems in the style of their characters. The green hat wearers can be creative and think outside of the norm, but maybe this is the stretch activity for the more able. http://www.mindtools.com/pages/article/newTED_07.htm
Learning Teams	Groups are identified early in the group's lifetime and become a static team throughout the learning programme or course. Groups of four work quite well as they can be split or joined to suit a broader range of activities. The teams form buddy groups to support each other and this cooperative approach creates a deeper understanding of how the group works, so teams can play to the strengths within the team. However, watch groups don't become overfamiliar and watch for personality clashes.

Further reading

Jacques, D. (2000) *Learning in Groups: a handbook for improving group work.* 3rd Ed. London: Kogan Page

Race, P. (2000) *500 Tips on Group Learning.* London: Kogan Page

Silberman, M. (1996) *Active Learning: 101 strategies to teach any subject.* Boston: Allyn and Bacon

Tuckman, Bruce W. (1965) 'Developmental sequence in small groups', http://dennislearningcenter.osu.edu/references/GROUP%20DEV%20ARTICLE.doc.

Glossary of terms

Academic relating to education, school or scholarships

Coaching encouraging learners to develop through problem solving techniques

Collaborative work jointly with other peers

Cooperative working jointly to shared goals, helping each other to learn

Differentiation catering for the needs of all learners to reduce barriers to learning

Facilitate supporting or stimulating learning

Generic referring to the whole or fundamental

Holistic the big picture; the whole qualification or curriculum

Hypothesis a supposition or belief

ILP Individual learning plan

Integrated the learning is comprised of a number of different learning methods and styles

IWB Interactive White Board

Mentoring supporting development by working with more experienced people

Participation to take part in

Pastoral concerned with the well-being of learners

Personalise to create for the individual

Self-directed under one's own control

Tutorial a one-to-one session to support learning

Workshop an area of learning to promote practical skill acquisition
    or group study

 SUMMARY

In this chapter we set out to achieve the following outcomes:

- To identify the main methods of delivering one-to-one
  learning.
- To identify the main methods of delivering group learning.
- To explore and analyse different strategies of creating
  groups.

Your personal development

In the first part of this chapter you explored the meaning of one-
to-one learning and how to personalise learning and use target
setting to create and use ILPs. Then you reviewed a number
of methods used to deliver one-to-one learning: workshops,
tutorials and virtual learning environments. You can look at Part 6
to develop this concept and learn more about motivation and
broader teaching and learning strategies.

In the next section, you looked at group learning and initially
discovered how to create groups. You thought about friendship,
ability, mixed-ability, competitive groups and considered the
theories put forward by Belbin and Tuckman about creating
groups.

Finally, you reviewed a number of methods used to deliver group
learning: workshops, think, pair, share activities, buzz groups,
circle activities, snowball/pyramid and jigsaw groups, round-
robin activities, fishbowl groups and learning teams. You can
look at Part 6 to develop this concept and learn more about
motivation and broader teaching and learning strategies.

CHAPTER 8
Monitoring and recording progress

LEARNING OBJECTIVES

The measurable outcomes that you will achieve by reading this chapter and completing the activities are:

- To list and explain methods of measuring progress of learners within the active learning environment
- To identify the purpose and describe strategies to incorporate starter and plenary activities into learning
- To explore strategies to promote stretch and challenge in learning sessions
- To analyse the importance of promoting independence
- To state the purpose of a range of records kept by teaching staff

Measuring and monitoring learner progress within individual and group settings

Having delivered learning, whether as a one-to-one or a group session, it is essential that you know how your learners are progressing. In this chapter we consider the formative assessment techniques that are used to measure individual progress either as individuals or as individuals within a group or session. More generic techniques are discussed in Chapters 11 and 12. The chapters do complement each other, particularly when considering questioning and feedback techniques – both very important strategies when establishing and assessing learning and should therefore be read together.

In addition to the measurement of progress, this chapter also considers the importance of maximising learner potential. You will hear this described as 'stretch and challenge' and 'promoting independence'.

Measuring progress

To fully understand how much a learner has learned, it is essential that you establish what they know at the start. Sounds obvious, but surprisingly many teachers teach their subject having gained only cursory information about what (some) learners may already understand about the topic and then teach everyone the same – maybe with a few nominated questions thrown in for those declaring some prior knowledge or experience. So how *do* you demonstrate that a) you know everyone's starting point and b) you know how far they have progressed during the session (as well as at the end of it)?

Simply:

Devise a strategy which enables the learner to tell you where they are at the beginning, middle and end of the session.

Some ideas

....

Share your desired learning outcomes at the start of the session. You will already have an idea about which ones *all* learners will achieve, which *most* of them will achieve and which only *some* will achieve. That will be based on your initial and diagnostic assessments and your knowledge of your learners. Then ask your learners to identify where they think they are at the start. You can do this by:

Sticking gaffer tape or similar onto the floor and asking learners to stand on the line according to what they know about the topic. The tape could be marked with their initials. This concept can be modified to become a 'learning ladder', a ruler or a 'thermometer of understanding'. The same principle is applied: at the start of the session a learner declares their state of awareness, using sticky notes to position their start point. At the end of the session or period of learning, the learner then revisits the tape, ladder, ruler or thermometer and reconsiders where they are at the end. Hopefully, they will be more aware and because this is a very visual identifier, it is also very motivational. To confirm that they are not just going with the flow, you can ask nominated questions applicable to their position on the measure to check.

Alternatively, write your differentiated learning outcomes on laminated cards – about A3 size. Pin or stick them to the wall, well-spaced. Refer to them in your introduction and deliver your session. At the end of the session, ask learners to stand by the outcome card that most represents their highest level of understanding from the session. Question or issue a quiz to the groups to confirm. Then in those groups, they create an action plan about what they need to do to achieve the next level. For those that have achieved the highest level they should write down how they are going to apply the learning in their assignment, at work or share their learning with a buddy, etc. This is called 'outcome cards'.

Use 'Learning Logs' to identify and reflect on individual learning development. The teacher presents a number of differentiated learning outcomes at the beginning of the session. The learners then identify and jot down in their notes or learning journal the outcome/s they want to achieve in the session, maybe with an explanation about why. Then, in discussion groups at the end of the session, talk about the next stages or why they didn't achieve the outcome/s they wanted to. The learner then makes comments in their notes or journal – thus developing their reflective practice.

Another idea allows you to intersperse the learning with mini plenaries or learning checks. Issue each learner with a laminated card, A4 folded is ideal, see Figure 3A:

Figure 3A	Example of folded laminated card

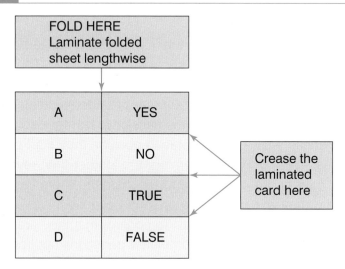

Frequently in the session, you ask verbal questions, which require either a multiple choice (A, B, C, D) answer or alternative answer type (yes/no or true/false) answers. All of the learners have to hold up their answer, say on a count of three, and you then know immediately who understands the topic and who doesn't. This is similar to the 'hands-up' method of seeking answers, but a little different. Vary the colour of the background paper to suit the needs of dyslexic learners – or just to add some colour to the activity!

Another variation uses Red, Amber and Green (RAG) cards to alert the teacher to the confidence of learners in answering questions, (see also p152).

A word of caution: informal assessments concerning where a learner 'feels they are' is not as accurate as a formal assessment to establish the learning. You will need to make a judgement about how reliable the emotional assessment is, based on how well you know your learners.

Independent learners will be able to identify their own learning outcomes. Encourage the use of learning logs or e-ILPs to record individual outcomes and then check progress towards these during and at the end of the session. This is particularly useful in workshop activities where learners are working on different aspects of the course. You can modify this, so that at the end of a session the learner is required to tell you what their personal learning outcomes were. These are then tracked on progress tracking sheets.

Ask learners to write 'one sentence summaries' of the session into their notes or onto personal laminated wipe-boards. This develops their comprehension and paraphrasing skills, as well as being a visual indicator of their learning. You can also ask them to note a 'muddy fact' – something they do not fully understand and need to do more research on before the next session. By transferring the responsibility you are promoting independence. If they get stuck you can always refer them to the VLE where you store your notes and other learning materials and are thus discretely encouraging them to study outside of the classroom.

Use peer- or self-marking to create a deeper understanding and promote independence. This will involve you creating marking frames or answer sheets for your learners, but might help reduce your marking load! Corrections or misunderstandings can be noted and discussed in plenaries.

Starter activities/plenary activities

In a session starter activity, the teacher is raising interest and establishing any previous knowledge or understanding of the topic. Starters can help to settle groups into learning – get the brain in gear! Basically, any activity that can introduce the session can probably close it as well and be used to consolidate, summarise or check learning. A quick search for 'starter or plenary activities' in your search engine will give loads of ideas. Ofsted take the view that 'the plenary ...is essential time for making sure that pupils have grasped the objectives and made progress, so that the next session can begin on firm foundations'.

Word-searches and crosswords using relevant terminology are popular and can be created easily using free software such as: http://www. wordsearchmaker.net/, http://www.puzzle-maker.com/WS/index.htm or http://www.puzzle-maker.com/CW/for crosswords, http://www.teachers-direct.co.uk/resources/wordsearches/, http://www.armoredpenguin .com/crossword/

Mind-mapping activities, for example 'Write down everything you know about…' aids the process of establishing previous learning and if appropriate the teacher can start learning from the missing bits. In the following example, the mind-map is started and then revisited mid-way and at the conclusion of the session.

Example starter activity: Learners complete column 1. Then the group discuss or **brainstorm** (also referred to as thought-shower or mind-map) the topic to establish where they are in relation to what needs to be taught and complete line 2. Finally line three is completed, but this could be mid-way through the activity as a consolidation activity.

What I know about the topic	What I want to know about the topic	What I have learnt

In any introductory session you could introduce a 'bouncing' activity in which the teacher asks learners to comment on others' answers or summarise others' answers following individual's responses. As a plenary, bouncing can be used to summarise the learning. 'Sammie, what have you learned today about …' 'Becka, can you summarise what Sammie has just told us about…' This type of activity would help learners to paraphrase views of others.

Most classic games can be adapted to suit learning: pass the parcel, Scrabble, bingo, charades, quiz games. TV programmes such as Blockbusters and Countdown can provide a model for an activity. Like any other teaching activity, variety is essential, so make sure you have a range available. A starter is also a very useful 'cover' activity as you can engage learners in games based on terminology (found in text books and schemes of work) and set them group activities to research the meanings – ideal – no previous knowledge or experience necessary!

Stretch and challenge

Every learner enters your classroom with a level of ability. Through initial and diagnostic assessments you will establish what those abilities are. In this section we consider the concept of stretch and challenge. If you were to research this, most links to stretch and challenge refer to the 'gifted and talented' groups of learners, but I take a broader view. Every learner should be pushed to maximise their potential. The level of support with which you would do this will differ between less and more able learners but the concept remains.

The idea starts with an analysis of the expectation. Learners entering post-compulsory education will do so with some previous experience. This might be qualification or it might be life or work experience. They will have a range of previous experiences which collectively will give an indication of the outcome of their current studies. You will hear the expression Minimum Target Grade (MTG). If a learner enters your organisation with six GCSEs at A*, then it is reasonable to expect that they will leave with distinctions in their coursework with you. Similarly, the learner with the minimum entry requirement for the course might be expected to exit with a pass. This analysis is known as MTG and is used during target setting to indicate the expected outcome of learners on your course. With 16 to 19-year-old learners it is one of the key measures of performance applied to organisations, however is more difficult to quantitatively measure for adults, for whom there may be few qualifications, but a wealth of experience. Within that group you would consider 'Value-Added' measures, i.e., how much does the learning contribute to employability, social and technological skills. This is probably a more qualitative analysis.

> You might therefore say that MTG + Value Added
> = Stretch and Challenge

Some ways to stretch and challenge:

- Use Bloom's Taxonomies (see Chapters 5 and 18). Bloom suggests levels of learning and there are links to a series of suggested verbs to use when setting learning outcomes and targets/actions. Ensure less and more able learners have outcomes with verbs to stretch them beyond the expectation. A good way of doing this is to use the expressions 'all, most and some learners will be able to...' setting the outcome verbs higher as you move from 'all' to 'some'.
- When asking for lists of things use the expression 'at *least* five (or any other appropriate number)'. This gives you the opportunity to stretch early finishers with finding more answers.
- Differentiation is the main method for ensuring activities are varied according to need and preferences. For example, including variety in: questioning techniques, teaching and learning methods, accelerated learning, supported learning.
- Setting targets to exceed MTG and not being frightened to address under-performance. A learner who is only achieving their MTG is coasting. Involve parents, carers and employers in promoting challenge in target setting.
- Setting extension work for more able learners. Try using the Apprentice/Dragons Den activities for entrepreneurial development, this will provide the more able with opportunities to transfer their skills and knowledge into new activities.
- Supporting learners through the use of LSAs, one-to-one coaching, cloze activities, etc. thus enabling them to achieve.
- Stretching through self-evaluation, for example, try the 'Two stars and a wish activity' – two good things about the work and one thing to improve. This will push at all ability levels.
- Consider depth and breadth of learning. In any syllabus there is a list of topics to be taught – this is the breadth of learning. The

teacher can then stretch and challenge through the depth of learning within the topic, i.e., the extent to which the topic is explored.

- Modify your questioning technique to reduce the fear of answering incorrectly. Use 'might' in your verbal questioning. For example: 'what are the key concepts of assessment?' This line of questioning infers that there is a right/wrong answer. However, 'what might be the key concepts of assessment?' infers a range of correct answers and as such is less intimidating.

Promoting independence

Independent learning does not mean learners working on their own. It means helping learners to take responsibility for their own learning and achievement, by providing opportunities for the learners to reflect and plan. Independent learners also appreciate the opportunity to give the teacher feedback on the effectiveness of the teaching and learning activities, thus making learning more effective. Independent learners are successful, confident and responsible. They are self-reliant and can make informed decisions about how they will learn. They enjoy setting their own targets and are competent in monitoring their own performance against them.

Independence does not always come naturally. Learners need help in learning the skills and this in turn will aid them after they have completed their learning programmes and have entered university or the world of work. Teachers are therefore tasked with promoting independence.

Some of the ways that this can happen include:

Using group and team work. Learners will develop target setting and team working skills whilst under the safety net of the classroom.

Enabling learners to choose learning options according to their preferences. This might be around activities or mode/frequency of attendance.

Offering marking schemes to allow learners to self- (or peer-) assess. Allow learners to develop their own action plans to address inaccuracies in their answers. Encourage learners to proofread and correct their written work and consider/promote the extent to which they can identify learning outcomes.

In tutorials or feedback sessions, use a coaching model of development. 'How do you think you could have done that differently?' 'what actions will you consider are most important in achieving a distinction grade?' etc. Help learners to do this by suggesting a tabular action plan.

What do I need to do to improve?	How will I achieve it?	By when and how will I know?	What else do I need to consider?

Help learners to understand how well they are doing or understanding the topic:

Flash cards or icons can be used to indicate the level of interaction the learner requires from the teacher. Laminated cards can be stood on tables, attached to the corner of the computer screen or displayed in the work area. They can also be used in questioning to indicate how confident they are in answering a question.

Traffic light cards to indicate level of help needed	HELP ME! (red)	NOT SURE (amber)	I'M FINE (green)
Smiley faces to show level of understanding	☺ ☺ ☹ Same principles as above		
Same with thumbs up, thumbs down, icons	👍 👎		
Scale of comprehension	⓪ ① ② ③ ④ ⑤		

Develop critical thinking and analytical skills by requiring learners to source their own research for arguments for and against a theme. Show a YouTube clip or a newspaper article as an introduction to a topic and create a discussion or debate.

Develop self-evaluation and reflection by the use of learning journals or diaries. Learners can reflect on learning, maybe comparing theory to practice, how core skills are transferred from one scenario to another or even whether the session was taught in a way they can grasp the topic.

Create a 'learning basket'. Fill it with activities and resources that a learner might use in activities or if they finish sooner than others. Flash cards, laminated personal wipe-boards, poster materials, word and number games, quiz sheets, a camera, maybe even a mobile technology device, etc.

Encourage learners to feedback to the teacher about 'how the learning was for them'. Were the methods appropriate, was the pace correct, what else could be included?

Record keeping

Finally, the teacher has responsibility for keeping records:

It will not take you long to recognise that part of the teacher's role is that of keeping records. They may be kept electronically or in paper formats. The documents are required for several reasons:

- Auditing purposes
- Information gathering
- Quality assurance systems
- Health and safety management
- Financial accountability.

Some of the documents used are:

Types of form	Use
Application, Admissions and Enrolment forms	Gathers personal details and information about declared learning and educational needs, marketing information and declarations prior to commencing a programme of study. Used to validate funding claims.

Types of form	Use
Qualification/ registration forms	Used to register a learner with an Awarding Organisation, thus notifying them of the intent to certificate following a period of study.
Learner preference analyses	Collecting details about preferred learning styles, used by the teacher to devise appropriate classroom activities.
Schemes of Work and Learning Plans	Provide the detail about the delivery of the subject at course and session level. Shared schemes of work promote learner independence by enabling them to better prepare for learning.
Profiles	May also be called 'pen portraits'. Information summarising learners' characteristics, ability, support needs, etc., used in planning differentiation.
Registers	An auditable document recording attendance and punctuality. More frequently these are electronic and might relate to staff timesheets or pay claims. Information informs statistical data regarding attendance.
Risk Assessments	Documents to identify the risks in learning environments and measures taken to minimise those risks. Personal Emergency Evacuation Plans (PEEPs) are written for individuals with physical difficulties to plan for incidents. Risk assessments are also required to cover medical contingencies, including supporting pregnant learners.
Individual Learning Plans (ILP)	Personal targets to aid the monitoring and development of learning, used to track progress and support study. Can be paper-based or electronically stored.
Induction records	Used to record what has been explained during induction, training on use of equipment and which documents have been issued.
Training and assessment plans	Used instead of, or in support of an **ILP** to plan and track progress through a particular qualification, particularly in employer-led provision.

Types of form	Use
Assessment records	Assessment plans, records of observations, records of questioning, assignment plans, feedback sheets, etc. (see Chapter 13 for detail and examples).
Progress and achievement trackers	Used to record where learners are in their programme. In general, progress trackers record at subject or session (micro) level and achievement trackers record at qualification (macro) level.
Progress Reports	Used to inform parents/carers and/or employers about the progress of their child or sponsored learners.

However time-consuming the paperwork is, it must be completed regularly and accurately. Other departments in the organisation will be relying on you to do this in a timely manner. They will also use these records to inform their workloads, claim funding, ensure examination entries are made at the correct time and allocate appropriate support for learners. Record keeping is part of the contract of employment, and whilst teaching is the more enjoyable part of the job, paperwork is similarly important to the efficiency of the organisation.

Glossary of terms

Brainstorm method of producing ideas

Buddy a peer, working companion or learning ally

Cloze an activity in which words or phrases are deleted

Comprehension understanding of an idea or concept

ILP Individual Learning Plan

Independent autonomous, working without supervision or dependence on another person

Laminated covered with a protective, usually plastic surface

Learning outcome the result of a learning session

Learning and educational needs the individual's favoured way of learning

MTG Minimum Target Grade

Paraphrasing rewording something with different (own) words

Peer someone of the same status

Plenary a conclusion, ending or summary of a period of learning

Qualitative data relating to opinions or thoughts

Quantitative data relating to statistics and number

Starter a short activity at the start of sessions to set scene, create learning ethos and engage learners quickly

Stretch and challenge a series of activities to maximise potential

Syllabus the structure of a qualification

Value-Added relates to activities that enhance learning and achievement

 # SUMMARY

In this chapter we set out to achieve the following outcomes:

- To list and explain methods of measuring progress of learners within the active learning environment.
- To identify the purpose and describe strategies to incorporate starter and plenary activities into learning.
- To explore strategies to promote stretch and challenge in learning sessions.
- To analyse the importance of promoting independence.
- To state the purpose of a range of records kept by teaching staff.

Your personal development

This section did not include any activities, but hopefully has given you lots of practical ideas to try in your sessions. The whole chapter is about ideas and if you attempt to try one idea every week you will develop significantly in your practice.

In the beginning of the chapter you explored ways of measuring progress. You established that in order to do this you need to know where every learner in your group is, prior to embarking on learning. You looked at progress gauges (ladders, thermometers, etc.), outcome cards, learning logs, mini plenary activities, and self and peer evaluative strategies. You are now able to express the importance of measuring progress and have a range of ideas to try in your sessions.

The concept of measuring progress was extended to discuss starter and plenary activities, both of which help to measure and demonstrate the progress of learners. You are aware of activities, such as word-searches and crosswords, mind-mapping activities, the bouncing activity and how to adapt classic games and TV programmes to become starters and plenaries.

In the next section you were introduced to the concept of 'stretch and challenge' and the importance of maximising learner potential. By identifying minimum target grades and adding value to learning, you will be able to demonstrate stretch and challenge. You also looked at how you can use verbs and Bloom's taxonomy to demonstrate the stretch and transfer this to your own sessions. The section continued with a number of other ideas to try in sessions.

In the section on promoting independence, again, you were introduced to some things to try in your sessions. Some of the ideas were very visual, others more practical.

Finally, you looked at record keeping. Whilst this is not the most exciting aspect of the teacher's role, you are now very clear about how important record keeping is to your learners and to the organisation. This section can be read in conjunction with Chapter 13.

Part four

Resources

9 Resources

....

This part and chapters relate to the learning outcomes in the following Units of Assessment:

● Using resources for education and training.

● Teaching, learning and assessment in education and training.

The learning outcomes relating to evaluation, reflection and professional/personal development are dealt with in Part 8 and the learning outcomes relating to your development of the minimum core are in Part 9.

CHAPTER 9
Resources

LEARNING OBJECTIVES

The measurable outcomes that you will achieve by reading this chapter and completing the activities are:

- To explore the purpose and range of resources
- To identify and select appropriate resources
- To analyse the advantages and disadvantages of using a range of resources and how they contribute to effective learning
- To suggest ways of modifying resources to meet the needs of all learners
- To review legislation relating to copyright

What are resources?

Resources are the equipment and aids that a teacher or learner will use to promote learning. They can be classified in the same way that learner preferences are classified and therefore a teacher will be able to choose resources to meet individual needs (differentiated). The more senses a resource affects, the more useful it will be. By linking suitable teaching strategies with professional resources, effectiveness and efficiency of learning will be increased. For example: if you are delivering a part of your session through verbal exposition, by listing key points on a hand-out and recording discussion points on a board or by encouraging learners to annotate their hand-out, most learners' learning needs will be met.

Resources will vary according to the subject, the learners, the accommodation and the skills of the teacher, but they should always be accurate in terms of content, spelling and grammar.

Some examples of resources and their link to the senses

Auditory (using the sense of hearing)

- Taped recordings
- Video, DVD
- YouTube or similar clips (auditory and visual).

Visual (using the sense of sight)

- Boards – wipe, chart or electronic
- Printed – hand-outs, posters
- PowerPoint presentation with note style hand-out (auditory + visual + kinaesthetic).

Kinaesthetic (using the sense of touch)

- Models
- Games
- Interactive activities.

Types of resources

Resources are not only the equipment and paper you take into the classroom, but you and your support mechanisms. A resource is anything which aids either the teaching or learning. Your LSA is a resource. The teacher is a resource. In this part we will focus on the more equipment-based resources.

There are some very simple rules when making sure that your resources are fit for purpose:

● Keep it simple, both in its creation and use.

● Ensure purposefulness – why create a resource that does not offer any value to the learning process?

● Be confident – practise how you will use the resource, especially if using it for the first time.

● Equipment – have you got access to what you need to use your resource?

Why do we use resources?

● To create interest
● To explain things visually
● To provide information
● As a memory aid
● To collect information
● To create active learners
● To promote autonomy and independence
● To offer variety
● To promote equality
● To communicate
● To differentiate.

The age of technology has increased the types of resources available and developed existing resources to the advantage of both teacher and learner. An interactive white board (iWB) or a computer attached to a projector enables anything created using a software programme to be displayed and modified in front of the learners; the Internet will become 'live' in the classroom; resources stored on Intranet or on virtual learning environments (VLE) are constantly accessible. Information communication technology (ICT) is the most popular means of communication and is used widely. Most commonly, it is used to email messages and information, to transmit/submit work, to call or send text messages to colleagues and learners using mobile telephones, to photograph and record learning activities and numerous other ways. Text writing is also being used to quicken learners' note-taking skills, but be careful that learners don't prepare their formal work in the same style!

According to Reece and Walker (2006: 157–158), the purpose of using resources is to:

- Increase understanding
- Reinforce key facts
- Create deeper learning
- Motivate
- Variety
- Effective use of time
- Simplify ideas.

The resources most commonly used in the classroom are:

- Wipe-board
- Flip chart
- Interactive board
- PowerPoint/Prezi presentation
- Hand-outs
- Augmented Reality (AR)
- Games
- Models
- DVD/flipcams/media systems
- Blogs/forums/wikis/podcasts.

Boards

Includes chalk boards, white or wipe-boards, flipcharts and stands, electronic boards. Chalk boards are outdated due to the dust they create, but may still be found in some older teaching venues. More commonly, you will see the dust-free wipe-boards or flip charts and stands. On a safety note, beware of the fumes that are given off by some permanent pens. More and more often you will see electronic or interactive boards in rooms (iWB). An interactive whiteboard is a large interactive display that connects to a computer and projector. A projector projects the computer's desktop onto the board's surface where users control the computer using a pen, finger, stylus or other device. The board is typically mounted to a wall or floor stand.

Every type of board uses the principle that words and drawings are displayed in front of the learners, using dry-wipe, permanent or electronic pens to write with. The electronic board has the additional facility that anything written on it can be saved for future use or printed to provide permanent copies. Flip chart paper can be peeled off the stand and displayed in the room to provide a reference point in sessions.

Unfortunately, wipe-boards have to be regularly cleaned to provide sufficient space, so make sure learners have taken information into their notebooks before erasing board-work. It is essential that words and drawings on the board are clear, accurate and written in a way to encourage note-taking and of course, visible and legible. The way you use the board is generally the same way that learners will create their own notes, so 'meckshure u cheque yorspellin' and learners understand your handwriting and the presentation style.

Ensure that boards are visible to all of your learners. Remember that visibility may be reduced for those sitting at the back of the room – the most popular seats – and things like colour blindness may limit visual impact for some learners. There is also a tendency to talk to the board whilst writing. Avoid this as it does reduce the audibility of the speech and disadvantages those with hearing impairments.

Using boards	
Advantages	*Disadvantages*
Cheap (except electronic)	Not permanent (except electronic)
Accessible	Teacher has back to room
Easy to use	Can be messy
Can be pre-prepared	Usually fixed position
Always in view	

Hint:

If you accidentally use a permanent pen to write on a wipe-board, overwrite it with a dry-wipe pen and it will come off easily. Baby wipes are also effective in removing smudges and stains.

Projectors

Projectors are used to display images usually visible on the computer's monitor to the wider audience. There are portable varieties for those working in community-based venues or in accommodation without fixed projectors. Projectors are usually connected to a laptop computer. Images are displayed onto a suitable pale coloured surface, screen or iWB. A useful addition is a laser pointer to focus learners' sight onto a particular word or phrase.

Liquid crystal display (LCD) projectors are used with electronic/ interactive boards, computers or video/DVD machines to display information to learners. They are either portable or ceiling mounted and offer a high quality method of display. They are, however, expensive and not always available in all teaching rooms. In order to use them efficiently and connect them correctly, a teacher needs to be trained in how to use the software and associated equipment and cables.

As projectors rely on an electricity supply and electronic components to operate them you should always check that they are working before the start of the session. You are advised to have a back-up plan just in case the equipment is faulty. Your organisation should also check that they are safe to use (portable appliance testing – PAT), and may insist that personal equipment has been safety checked.

Using projectors	
Advantages	*Disadvantages*
Colourful	Prone to breakdown
Interactive	Slightly noisy to use
Can pace learning by slowing or quickening pace in revealing images	Needs window blinds or dimmed lights to be clearly visible
Versatile	Light from projector can shine in teacher's eyes
Easy to use once trained	
Professional	

Hints:

- Use sentence case when preparing PowerPoint slides
- Stand to one side and face learners
- Do not overcrowd slides
- Read from notes not projected image
- Use legible font style and size.

Note: Enhancing PowerPoint presentations using Prezi creates a more modern and professional style; they can also include animations which add interest. Beware of 'death by PowerPoint' in which sessions are repeatedly taught based on a PowerPoint or the presentation contains annoying features.

If you have ten minutes to spare, this is a link to a YouTube clip highlighting the dangers of bad presentations. http://www.youtube.com/watch?v=KbSPPFYxx3oDonMcMillan (2008). A shortened version (four-and-a-half-minutes), suitable for use with learners is found at: http://www.youtube.com/watch?v=IpvgfmEU2Ck (accessed November 2012)

Hand-outs

Hand-outs are the most commonly used resource due to availability of photocopying and printing facilities. Their versatility makes them useful in the classroom as information sheets, records of key words, *aides-memoire,* question sheets or notes pages. When creating a hand-out, the teacher should always consider the purpose of the resource:

- Is it to be used to support the session or as additional information?
- Are learners expected to write on it?
- Does it need hole-punching to put into files?
- Would it be better with pictures?
- Does it comply with copyright guidance?
- Is it user-friendly and does it respect equality of opportunity?
- Is the text legible?
- Will learners read it or just file it?
- Would coloured paper or coloured font make it clearer to read?
- Would it be better enlarged onto A3-sized paper?
- Would it be enhanced by borders, bullet points, etc.?

There are several different types of hand-out, the main ones being:

Information sheets. Usually text-based, but there is a danger that they will be distributed and filed before being read and understood, thus rendering them useless in terms of learning. If a hand-out is used in that way it is a waste of paper! It would be better to write key words, maybe using a bullet format and have plenty of white space on the sheet for learners to annotate with meaning, paraphrasing or similar explanations. Or ask learners to highlight key words as you are discussing the topic. Hole punch hand-outs before issuing to learners – it saves time whilst waiting for the hole punch to follow the distribution and/or saves them falling out of their files on the way home!

Gapped hand-outs are ideal as a means of differentiating information according to ability. They can be used to aid learning by getting learners to complete them during discussions or as a test to check that a topic is understood. A PowerPoint can also be adapted in this way. The version printed for learners has gaps; they need to be attentive to the displayed version to see and hear words to fill those gaps. For example:

Text	Level	Strategy
'Resources are the equipment and aids that a teacher or learner will use to promote learning. They can be classified in the same way that learner styles are classified and therefore a teacher will be able to choose resources to meet individual needs (differentiated). The more senses a resource affects, the more useful it will be.'	Difficult	Omit words. 'Resources are the ... and ... that a.... or learner will use to ... learning. The more ... a resource affects, the more ... it will be.'
	Average	Omit words – leave correct number of dashes to replace letters: 'The more ------ a resource affects, the more ------ it will be.'
	Easy	Omit words – leave first letter and dashes to replace words. 'The more s----- a resource affects, the more u----- it will be.'
	Very simple	As above but list the missing words at bottom of sheet. 'The more s----- a resource affects, the more u----- it will be.' senses, useful

Help sheets are a means of developing learning by interacting with the learners. By leaving white space on the page, learners can be encouraged to add their own notes. The printing of PowerPoint slides as 'hand-outs – three per page' is a very professional style of presentation. Add label tags to diagrams so that learners can complete them as you say the words or copy them from the board as you complete them. Just the simple strategy of leaving lines under a question for the learners to answer, helps them to understand how much to write in their response.

Posters and display materials are useful tools to consolidate learning. They can be created by learners, who will, hopefully, be quite proud to display their work, or created by the teacher. A poster displayed in the room will be looked at during the session as eyes and concentration wander; the content is then subconsciously noted. It is a good way of using colour to stimulate learning and is seen as a fun exercise rather than hard work. Teachers can laminate key hand-outs to ensure that they are kept in pristine condition; small activities used with learners will also keep longer if preserved by laminating them.

 **ACTIVITY 1**

Creating and adapting handouts

Choose a topic from your current scheme of work or training plan and create an informative hand-out. To develop your IT skills use MS Word, PowerPoint or Publisher or similar software programme.

Modify this hand-out to enable learners to interact with it. Differentiate the levels of interaction as described in the example above. The hand-out can be used in paper format or displayed electronically.

Deliver your session and evaluate the usefulness of the activity in terms of:

Engaging learners

Supporting study skills

Meeting the needs of all learners in your session

Models and games

These offer visual and kinaesthetic learners the opportunity to see or feel an item, albeit a model. A model is three-dimensional and can be a tactile way of looking at something. Games provide fun activities to experience or practise topics. Think about how different spelling tests would become using word games rather than a pen and paper. However, games and models tend to be expensive and the use of a particularly costly item has to be supervised. There are also problems associated with obtaining and storing such things. Examples include model engines, skeletons, etc., or games such as Monopoly, Pictionary, Scrabble, playing cards. Activities are created around the model/game to develop understanding or skills.

Audio-visual resources

For example, DVD, video, slide shows. These are frequently used resources and offer good ways of visualising an activity or initiating discussion. They are usually of a high standard. If recording items from the television or radio, you should ensure that you have the necessary permissions for use. Podcasts and YouTube provide a wide variety of topic material to stimulate interest. The teacher should prepare well – it is not usually just popping the thing into the recorder or projector. A good session around a video clip or DVD will have a list of prepared discussion points or questions. This focuses the learner on things to look for during the screening and is a basis for a later discussion or question activity. Flip-cams can be used to record learner activity and played back to analyse, critique or assess performance. The necessary equipment must be available: this might mean hiring equipment or moving to a room with equipment already in it. In most cases there will be a key or password involved – who's got it? What is it? Where is it? What will I do if it doesn't work?

Again, as with teaching and learning activities, the success of resources will be *variety*: variety in terms of resources used and the way in which the teacher uses them, but also in terms of meeting needs of learners.

ACTIVITY 2

Personal development

Book a room with an iWB or ask (your mentor) where you can borrow specialist equipment, for example a portable overhead projector.

Practise using the equipment to project an interactive resource, YouTube clip and/or use the iWB software to make and save notes.

Ensure that any projected material is checked to make sure that your spelling and grammar is correct. Ask a colleague to proofread for you.

Do an assessment to identify your IT skills and identify any additional training needs required to develop your use of e-learning in the classroom. Unlike literacy and numeracy, there are few free diagnostic tests, but you may find that the ones used in your own organisation to assess learners will be sufficient to test your skills.

Resources generally enhance the verbal (auditory) teaching methods by providing a visual stimulus. Some resources can engage learners when being used so they meet kinaesthetic learning preferences.

Resource	Strengths	Limitations
Wipe-board	Role models note-taking skills, notes key words and spellings, can be colourful, widely available, easy to use, can pre-prepare headlines, visible, cheap, doesn't break down	Non-permanent record, need to keep cleaning board to make space, slippery surface may make handwriting illegible, sustained use makes them difficult to keep clean, fixed position, encourages teacher to have back to room
Interactive Board	Writings can be saved/ printed, modern,	Semi-permanent record, very expensive to purchase,

▶

Resource	Strengths	Limitations
	professional, versatile as write-on board or display board, anything visible on computer screen can be displayed in a group setting and retrieved at a later date, suits modern technologically minded learners	not widely available, training needed before effective use, needs a special pen to write with, writing looks odd, easily damaged and expensive to repair, fixed height boards not always easy to reach.
Flip chart	Paper can be distributed around learners for interactive group work/ display, moveable, can double as small wipe-board, pads can be pre-prepared	Paper not always available, bulky if moved any distance, small writing space
PowerPoint Presentation	Updated version of overhead projector and slides, graphics and animations aid interest, speed of use can dictate pace of session, modern, professional delivery with large audiences	Projection equipment needed which is expensive and noisy, tends to be over-used or poorly used, reliant on hardware which may not work, not widely available in community or workplace environments
Hand-outs	Easy to create, copy and use, versatile, wide variety of formats, permanent record to take away, printed versions make good quality editions, can be laminated to preserve, easy to adapt for differentiation, wide range of styles and uses	Overused at times, learners don't always read them fully, can get tatty when continually reproduced, especially copying from copies or reusing, need to consider copyright when copying from texts
Mini Wipe-Boards	Simple to make by laminating A4 paper, although card is stronger. Used to check learning or collating ideas. Can	Can be messy when dry-wipe pens smear, non-permanent record. Need to be replaced regularly.

Resource	Strengths	Limitations
	include coloured sheets to aid clarity of text for dyslexic learners	
Projector	Portable or fixed; can build up pictures and diagrams, colourful, relatively easy to create, can be retained for future use if saved on computer, can be used to pace session, good with large audiences	Projector may be noisy and relies on power source. Lighting in room may impact on visibility.
Games/ Models	Fun activities, tabular/text formats can easily be made into games for group work. Three-dimensional, either life-sized or scale versions, good to feel/see/smell, ideal in 1:1 or small group settings, ideal to use/ prepare for dangerous or expensive situations	Time-consuming to create or expensive to purchase Difficult to store, difficult to make
Media: DVD/video clip	Good method of aiding comprehension, appeals to all age groups, visual, stimulates discussion	Display equipment required which is expensive, not widely available and reliant on power sources

Resources are used either to aid teaching or to aid learning. The most effective resources stimulate a number of senses, are versatile and easy to use, achieve what they set out to achieve and are simple. There is no single resource that is purely advantageous to prepare and use, so the teacher must weigh up the strengths and limitations, and consider their learners and the environment in which they work. Then they can make informed decisions about what resources they should use.

E-learning

'Learning facilitated and supported through the use of information and communication technology'

JISC (www.jisc.ac.uk)

Most new and emerging e-learning technologies are associated with either computers or microchip technologies. It is obvious that teachers will use these (sometimes) labour-saving devices to appeal to their modern learners. In Chapter 11 we consider e-assessment to support e-learning.

However, there is still a place for tried and tested methods and the key to successful teaching is a blended approach, i.e., complementing traditional and e-learning technologies to aid effective learning. The interaction between the modern and the traditional adds variety, meets different needs and doesn't compromise the skills of the teacher. E-learning is now a typical feature in better sessions.

E-learning can be:

Asynchronous – i.e. used independently of the teaching environment. For example: VLE platforms, online courses, blogs/forums.

Synchronous – i.e. used with others. For example: live chat rooms, Skype.

Some of the e-learning technologies, very often referred to as ILT or ICT, are listed below:

● World Wide Web (www)/Internet – a vast array of useful (yet sometimes useless) information. Learners can be directed to sites for further reading or research or the sites can be downloaded (displayed) for use in session and for learners to engage with the activities contained within the sites. Copyright laws apply to how the Internet is used and transmitted. The teacher should be cautious about its use: a web page can be written by anyone and there are no guarantees about the accuracy of the information they contain; sometimes a very innocent word used in a search engine has different connotations – check it out first, especially with younger or vulnerable learners. The ease of the use of 'cut and paste' sometimes incites the learner to plagiarise work by inaccurate referencing.

- Intranet – organisational-based web pages, similar to the Internet, but more reliable in content as it is approved prior to uploading. Specific readings or information pages can be uploaded (put onto the Intranet) to support learning.

- VLE – (virtual learning environment) provides alternative learning strategies, without the need for direct contact. Brands commonly seen are Moodle, Blackboard and LearnWise, etc. They can support distance learning packages, support material, tracking systems, chat areas and email functions. Usually accessed and protected through password protection software.

- Mobile/Smart phones – to text, email or surf the Internet, take photographs or to make video clips, download Apps to link to pertinent sites.

- Digital cameras – a permanent record of practical activities.

- Presentation software – PowerPoint, Prezi.

- Interactive boards – used as a board or display screen, touch or mouse-controlled through a PC or laptop or with a DVD player.

- Electronic voting systems – an interactive version of multiple choice questioning seen on TV as audience-interactive answer systems.

- Weblogs (blogs) – discussion sites for personal diary and chat facilities. Their educational use is not yet proven, although it has potential, it is not reliable in terms of content or accessibility. Forums contained within the organisation's VLE are likely to be safer for learners. Modifications include v-logs (sharing videos), photologs, edulogs (for educational use). Blogs emerged from about 1999. Most learners are familiar with social networking sites, so an educationally-based forum is a useful method of exploiting the preference to communicate in this way.

- Wikis – a web-based application which allows learners to collaboratively create documents. They can be edited by the group and can include hyperlinks to websites and other documents.

- Podcasts – a media recording from TV or radio downloaded to a PC, tablet or mobile device. Once downloaded they can be screened offline to support learning. They are most effective when linked to question or discussion sheets.

- Webinar – a presentation/seminar transmitted over the web, the term being a mutation of web and seminar. A webinar is a two-way dialogue, webcasts are one way presentations. Webinars can be used to link groups learning at different locations.

- Augmented Reality (AR) – reading materials containing embedded markers which when scanned provide supplementary information on a topic. An App is downloaded to a mobile device which when placed near the marker creates a virtual imagery. Originally used in military and medical applications to simulate events, the technology is now extended to entertainment and educational use. In an educational use, learners use their phone to scan a barcode which uploads a video clip. This is effective when teaching skills in a workshop. If, following the initial demonstration, a learner forgets the next step, they can use AR App rather than wait for the teacher to re-explain. The clips will be available for constant reference on the VLE to those without the App.

Resources needed to facilitate the use of e-learning technologies:

- A computer (PC or laptop)
- A screen/iWB
- A projector
- Speakers
- Peripherals (devices associated with a computer: keyboard, mouse, etc.)
- Software
- Smart phone.

The technological era has opened up an exciting variety of resources for the teacher and a wide range of resources is the key to successful sessions. Sessions including e-learning will need enhanced preparation – finding websites, checking rooms for working equipment, etc. Also, when incorporating ILT or ICT into your teaching you should bear in mind how it is accessed by learners. Not everyone has a computer or smart phone, nor does every learning environment support the use of e-learning technologies. Thus a totally ILT/ICT-based learning medium would not be inclusive. This further supports the earlier suggestion of a blended approach. By all means offer it as an alternative or supplementary means of learning and include it in teaching if you can, but remember that it doesn't suit everyone, nor is every teacher comfortable with its use and by offering both traditional and e-learning strategies you will be able to differentiate and vary your teaching.

Adapting resources

Adapting resources to meet needs, both yours and your learners', is similar to adapting methods of presentation and assessment to benefit learners.

The adaptations that are made depend on what resources you use, how you use resources, and when you use resources. Adapting resources aids the inclusive learning environment, in that you will modify resources to suit everyone in your session. This involves considering your learners, what they are studying, how they are studying and all the variables that emerge as you get to know your learners.

Some of the simplest and more common adaptations that can be made are:

- To include white space – learners can add notes during your presentation, thus engaging with the resource.
- To include images – to enhance visual appearance and create interest.
- To create positive images in order to enhance equality and diversity themes.
- To word process hand-outs, with appropriate font styles and sizes.
- To use sentence case, avoiding CAPITAL LETTERS – which as well as being more difficult to read, appear to 'shout' at the reader.
- To use short, simple sentences which are easier to understand and leave more complex sentences for those more able to comprehend such styles. Complete a SMOG test to determine the readability of the text.

- To miss out words – again to engage learners with the hand-out or PowerPoint.

- To address inclusivity (paper/print colour, size, language, expression, etc.).

- To slow down your speed of writing on the board, which helps to improve legibility.

- To use reveal techniques to create pace in the session and gradually introduce the topic in smaller chunks.

- To use key points or bullet points rather than lots of text.

To consolidate this section, try this activity to analyse one of your resources:

 **ACTIVITY 3**

Adapting resources

Take one hand-out or print out from a PowerPoint presentation or web page (or similar text-based resource) that you have used in the last few weeks.

Analyse the following:

- What percentage of the resource is white space?
- Is it read-only or is the learner required to interact with their resource?
- How many images are in the resource?
- What is the presentation style?
- Is the resource prose, subtitle/text, bullet point or key word?
- What is the balance between the presentation style (same/varied)?
- What is the font style and font size?
- How do you know if the information contained within the resource is understood?

How can you improve the resource to meet the needs of:

- Visual learners?
- Kinaesthetic learners?
- ESOL learners?

- Entry Level learners?
- Level 3+ learners?

Is the resource fully referenced?

Are there additional links to further information or websites?

How is the resource effectively used as:

- A teacher's aid?
- A learning aid?
- A revision tool?
- An assessment tool?

Review the resource and adapt it accordingly. Keep before and after versions to show your personal development, and reflect on this activity with a colleague or tutor.

Assistive technologies

Some learners experience difficulty in accessing learning environments, using computers or other learning resources and benefit from using equipment which aids accessibility. This equipment is known as Assistive Technology (AT). Equipment might be adaptions or modifications to customary equipment. Some assistive technologies are off the shelf versions, some can be homemade devices; all enable a learner to participate in learning. Some examples of AT seen in educational settings include:

- Wheelchairs and other mobility devices
- Tools to reach, grab or pick up small items
- Personal Emergency Response Systems (PERS)
- Computer accessibility software to aid keyboard use
- Screen readers, magnifiers to aid visually impaired learners
- Alternative communication strategies to aid those who have difficulty with spoken language
- Prosthesis and adaptive sports devices.

Advice and guidance to support educationalists and other professionals can be found at the British Assistive Technology Association (BATA). They define AT as:

> 'Assistive technology is any product or service that maintains or improves the ability of individuals with disabilities or impairments to communicate, learn and live independent, fulfilling and productive lives.'

Barbara Phillips, Executive Director, BATA (March 2012).
http://www.bataonline.org/

Resources and health and safety

Standard rules apply when using resources in the classroom; teachers have a responsibility for the safety of themselves and those around them. Some things to consider:

- Safe movement around the room when using resources or working in groups
- Possible risks associated with changes in intensity of light to cope with visibility of projected images – from bright to dim lighting
- Safe electrical usage – PAT testing, trailing cables, no overloading of plug sockets or extension cables, etc
- Safe use of photocopiers, printers, etc
- Eye care/safety resulting from prolonged use of visual display units (VDUs)
- Fumes from some permanent markers and board cleaning sprays.

Legislation and copyright

Copyright legislation and guidance protects the originators of material against plagiarism and compromising intellectual ownership. Materials include books, newspapers, journals, material downloaded from the Internet, broadcasts – in fact anything which is not your own original material. It is against the Copyright, Designs and Patents Act 1988, and the subsequent amendment Copyright and Related Rights Act 2003, to reproduce material in any way without acknowledging the originator.

Plagiarism is when a writer uses somebody else's work without saying so, or expresses someone else's opinions as their own. Even if you reference the work, you are only allowed to use a small amount of that text (the copyright and licensing laws govern this). This is a problem given the amount of information on the Internet, which is easily pasted into learners' essays. Educational organisations do not tolerate plagiarism and it is easy to prevent being accused of plagiarism if sources are referenced. Referencing, therefore, is used to acknowledge the rightful owner (the author, the learner or the teacher). Relating this to the learning environment, it means that during research activity learners are required to use a system like Harvard when referencing, to cite the source of their research.

More Information:

Part 5 Assessment – authenticity and spotting plagiarism.

In order to devise a fair system of paying royalties to originators, the Copyright Licensing Agency (CLA) offers licences to educational establishments so that teachers can photocopy, scan or digitally reproduce information for their learners. It extends to include the re-use of cuttings from magazines, journals and newspapers. Usually, close to every photocopier there is a charter explaining how much can be reproduced. Your reprographics or Academic Standards department will advise on this. Exercise caution when copying anything, as the CLA can carry out spot checks and could ask for access to filing cabinets/shared e-storage to check that information is not being illegally copied. Always state the originator's name, even if it is a hand-out devised by a colleague.

Two more recent pieces of legislation are under review due to the controversy around its implementation. These two laws are: Digital Economy Act 2010 and Communications Data Bill 2012. Both relate to digital media and attempt to regulate browsing and storage using the Internet.

Glossary of terms

Annotate to add notes to something to add explanation or context

App software programme for Mobile applications and Smart phones

Blended (learning) a mixture of traditional and modern/computer-based learning technologies

Collaborate to work jointly with other peers

Copyright legal ownership of text or images

Download copy data from one system to another

ESOL English for speakers of other languages

Hyperlink an electronic link between documents

ICT Information Communication Technology

Interactive have an effect on, engage with

iWB Interactive White Board

Laminate cover with a protective, usually plastic surface

Offline not connected to a network, Internet or similar

Plagiarism the passing off of someone else's work as your own without reference

Resources a teaching aid to support learning

Revision to repeat the content in order to refresh understanding

SMOG a readability test

Stimulus to initiate a reaction; to motivate

Upload to transfer data to a larger computer or network

Variables the analysis or acceptance that not everything will fit in the box

Verbal exposition teacher-talk

VLE Virtual Learning Environment

SUMMARY

In this chapter we set out to achieve the following outcomes:

- To explore the purpose and range of resources.
- To identify and select appropriate resources.
- To analyse the advantages and disadvantages of using a range of resources and how they contribute to effective learning.
- To suggest ways of modifying resources to meet the needs of all learners.
- To review legislation relating to copyright.

Your personal development

In this section you have had the opportunity to compare many different types of resources and considered how you might use them in your teaching sessions. You have looked at descriptions of the main types of resources, including those which are classified as e-learning resources. For many, you have challenged your ideas about when and how to use them to create purposeful learning and to ensure that they meet the needs of all learners in your sessions. In reviewing e-learning resources you have learned about new ideas or confirmed your understanding of the many new expressions which seem to appear in the teachers' language.

You have completed three activities to develop, explore and evaluate the resources available to you, and in some instances you will have identified additional training that you need to use them to the maximum value.

You have reviewed a number of assistive technologies and how they are used in the inclusive learning environment.

Finally you have considered the impact that legislation has in terms of using resources and in protection the ownership of published material.

Part five

Assessment

This part and chapters relate to the learning outcomes in the following Units of Assessment:

- Understanding assessment in education and training.
- Understanding the principles and practices of assessment.

- Assessing learners in education and training.
- Teaching, learning and assessment in education and training.
- Developing teaching, learning and assessment in education and training.

The learning outcomes relating to evaluation, reflection and professional/personal development are dealt with in Part 8 and the learning outcomes relating to your development of the minimum core are in Part 9.

CHAPTER 10

The principles of assessment: functions and concepts

LEARNING OBJECTIVES

The measurable outcomes that you will achieve by reading this chapter and completing the activities are:

....

- To explain the functions of assessment in training, learning and development
- To define and explain the key concepts (ideas) and principles (values) relating to assessment
- To define the rules associated with assessments to ensure valid, reliable and accurate assessments
- To describe the meaning of words associated with assessment
- To state the roles and responsibilities of the teacher/assessor
- To summarise the main legislative and regulatory factors
- To describe and explain the meaning of ethics and values in assessment

Assessment basics

Assessment is the term given to checking that learning has occurred. It is the way teachers and trainers know whether learning is complete.

> Assessment is the process by which evidence of
> student achievement is obtained and judged.
> Ecclestone, (1996) points out that assessment
> requires two things: evidence and a standard or scale.
>
> *Gray (2005:50)*

Some of the first things you need to grasp in assessment are: how, what, when, where, why. You cannot assess somebody or something without telling them about the expectations or setting the standard. The standard may be role-modelled, industry-based, competence-based or theoretically driven; they may be from accredited qualifications or in-house training programmes. Whichever applies, the standard should come from the national occupational standards or programme assessment criteria. In recreational or work-based training provision it is possible that the standards are less formal; the goals are likely to be devised by the teacher, the employer and/or the learner. Therefore, in essence, standards and goals are the keys to successful assessment.

> If you know where you are going, you'll be able to
> tell when you've got there.

The output of assessment is 'evidence'; evidence is the confirmation that assessment has occurred and the way it is proven. To summarise, assessment means 'a method of confirming learning'.

Why assess?

Businesses and training institutions are driven by the need to have a qualified workforce. In both the private and public sectors this need is met through a range of opportunities delivered either on their premises or in conjunction with a college or private training provider. Education and training is delivered as part of a professional development programme, apprenticeship, day-release or full time education programme. Whichever way the education or training is delivered there is a need to ensure that the standards are consistent and recognisable. To this end each occupational sector has a series of qualifications. Where qualifications do not exist, perhaps because the employer has their own specific training needs, there is still a need to produce standards by which to measure learning.

The need for assessment is therefore linked to national or organisational standards. Assessment is required to ensure the integrity of those standards.

There is increasing focus on ensuring that assessment is meaningful and understood by all. Assessment is no longer solely a vehicle to complete a qualification (assessment OF learning), assessment now is a tool to develop and monitor progress within a qualification or training programme (assessment FOR learning).

ACTIVITY 1

Self assessment

Where are you now in terms of how you assess learning?

Key stages of learning	How do you currently assess this stage? If not yet teaching, how might you assess this?	Why do you do this? (self, learners, managers)
Initial assessment of a skill at entry to a qualification		
Getting to know your learners		

Key stages of learning	How do you currently assess this stage? If not yet teaching, how might you assess this?	Why do you do this? (self, learners, managers)
Planning learning for groups		
Planning learning for individuals		
Monitoring progress in sessions		
Checking learning of topic: Checking learning of unit/ module		
Checking retained information and/or transferability of information/skill to another context		
Responding to needs of learners		

The purpose of this activity is to establish your starting point in developing your skills in assessment. You should use this activity to create opportunities to increase the frequency and range of assessment. Assessment is essential to learning. Teachers must know whether their teachings are comprehended and the learning has been learned, i.e. teaching for learning. Otherwise we are setting up our learners to fail once outside of the learning environment.

The language of assessment

The terminology or language of assessment leads to the introduction of words which demand further explanation. This section introduces the reader to the technical language of assessment through investigating the process of assessment.

Assessment can be carried out before enrolment (at interview), at commencement (diagnostic and initial assessment), during and at the end of the learning or training activity and at the end of the module, unit or programme. It may be pertinent at this point to look at how qualifications are structured, as this will lead us to the points at which assessment should occur.

Programme of learning

A Programme is a collection of qualifications which create a college course, an apprenticeship framework or a training programme. This is described as the curriculum (see also Chapter 21 onwards). A qualification is made up of a number of Units of Assessment.

In September 2010, a new qualifications framework was launched, replacing the old National Qualifications Framework (NQF). The Qualifications Credit Framework (QCF) continued to list a hierarchy of levels of qualifications, however, in the new system, a tariff was issued with a greater number of levels (eight) of increasing difficulty. These levels meant that qualifications could be matched against each other – for example at Level 3 you will be able to undertake an A level, an Advanced Apprenticeship or a BTEC Extended Diploma. Whilst qualifications might be of different sizes within the Level 3, they all have parity in terms of difficulty. The following diagram (Figure 5A) shows the QCF.

In the vocational sector, National Occupational Standards (NOS) are written by the Sector Skills Councils (SSCs). These standards form the basis of the Units of Assessment (UoA) and the resultant qualifications created by Awarding Organisations.

Qualification

A certificated qualification, endorsed by an Awarding Organisation and approved through the Qualifications and Credit Framework.

Figure 5A   The qualifications credit framework

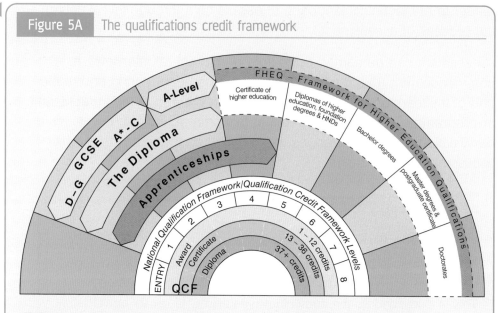

(QCF, see: http://www.ofqual.gov.uk/qualification-and-assessment-framework/89-articles/145-explaining-the-qualifications-and-credit-framework)

For example, some qualifications you may come across include:

Level 4	Certificate in Teaching in Education and Training
Level 2	Certificate in Health and Social Care (QCF)
Level 1	NVQ Diploma in Hairdressing and Beauty Therapy (QCF)
Level 3	Extended Diploma in Public Services (Uniformed) (QCF)
Level 5	HND Diploma in Business (QCF)
Entry	Functional Skills Mathematics

A qualification consists of a number of Units of Assessment, clustered to create a certificated qualification.

Units of Assessment (UoA)

The smaller subsections of the qualification which focus on a particular aspect. There will usually be several units in a qualification.

Each unit will have its own specified learning outcomes and assessment criteria. Each will have a specified level and credit value. Additional information may be provided to guide the assessment process. The documentation will also state the name of the sector skills area which owns the unit. In some qualifications, units of assessment from different sector areas will be combined to create meaningful qualifications.

Teachers and trainers are required to assess competence or knowledge and understanding relating to the UoA.

Content

Each Unit of Assessment will have statements relating to what has to be covered in order to achieve the unit. These statements about content are written in terms of what the learner will know or be able to do on completion of the Unit of Assessment. In some qualifications not all of the content is assessed. In some the breadth of the content requires clarification. The extent of the assessment will be stated in assessment guidance provided by Awarding Organisations. The 'Assessment Guidance' therefore is an essential document in making assessment decisions.

Rules of combination

Qualifications consist of Mandatory and Optional units. As their names infer, mandatory units are those which must be achieved and optional ones are usually from a list of units arranged singularly or in groups from which the learner must select a specified number. The purpose of grouping units is to ensure that qualifications contain the range of competence expected in the industry.

Version 4 http://www.paa-uk.org/Qualifications/Regulated/Qualifications/QCF% 20Info/QCF%20Support%20Pack/Rules%20of%20Combination%20in%20the% 20QCF.pdf (accessed March 2011)

Accumulation and transfer of credits

In order to provide benchmarks for qualifications, the regulatory body: Ofqual requires that each unit in a set of National Occupational Standards is set at a *level* of learning. This determines the level of difficulty of the unit. It varies from Entry (entry 1, entry 2 and entry 3); through Level 1 to Level 8. Level 2 is roughly equivalent to GCSE level and Level 3 at A level standard, Level 8 is PhD (see diagram above). Another benchmark is that of *size*. This refers to the volume of learning and is stated as a 'credit'; an award comprises one to twelve credits; a certificate comprises thirteen to thirty-six credits; a diploma comprises of thirty-seven credits or more.

> **Watch point**
>
> This change is different to the earlier framework in which a diploma
> was at a higher level than a certificate. Now there are awards,
> certificates and diplomas at all levels; they are now determined by
> their size, not their difficulty.

The final benchmark relates to *subject*; qualifications are categorised into
the subject sector classification scheme. For example, Award, Certificate
and Diploma in Teaching in Education and Training units are in subject
area 13 – Education and Training, sector area 13.1 – Teaching and
Lecturing (see also Chapter 28).

Programmes of Learning and Apprenticeships are arranged around
these frameworks; so you may be employed to deliver a particular unit or
module or you may work within a team of people to train towards a
whole or part qualification. Whichever strategy is used, the teacher or
trainer will have to assess that learning has occurred. In some
qualifications this learning is referred to as 'demonstrating competence'.

Unfortunately, assessment is such a wide topic and the qualification
frameworks are so varied that there are many different terms used
(assessment jargon) and it sometimes takes a while to learn the words;
usually when you do discover their meaning it is broadly the same as
another similar word used by a different qualification team. Let us look at
some of those terms:

Term	Alternative expressions
Qualification	Standards, specifications, course, syllabus, programme, apprenticeship. Written by an Awarding Organisation following a set of National Occupational Standards
Learning Outcome	Objective, range statements, content, statements of competence
Evidence requirements	Assessment guidance, evidence, portfolio, assignment, assessment criteria

Term	Alternative expressions
Grading	Grading criteria are the level at which the outcomes are met – e.g., pass merit/credit or distinction
Quality Assurance	Verification, moderation, standardisation
Assessment	Test, exam, evidence (proof)

Command words

Within every set of Units of Assessment (UoA), there are a series of statements to define exactly what a learner has to do in order to demonstrate their competence against a specific set of standards. We have already seen these words in connection with the writing of learning outcomes for sessions.

For example: 'explain....' is frequently seen. Explain can be defined as 'to make something clear by giving a detailed account of relevant facts or circumstances'. How a learner does this will be 'explained' later in the chapter, but suffice to say, at this point, it could be written, verbal or demonstrated, or a combination of these strategies. It is the skill of the teacher/assessor that will guide the learner towards an effective method.

 ACTIVITY 2

Command words

Make a list of any similar command words you use in your training or learning environment when 'explaining' the subject or how it will be assessed.

Consider:

Wording in assignments or instructions to complete question sheets.

▶

e.g.: Explain

                    *

*   *

*   *

*   *

*   *

*   *

Extension Activity:

Create a dictionary of terms that your learners may find helpful.

Clue: look at the learning outcomes in a qualification. Sentences usually start with a word that indicates what needs to be done in order to meet the requirements of the outcome. Awarding Organisations also have resources to explain their command words.

Concepts of assessment

A concept is an idea, in this instance, about assessment. The concepts that you will commonly see are:

- Norm referencing
- Criterion referencing
- Formative assessment
- Summative assessment
- Ipsative assessment.

Norm referencing is when learners are assessed against each other. It is quite an old-fashioned concept. For example, if you were to set a test where the top 10 per cent were able to progress to a higher level or rewarded in some way, and the lowest 10 per cent were penalised in some way, perhaps by going down a grade of class, then this would be norm referencing. The learner's ability is measured (and compared) against other learners. This is very common in educational establishments, when learners are split into sessions according to ability rather than year or house groups. The percentiles can also be varied: for example if there were a lot of learners who gained high marks in their test, but you only had reward spaces for half of them, it is possible to raise the pass mark to match the figure of 'top 10 per cent of learners,' equally if the tests were very difficult, you can lower the pass mark to reward the 'top 10 per cent'. In this way, you will consistently have a top 10 per cent, although their pass marks may have been different.

Criterion referencing is when a learner (trainee, candidate, student) achieves a standard, they either can (or can't) do the task, answer the question or demonstrate competence. They can continue in their attempts until the criterion is achieved (plural is criteria). Therefore in this style of assessment the teacher is measuring what a learner can do. Whilst it is generally associated with a 'can do-can't do' (pass-fail) assessment, it may be linked to a grading scale which determines how well a learner can do something. In this strategy a learner can pass, pass with merit or pass with distinction.

Formative assessment is an interim judgement and is key to any 'assessment for learning' strategy. It is also known as 'continuous assessment'. It has the advantage of being an ideal opportunity to tell a learner how they are progressing and giving them the chance to improve. This type of assessment is very motivational because it is seen as a review rather than an assessment. It helps learners to progress and maximise their potential. There is life after formative assessment! One of the disadvantages of formative assessment (although significantly outweighed by the advantages) is that continuous assessment may feel like *continual* assessment.

Kolb's learning cycle (see Figure 5B) advocates the concepts of formative assessment and feedback clearly within the cycle, indicating their value in personal development and progression. Formative assessment aids learning.

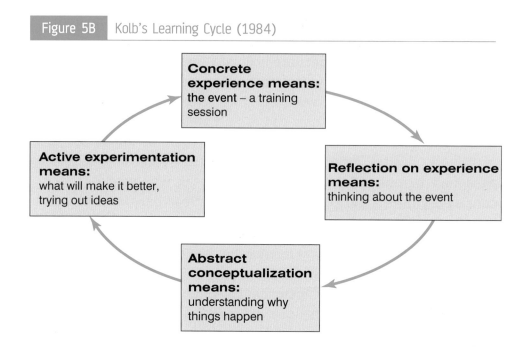

Figure 5B   Kolb's Learning Cycle (1984)

Summative assessment is usually associated with tests and exams. It is 'assessment of learning' and is a formal process to close a stage of learning or training; thus enabling the whole programme to move forward. In summative assessment styles, a learner progresses through their qualification or unit of assessment until the time comes that learning is complete and they are tested on their knowledge or skills. A judgement is made, which is then expressed on a certificate. If a learner wishes to improve they usually have to 'sit' the examination again. This does put enormous pressure on learners as the outcomes may determine their future, however with teaching that prepares a learner well for their test, such apprehension and anxiety can be lessened. (See also Chapter 23: assessment emotions). In a less formal situation the summative assessment is usually completed in smaller chunks to build up to the whole qualification. This is where formative and summative concepts overlap and the meaning of the terminology becomes less black and white.

Ipsative assessment is relatively new in assessment concepts. It is used within self-assessment when an individual is matching their performance, knowledge or ability against a set of standards. It is a useful way of undertaking an initial assessment or, alternatively, a way of summarising learning; it can also be used whilst learners are on their programme of study to encourage reviews of progress. Profiling is a method of recording ipsative assessment.

ACTIVITY 3

Self-assessment against criteria

Assess your own performance against statements of competence:

If you were to measure your performance as a teacher or trainer against the, 'New overarching professional standards for teachers, tutors and trainers in the lifelong learning sector' (LLUK, 2006), you would be undertaking an assessment using criteria. For example: This is an extract from Domain E – Assessment for Learning, using criteria related to professional practice (LLUK 2006: pp 11, 12). By comparing your status against a standard you are self-assessing yourself.

	Standard	How do you measure up to the standard? Do you do this? How – what evidence do you have to prove this?
EP1.1	Use appropriate forms of assessment and evaluate their effectiveness in producing information useful to the teacher and the learner	
EP1.2	Devise, select, use and appraise assessment tools, including where appropriate, those which exploit new and emerging technologies	

▶

	Standard	How do you measure up to the standard? Do you do this? How – what evidence do you have to prove this?
EP2.1	Apply appropriate methods of assessment fairly and effectively	
EP2.3	Design appropriate assessment activities for own specialist area	
EP3.2	Ensure that access to assessment is appropriate to learner need	
EP4.2	Use feedback to evaluate and improve own skills in assessment	
EP5.3	Communicate relevant assessment information to those with a legitimate interest in learner achievement, as necessary/appropriate	

In the boxes on the right you will write statements, make lists, justify your choices and opinions, describe strategies and give examples of instances when the competence is demonstrated. As this is a self-assessment, and therefore only an individual's opinion of their ability, the judgements will usually be supported by other assessments (see Chapter 11: triangulation).

This strategy can be used to self-assess yourself or assess your learners. Once you have a set of standards, you are able to make judgements against knowledge and skills.

Principles of assessment

A **principle** is a rule that you will follow; it is an underlying standard that you will not compromise. Some of the principles that you should advocate are:

- Consistency – you will always ensure that the methods and timeliness of your assessment is at a level standard, making certain that irrespective of how and when your learners are assessed, the outcomes are constant.
- Accessibility – you will always ensure that all of your learners are able to access your assessments and follow systems of equality and inclusion.
- Detailed – you will always ensure that your assessments cover your curriculum or unit fairly and evenly, leaving no part undecided.
- Earned – you will always ensure that your learners have achieved their qualifications with rigour and others will respect the integrity of the assessment.
- Transparency – you will always ensure that everyone involved in the assessment is crystal clear about its purpose and meaning.

These principles form the acronym **CADET**©.

C	Consistent
A	Accessible
D	Detailed
E	Earned
T	Transparent

So, these are the values and principles that you follow when preparing, implementing and evaluating assessment. It will be these values that will help to determine the effectiveness of your assessment.

It should be remembered that assessment is not merely something which occurs in the workplace or end of year test. In every training session that you do you will set learning outcomes, deliver your topic and then close the session. The notion of teaching FOR learning means that to truly know if you have achieved the learning outcomes you must set an assessment activity. If the close of your session is: 'is everybody OK with that?' you may be able to claim that you have 'taught' your topic, but you cannot claim that your learners have learned anything! You must, therefore, include into the structure of your training session, small assessment activities which help you to confirm learning. The easiest to prepare are verbal or written questions – but make sure everyone contributes and remember that you can use similar activities in the follow-up session as a recap activity, before moving forward to the next topic. In the next chapter we will review the different ways that this can be achieved.

The rules of assessment

Once you have sorted out the basics of assessment, you can get down to the actual assessment. There are a number of different ways of assessing, but all rely on the fact that you need something to measure against. These are usually written by Awarding Organisations but there are some courses where you may have to devise your own standards, for example non-qualification courses, industry training schemes or recreational programmes.

Some words of caution here: NEVER substitute your own standards onto qualifications which are approved within the QCF, however well intentioned.

Qualifications are written against National Occupational Standards (NOS) and approved as such by bodies charged with the remit to create a standard across the country – for example: City and Guilds (C&G). If you change the specifications contained in the qualifications you will disadvantage your learners, because you are creating your own qualification, which will not be recognised within your professional area. A similar rule should apply to the delivery of industry training courses; these courses are agreed at head office level and provide a standard across the company.

The first task when planning assessment is to gain sight of the Awarding Organisation's specifications for your unit/module or qualification. In it you will find a series of paragraphs telling you what a learner will know/ be able to do/demonstrate at the end of the unit or module. Some qualifications/units will tell you that you need to collect two of this, a report on that or an observation for the other, but more often it will be up to you to decide on the appropriate assessment task and the method, usually under the supervision of the internal quality assurer (IQA). There are some rules that will help you make informed choices. You should ensure that your assessments are:

- Valid/Relevant – assesses what it is supposed to, according to the curriculum, in an appropriate manner.
- Reliable/Fair – assesses in a consistent manner to the expected standards, regardless of who makes the judgement or when the judgement is made without any bias or preference.
- Authentic – is able to be attributed to the learner.
- Current/Recent – is up to date and recently written.
- Sufficient – is enough to cover the content/performance criteria.
- Power of discrimination – a balance of easy and difficult questions, so that learners are not disadvantaged.
- Objective – judgements made are not personal opinion, which means that marking criteria need to be clear and not open to interpretation.

ACTIVITY 4

The rules of assessment

Consider the rules listed above, decide which rule applies in the statements below:	Record your answer here:
• Poor wording of questions and assignments leads learners in a wrong direction, causing their assessment to be completed inaccurately.	This is an example of an assessment that *lacks validity*. To be *valid* an assessment must provide opportunities for the learner to collect evidence to meet the standards being attempted

Now continue to identify which rule is tested in the following examples:

1. Future criticism of competence, usually from future employers, because learners have not been tested across the breadth of the syllabus.	
2. Ambiguous or inaccurate marking by staff who do not communicate well leads to different standards of competence of learners	
3. Teachers inventing their own standards that can lead to varying degrees of competence.	
4. Poor research skills leading to inaccurate citation and/or plagiarism	
5. Work presented in a portfolio is not signed or dated	

To overcome these issues, you should follow the rules of assessment, by:

- Always ensuring that your learners are prepared for their assessments
- Devising tasks that test what you have taught.
- Telling learners how, when and where assessments will happen.
- Offering study skills to support presentation of research in work.
- Asking colleagues (or internal quality assurer) to review the task before submitting to learners (when devising assessments).
- Creating varied assessment tasks to give good coverage of material and opportunities for differentiation.

Answers to Activity 4: 1, Sufficiency; 2, Reliability and objectivity; 3, Validity and reliability; 4, Authenticity; 5, Authenticity and currency.

The role and responsibilities of the teacher as an assessor

Further to the explanations relating to the role of the teacher explained in Chapter 1, this section develops your understanding of the role of the teacher as an assessor. It is helpful first to consider who else is involved in an assessment and their role. The process starts with the learner, who is assessed by the teacher/assessor, who then submits work to the quality assurer. This simplistic process is further explained as:

Title	Role	May also be known as:
Learner	Assessment can't happen without a learner To attend regularly To achieve award in a timely manner To respect the rules of the organisation	Trainee, candidate, student
Teacher	In some instances this person may be different to the person assessing To demonstrate skills To teach underpinning knowledge (UPK) To raise confidence To monitor progress towards assessment	Tutor, trainer, coach, facilitator

▶

Title	Role	May also be known as:
Assessor	To make judgements about knowledge and understanding and skills, including those in the workplace To ask oral questions to test knowledge related to the task To check validity, currency, authenticity and sufficiency of evidence To feed back the outcome of assessment To make records To process assessments to the quality assurance stage	Teacher, skills assessor, trainer, observer
Internal Quality Assurer	To confirm that assessments are valid, current, authentic and sufficient to meet the assessment criteria To support and guide teacher/assessors To make records To lead on standardisation activities To plan external QA visits To liaise with Awarding Organisations	Internal verifier Internal moderator
External Quality Assurer	Appointed by the Awarding Organisation To confirm assessment and QA procedures comply with Awarding Organisation assessment guidance	External verifier External moderator External examiner

The teacher will work with the learner in the following ways:

- Providing initial advice and guidance prior to enrolment.
- Preparing and delivering an induction to the programme, qualification and organisation.
- Undertaking initial assessment to ascertain the best pathway.
- Undertaking diagnostic assessment to check or confirm previous learning.
- Identifying additional learning requirements.
- Introducing the learner to the framework or qualification.
- Preparing the programme of study and long and short term targets.

- Providing a platform for learning.
- Planning assessments.
- Reviewing targets and progress.
- Undertaking a range of assessment activities according to need.
- Supporting and advising the learner on methods of collecting evidence to support competence.
- Giving feedback to the learner.
- Confirming validity, sufficiency, authenticity and currency of evidence.
- Keeping records of assessment.

In addition, the teacher is required to participate in quality assurance processes, many of which are described briefly later in Chapter 15:

- Be the first point of contact between the learner and the quality assurer.
- Contribute to quality assurance procedures.
- Attend standardisation activities.
- Fully understand the qualification.
- Maintain and update own expertise and professional development.
- Maintain own licence to practise.

The qualities the teacher will possess include:

- Organisational skills
- Time management skills
- Patience
- Communication skills
- The ability to evaluate/assess objectively and accurately against units of assessment and National Occupational Standards
- An approachable manner within boundaries of role
- Perception
- The ability to judge without appearing to interrogate or sanction
- An ability to create relationships built on trust and integrity
- Knowledge of systems and procedures and the ability to be the 'guardian of the rules'
- Advocacy of high standards.

Qualifications for assessors

Awarding Organisations will set the standards required of people who undertake assessments in relation to their qualifications. One of the most obvious is that of personal competence. Teacher/assessors are required to be competent in their subject themselves to at least a level higher than that which they assess. For example, the assessment guidance might recommend that this is a minimum of Level 3 (A level on the QCF) and between three and ten years' experience in the field of expertise. Where there are no appropriate Level 3 qualifications available, lower levels are acceptable, supported by relevant industrial or commercial experience. Secondly, they look for competence in assessment. Depending on the type of qualification this may be a generic teaching qualification, which includes modules on assessment, or specialist assessment modules from the Learning and Development suite of modules. You may hear these called D units or A&V units or the up-to-date Assessor and Quality Assurance Awards (Wilson 2012).

Additional information

Education and Training Foundation/IfL – regarding standards and regulations for teachers

Sector Skills Councils – for information regarding occupational competence

Legislation: The main acts and rules

The main pieces of legislation concerning teaching, learning and assessment are covered within Part 1. In addition, with regards to assessment and quality assurance, there are some regulatory requirements which apply.

In England, the Office of the Qualifications and Examinations Regulator (Ofqual) is bound under statute to ensure that Awarding Organisations and their approved centres comply with a set of regulations relating to quality assurance. They are also responsible for vocational qualifications in Northern Ireland. University degrees are regulated by the Qualifications Assurance Agency (QAA).

In respect of Ofqual, the regulations are:

- The statutory regulation of external qualifications in England, Wales and Northern Ireland (2004)
- NVQ Code of Practice (revised 2006)
- Regulatory principles for e-assessment (2007)
- Regulatory Arrangements for the Qualifications and Credit Framework (2008)
- Operating rules for using the term NVQ in a QCF qualification title (2008)
- The Apprenticeship, Skills, Children and Learning Act (2009).

You do not need to be able to recite these, but you should know that they underpin the values of delivering and assessing accredited qualifications. The various regulations aim to meet the needs of learners, maintain standards and comparability, promote public confidence, support equality and diversity and ensure value for money. To this end they specify that Awarding Organisations and approved centres must:

- Maintain standards by confirming compliance to approval criteria.
- Offer a robust, consistent approach to Quality Assurance (QA) processes such as Internal Verification (IV) and Internal Moderation (IM).
- Sample assessment decisions to confirm validity and authenticity.

- Provide valid and reliable outcomes against National Occupational Standards.
- Keep accurate records relating to assessment decisions.
- Have policies and procedures in place for assessment and Internal Quality Assurance (IQA).
- Provide administrative systems to support registration and certification.
- Ensure that QA systems are consistently applied.
- Recruit appropriate staff to ensure integrity in all aspects of provision.
- State clear roles and responsibilities of staff to maintain high standards.
- Ensure staff have relevant qualifications and experience to undertake their roles.
- Review and evaluate to promote improvements.
- Have effective systems to recruit learners and ensure their needs are met.
- Provide human and physical resources to support the delivery and assessment of accredited qualifications.
- Ensure fairness in assessment with appropriate references to appeals processes.

Ofqual also regulates vocational qualifications in Northern Ireland, with the Council for the Curriculum, Examinations and Assessment (CCEA) which regulates other qualifications in Northern Ireland. In Scotland, qualifications are regulated by Scottish Qualifications Authority (SQA). In Wales, the regulatory body is the Department for Children, Education, Lifelong Learning and Skills. (DCELLS). In Eire, the National Qualifications Authority of Ireland (NQAI) has responsibility.

Useful resources

Ofqual: http://www.ofqual.gov.uk/
CCEA: http://www.rewardinglearning.org.uk/
SQA: http://www.sqa.org.uk/
DCELLS: http://wales.gov.uk/
NQAI: http://www.nqai.ie/

Diversity and assessment

REVISION

In Chapter 2, we reviewed additional information regarding legislative guidance on equality. In Chapters 16 and 17, we look at the inclusive learning environment and summarise the way teachers should work to maintain an equal and fair atmosphere whilst promoting diversity.

Ensuring that learners have fair and equal access to assessment is as important as that of equality of teaching and learning. Equality does not mean treating all people the same; it means to value and support different groups appropriate to their needs and requirements. It does require teachers to design training and assessment around the individual needs of all learners. Diversity in teaching, learning and assessment requires teachers and assessors to respect the difference between individuals.

The current diversity within the population of the United Kingdom is extremely broad. Embedding equality and diversity into all aspects of the programme is now seen as standard practice in helping to raise cultural awareness and prepare learners for their future experiences in the world of work. Some groups that you will need to support, stretch and challenge include 'those whose needs, dispositions, aptitudes or circumstances require particularly perceptive and expert teaching and, in some cases, additional support'. You will also hear the expression 'those with protected characteristics'. Such learners may include:

- disabled learners, as defined by the Equality Act 2010, and those who have special educational needs
- boys/men
- girls/women
- groups of learners whose prior attainment may be different from that of other groups
- those who are academically more or less able

- learners for whom English is an additional language
- minority ethnic learners
- Gypsy, Roma and Traveller learners
- learners qualifying for a bursary scheme award
- looked after children
- lesbian, gay and bisexual learners
- transgender learners
- young carers
- learners from low-income backgrounds
- older learners
- learners of different religions and beliefs
- ex-offenders
- women returners
- teenage mothers
- other vulnerable groups.

(Ofsted, Common Inspection Framework 2012, p38-39)

Ethics in assessment

This section is for guidance: it does not constitute legal advice. Organisations will have their own codes of practice and teachers should always seek advice from colleagues and managers. Most teachers automatically respect the position they are in and understand the need for confidentiality. This is likely to be two tiered: that which is confidential to the organisation and that which is confidential between the teacher and the learner/s.

Confidentiality is required in all aspects of the role:

- in planning to ensure timely preparations
- in appeals and disputes to ensure impartial outcomes
- in feedback to ensure appropriateness of location and outcome
- in evidence to ensure the security of information contained in personal journals, portfolios, or corporate information
- in records to protect learners' personal information, progress and assessment records.

The Freedom of Information Act 2000 is the public's right to know. It gives individuals the right to request information you are keeping about them both on paper and electronically. The Data Protection Act 1998 requires organisations to store information securely and lawfully. It protects the personal data that is stored within an organisation against unlawful disclosure.

Teachers should be mindful that there are certain circumstances under which they must pass on information – even if told in confidence, for example matters concerning illegal acts or child abuse.

Finally, the teacher's attitudes, values and beliefs should never influence assessment practice or the way a learner is treated (see also Equality and Diversity). As a professional occupation a code of conduct is required of trainers and teacher/assessors.

The Institute for Education Business Excellence sets a code of practice for assessors, which is easily attributed to teachers. It requires teachers/assessors to:

- evaluate objectively, be impartial, with no bias, declaring any conflicts of interests which may undermine their objectivity.
- report honestly, ensuring that judgements are fair and reliable;carry out their work with integrity, treating all those they meet with courtesy and sensitivity.
- do all they can to minimise the stress on those involved in the assessment visit, taking account of their best interests and well-being.
- maintain purposeful and productive dialogue with those being assessed, and communicate judgements clearly and frankly.
- respect the confidentiality of information, particularly about individuals and their work.
- attend assessment visits well prepared, having read pre-visit documentation.
- dress in a professional manner and be punctual.

http://www.iebe.org.uk/index.php/code-of-conduct-for-assessors

Glossary of terms

Approval permission to deliver qualifications on behalf of an Awarding Organisation

Assessment the checking of learning and demonstrating competence

Authenticity to establish who wrote/owns the subject

Awarding Organisation a body approved by Ofqual to create and certificate qualifications (AO)

BTEC Business and Technology Education Council; a qualification title part of Edexcel; an Awarding Organisation

C&G City and Guilds; an Awarding Organisation

CADET$^©$ consistent, accessible, detailed, earned, transparent – principles of assessment

Competence the knowledge of or ability to do something

Concept an idea

Criterion (pl: criteria) a standard of competence

Currency up to date, reflecting current practice

Evidence the output of an assessment activity; evidence of a learner's knowledge, understanding, skills or competence that can be used to make a judgement of their achievement against agreed standards/criteria

Formative continuous assessment

Formative assessment interim or on going assessment

Goals an aim or desired result

Grading the degree of competence, pass, merit, distinction

Hierarchy ranking according to status or authority

HND Higher National Diploma

Ipsative self-assessment against standards of competence

IM Internal Moderator

Internal Quality Assurance (IQA) validating the integrity of the assessment

IQA Internal Quality Assurer/Assurance

IV Internal Verification

Jargon language, words or expressions of a specialist occupation

Level 3 a position within the QCF indicating the value of a qualification

National Occupational Standards (NOS) nationally set guidelines defining the level, size and subjects used in designing UoA

NQF National Qualifications Framework

NVQ National Vocational Qualification

Objectivity without bias

Ofqual regulatory body, Office of the qualifications and examiners regulator

Pathway a route. Usually describing the combination of units to achieve the learner's goal

Performance criteria standards of required competence

Plagiarism the passing off of someone else's work as your own without reference

Portfolio a storage tool, used either paper-based or electronically to collect evidence

Principle a set of values or beliefs promoted by the teacher; a rule or moral code

Profile how information about a thing or person is recorded

Profiling identifying characteristic traits or skills/knowledge against a set of standards

QCF Qualification and Credit Framework

Qualification a set of specifications (UoA) leading to an award, certificate or diploma of achievement, a skill that makes someone suitable for a job

Quality Assurance (QA) a system of review to confirm that processes are in place and applied to guarantee the quality of the service or product; systematic checks to provide confidence

Referencing a source of information

Rules validity/relevance; reliability; authenticity; currency/recency; sufficiency; power of discrimination; objectivity (rules of assessment)

SSC Sector Skills Council: responsible for writing Units of Assessment

Standards an agreed level of competence

Sufficiency to check that there is enough evidence to cover the criteria

Summative assessment final or summary assessment

Target an objective or focused path towards a specified outcome

Units of Assessment (UoA) statements of knowledge and/or competence, clustered to make a qualification

Valid (in research) measured accurately to elicit reliable outcomes

Validity a strategy to ensure that judgements are made against criteria

SUMMARY

In this chapter we set out to achieve the following outcomes:

- To explain the functions of assessment in training, learning and development.
- To define and explain the key concepts (ideas) and principles (values) relating to assessment.
- To define the rules associated with assessments to ensure valid, reliable and accurate assessments.
- To describe the meaning of words associated with assessment.
- To state the roles and responsibilities of the teacher/assessor.
- To summarise the main legislative and regulatory factors.
- To describe and explain the meaning of ethics and values in assessment.

Your personal development

You have reviewed the basics of assessment and confirmed your understanding of why assessment is important. You have completed a couple of activities to identify your starting points in understanding assessment and developed your knowledge of assessment in the context of current curriculum.

In considering the language of assessment you have raised your awareness of the terminology and variants in current use, undertaking further research on the topic by following links to relevant websites and reading.

You have looked at the main concepts of assessment and what is meant by the terms norm and criterion referencing, ipsative, formative and summative assessments. You have compared and contrasted the notion of formative and summative assessment and are aware of how to use these in promoting improvement and testing competence, whilst taking into account the importance of Kolb's Learning Cycle. You may have completed the activity to analyse and reflect on your own competence against one of the LLUK standards.

You have explored the use of command words in setting assessment tasks and, in the activity may have developed a dictionary for your learners' use.

You have investigated both the principles of assessment – CADET© – and the rules of assessment: validity, reliability, authenticity, currency, sufficiency, objectivity and the power to discriminate with reasons why problems occur if the rules are not followed. In focusing on the principles of assessment you have decided on the values you will advocate when carrying out assessments.

Finally, you have examined the roles and responsibilities of the teacher as an assessor and the link between that role and those of the learner and quality assurer. You can explain the roles of those within the assessment process and their contributions to the quality assurance processes.

You have perused a list of legislation factors and ethics which should be considered when assessing learners.

CHAPTER 11

Planning and delivering assessment

LEARNING OBJECTIVES

The measurable outcomes that you will achieve by reading this chapter and completing the activities are:

- To describe the planning process and apply in the organisation of assessments
- To describe the advantages and disadvantages of each assessment method and make informed decisions about which to choose
- To evaluate your choices of assessment methods and identify what makes assessment effective
- To compare and contrast the range of assessment methods available to use
- To review the use of electronic assessment and technology in assessment

Effective assessment

If assessment is to be seen as a valuable tool and respected by learners, colleagues and other stakeholders, then it must be seen to do what it purports to do, i.e. it must be effective. Effectiveness means producing the intended or desired result. This chapter looks at various aspects of planning and delivering assessment to ensure that you assess effectively.

Before commencing any form of assessment, the first thing you should establish is what you intend or want from the assessment.

- To demonstrate practical skill (psychomotor skills)
- To recall knowledge (cognitive skills)
- To value or appreciate an opinion (affective skills).

In the example above, Bloom (1956, 1964, and Dave 1967) are used to identify the desired outcomes. (See also Chapter 5; session planning skills). Equally, you may want to assess your learners' progress through the learner journey to establish the extent of their learning. Assessment of progress within sessions is a key theme in ensuring learners are developing their learning. The same skills apply in interim assessment as apply to the more usual forms of assessment.

Once you have established what you want, then you should select methods of assessment which will deliver the products of assessment you need in order to make the judgement.

To make decisions about effectiveness you should consider:

- the desired outcome
- the methods of assessment
- justify the choices you make
- gather evidence – the products which demonstrate competence.

The products of assessment are:

- Documents – letters, printouts
- Posters, reports, homework
- Photos

- Portfolios of evidence
- Essays, reports, presentation notes
- Artefacts, artwork, finished items
- Models and diagrams
- Testimonials, references
- Personal statements, CVs
- Certificates
- Observation reports
- Responses to questions.

Communication aids effectiveness. By agreeing, sharing, negotiating and discussing plans, methods and outcomes, the teacher (or assessor) will be able to justify and evaluate their assessments. It will also aid some 'joined-up thinking' – many requirements contained in standards are common across a range of units or modules. Communication about these common factors will lessen the assessment load on learners by consolidating tasks to cover more than one unit or module (a holistic approach). This can also apply to functional skills – why can't presentations be assessed for communication skills as well as content?

Finally, in trying to establish effectiveness, the teacher should consider the values, ethics and safety of the assessment. The values (CADET) should not be compromised when aiming for effectiveness: the ethics concerning confidentiality and integrity in assessment are paramount and we should never forfeit standards of safety when creating or carrying out assessments.

All of this is put together as a plan.

Planning assessment

What is a plan? In short, it is a detailed breakdown (or formal contract) about how the learner is going to achieve their desired learning outcomes. In sessions the statements are included in the Learning Plan, but where assessment is separated from the learning it might be necessary to plan separately (for example in work-based programmes or externally tested qualifications). Planning is one of the first stages in the assessment process, namely: plan – collect evidence – make a judgement – give feedback and review, and then you are back to the beginning and ready to repeat the process (see Figure 5C).

Figure 5C The assessment cycle

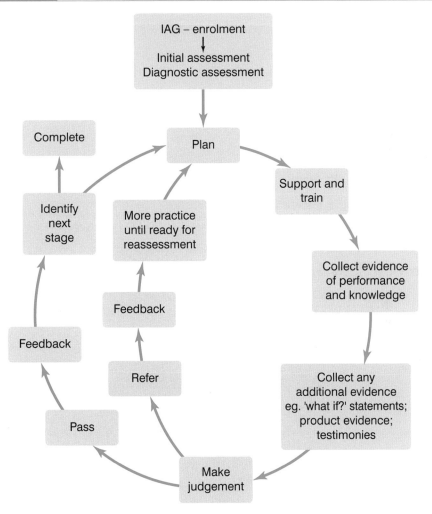

There are some protocols to observe when planning assessments:

- Ensure the assessment is fair (equality and diversity).
- Explain the process to the learner – how, why, where, when, with whom, what?

- Link the plan to the assessment criteria – be transparent.
- Negotiate with the learner and the employer and get agreement from all parties.
- Ensure that the planned assessment causes minimal disruption to the routine work of the employer's business.
- Confirm shift patterns and resources are available and suitable.
- Factor in any special assessment needs – to suit disability or difficulty.
- Plan to achieve success, not to fail – is the learner ready for the assessment?
- Always prioritise naturally occurring performance over simulated or contrived performances.
- Maximise assessment opportunities – look for holistic assessments rather than unit driven.
- Ensure that the learner fully understands the whole process and what to do if they do not agree with the outcome – i.e. the appeals process.

A plan might look like this:

SUMMATIVE ASSESSMENT PLAN	
Name: A Learner	Date of proposed assessment: 14th January 2014
Planned activity: To prepare short crust pastry and fruit for 24 portions of apple pie	
Expected outcomes/criteria/evidence (Units: Prepare and cook pastry products, Prepare and cook fruit dishes, Working safely and hygienically) Select and measure ingredients accurately Wear appropriate work wear and ppe Select equipment to prepare pie	

Demonstrate health and safety practices throughout activity

Follow the recipe accurately

Assemble prepared commodities for the apple pie, continue to assemble and cook dish for lunchtime customers

Take photographs of product at various stages of the process

Evaluate how successful you were in achieving the outcomes

Evidence Methods:

Observation by assessor in the workplace

Oral Questions

Photographs

Plan Signed/dated by teacher/ assessor:	Plan Agreed, signed/dated by learner:
A.N. Assessor 7th January 2014	A Learner 7th January 2014

Special considerations:

Confirm with employer that menu is as agreed and products are available

Prepare recipe card in large font

Feedback after lunch to minimise disruption

Feedback following assessment:	Actions for development:

Outcome:	Teacher/assessor signature:
Pass ☐	Learner signature:
Needs further training ☐	Date:

Planning assessments are key to a problem free process. By observing the protocols in the bullet points earlier, you can ensure that planning is effective, comprehensive and meets the standards expected in assessment.

The what, why, when, how, where, who considerations

Most often used in questioning, the 'w' words are equally important in planning assessment.

> *I keep six honest serving men*
> *(They taught me all I knew);*
> *Their names are What and Why and When*
> *And How and Where and Who.*

Rudyard Kipling, Just So Stories 1902, The Elephant's Child

In your planning session, you will not go far wrong if you answer the questions:

What: what will be assessed – you may need to write this both formally (using the Units of Competence) and in a way the learner will understand (task related). The goals or short term targets need to be specific, measureable, achievable, relevant, time bounded, ethical and reviewed (SMARTER).

Why: to achieve success in the chosen qualification, this may be the long term target.

When: specify the date and time of the assessment

How: how will the assessment be carried out, by what method/s? The methods will be determined by the type of assessment: Is it a practical assessment or is underpinning knowledge to be tested? Any contingency plan should be mentioned in case for any reason the assessment is interrupted.

Where: specify the location of the assessment, for example, in the workplace

Who (with whom): who will be involved, for example a teacher/assessor, a witness in the training environment? Is the teacher/assessor someone who works in the environment or a peripatetic assessor visiting from a training provider? Are there others in the workplace who may be affected by the assessment?

This detail is required to both create the contract and alleviate any misunderstandings. By being clear about the expectations (from all parties involved), the learner will be more comfortable in the assessment situation. Irrespective of how much practice a learner has, and how confident they are in their surroundings, very often the mere mention of the assessment word sends a shiver of trepidation.

In order to meet the 'HOW' statement, a teacher/assessor needs to be sensitive and aware of the characteristics of their learners. 'HOW' is mainly concerned with the method of assessment, but some learners require special assessment arrangements, which cause an amendment to a selected assessment strategy. Barriers to assessment or special assessment considerations come in many forms, but are usually the same as those relating to learning in general (see Chapter 6).

When to assess

Assessment can occur at any time during a programme or course. Pre-course, initial, diagnostic, formative and summative are the words associated with assessment and to a certain extent identify the stage they are used. This process, from the learner's very first contact to their successful completion, is very often referred to as the learner journey.

There is a lot of cross over and similarity in the expressions and some differences in how teachers interpret the words.

Pre-course or interview stage

An interview enables teachers to assess potential or a learner's suitability for a course or programme. Younger learners may need to refer to schools grades or predicted grades to meet entry requirements. Adult learners may cite employment history and experience in the form of a *curriculum vitae* (CV). The interview should be a two-way process to ensure that learners fully understand expectations of the programme before committing themselves. The pre-course interview is therefore a means of ensuring that the right people are on the right courses. On occasions learners will want to use their previous experience, learning or achievement to their new course. This is called Recognition of Prior Learning (RPL).

Beginning of course or programme

Carrying out an initial assessment helps you to plan appropriate courses or sessions for your learners. You may use assessment to identify specific needs of learners, and using the results to influence assessment should be an integral component of your teaching and learning plans. See also Part 2.

Whether a learner is enrolled onto a full-time or part-time programme, there should be an induction. The induction provides the opportunity to introduce the learners to the programme, to each other, to the teacher/s and to the programme or module. This is another opportunity to carry out initial assessment and use this to create a profile of the learners on the course:

- Why are they there?
- What is their previous knowledge or experience?
- What are their strengths and weaknesses?
- How confident are they?
- Will their personal circumstances influence their progress?
- What is their character?
- What do they enjoy or dislike?
- What are their expectations and aspirations?
- Are they motivated?

It would be very easy to make assumptions at this point and break the first rule of teaching, the most common assumption being 'they're here and want to learn'. That may be so, but there will be degrees of desire and these will influence the learner! There are some useful yet informal strategies which can be used to find out about your learners. One of these is to use an ice-breaker activity. Another even less formal way is to set a simple activity or questionnaire, maybe associated with previous knowledge, skills or experience and whilst the learners are completing it you can go around the room talking to each person on a one-to-one basis to find out something about them and why they are there. The more formal strategies are often collectively known as diagnostic assessment. These identify and assess learners' capabilities in order to inform the structure of the programme or scheme of work; they will also identify learning needs and therefore the support needed to ensure progress. Such diagnostic assessments include:

Learner needs analysis	To ensure that teaching methods are suited to individuals
Preferred learning styles	To find out how your learners like to learn
Initial screening	To check basic skill levels to identify level of support needed
Prior learning	To identify previous experience, learning
Skills test	To check current level of competence

As many organisations are measured and funded on their success, it raises the importance of ensuring that:

the right learner ⟶ is on the right course ⟶ and receiving the right support.

This contributes to learners staying until the end of the course and therefore maximises their potential to achieve their learning goal. Effective initial assessment will record plans and development needs in an action plan or individual learning plan.

During the course or programme

Assessment during the course is usually formative. This means that it is an interim judgement or decision about progress, which is reported to the learner as feedback. This enables them to consider what they are good at and build on their strengths, whilst informing them of improvements that need to be made to meet the requirements of the assessment or qualification. There is always 'life after formative assessment'. Careful feedback can motivate, enlighten and provide a vehicle for development. Bad feedback can destroy confidence. Feedback (sometimes called 'constructive' feedback) should follow a pattern of identification of what is good or what has been achieved successfully, followed by the 'in order to improve you should' statement and finished with a praise or motivational statement to leave the learner feeling confident and willing to carry out the developments you have identified. The feedback should include the judgement made, for example: pass or refer; satisfactory or needs further development; competent or needs further training or experience, but *never* fail. Formative assessment can relate to a piece of assessed work or as a meeting to discuss progress (a tutorial, see page 46–47). Both require skilled practice in feedback and setting of targets.

At the end of the course/module/unit

Assessment at this point is usually referred to as summative. It is a final decision or judgement about competence or ability. Dependent on the programme, learners may be offered another chance to improve their result, but in the case of examinations it is generally a 'one-opportunity'. It is worth reminding teachers that summative judgements can have a significant impact on learners, hence their learners' apprehension before test periods. The teacher should therefore prepare learners not only by revising content but in how the examination is conducted. Past papers or simulations can provide confidence pre-exam. Some courses have assessment strategies which enable learners to be graded on their work. Clear marking criteria are required, which should be shared with learners – 'in order to receive a merit you need to ...'

After the course

....

Some organisations will gather information to provide a statistical picture of their institution, for example, the percentage of learners progressing to higher level courses or employment. This may be done at exit interviews or by customer satisfaction questionnaires. It is used to measure the effectiveness of their programmes and their contribution to economic targets.

Types of assessment methods

Assessment is the term given to checking that learning has occurred and that the learner is competent in the skills and knowledge of the occupational area. Assessment is not just something that will occur summatively, it will happen throughout the programme as a means of monitoring progress and is essential at the commencement of the programme to identify appropriate training and assessment strategies to meet your learner's needs. Assessment also refers to the process of collecting proof of competence; this is frequently referred to as 'evidence'. This evidence is generated by undertaking an observation, questioning session, review of products, completion of assignments or another assessment method.

The methods which generate the evidence can be described as being direct or indirect. **Direct assessment** means that the evidence is the learner's own work; **indirect assessment** means that the evidence is the view or opinion of others.

There are several different ways of assessing or collecting evidence to demonstrate competence. The table below describes the main ones that you will come across:

Observation (direct assessment)

Description:

Used in practical situations when a learner demonstrates their competence (natural performance) whilst being observed by their teacher/assessor. This is considered one of the best forms of assessment – primary

Observation (direct assessment)

assessment – because there can be no doubts that the learner knows how to do something. The observation should be recorded either on film, electronically or on paper. A phone with a camera is quite useful, but ensure that you have relevant permissions before photographing or filming a learner, especially if they or those around them are minors; equally, employers might be quite sensitive to filming in their offices or shop floors. There may be occasions when the verifier needs to observe observational evidence to verify standards. Observation is very versatile in assessment as learners are usually repeating their everyday activities and so will always perform at a level appropriate to their need and ability. Verbal questioning complements observation well. Observations will be planned in advance in order to ensure that learners are prepared and, if relevant others involved in the process, for example employers, can expect additional people attending their establishment. Observation Records would record the context and describe what has been seen.

Advantages:	Disadvantages:
● Primary assessment method for practical skills	● No permanent record of performance
● Able to see naturally occurring practice	● Expensive
● Ideal opportunity to see if theory is applied in a practical situation	● Needs to be verified to confirm judgements
● Can be used formatively or summatively	● Can be intrusive
● 'Can do' or 'can't do' outcomes	● Can't check theory or underpinning knowledge
	● Detailed preparation and organisation required
	● May be subjective

Assessment conditions and environments

The environment in which assessment occurs is as important as the type of technique used. In some instances the technique used will directly impact on the environment and conditions.

● Observations need to occur where the task regularly takes place; after all it is frequently referred to as naturally occurring evidence. A teacher/assessor must neither help nor hinder the learner who is being observed, nor must other colleagues.

Simulation (direct assessment)

Description:

This is similar to observation, but uses a simulated activity rather than natural performance. The rules associated with observation (above) apply. Whilst many qualifications do not generally support this type of evidence, there may be occasions when it is deemed appropriate, for example when using high cost materials or in dangerous situations. You would not expect an airline pilot to be assessed on his ability to crash land in a 'natural performance' scenario – this is best done under simulated conditions, which should mirror reality. Fire drills and first aid are other commonly simulated assessments. Teacher/assessors should always confirm the validity of using simulation as an assessment method by reading Awarding Organisation guidance on assessment.

Advantages:

- Can be used to assess when circumstances involve dangerous or expensive resources

- Can be used formatively or summatively

Disadvantages:

- Does not match the real thing in terms of senses and emotions

Assessment conditions and environments

The environment in which assessment occurs is as important as the type of technique used. In some instances the technique used will directly impact on the environment and conditions.

- Simulations may occur under replicated or virtual conditions – but these should be a realistic as possible to ensure that the scenario mirrors the event.

- Some college environments may be considered as simulated; the exceptions are those where members of the public pay for services, such as in hair salons or training restaurants.

Project and assignment (direct assessment)

Description:

These are usually a series of activities which collect together to make a project or assignment. For example, task one may be a written description of

Project and assignment (direct assessment)

something, task two may be a presentation of some findings and task three may be a booklet or poster. Generally, a project is designed by the learner and an assignment is designed by the teacher/assessor; both include a 'brief' which is related to the learning outcomes. Awarding Organisations may pre-set assignments in order to standardise practice. Internally set assignments should be quality assured before launching to learners. There may be different assessment methods within an assignment or project depending on the tasks. The teacher/assessor will be assessing learning outcomes which relate to the proposed content of the assignment or project and are used during marking. Some qualifications also include levels of understanding, which are reflected in grading criteria. Teacher/assessors can differentiate outcomes of assignments and projects to suit learner's needs.

Advantages:

- Can be used formatively or summatively

- Allows individual creativity to develop

- Develops research skills

- Collection of tasks which can be differentiated easily

- Assesses wide range of skills and knowledge

Disadvantages:

- Confused in meaning – project is learner-derived, assignment is tutor-derived

- Poorly used – preparation only concerned with single subject, whereas it may be applicable across a broader range of topics

- Time-consuming

- Over-reliance on written work in more academic subjects

Assessment conditions and environments

The environment in which assessment occurs is as important as the type of technique used. In some instances the technique used will directly impact on the environment and conditions.

- Projects and assignments are frequently completed in a more traditional learning environment. A teacher/assessor needs to establish to what extent research is a requirement and ensure that the learner has access to journals, books or the Internet. They should be written holistically to assess as wide a range of skills as possible

Case study (direct assessment)

Description:

Case studies are scenarios prepared by the teacher/assessor to test aspects of the qualification which are not able to be assessed in other ways. Alternatively, case studies can be used to confirm that knowledge achieved in one situation can be applied in other situations or answer 'what if' questions. A case study will describe a specific scenario and have questions about the given situation.

Advantages:	Disadvantages:
● Allows description, comprehension and analysis of facts	● Need detailed marking criteria to avoid subjectivity
● Opportunity to answer 'what if' scenarios	
● Aids reflection	
● Can include personal values and opinions	

Assessment conditions and environments

The environment in which assessment occurs is as important as the type of technique used. In some instances the technique used will directly impact on the environment and conditions.

● A case study can be completed as an open book assessment (learners are allowed to use their notes, a text book or perhaps, the Internet to seek their solutions) or under examination conditions. They can be completed as an individual, paired or small group activity.

Written questions – Essays (direct assessment)

Description:

A discussion type of question which can be structured, semi-structured or unstructured. The teacher/assessor will need detailed assessment marking plans to ensure fairness, especially if the essay is around opinion and therefore has no right or wrong answer. The teacher/assessor should also consider what

▶

Written questions – Essays (direct assessment)

proportion of marks will be attributed to spelling and grammar, content, structure and argument etc. To be considered fair, the assessment marking strategy should be shared with your learners. Marking is quite complex. Marking could be subjective. Questions can be posed as tests or exams with time constraints. Under certain conditions the use of texts to complete the questions (i.e. open book questions) is permissible.

Advantages:

- Assesses understanding and high order cognitive skills
- Can gain insight to opinions/ arguments relating to an issue
- Can assess literacy
- Can be closed (no reference), open book, or open (later submission) styles
- Can be used formatively or summatively
- Appropriate as exam or a stand-alone piece of work

Disadvantages:

- Takes time to write and mark
- No single answer
- Limited preparation time
- Limited coverage of the subject/ syllabus
- Prone to subjectivity in marking

Assessment conditions and environments

The environment in which assessment occurs is as important as the type of technique used. In some instances the technique used will directly impact on the environment and conditions.

- Essays, especially those undertaken under examination conditions, need careful planning. A teacher/assessor must consider privacy, quiet, desk space, timing, allowable resources and plan to accommodate the needs of the learner, especially for those who might need additional support (extra time, signers, scribes, specialist resources, etc.). A teacher/assessor needs to establish how much help is allowed, before it would be considered inappropriate. Guidance on this should be taken from the Awarding Organisation, as permission is needed to change formal assessment arrangements.

Written questions – Reports (direct assessment)

Description:

A descriptive account generally used to explain a particular topic. Reports provide the opportunity to link theory and practice and offer chances for the learner to cover 'what if' scenarios. There is rarely a right or wrong answer, so marking the report is best linked to the standards of competence or Units of Assessment to provide validity to the assessment. As they are written by the learners the level is reflective of ability. Structured reports offer guidance on how much detail to include in the answer and can be helpful to learners.

Advantages:	Disadvantages:
• Less formal than an essay	• Need detailed marking grids
• Allows description, comprehension and analysis of facts	
• Opportunity to answer 'what if' scenarios	
• Aids reflection	
• Can include personal values and opinions	

Assessment conditions and environments

The environment in which assessment occurs is as important as the type of technique used. In some instances the technique used will directly impact on the environment and conditions.

● Reports, especially those undertaken under examination conditions, need careful planning. A teacher/assessor must consider privacy, quiet, desk space, timing, allowable resources and plan to accommodate the needs of the learner, especially for those who might need additional support (extra time, signers, scribes, specialist resources, etc.). A teacher/assessor needs to establish how much help is allowed, before it would be considered inappropriate. Guidance on this should be taken from the Awarding Organisation, as permission is needed to change formal assessment arrangements.

▶

Written questions – Short answer questions (direct assessment)

Description:

A series of questions where the answer is usually about a few sentences long. In some cases (the 'state four reasons for…') type of questions, only a few words are required. Ideally questions start with how, why, what, etc. The marking plan should include all possible answers that could be offered by learners to increase the objectivity. Short answer questions are quite easy to mark and are suitable for checking knowledge and understanding. They offer many opportunities to differentiate to meet learner needs in that the complexity of the questioning is easily varied to suit ability. If completed independently, the teacher/assessor needs to check that it is the learner's own work, maybe by asking a few oral questions or comparing the writing style with the learner's usual style. These are likely to be pre-set by the teacher/assessor and used to confirm knowledge and understanding. Questions can be posed as tests or exams with time constraints or as group activities, homework or recap activities. Scripts can be exchanged between learners to mark each other's work – under supervision.

Advantages:	Disadvantages:
• Versatile – ideal as introductory, plenary, homework or exam questions	• Answers can lack depth unless extended answers are requested
• Used to reinforce learning	
• Ideal when information needs to be remembered as opposed to recognised	
• Assesses comprehension	
• Quick to mark	
• Can be used formatively or summatively	
• Can be used as one word, simple sentence or extended answers	

Assessment conditions and environments

The environment in which assessment occurs is as important as the type of technique used. In some instances the technique used will directly impact on the environment and conditions.

Written questions – Short answer questions (direct assessment)

- Short answer questions, especially those undertaken under examination conditions, need careful planning. A teacher/assessor must consider privacy, quiet, desk space, timing, allowable resources and plan to accommodate the needs of the learner, especially for those who might need additional support (extra time, signers, scribes, specialist resources, etc.). A teacher/assessor needs to establish how much help is allowed, before it would be considered inappropriate. Guidance on this should be taken from the Awarding Organisation, as permission is needed to change formal assessment arrangements.

Written questions – Multiple choice questions (direct assessment)

Description:

A question with (usually) four possible answers. The learner has to identify which of the offered answers is correct. As a learner selects an answer there is little opportunity to expand or probe understanding. They are very simple to mark; the Awarding Organisation may use computers to scan answer sheets and calculate the number of correct answers. They are quite difficult to write in the first instance but for the learner they are relatively easy to undertake. This method does not support any differentiation of individual need, but is a very objective way of marking. These are likely to be pre-set by the teacher/assessor and used to confirm knowledge and understanding. Questions can be posed as tests or exams with time constraints or as recap activities. Often called multiple-guess by learners inferring that correct answers do not always test learning.

Advantages:

- Good way to check facts
- Low to high order cognitive test
- Checks recognition and recall
- Can test a lot of things as questions are short
- Answers are easy to mark
- Outcomes are reliable

Disadvantages:

- Answers may be sorted to get a 50/50 guess scenario
- Difficult to prepare
- Needs careful testing before launch to check for frequency of answers

▶

Written questions – Multiple choice questions (direct assessment)

- Questions can be 'banked' and selected to make different tests each time they are used

- High level of objectivity in marking

- Can be used formatively or summatively

Assessment conditions and environments

The environment in which assessment occurs is as important as the type of technique used. In some instances the technique used will directly impact on the environment and conditions.

- Multiple choice questions, especially those undertaken under examination conditions, need careful planning. A teacher/assessor must consider privacy, quiet, desk space, timing, allowable resources and plan to accommodate the needs of the learner, especially for those who might need additional support (extra time, signers, scribes, specialist resources, etc.). A teacher/assessor needs to establish how much help is allowed, before it would be considered inappropriate. Guidance on this should be taken from the Awarding Organisation, as permission is needed to change formal assessment arrangements.

Verbal/oral questions (direct assessment)

Description:

These are questions which try to establish depth of knowledge and are a useful assessment tool to complement observation in order to check understanding. For example – 'what would happen if...' or 'can you explain why...' type of questions. Verbal questioning is usually informal and sometimes unprepared in that the teacher/assessor sees something during an observation and wishes clarification or further information on a particular issue. Verbal questioning should be recorded on either tape, electronically or paper and the learner should sign to confirm accuracy of answers recorded. Verbal questioning is a very versatile method of assessment and is so easily adjusted to meet individual need that it is considered a primary method of assessment. Oral questions are not exclusively part of an observation; they are used as a method

Verbal/oral questions (direct assessment)

of testing knowledge evidence. Verbal questions can be pre-set by the teacher/assessor.

Advantages:	Disadvantages:
● Can be used formatively or summatively	● Sometimes difficult to devise questions
● Informal in style	● May be posed as closed questions
● Supports theory in practical situations	
● Responsive to needs	
● Open questions probe knowledge	

Assessment conditions and environments

The environment in which assessment occurs is as important as the type of technique used. In some instances the technique used will directly impact on the environment and conditions.

● Verbal questions will often be executed in the same environment as the observation or simulation. However a teacher/assessor needs to be mindful that workshops are often noisy or learners might be distracted, so consideration of the appropriateness of the environment needs to be factored into the assessment plan.

Professional discussion (direct assessment)

Description:

This is a semi-structured interview where the teacher/assessor and the learner discuss an issue and the teacher/assessor prompts the learner into answering questions related to subject outcomes. It is very often used to link workplace practice to standards of competence or Units of Assessment. The method is particularly suited to qualifications which require deeper understanding of a topic or learners who prefer the autonomy of free expression in their own assessments. It is an effective tool because an experienced teacher/assessor will lead the conversation to ensure all aspects are covered, however,

▶

Professional discussion (direct assessment)

authenticity could be questioned – did the teacher/assessor lead in a way that would elicit only correct answers? Is it really the learners own words/actions?

Advantages:

- Generally used supported by other assessment methods

- Allows for description, evaluation and reflection

- Structured discussion allows for gaps to be covered

Disadvantages:

- Expensive as it is 1:1

- Can be too leading

- Can be disjointed; learners need preparation time to ensure logical flow of ideas

- Recording of discussion needs to be prepared (audio/writing)

- Sometimes delivered as a Q&A session

Assessment conditions and environments

The environment in which assessment occurs is as important as the type of technique used. In some instances the technique used will directly impact on the environment and conditions.

- The professional discussion needs to be conducted away from noise or influence. In cases where the discussion is recorded, permissions to record should be gleaned in advance with a clear explanation of how the recording will be used and stored.

Peer and self-assessment (indirect assessment)

Description:

Both peer and self-assessment generally lead to reflective practice. Both are concerned with the ability to judge oneself and involve a critical analysis of the individual learner. It is useful when trying to develop a learner's evaluative and feedback skills. Peer assessment is based on learning from each other and is therefore a good way to share ideas and best practice. Self-assessment is a personal review of learning.

Peer and self-assessment (indirect assessment)

In managed self- and peer assessments, the strategy usually starts with some carefully posed questions, ideally devised by the learner although teachers can guide them to reach solutions and standards. The questions should be open and probing.

As an informal strategy it is very common. Reading through a piece of work to ensure everything is covered before handing it in is a form of self-assessment. As a formal assessment strategy it can be used in the format of personal statements, journals, diaries or profiling. All of these assessments require the learner to write down what they did or would do in a given situation; this is then linked to a set of standards or criteria (as opposed to a rambling piece of text about general issues. There may be a witness testimony to authenticate the validity of the statements. This assessment method requires a good level of self-criticism and personal awareness and may need to be 'taught' before embarking on as a reliable method of assessment. Peer assessment follows the same principles although the review is undertaken by a fellow learner. Authenticity is the main risk associated with this method of assessment in that learners may not be familiar with the Units of Competence or be as confident in deciding sufficiency. These can be used as an alternative to professional discussion.

Advantages:

- Generally used supported by other assessment methods

- Enables evaluation and reflection

- Allows learners to develop responsibility for own learning

- Learning logs can record progress and aid reflection

- Gathers ideas and emotions from similar people

- Informal feedback

Disadvantages:

- Judgements made by self rather than an expert

- Difficult to be objective

- Limited to the extent of the profile document

- Peers may not know the standards and so compare with what they do

Assessment conditions and environments

The environment in which assessment occurs is as important as the type of technique used. In some instances the technique used will directly impact on the environment and conditions.

Peer and self-assessment (indirect assessment)

- There are no particular conditions required for assessment, other than common sense in respect of suitable environment. However, it should be clarified how much of the evidence will be deemed valid without additional evidence to support statements or assumptions made.

Recognition of Prior Learning (RPL) (indirect assessment)

Description:

Previously known as 'accreditation of prior learning, achievement or experience' (APL, APA or APE respectively)

A system of recognising the skills a learner comes into training with. The process of claiming RPL requires a learner to work either independently or with a teacher/assessor to match their previous skills or knowledge with the criteria contained in the qualification they wish to achieve. The assessment of RPL requires the teacher/assessor to validate the claim and ensure the authenticity of the evidence and confirm that the skills and knowledge are current. Testimonies, product evidence and a skills test may form part of the claim. The complexity of gathering evidence may be perceived as a barrier to using RPL as an assessment method.

Advantages:

- Generally used supported by other assessment methods
- Values previous learning, achievement and experience

Disadvantages:

- Need to validate all claims
- May not cover current competence
- Difficult to prove
- Time-consuming to analyse
- Needs specialist staff

Assessment conditions and environments

The environment in which assessment occurs is as important as the type of technique used. In some instances the technique used will directly impact on the environment and conditions.

Recognition of Prior Learning (RPL) (indirect assessment)

- In its most simple application, i.e. a previously acquired unit of assessment is used to exempt re-assessment in a larger credit value qualification, the production of a certificate from a recognised Awarding Organisation is sufficient to claim previous competence. However, in more complex scenarios, the teacher/assessor should explain that the responsibility for proving existing competence against current standards remains with the applicant and in some instances this can be an extensive piece of work.

Reviewing products or artefacts, portfolios (direct assessment)

Description:

Many assessments generate products which will form part of the assessment. Things such as print outs, letters, booklets, photographs and video clips are frequently submitted to prove a learner has developed skills to the required standard. The use of mobile technology and e-portfolios provides a mechanism to produce a sustainable (i.e. paperless) portfolio.

Advantages:

- Items generated outside of the classroom can be used to support demonstration of competence

- Generally used supported by other assessment methods

- Links the importance of classroom and work-based assessment

Disadvantages:

- The authenticity (ownership) of the product is not without doubt

Assessment conditions and environments

The environment in which assessment occurs is as important as the type of technique used. In some instances the technique used will directly impact on the environment and conditions.

- Work products are items, for example, business/service documents (minutes, print-outs, forms, procedures, diagrams); finished goods, commodities or commissions, or anything similar produced during normal

◀

Reviewing products or artefacts, portfolios (direct assessment)

work activities. Learners should obtain authorisation to use any document or procedure.

- If using mobile technology to video an assessment or take photographs of others, learners and teacher/assessors must ensure that appropriate permissions are sought and received before using them in evidence.

Testimonials (indirect assessment)

Description:

The use of testimonials is important when the teacher/assessor needs to rely on others who have a closer contact with the learner. Workplace supervisors are a valuable source of evidence to prove that a learner consistently works to a prescribed standard. Testimonials should be written against the Units of Assessment, however, frequently workplace staff are less familiar with the criteria and therefore the teacher/assessor would be required to annotate the testimonial during the assessment process. A witness is someone who is able to testify (validate) what they have seen. A witness might be an employer, customer or team member.

Advantages:	Disadvantages:
- Able to collect information from work or other activities to support studies - Generally used supported by other assessment methods	- Reliability of witness cannot be guaranteed

Assessment conditions and environments

The environment in which assessment occurs is as important as the type of technique used. In some instances the technique used will directly impact on the environment and conditions.

- Authenticating the testimony is essential in making judgements about the content. If presented in a more *ad hoc* manner, then a quick phone call to the writer of the testimonial should satisfy the teacher/assessor that it is a true reflection of competence.

Testimonials (indirect assessment)

- Pre-set or semi-structured testimonials are invaluable for the busy work-place supervisors who have limited experience of what or how to write a witness testimony.

- Always triangulate evidence presented by third parties, perhaps with some verbal questions, some artefacts or a professional discussion with the learner.

e-Assessment or online tests

Description:

All or parts of qualifications can be achieved using learning technologies. Paper-based examinations can be replaced by online tests which give instant results. Paper-based portfolios are being replaced by e-portfolios which require all evidence to be stored in a more environmentally friendly manner. The evidence is stored electronically on either personal media storage devices, using a training organisation's servers or specialist software.

Advantages:	Disadvantages:
- On demand assessment	- Expensive to resource
- Immediate feedback	- Licences may be needed
- Objective	- Reliant on power and network access
- Inclusive	- Not everyone is confident with technology
- Sustainable – paperless	- Cut and paste is common

Assessment conditions and environments

The environment in which assessment occurs is as important as the type of technique used. In some instances the technique used will directly impact on the environment and conditions.

- Authenticity is the main risk area here, especially if the test is undertaken without the rigour of invigilation by independent staff.

- Always seek some photo identification to prove that the person doing the online test is the correct learner.

▶

e-Assessment or online tests

- Usual examination conditions are expected to reduce the risk of copying or eliciting correct answers from texts etc.

Group activities (direct assessment) (see also Part 3)

Description:

A range of activities can be used to assess, however assessment is difficult. It is commonly a classroom-based activity but requires accurate records to split the individual performance from the group. It is very often accompanied with other assessment methods to aid authenticity of evidence. Group work aids collaboration and teamwork, both useful as future employability skills. Assessment in groups will aid depth of knowledge and aid more holistic views on a topic.

Advantages:	Disadvantages:
● Motivational as tasks are shared	● Difficult to attribute results to an individual or particular skill
● Less intimidating	
● Individual strengths can be played to maximise results	● Weaker learners can hide
	● Can disadvantage some learners
● Can be used formatively or summatively	● Marking can either encourage or disadvantage collaboration

Assessment conditions and environments

The environment in which assessment occurs is as important as the type of technique used. In some instances the technique used will directly impact on the environment and conditions.

- Decide how to allocate marks. For example is the product or the process to be scored? Do you allocate the same mark for everyone or mark according to the specific role within the group?

- A solution could be to award the same mark to the group for the product, but mark within a band for individual contribution. In more mature thinking groups this could be done by the group. Alternatively, observation, a viva or personal log could be used to attribute individual scores.

 ACTIVITY 1

Assessment methods

How do you know everyone has learned the topic?

Quite simply, you don't unless you assess.

From the lists above, give two examples of how you might assess each item in the list below. State why you think your chosen examples are the right ones:

- Discuss the effects of the Second World War on the economy of Britain.
- Identify road signs for crossroads, T-junctions, speed restrictions, etc.
- Using a photocopier.
- Baking a cake.
- Reviewing and evaluating teaching methods.
- Comparing and contrasting two issues.
- Preparing for a job interview.
- List the correct flag for a list of countries.

Describe how will you know if your assessments are effective (i.e. valid, fit for purpose, etc.)?

Controlled assessment

In some qualifications, a percentage of the assessment is now completed under supervised conditions. This was introduced in response to varying standards in the marking of learner portfolio work in a bid to raise the reliability of the tests. The assessment is 'controlled' by way of pre-set assessments marked independently. Either the Awarding Organisation sets the assessment and the teacher marks it using

detailed marking schemes, or, the teacher sets it and sends it to the
Awarding Organisation who mark it.

Quality versus quantity

Trying to collect sufficient evidence to meet the scope of the assessment
criteria has long been a challenge for teachers. There is a tendency,
particularly with inexperienced teachers to collect too much, 'just in
case' or at the opposite end, not have enough. This balance is
something teachers must confront and test frequently. It is better to
collect one piece of really useful evidence rather than a collection of
things which only relate to parts of a learner's qualification.

There are a couple of suggestions which may be useful:

- Read and comprehend the assessment criteria for the whole
  qualification, not just part of it. By doing this you will see where there
  is repetition and be able to attribute evidence to more than one
  aspect of the qualification – this is generally referred to as cross
  referencing.

- Consider linking the job to the qualification rather than the other way
  around. Many jobs completed by the learner cover a range of units
  of assessment and therefore will be easier for the learner to
  understand. This is referred to as holistic assessment – where the
  teacher/assessor considers the bigger picture. An example of this
  would be a health and safety unit. It is possible to collect a range of
  evidence to confer competence in health and safety, but then every
  job a learner does in their work environment will enable them to
  demonstrate their application of health and safety, supported by
  some 'what if' questions to check understanding or contingency
  plans. This would reduce the amount of evidence required and
  embed it fully into every task completed.

Wherever possible, always try to assess learners to minimise the
amount of work, whilst maximising the usefulness of the evidence; this
enables efficient assessment.

 ## ACTIVITY 2

Holistic assessment

Consider one of the following scenarios and, using your National Occupational Standards, create a grid (may also be called a plan or matrix – an example of one is shown below) which shows which parts of the qualification can be assessed whilst observing the task.

	REF	Unit 1.1	Unit 1.2	Unit 1.3	Unit 2.1	Unit 2.2	Unit 3.1	Unit 3.2	Unit 3.3	Unit 4.1	Unit 4.2	etc.
xyz document				✓	✓		✓	✓		✓	✓	
Observation		✓	✓	✓	✓	✓		✓				
Oral Question					✓	✓						
etc.												

To start this task you will need to break your chosen task into its component parts. You should also consider additional skills such as customer service, health and safety, equality and diversity. You may wish to expand the case study to set the context.

Example: Restaurant – taking a customer's order.

Main Observable items within a job: customer service, using order systems (e.g. written pads, electronic systems), customer information (table, extras required, food choices and preferred cooking style, etc.)

Secondary skills demonstrated during the job: approaches to hygiene and safety, appearance, communication with customers and staff, knowledge of menu (food and drinks), how item is served, organised approach – table laid, crockery, accompaniments, dealing with problems or unexpected situations. Each of these topics is contained in the Level 2 Diploma in Professional Food and Beverage Service, City and Guilds 7103-02, Qualification handbook, 500/7478/7.

▶

Now think about these workplace routines and select an appropriate idea to plan your own holistic assessment:

1 Hairdressing Salon: shampooing a client's hair in preparation for a cut

2 Construction Site: Laying a foundation course of bricks for a garden feature

3 Garage: Changing a tyre on a vehicle

4 Office: Typing a set of minutes from your supervisor's notes

5 Veterinary Surgery: Preparing a rabbit for a non-surgical procedure

6 Cafe: Preparing a steak and kidney pie for a lunchtime meal

7 Care Home: Helping an elderly patient to dress

8 Nursery: Supervising a play session with a group of three-year-olds

9 Office: Retrieving a document from a computer for your supervisor

10 Reception Desk: Dealing with a delivery of office stationery

11 Leisure Centre: Preparing an exercise plan for a guest

12 Beauty Salon: Preparing a client for a neck and back massage

13 Newspaper Office: Receiving an advert for this week's edition

14 Farm: assisting the farmer with preparations for lambing

15 Restaurant: serving wine at the table.

Always apply the rules of assessment to the chosen assessment method (validity, authenticity, currency, sufficiency). Is the method a reliable way of providing valid evidence, authentic to the learner, demonstrating current practice and will it provide enough (sufficient) evidence to meet the standards? (See also Chapter 10).

In helping you to compare, contrast and decide upon appropriate assessment methods for a given assessment, consider the following scenarios:

CASE STUDY

The learner works in a hairdressing salon and the assessor is the senior stylist. They work together daily. Clients book in to the salon for various services, usually regular clients but sometimes they are 'walk-ins'. In addition, the learner needs to demonstrate their understanding of how to respond to spontaneous bookings as opposed to regular clients? How does the assessor need to plan this assessment?

CASE STUDY

The learner works in a Vehicle Repair Station. Every day work is allocated to the learner in the form of a job-card; he usually works with one of the mechanics, but is well able to do some tasks with minimal supervision. The assessor is from a local training provider and meets the learner on their day release day and visits the garage monthly. The assessor always meets the Garage Supervisor when he visits. How should the assessor plan assessments for this learner?

CASE STUDY

A learner visits the training provider having returned to work following maternity leave. She is now a receptionist and is the first point of contact for employees and guests visiting the company. She worked in an office as an administrator prior to having a baby and is now considering an apprenticeship in Customer Services. How will you advise the learner in presenting her previous experience towards her new qualification?

CASE STUDY

Learners in the College have to attend sessions in the Training Restaurant as part of their hospitality and catering course. They have a rota which requires them to work in the kitchen, restaurant, reception desk and bar. In addition they have practical sessions in a skills kitchen. How can the college activities link to the assessments for their course? How would you explain the difference between activities undertaken in skills development, the training restaurant and their theory sessions? How can these contribute to a holistic method of assessment?

In summary, choosing assessment methods should always be linked to the learner's needs and appropriateness of the environment.

Electronic and mobile learning and assessment technologies

ILT is used increasingly as a teaching tool (see Chapter 9: resources); it therefore follows that it will be seen as an assessment tool also. For teachers and learners who enjoy this style (but remember this doesn't include everyone), it is merely a continuation of their learning when they are assessed in this way.

Some of the ways in which ILT/ICT can support assessment are:

- word processing work
- using presentation software, e.g. PowerPoint or Prezi, for presentations
- using interactive boards in question sessions
- using the Internet for research
- using forums, Virtual Learning Environments (VLE) and social networks to share ideas and questions
- using databases and spreadsheets to track progress

- using email to submit and return work
- storing evidence in e-portfolios
- online screening or diagnostic assessment
- course material uploaded to VLEs
- using smart phones or i-touch to record performance evidence
- questioning using electronic voting systems.

Most organisations now express a commitment to the development of e-assessment.

Advantages to e-assessment:

- Learners can take tests as they become confident/competent.
- Immediate feedback and results.
- Objective marking, especially when computer marked.
- Less requirement for paper records, results stored electronically.
- More inclusive.

Disadvantages to e-assessment:

- Expensive technology and specialist software necessary.
- Reliant on power, servers, Internet links – what if this is not available due to location or supply?
- Not everyone is comfortable with technological advances.
- Difficult to assess values and attitudes, typically presented in essay format.
- Overuse of 'cut and paste'.

Progress around ILT in assessment needs to be concerned with a blended learning approach. This will offer alternatives according to levels of confidence in using computerised technologies and provide changes in style (as opposed to death by computer technologies). E-assessment should be offered as an acceptable alternative rather than a required option.

Supporting assessment through (electronic) e-technologies and (mobile) m-technologies is becoming increasingly popular as the technology, equipment and access is improving. In an era of environmental sustainability the days of lever-arch files full of evidence is diminishing in favour of alternative storage strategies.

Online assessment has been a feature of many qualifications for a number of years. When assessment is undertaken through multiple-choice questioning many Awarding Organisations host this through easy to access online testing software such as Global Online Assessment (GOLA) or e-volve. Marking through the use of scanning software has been used for many years where multiple-choice questions or Likert scales are used to analyse answers.
(http://psychology.about.com/od/lindex/g/likert-scale.htm)

Many organisations now have Virtual Learning Environments (VLEs), for example Moodle or Blackboard. These are hosted through the Internet or through an organisation's servers and Intranets. They include access to resources, links to websites and documents, provide email facilities and support wikis, blogs and chat rooms. They complement, or offer an alternative to, managed learning environments and have the added benefit of being available 24/7. The VLEs can host forums on which learners can have conversations, meetings or share ideas. These can be synchronous or asynchronous (see Chapter 9).

E-assessment is supported by recent developments in software and hardware resources. Digital cameras can easily provide still or video evidence of competence or products. Flip Cams record activities and are easily uploaded (transferred) to computer storage systems. Similarly, the Internet provides valuable links to downloadable material to support assessment activities. Voting systems provide interesting mechanisms to vary traditional questioning sessions. The increased access to Wi-Fi and the development of Smart phones and associated apps (for example: Augmented Reality app) are really broadening the scope of assessment and learning.
http://www.jiscinfonet.ac.uk/InfoKits/effective-use-of-VLEs/e-assessment

Teachers can accept electronic copy of assignments and other written pieces via email and, by using 'review' in Word applications, are able to provide a timely and trackable marking system. These, and other electronic files used to collect evidence, can be uploaded to e-portfolios using software systems such as Smart Assessor, Learning Assistant, Pass-Port, Pebble-Pad or iWebFolio.

Assessment decisions

Following an assessment and the resultant feedback, you will have to make a judgement. The decision will be a summary of what you saw that was good, the standard achieved, how much further development is needed. There will usually be parts of the assessment that are satisfactory, but there may be parts that were not so good – this may be reflected in the grade or pass mark. All criteria contained in the Units of Assessment must be met, which is why an assessment may consist of more than one method of assessment to cope with the things that don't naturally occur.

Depending upon the type of qualification, purpose of assessment and level of formality in the assessment, the decision will either be:

- Pass or Fail – the assessment either meets or doesn't meet the standard required.
- A graded result – pass, merit [credit], distinction which describes how well a learner has achieved, but your feedback needs to explain the development between levels.
- Marks – out of 10, 20, 100, etc., usually expressed as percentage.

The teacher should be quite clear in stating the outcome of the assessment. Saying the words 'you've passed' is very often the thing that is forgotten at the expense of creating good feedback. Also, sometimes the feedback is so positive that a learner can misunderstand the outcome, maybe thinking that they've passed or achieved a higher grade than they actually have.

The 'F' word

The word fail is rarely used. This is because it is highly demotivational. Although, teachers need to remember that some learners will fail and should consider when and why this is acceptable, and equally how to manage it fairly and respectfully. Rarely is everything so bad in an assessment that the teacher cannot comment positively on some aspect. If an assessment is not at the required standard, i.e. fails, you should consider alternative expressions such as 'needs further training' or 'not yet competent' or simply 'refer'.

When making an assessment decision or judgement it is important that the teacher remains objective. The best way of doing that, to guarantee the reliability and fairness of your decision, is inherent in the make-up of the qualification and the rules of assessment.

- Always use the units of assessment specified in the assessment plan (validity).
- Always check that documentation is signed and can be attributed to the learner (authenticity).
- Always check that documentation is dated and that the evidence reflects current industry standards (currency).
- Always check that there is enough evidence to cover all aspects of the targeted assessment criteria (sufficiency).
- Always apply the rules of assessment consistently without bias in all decision making (reliability/fairness).

It is worth commenting here about authenticity and plagiarism. All evidence presented to confirm competence must do that. Teachers and assessors must ensure that all work submitted for assessment is the work of the individual learner. It must not be someone else's work. For example, in an office a learner presents to you a number of letters that the learner alleges to have composed and sent to customers. How do you know? You cannot assume that just because these letters were presented by the learner that they were created by them.

Plagiarism

Plagiarism is similar but refers to the passing off as someone else's published material as their own. Plagiarism is the result of a naïve belief that it can be copied or a deliberate act of passing off someone else's work as their own. By teaching about referencing and advocating good standards in study skills, we can ensure that learners do not fall foul of accusations of plagiarism. It is more usually seen in written statements or assignments where articles, particularly, from the Internet, are included into a learner's work without any citation or reference. Plagiarism breaches the Copyright, Designs and Patents Act 1988 in which it is against the law to reproduce material without acknowledging the owner. The acknowledgement is usually in the format of a reference citing the name of the author, the title of the product and the publisher. If using larger pieces of work then permissions from the owner need to be sought.

Unfortunately, one of the downsides of the Internet is the apparent ease in which people can download information and cut and paste it into their work, or even acquire whole assignments.

How to spot plagiarism:

- Different writing style or writing level to that seen in usual work.
- Variants in fonts and font size within text.
- American spellings (…ize, color, center, program).
- Different referencing system to that which has been taught.
- Word processed work when hand written is usual.
- Obscure references or sources of information.
- Different opinions/context to those made in a session or text books.

If you suspect something, you don't need fancy software tools to detect it. Just type the sentence, without the smaller words (e.g. of, and, the, etc.) or key words that seem obscure, into a search engine – like Google™ – and generally, it will appear verbatim in the list of 'hits' that appear as search findings. Wikipedia is a frequently abused reference used by learners.

In terms of authenticity, it doesn't hurt to get learners into the habit of signing and dating their work.

I confirm that this [assignment/essay etc.], is all my own work.

Signed: A Learner.

Today's date

This does not stop plagiarism, but it enters the learners into a contract concerning ethics.

Triangulation

There are various ways to achieve confidence in your assessment and thus promote effectiveness. One of the easiest is to triangulate judgements. This means to use more than one assessment method to confirm competence. For example, would you allow (believe) a learner who presented a photograph and told you it was their work? It is more likely that you will check this out by asking some verbal questions to elicit information about how they did it. You may add to this by considering previous classwork activities they have done or by setting another practical task to confirm their ability. In an alternative example, a learner presents some product evidence from their workplace; you check out understanding with some oral questions and seek testimony from a workplace supervisor. If the results of all of these assessment methods say the same thing then you can confirm competence. Each method is therefore contributing effectively to produce an assessment that is reliable and authentic and provides sufficient evidence on which to confirm competence.

Triangulation also provides variety. By testing learners in different ways, not only does it triangulate providing confirmation that decisions are accurate and consistent, but it adds interest and meets different learning styles.

Portfolios

Portfolios are a collection of evidence. Evidence is defined as the output of an assessment activity; evidence of a learner's knowledge and understanding, skills or competence that can be used to make a judgement of their achievement against agreed standards/criteria. As such, evidence collected by teacher/assessors can be:

- Observation of performance
- Oral questions

- Written questions
- Products, documents, artefacts, photographs, video clips, records
- Professional discussion
- Personal statements or logs, reflective accounts
- Witness Testimony
- Supplementary evidence – i.e. that which contextualises or explains the context of other pieces of evidence.

Each of these is discussed as an assessment method earlier in this chapter.

Unfortunately, it is not possible for the teacher/assessor or learner to just say 'I do that'. They need to be able to prove it.

What is a portfolio?

Records are kept by learners in the form of portfolios. Portfolios will include records and evidence, derived either in the classroom or from the workplace, and documents created by their teacher/assessor to record observations, testimonies and questioning. A portfolio is a collection of evidence or proof – this is more likely to be the best or final copy rather than everything created during the training process. The portfolio tells the story of the learner's journey from trainee to competence.

A portfolio of evidence, therefore, is a term used to describe the way in which the evidence required to demonstrate competence in a particular qualification is kept. A portfolio can be paper-based, electronic (either through an e-portfolio or portable storage device), or a combination of both. Brown (1992) defines the term 'personal portfolio' as follows:

> '...a private collection of evidence which demonstrates the continuing acquisition of skills, knowledge, attitudes, understanding and achievement. It is both retrospective and prospective, as well as reflecting the current stage of the development of the individual...'

Whilst the portfolio belongs to the learner, it is important that the teacher/ assessor and the quality assurer (verifier) have access to it. The assessor needs to see the evidence in order to make judgements about the validity, authenticity, currency and sufficiency of the contents. The internal quality assurer needs to see it to sample the decisions made by the teacher/assessor for accuracy and transparency. The Awarding Organisation will also require access, via an external quality assurer, to the information for sampling purposes.

A portfolio, despite the fact that it is an individual's record, does not need to include personal or learning materials as that part of the learner journey towards competence is not assessed. It should be evidence relating to how competencies were demonstrated against whichever qualification is being achieved. The evidence should be collected and presented in a logical manner not only to enable the person collecting the evidence to reflect on their progress, but to aid those assessing the qualification to 'find' the evidence. So by keeping a list of contents, referenced to what is being demonstrated, the learner will always know how much more needs to be done in order to complete the qualification. Most learners need help to compile a portfolio.

On the occasions when a portfolio is paper-based, it is generally stored in a file or folder. However, it is not essential to copy absolutely everything. Where evidence comes from work or work experience, and teacher/assessor will view evidence in its normal location and 'testify' to its existence. This will ensure that folders do not become excessively large with lots of photocopies of documents. It also supports the notion that confidential material or records can be retained within the organisation. Similarly, products, for example, brick walls, cooked food items or clients hairstyles cannot be 'put' into a folder. Admittedly, photographic evidence can be made, but teacher/assessors observing the real thing is sufficient. If necessary, as part of QA sampling, QA teams might request site visits to view the evidence judged as competent by the teacher/assessor.

In these instances, one Awarding Organisation, City and Guilds, recommends that when evidence is assessed *in situ*, the record of that assessment must state:

- Who and what was assessed and by whom
- The date and location of the assessment

- The assessment methods used to collect the evidence
- The assessment decision
- the units, learning outcomes and assessment criteria achieved
- the location of the supporting evidence.

Qualification Handbook for Centres (Feb 2011 p11)

ACTIVITY 3

Portfolio contents

Make a list of five typical pieces of evidence that could be retained in the workplace or work experience placement.

1

2

3

4

5

Answers:

Fire Evacuation procedures, office procedures, cooked products from a catering outlet, staff appraisals, environmental/ layout of space, safe working practices, clients' treatments, confidential files, etc.

Portfolio extras

Some teacher/assessors find it useful if their learners' portfolios contain the Units of Assessment to save them time when assessing. Other teacher/assessors provide grids which link the specifications to the evidence – called tracking sheets (see page 263).

Teacher/assessors need to mark according to professional standards, particularly relating to presentation of work, accuracy of spelling, grammar and the use of English. Teacher/assessors should always correct inaccuracies.

Confidentiality in assessment is part of the ethical responsibilities of a teacher/assessor and an IQA. A teacher/assessor/IQA is required to keep records securely, and respect the confidentiality of learners and their employers. For example, a teacher/assessor will more than likely come into contact with systems and procedures in many different organisations. They must be mindful of 'commercial in confidence' which requires them to look at documents only for the purpose of assessment and not divulge information to others. If you use photographs in your portfolio, you must seek permission to use them. If people are in the photograph, especially minors or vulnerable adults, this should be in writing (from parents/guardians/carers of minors or vulnerable adults).

Copyright legislation exists to protect intellectual ownership and misuse of published materials. Plagiarism is when there is a lack of accurate referencing of published information. To overcome this learners should not 'cut and paste' or cite published works without referencing the source. For example, to cite a part of this paragraph the writer should write it as follows: Wilson (2013) states: 'Plagiarism … is a lack of accurate referencing of published information'. Then, in a bibliography or reference list at the end of the essay or statement, you would include the reference: Wilson, L. (2013) *Practical Teaching: A Guide to Teaching in the Education and Training Sector*. Andover: Cengage.

Supporting learners to complete their portfolio is common. A teacher needs to decide at what point the support is complete and assessment starts. The evidence contained in a portfolio must be authentic – i.e. the learner's own work, so it cannot include work which has been created by the teacher/assessor (with the exception of records created by the teacher/assessor to record observations, questioning, etc.). There are ways of showing development within a portfolio, for example to include draft versions of evidence and final copy. This way, internal and external QA staff can see the learner's journey to competence. In discussing authenticity, it should be noted that everything contained in a portfolio should be signed and dated. When assessing e-portfolios, signatures are not possible (in that e-signatures could be attached by anyone), so the teacher/assessor must make other investigations to ensure that the work is authentic and owned by the learner.

Portfolios do have a shelf-life. Evidence contained in a portfolio is required to be current practice. This means that evidence contained in a portfolio which is more than 12 – 24 months old (depending on the sector) is likely to be considered too old to be valid. Awarding Organisations will provide advice on currency of evidence and it will change according to the sector. For example: the technology sector is advancing very quickly, so the evidence needs to reflect current versions of hardware and software. The Arts sector is likely to allow evidence built up over a longer period of time.

Exemplar Portfolios are commonly requested by learners. These are not advised because they remove the spontaneity of the evidence methodology. Learners (and teacher/assessors) tend to replicate the style of the example and this restricts the efficiency of assessment.

Tracking evidence

In this context, the tracker is used by the learner to track their own progress and link their evidence to the criteria of the qualification. Once a learner has collected all of their evidence it will need to be indexed it and linked to the assessment criteria of the qualification.

Depending upon the type of qualification the learner is undertaking, one of the following would be an appropriate method to track evidence.

	REF	1.1	1.2	1.3	1.4	1.5	2.1	2.2	2.3	3.1	3.2	etc.
xyz document	Pg5			✓	✓		✓	✓		✓	✓	
Observation 30/11/11	Pg8	✓	✓	✓	✓	✓		✓				
Oral Question record 1	Pg12						✓	✓				
etc.												

	REF	P1	P2	P3	P4	P5	P6	M1	M2	D1
Assignment 1	Doc1	✓	✓	✓				✓		✓
Assignment 2	Doc2				✓	✓	✓		✓	

In these tracking grids each piece of evidence is given a reference (or a page number) to indicate where it is located. Remember this could be at the workplace or saved to a file or folder on a portable storage device. Then the evidence is linked to the standards. In the first example you will notice that there is no piece of evidence that is recorded against 2.3. This means that any reviewer of this tracker would alert the learner to gaining some evidence to evidence it – alternatively it might be an error in the tracking.

Watch point

- Teacher/assessors should always check the tracking sheets as they will need to sign to say that the evidence they have assessed does in fact cover the criteria claimed.

- Tracking is a difficult task if a learner is not very organised or the qualification has some complex cross referencing – so as a teacher/assessor you should be prepared to support them in this task.

Glossary of terms

Bibliography a complete list of everything investigated during the research, in alphabetical order

Blended learning a mixture of traditional and modern/computer-based learning technologies

Confidentiality secrecy of information

Contingency plan planning for the unexpected occurrence

Cross reference linking evidence to more than one aspect of the qualification

Diagnostic (assessment) assessment occurring early in the learner journey to establish starting points or identify capability or skill level, particularly in relation to functional skills

Direct assessment evidence of the learner's work

E-assessment electronic versions of assessment

Effective (assessment) to produce the intended or desired result or outcome

Ethics the acceptable rules or behaviours

Fail an assessment decision; not at pass standard

Feedback verbal or written comments about the assessment intended to bring about improvement

Grade a level or degree of competence

Holistic the big picture; the whole qualification or curriculum

Indirect assessment evidence or opinion from others

Initial assessment assessment occurring very early in the learner journey to establish potential, aspirations, suitability or existing level of learning/experience

Integrity having values and principles

Judgement a decision about an assessment

Outcome the consequence or impact of the learning and assessment strategies

Pass assessment decision relating to satisfactory performance

Reference a list of material cited in the research essay, in alphabetical order

Reliability a strategy to ensure that assessment decisions are consistent

RPL Recognition of Prior Learning

Sampling the probability or non-probability of the data

SMARTER specific, measurable, achievable, relevant, time-bounded, ethical and reviewed

Subjective decisions influenced by other factors

Tracking a method of recording progress

Triangulate measuring by different perspectives

Triangulation/Triangulated the validation of one set of data against other sets.

 # SUMMARY

In this chapter we set out to achieve the following outcomes:

- To describe the planning process and apply in the organisation of assessments.
- To describe the advantages and disadvantages of each assessment method and make informed decisions about which to choose.
- To evaluate your choices of assessment methods and identify what makes assessment effective.
- To compare and contrast the range of assessment methods available to use.
- To review the use of electronic assessment and technology in assessment.

Your personal development

You have looked at the planning process and studied its position within the assessment cycle. You are able to explain the protocols and design features of effective planning and have reviewed the factors which may provide barriers to successful assessment. In this section you have had an opportunity to revise how Bloom's Taxonomy can be used to differentiate and develop learners.

You can describe and compare the various methods of assessment and have considered how they are appropriate within different assessment situations. This section described, compared and reviewed special conditions in observation, simulation, project/assignment work, case studies, various styles of written questioning, oral questioning, professional discussion, self/peer assessment, RPL, reviewing products of assessment, testimonials and e-assessment. This will enable you to make better choices about the assessment methods you plan to use and to justify your selection.

By completing the case studies you have shown how you devise assessments to ensure that they meet the rules of assessment, i.e. validity, reliability, authenticity, currency and sufficiency. Further you have developed this concept by exploring how using holistic assessment minimises the quantity of evidence required to demonstrate competence.

Finally you have looked at portfolios, what they are and how they support the assessment process.

CHAPTER 12

Questioning and feedback in assessment

LEARNING OBJECTIVES

The measurable outcomes that you will achieve by reading this chapter and completing the activities are:

....

- To compare and contrast a variety of different questioning techniques
- To consider the strengths and weaknesses of each method and make informed decisions about selection of questions
- To explain and evaluate the effectiveness of questioning techniques
- To describe the method of constructive feedback
- To identify the value of feedback, especially relating to assessment and progression
- To explain and evaluate the effectiveness of feedback techniques
- To describe the skills required to provide effective feedback

Questioning techniques

Questioning refers to a process designed to find out what someone understands (or knows) about a topic. It is one of the most commonly used, successful and versatile methods of assessment, so worthy of some additional hints and tips. In this part of the chapter, we revisit the main questioning methods and look at each in detail to help inform effective use of questioning.

The variety of methods within the category of questioning is large and the way it can be used to differentiate, motivate and develop learners is very broad. Equally, it is the assessment method that is most criticised and open to inefficient and ineffective use.

1 Essay type	
Description	A structured, semi-structured or unstructured piece of writing on a topic.
	The level of structure is determined by the question posed.
	May also be called extended questions.
Main uses	Depth of subject knowledge is tested.
	Tests values, opinions and argument.
	Academic/research investigative pieces.
	Creative, evaluative or descriptive writing.
	Unsuitable as oral questioning.
Designing Questions	Very easy, questions can range from unstructured, when learners decide upon their own topics as in dissertations, to semi-structured, when broad topic titles are given, to structured when learners answer a series of questions making up the topic title.
	Categorised as supply type of questions.
Making judgements	Difficult to mark – detailed assessment criteria required to allocate set marks for specific component of essay (e.g. ten marks for …, 50 marks for …, etc.).

▶

	Difficult to mark objectively so results may lack consistency.
	Generally marked as a percentage or grade.
Assessment Rules	Formative or summative applications.
	May cover only a small aspect of the curriculum so impacts on validity and sufficiency.
	Open to plagiarism and cheating thus questioning authenticity.
Differentiation	Assesses understanding and cognitive skills.
	Assesses literacy skills (and numeracy when data collection requirements are included).
	Can be intimidating for learners, as essay writing is a skill in itself.
	Level of high order skills makes them highly suitable for learners at Level 3 and above.

2 Short answer type

Description	Specific questions on a single or multiple topics, requiring a few paragraphs of text as an answer.
Main uses	Very versatile style of questions, which can be oral or written, requiring one-word, sentence or extended answers.
	Tests cognitive skills and either depth of knowledge or breadth of knowledge – dependent on questions asked.
	Good homework questions as they do not take too long to complete.
	Requires learners to remember information.
	Ideal as extended oral questions.
	Often called 'open' questions.
	Very effective when used orally in a nominated questioning style, so that questions are linked to learner ability.
Designing Questions	Fairly easy to design using words such as How? Why? When? Where? What?

	Create open questions, requiring responses covering fact, opinion.
	Can design should/could/would options in questions.
	Categorised as supply type of questions.
	Can be one-word or sentence/paragraph length responses.
Making judgements	Marking grids are required as answers will vary.
	Objectivity increased due to more focused responses.
	Weight of questions is usually reflected in number of marks available for each question.
Assessment Rules	Formative or summative applications.
	Covers a wider range of topics in the curriculum and improves sufficiency in coverage.
	Widens opportunities to collect valid, reliable and qualitative responses.
	When questions are asked verbally it is absolutely authentic – unless the question is posed in advance and answered at a later time.
Differentiation	Less frightening than essay type questions.
	Develops essay writing skills, therefore ideal for learners progressing to or aspiring to higher academic levels.
	Degree of difficulty can be varied to support different needs of learners.
	Less analysis and argument needed, questions usually relate to fact or opinion, which makes them more suitable for Level 1 and 2 learners.
	Can be used to probe deeper into a subject to ascertain levels of understanding.
	Opportunity to collect ipsative/profiling information.

3 Multiple-choice type

Description	A question with (usually) four possible answers, which requires learners to identify the correct answer.
	Sometimes called restricted response or expressed as multiple-choice questions (MCQs).

▶

Main uses	Requires learners to recognise information. Possible as oral questions if planned in advance. Very often used in summative tests. Easily adapted to suit e-assessment.
Designing Questions	Very difficult to prepare. Questions (the stem) have a correct answer (the key) and several (usually 3 or 4) incorrect answers (distractors). The key and distractors are collectively called 'options'. Learners call them multiple guess questions as once the obvious distractors are removed; it usually leaves two possible answers. C is the most common correct answer so the test needs to be tested so that correct answers are evenly distributed. Categorised as selection type questions.
Making judgements	Very easy to mark as only one answer will be correct. Computerised marking software and voting systems can be used. Learners can participate in marking if given answer frames. Very objective way of testing. Opportunities to vary levels of questions to test range of ability – power of discrimination.
Assessment Rules	Questions can cover a large part of the curriculum. Large numbers of questions can be asked in a relatively short space of time. Can be used to gather quantitative data in larger research studies. Can be used formatively or summatively.
Differentiation	Questions can vary in level of difficulty. No test of writing skills, but good to develop reading and comprehension skills. Questions can be 'banked' and reused at a later date. Generally MCQs test recall rather than comprehension, however, more complex questions can be formed to test higher order skills.

4 Alternative answer type

Description	Either yes/no, true/false answers to specific questions resulting in very restricted responses.
Main uses	Requires learners to recognise information by giving limited answers. Very little depth of knowledge required. Tendency to guess, therefore low order cognitive skills are tested. Used in questionnaires to gather data. Often called 'closed' questions.
Designing Questions	Simple to answer and prepare. In more complex questionnaires, avoid an odd number of responses as this allows people to remain undecided (sitting on the fence), which may not be helpful in eliciting data. Categorised as selection type questions.
Making judgements	Easy to mark, learners can participate in marking. Objective method of marking, but limited reliability due to guesswork.
Assessment Rules	Doesn't test reliably due to chance of guessing answers correctly. Due to lack of reliability, they are more suitable to formative assessment.
Differentiation	Does not test writing skills. 50 per cent chance of correct answer. Use of Likert scale can bring in more responses (strongly agree, agree, disagree, strongly disagree).

5 Matching answer type

Description	Two lists of data or facts are written which have to be matched.
Main uses	Used to match, for example: events and dates; terms and explanations; facts and figures; etc.

	Can be used with individuals or groups. Unsuitable as oral questions.
Designing Questions	Average ease to design, but messy to answer; answers tend to be lines drawn from one correct answer to the corresponding fact in other list, so may need to prepare answer sheets. Categorised as selection type questions.
Making judgements	Easy to mark, although answer sheets may be difficult to read. If one question is wrong it may limit opportunities to get all other answers correct. Very objective in scoring/result.
Assessment Rules	Valid and objective method of testing factual data. Difficult to include the power to discriminate because of limited answer frameworks. Ideal formative assessment for low order skills.
Differentiation	Suits fun activities and opener/closure activities. Very few literacy skills assessed. Can test whether learning outcomes are met. Covers wide curriculum or can link separately delivered topics to create learning links.

6 Completion type

Description	Text or diagrammatic sheets in which key words are omitted. Sometimes called gapped hand-outs.
Main uses	Can be used for recall tests at beginning and end of sessions or to create interaction during session time. Can be used as oral questions if planned in advance. Useful to create *aides-memoires* for learners.
Designing questions	Any document can be adapted to become a completion-type test.

	Cloze technique (missing out letters in regular patterns) can be used to determine reading ages and comprehension levels. Categorised as supply type questions.
Making Judgements	Objective as there should be only one correct solution. Marking is usually correct responses out of maximum.
Assessment rules	Valid, in that tests are usually about current topics being taught in the curriculum. Formative strategy to check classwork progress.
Differentiation	Can be used with or without answer options to differentiate between abilities. Can test spelling and comprehension of technical terms.

General hints and tips about questioning

- Make sure that learners know how to answer the questions – special answer sheet, black ballpoint pen or pencil, style (essay, report or bullet points), word count.
- Make questions short and precise.
- Use a 'tell me' style of opener to questioning.
- Avoid two questions in one sentence/question.
- Avoid negatives in questions – 'which of the following is not …' and multiple correct questions – with questions like 'which is the main reason for …' If these *must* be used then highlight the command word using **bold**, *italics* or <u>underline</u> formatting.
- Arrange questions logically and avoid repetition in subject type.
- If suggesting a word count, it is usually acceptable to add a '+ or – 10 per cent' rule, before marks are deducted for too few or too many words.
- The more unstructured the question the more creative and diverse the answer because of the freedom of ideas allowed.
- Reduce misinterpretation of questions by avoiding words like 'some', 'a few', 'a range'. How many *is* a few?

We have already learned that there a number of different questioning methods, but within those methods there are a number of different techniques to asking questions. However, before moving onto techniques there are some basics that underpin each technique.

The basics: open, closed and leading questions

Good questioning should be of an 'open' type, which means that the learner has to think of the answer. A good open question will test knowledge or understanding and contain opportunities to provide a full answer. Closed questions have limited responses, for example, yes/no or true/false solutions – so a learner could guess the answer. In leading questions the teacher includes a key word which might indicate a preferred response from the learner – or even suggest the answer.

 ACTIVITY 1

Open and closed questioning

Following on from the descriptions of closed or leading questions, how would you re-write them to become open in style?

Closed Question	Open Question
Are there seven days in a week?	How many days are there in a week?
Is it correct that you inform your manager if you encounter an unexpected situation?	
Are you OK with that?	
Are you happy with the evidence in your portfolio?	
Do you know where your supervisor is?	

Leading Question	Open Question
I can see that you understand about PPE because you are wearing your boots. Do you understand about PPE?	What does PPE mean?
Is it true that blue and red mixed together make purple?	
How well do you get on with the people in the office?	
Have you improved your punctuality on site?	

Other questioning techniques

Nominated or directed questions In group situations, a nominated or directed style of questioning ensures that everyone contributes and that questions offered to learners are pitched at the learner's known ability. They are an effective means of differentiating or meeting learners' needs. In a nominated style the teacher poses the question to the group, then pauses so that all learners can all create their own answer, the teacher then nominates (or directs) the learner to give the answer. It can be made fun by offering play or pass options to minimise embarrassment if learners do not know the answer. You may also try the 'ask a friend' strategy, in which a learner can elicit the help of someone else in the group. In the worst questioning scenarios, the teacher leaves insufficient time for the learner to answer and completes the question themselves. Some teachers create some innovative ideas to vary the nomination technique; they use lollipop sticks, bingo balls or identity badges – anything to help distribute their questions.

Scaffolding questions Scaffolding questions are those that build on a learner's existing knowledge of understanding. They enable the teacher to take forward the learner and explore the extent of their knowledge and if they are able to apply it in other contexts or in problem solving. The example shows how scaffolded questions develop: List three kinds of carnivores. Explain the typical diet of your chosen carnivores. Compare your carnivore's diet with a herbivore's diet. What would happen if a carnivore ate a herbivore's diet?

Funnel questions A technique which will take a broad topic and go into it in more detail thus channelling the information. The teacher can use an open question to launch the discussion and then use probing questions to delve deeper into the subject. How or why did that happen? What would happen if…? Can you give me more information about…?

Probing questions The use of How? Why? What? When? Where? To establish more detail from the first response. A useful technique to challenge more able learners to think more deeply on a topic.

Rhetorical questions These questions are statements posed as questions, and whilst they don't need an answer, they can stimulate discussion on the topic. For example: 'doesn't the light cast some lovely shadows on that picture?'

Socratic questions Based on the Greek philosopher, Socrates, these types of questions encourage deeper thought and challenge assumptions. They are very good for stretching more able learners. For example: 'why do you believe that…?', 'why is x better than y?'

Using silence Using silence is effective in allowing time for the information to 'sink in'; alternatively, silence allows learners waiting time to formulate their replies.

Using paraphrasing Allows the teacher and the learner some time to reflect and confirm understanding. It is used after periods of silence to re-energise a conversation.

Using positive words and behaviours The use of short words or non-verbal body language can encourage learners to continue on a train of thought, without significantly interrupting the conversation. Our body language can also express interest and therefore keep a reply or discussion on a topic going. For example, pepper the conversation with a nod, lean forward, use little words like OK, and…, good, or just mmm! or humph!

Using movement Kinaesthetic learners do not particularly enjoy questioning sessions, they become bored. So why not try posing your question as a statement which has levels of agreement as a response, or verbally posing multiple choice questions with a range of feasible answers. Learners then move to the appropriate corner of the room according to their answer and discussion can commence!

Reverse questioning Try flipping your questioning! Give the answer and ask learners to identify the question. This gives learners the opportunity to see the bigger picture.

ACTIVITY 2

Identifying good questioning

Arrange to observe a peer (preferably one noted to be good at questioning) and focus on their questioning techniques. Pre-service teachers can complete this activity during micro-teach sessions or observe their teacher training tutor.

What types of questioning do they use?

When do they use questioning? (recap, checking progress, plenary)

What do they do with incorrect answers?

How do they differentiate? (Nominate, probing questions)

Draw a seating plan and mark each time the teacher asks a learner a question to see the range or distribution of questioning. Is everyone included?

Effective feedback

Feedback is the conversation between the teacher and learner. It aims to celebrate strengths, give constructive advice on weaknesses and identify areas for further development. It is essential in the assessment process; the main purpose being to let learners know how well (or not) they are doing.

Feedback is the key to successful development of potential, increasing motivation and assessment. It is part of the learning process, because it tells the learner how well they are doing. The quality of the feedback is as important as the quality of the teaching or training. Feedback should be frequent and meaningful. There are two types. The praise and criticism model is that which is based on personal judgements and is therefore subjective. In this model you list the strengths and the weaknesses. The constructive feedback model is preferred and more objective, because it is based on specifics and related to the assessment against standards or criteria. Constructive feedback can be positive, when good practice is praised. The teacher will appreciate and value what has been done and comment on how well it has been achieved. Constructive feedback can be negative, when improvement needs are discussed. Giving negative feedback does not mean giving the feedback in a negative (i.e. unsupportive) way. The person giving the feedback should not use sarcasm or anger. Be helpful – start with a positive statement and then comment on the improvements that are needed.

Watch point

Don't get over enthusiastic with the praise; it is far more effective when offered as a result of something achieved, rather than responding to everything as 'brill!'

You may also hear the expression feed-forward. Whereas feedback is based on a response to what has occurred, feed-forward is based on the notion of motivating a learner to develop. It aims to address the difference between 'assessment OF learning' (feedback) and 'assessment FOR learning (feed-forward)'. This might merely be an up-to-the-minute response to research in the field as effective feedback in its existing format has always been a method of aiding improvement, but it does reflect the fact that feedback tells someone how they have done and does not necessarily move them forward.

Feedback skills

Giving feedback is not easy; it is particularly difficult at the opposite ends of the feedback spectrum. If observed practice or an assessed piece is particularly good, it is difficult to identify development suggestions, or, conversely, it is difficult to feedback to learners without destroying confidence when the required standards are not met. Giving effective feedback will test your own skills in listening, objectivity and explaining. It will improve the confidence of your learners and develop their potential, but it takes time to get it right. The hint here is that, although you will be encouraged to give immediate feedback, in the early days you may wish to consider what you want to say before diving in – so give yourself a few minutes to think and plan what you are going to say.

Feedback should:

- Always be planned and carefully thought about.
- Be delivered promptly after the assessment, preferably immediately, especially after observation or verbal questioning sessions.

- Be a two-way process – you can always ask the learner to say how they think it went and get an idea of their understanding, checking their ideas for development. However be cautious, because the learner might think differently to the teacher, which gives rise to conflict of opinion immediately within the feedback.

- Be motivational – feedback increases confidence and self-esteem and therefore potential attainment.

- Be specific – feedback should only be about the assessment; it should be unbiased, without opinion, unnecessary digression or imposing your own standards.

- Offer choices and solutions or coach new ideas from learners – this develops potential.

- Only comment on things that can be changed – e.g. behaviours or values, not appearance or inner character.

- Positive – use strategies that will encourage a learner to develop.

- Be constructive – a balance of positive and negative comments.

- Feedback should be offered on a one-to-one basis and as privately as possible.

- If circumstances mean that feedback cannot be immediate, then tell the learner when it will be possible. For example: after the shift, when it quietens down a bit, when you get your next break, etc.

Constructive feedback is helpful and supportive. It is motivational in that it neither gives false descriptions of a learner's ability nor does it destroy their self-esteem, but aims to develop and fine-tune skills. Whether produced verbally or in writing, this effective style of feedback follows a distinct pattern of:

- A positive opener
- A developmental statement
- Motivational close

This is called 'the feedback sandwich'

By starting with a positive statement, you will reassure and relax the recipient of the feedback. Always identify something good, even if it is only the fact that they turned up on time! The comments you make should always link to the standards being assessed. The feedback should always be about the individual and you should never compare their performance with anyone else or anything other than the standards expected.

Developmental statements are the point at which you should make comments about things which need to be improved. It is good to get contributions from the recipient of the feedback. Using open questions or coaching techniques will aid this process and together you will formulate your future plans.

Some questions you might wish to consider are:

- How do you think that the customer felt when you...?
- What would you do if...?
- What alternatives are there to...?
- Why did that happen?
- At what point in the process would you think about...?

If there is going to be a 'but' the person giving the feedback should build up confidence (i.e. discuss the positive aspects of the work) before delivering the shock. The use of the word 'but' should also be used cautiously. 'But' muddles what you are trying to say and confuses the message. 'It was OK, but, ...' (*Is it OK or not?*)

A contextual example of this is:

'It was alright but it wasn't very welcoming' is not particularly helpful. It seems to suggest a negative outcome. An alternative suggestion might be:
'I liked the way that you welcomed the customer and believe it would be improved if you'd stood to greet them.' This is of the same flavour but not as hard as a 'but' statement. In the second statement the 'but' is delivered as an 'and'. Therefore, is not as critical and more developmental.

Ending the feedback in a motivational way will incite the learner to take on board recommendations and leave them feeling positive about their performance, even if not ecstatic about the outcome. Ideally in a feedback session, you should try to get the recipient to identify their own way forward. This ownership of the actions needed to improve will result in a high level of motivation. It is at this point you can develop reflective skills in your learners.

The typical feedback conversation:

State what the standard is or what the assessment was about. Describe what has been observed or reviewed, without side tracking.

Make a comment about what has been achieved.

Offer alternatives like: have you considered…, you could try… Avoid 'BUT'

Summarise the key achievements. Make and state your judgement – you meet/don't meet the standards, you've passed or you need more practice.

In discussing feedback, it is worth noting the research of Professor John Hattie of Auckland University (1999 and 2003). He investigated the effects of feedback on achievement and the ability of teachers to influence learning.

Having dissected the factors associated with teaching and learning and categorised them into responsibilities, he discovered, not surprisingly, that the teacher has a significant influence on learning. This furthered his earlier research which identified the extent to which feedback impacts on achievement, all of which supports the current beliefs in assessment *for* learning rather than the assessment *of* learning. In summary, effective feedback is more effective in developing learner progress than merely providing grades. This is generally because if a learner is told 'that's a pass' or 'it's a grade B' they are more likely to accept that outcome without seeking development or improvement. When given feedback, most learners will attempt to develop future work. In combination they are able to meet both learners' values and aspirations.

Additional reading

Additional reading on this research is widely available on the Internet using Hattie, feedback and assessment as key words in a search engine.

Glossary of terms

Closed (questioning) limited response type of questions

Constructive a term used to imply helpful feedback

Distractor incorrect answer choices in MCQs

Extended question a question that involves a long answer

Key the correct answer in a MCQ

Leading (questioning) a question (with an indicated answer contained within the question)

MCQ multiple choice question

Open (questioning) question designed to elicit a detailed response

Qualitative data relating to opinions or thoughts

Quantitative data relating to statistics and number

Questioning queries inviting responses

Restricted response limited choices in answers

Stem the term given to a question in a MCQ

 SUMMARY

In this chapter we set out to achieve the following outcomes:

- To compare and contrast a variety of different questioning techniques.
- To consider the strengths and weaknesses of each method and make informed decisions about selection of questions.
- To explain and evaluate the effectiveness of questioning techniques.
- To describe the method of constructive feedback.
- To identify the value of feedback, especially relating to assessment and progression.

- To explain and evaluate the effectiveness of feedback techniques.
- To describe the skills required to provide effective feedback.

Your personal development

You have analysed the meaning and purpose of assessment in the context of questioning and feedback. You can recognise key terms relating to feedback and questioning.

You have investigated a wide range of questioning methods and looked at the advantages and disadvantages of each. This will enable you to make better choices about the questioning methods you plan to use and to justify your selection. Then you have reviewed several types of questioning techniques and can distinguish between the main types of questioning, considering their value to both teacher and learner in achieving valid and reliable data about progress.

You have analysed how you can modify your questioning techniques to ensure that you are able to assess the knowledge and understanding of your learners. You can differentiate questions by using different techniques for individual and group situations. You have practised re-writing questions to make them more efficient in gathering accurate information.

You have identified strategies to offer and deliver feedback and reflected on the possible outcomes of assessment. You can explain how feedback is a valuable tool in developing learning, including reference to the work of Hattie.

You can explain the importance of effective feedback in both assessment of learning and assessment for learning. In each you can use feedback to express achievement and development of learners' competence, following a constructive feedback model. You have scrutinised the protocols required in delivering an effective feedback session.

CHAPTER 13
Recording progress and achievement

LEARNING OBJECTIVES

The measurable outcomes that you will achieve by reading this chapter and completing the activities are:

....

- To state the importance of record keeping during and after assessment
- To describe the purpose of assessment in terms of measuring achievement and progress
- To describe the need for record keeping at individual and organisational level
- To specify procedures and documents relevant in the planning, implementation and decision making processes of assessments
- To recognise some simple designs for basic record keeping documents
- To describe how and why progress is reported, to whom and about whom

REVISION

Ways of measuring progress of learners within sessions is explained in Chapter 8. Those same strategies can apply to any formative assessment strategy and some modified to suit summative assessment. This chapter suggests ways of recording progress

Assessment procedures

Procedures are defined as 'the official way of doing things'. These routines are usually specified or informed by legislation or in the case of assessment by codes of practice regulated by Ofqual. There are procedures associated with the planning, implementation, feedback and judgements of assessment. Some qualifications have specific codes of practice relating to the delivery, assessment and quality assurance of programmes and the qualifications of assessors and verifiers. The guidance exists to ensure that learners, teachers, trainers and assessors, delivery and assessment institutions and Awarding Organisations are clear about strategy, method and role and that practices are able to stand up to scrutiny by inspectorate and audit teams.

Awarding Organisations will also provide information on quality assurance (QA) processes.

The importance of record keeping

Records are an essential part of the assessment process; they provide evidence of achievement and competence. They also have a wider purpose in respect of supporting organisational processes.

The part of the job associated with record keeping often seems bureaucratic and repetitive. It sometimes takes longer to prove you did the job than it took to do the job in the first place. These feelings are quite common and you should not feel guilty about having them, although to move on you need to see the value in the process, so here goes...

Paperwork: The necessary evil or the answer to your prayers?

The need to record assessments or in fact any other aspect of the role is essential to you, your learners, your colleagues and your managers. Completing the necessary paperwork on time and distributing it to those who need it is essential to support efficient and effective working practices.

Record keeping is best done in smaller chunks and not all left to the end of a programme; this ensures a distribution of the workload and timely completion of records which ultimately saves time. Records help you to remember what has occurred and act as a guide to others in case you are not available. A filing system suits methodical workers but not spontaneous types and so it is something that may need personal development time to fine tune. Records need to be kept in a logical sequence; chronological, alphabetical, by name, by programme or any combination of those. They may be stored as a paper record or saved electronically.

So that you can understand the importance of recording progress and keeping records, it might be useful to identify the stakeholders in the process (see Figure 5D).

Figure 5D Stakeholder Table

Who needs records and why:

Who	Why
Learners	● to provide records to evidence achievement, progress and support needs Learners will need support in storing their information.

▶

Who	Why
Teachers (Assessors)	<ul><li>to replicate progress records of learners (in case of loss); to inform reports to others</li><li>to inform reflective personal and professional practice</li><li>to know who has done what and when</li><li>to provide a record of the variety of assessment methods used</li><li>to raise awareness of the overall assessment strategy of a learner</li></ul>
Colleagues	<ul><li>to support team members during absence</li><li>to share in team meetings and self-assess the effectiveness of their programmes</li></ul> Colleagues need your records to be assembled logically and accessible.
Managers	<ul><li>to monitor performance</li><li>to plan for responsive provision</li><li>to make strategic and financial decisions</li></ul>
Quality Unit	<ul><li>to generate comparative analysis across the organisation</li><li>to compare performance with national averages and organisational trends</li><li>to identify interventions</li></ul>
Parents and carers	<ul><li>to inform about the progress of their child on the programme</li></ul> Learners may not communicate well with their parents and so this is the only link. Don't rely on learners giving reports to their parents, especially if they are anticipating less complimentary reports.
Schools	<ul><li>to create a link between vocational and academic studies</li></ul>

Who	Why
	● to develop a standardised approach to a learner's development
Employers	● to inform about the progress of their employee on the programme As the financial sponsor, they require accurate and reliable progress information. ● to inform their business processes
Awarding Organisation	● to register and certificate achievement ● to action and record external quality monitoring processes ● to inform responsive development
Auditors	● to check funding claims are legitimate and business processes are legal and above question ● to scrutinise accountability and responsibility
Inspectorate	● to quality assure performance at organisation level against national standards ● to justify appropriate use of public funds

What are the consequences of failure to keep records?

● Learners' progress is haphazard and unstructured.

● Mistakes and trends are not noticed so they continue to impact on practice, possibly in a downward spiral.

● There is a lack of accountability with no-one taking the lead on responsibility to learners and other stakeholders.

● Learners don't gain their qualifications, or if they learn the required elements they will not be accredited through a recognised organisation.

● Public confidence is reduced, which results in lower enrolments, which leads to fewer sessions, fewer jobs, and eventually the demise of the organisation.

Hints and tips for record keeping

- Keep copies for third parties.
- Write in an appropriate style for the reader – the learner, parent, Awarding Organisation, etc.
- Keep notes about informal processes – development needs and actions, late work, re-submission dates, problems, etc.
- Documentation should give an overview rather than record every 'if, but and maybe'.
- Documents should be fit for purpose.
- Keep records relating to the process and product of assessment.
- Records may be self-devised or devised by the organisation – ask what is in use before going your own way.

Assessment documentation

Documentation is an essential component of assessment. However, before going blindly into your document collection, remember that:

- Methods of recording assessments will differ according to the qualification type.
- Always use the forms agreed within the organisation.
- Suggestions for improvements should be made through the Internal Quality Assurer/quality department.
- All forms should, at the very least, include the qualification title, names of the teacher/assessor and the learner and the date.

Forms below are examples of format in order to recognise style. They should not be considered as 'approved' documents. The forms described, which are examples and not an exhaustive list, are:

- Assessment Planning
- Assessment Implementation
  - Observation Records

- Records of Questioning
- Assignment Front Sheets
- Assessment decisions
  - Feedback
  - Judgements
  - Tracking Sheets.

Planning

Assessment needs to be planned (see Chapter 11, Planning and delivering assessment and Chapter 5, Session planning skills). In the same way that teaching is planned in order to meet need, produce variety and structure, so assessment should be organised similarly.

Some of the reasons for this include:

- Learning outcomes need regular assessment to ensure learners are on target to achieve their goals.
- Assessments in the workplace need to be arranged with supervisors, to minimise disruption to the business.
- Recreational courses will have learners working on their own projects, so the teacher needs to liaise closely to ensure learners goals are recognised, realistic and monitored.
- Special arrangements may need to be made – access to specialist equipment and resources.
- Complex programmes of study need to have all assessments plotted to ensure even distribution across the programme.

Planning, especially for one-to-one assessments, needs to be recorded and agreed. The learner should have clear guidelines about what they are expected to do and what the outcomes are likely to be. In some, particularly vocational courses, assessment strategies require a number of successful formative assessments of practical skills, before a summative assessment of practical skill or knowledge tests.

A suggestion for an assessment plan is:

SUMMATIVE ASSESSMENT PLAN	
NAME:	Date of proposed assessment:
Planned activity:	
Expected outcomes/criteria/evidence:	
Other who might be affected or need to be involved in the assessment:	
Plan signed/dated by teacher/ assessor:	Plan agreed, signed/dated by learner:
Feedback following assessment:	Actions for development:
OUTCOME: Pass ☐ Needs further training ☐	Teacher/assessor signature: Date: Learner signature: Date:

In this example the plan is in two parts, the top part being completed before the assessment and the lower part after the assessment, thus combining the plan and a record of the outcome (see also Chapter 11: Planning and delivering assessment).

In planning for more academic subjects, the teacher should consider the total number of assessments (which may consist of a number of tasks) and plot these into a calendar to distribute them across the programme of study. This involves liaising with other teachers on the team, whilst working within Awarding Organisation deadline dates. By undertaking this activity you will help your learners to manage their workloads. This kind of document is especially important when a number of different people all work on the same qualification; it works by minimising the risk of having all due dates crammed into a short period. A suggestion is:

Unit	September	October	November	December	January	February	March	April	May	June	July
1		X									
2				X							
3						X					
4							X				
5									X		
6											X

In modular or unitised programmes, for example Extended Diplomas, then assessment will take the format of an assignment which includes a number of tasks, which relate to unit criteria and the demonstration of embedded functional skills. In this instance, an assessment plan may follow this style:

Unit title:			
Task	Interim due date	Links to criteria	Links to functional and PLTS skills
Task one Description of what a learner must do or present for assessment		e.g. P1, P3, M1	English, mathematics and ICT Personal learning and thinking skills (PLTS) Personal social development (PSD) (use words or the numeric references)

Task two *Description of what a learner must do or present for assessment*	*e.g. P2, M2, D1*	*English, mathematics and ICT* *PLTS* *PSD* *(use words or the numeric references)*
Task three etc. *Description of what a learner must do or present for assessment*	*e.g. P4, P5, M3*	*English, mathematics and ICT* *PLTS* *PSD* *(use words or the numeric references)*

To achieve a pass, the learner must:

This section will specify the P criteria using command words such as describe, identify, etc.

To achieve a merit, the learner must:

This section will specify the P and M criteria using command words such as analyse, etc.

To achieve a distinction, the learner must:

This section will specify the P, M and D criteria using command words such as evaluate etc.

The completed assignment must be handed in by:

Signatures: *Teacher and Quality Assurance Coordinator*

Implementing

The processes involved when implementing (doing) the assessment are related to ensuring that the rules of assessment are being met (Chapter 10). You should consider what type of assessment method is being used (Chapter 11), whether or not it is formative or summative

(Chapter 10) and what you need to achieve in terms of outcomes and the time/location available.

Some of the things you may need to consider during formative and summative assessments are:

- Is the learner sufficiently prepared for the assessment?
- Do you have access to registration numbers; have you confirmed the eligibility to enter the assessment process?
- Do you and the learners have access to sufficient, adequate resources for the assessment?
- Does the arrangement of furniture facilitate equality and honesty?
- Has there been an accurate briefing of expectations and statement of proposed outcomes – shared planning?
- Is there a quiet area for oral questioning (if necessary)?
- Are you able to identify individual progress within the group?
- How will the assessment be recorded?
- Does the assessment need third-party intervention (an invigilator) to ensure impartiality?
- Can you guarantee accuracy in timing of assessment – start and end times, a visible clock, adherence to specified durations?
- Have you checked the authenticity of learners – are they who they say they are?
- Have you considered how the results of the assessment are to be conveyed?
- Do you need a feedback session afterwards?

During the assessment, dependent upon the method of assessment chosen, you will need to keep records to aid the process of making assessment decisions. Some examples are:

Observation records

These forms are most commonly associated with the recording of observed evidence. The purpose of keeping documents relating to observation is to ensure that what is seen is accurately matched to the assessment criteria. Whether this is completed by the teacher or the learner will depend on how confident the learner is and how familiar with the criteria they are. In my experience it is usually the teacher's job! The observation record would be a piece of evidence to demonstrate what was seen, when, and should be confirmed or 'witnessed' by the parties involved – usually in the form of signatures. The most common use of observation documents is to record work place activities. They are usually descriptive and are written as a chronological record. For example:

2nd November 2012

Reception area of Smith's Engineering, Sometown.

At 09.15, Sheila greeted the customer in a polite manner, asking the purpose of their visit and who they wished to see. She then used the telephone to inform the Director's secretary that the visitor had arrived. Sheila gave the visitor's name and the company they represented. Whilst waiting for the visitor to be collected, she issued a visitor's badge and asked the visitor to 'sign-in'. Two incoming calls were taken using the standard greeting and directed to the extension required. At 09.20, as the secretary still hadn't arrived to collect the visitor she invited them to take a seat in the waiting area. A package arrived and was signed for; rang to inform addressee of its arrival. She smiled when the visitor left reception with the secretary at 09.25.

When writing up observations, it is useful to have a copy of the assessment criteria to hand and to be mindful of everything that is occurring; this will enhance the holistic approach to assessment. Using the same example and the UoA (to make the link to the standards), an observation record might look like:

Name of Learner: Sheila Learner	Date: 2nd November 2012
Qualification: Award in business Administration	Level: Level 2
Location of Assessment: Reception area of Smith's Engineering, Sometown	

A description of the event or activity	Links to performance criteria
At 09.15, Sheila greeted the customer in a polite manner, asking the purpose of their visit and who they wished to see. She then used the telephone to inform the Director's secretary that the visitor had arrived. Sheila gave the visitor's name and the company they represented. Whilst waiting for the visitor to be collected, she issued a visitor's badge and asked the visitor to 'sign-in'. Two incoming calls were taken using the standard greeting and directed to the extension required. At 09.20, as the secretary still hadn't arrived to collect the visitor she invited them to take a seat in the waiting area. A package arrived and was signed for; rang to inform addressee of its arrival. She smiled when the visitor left reception with the secretary at 09.25.	Meet and Welcome: 2.1,2.2,2.3,2.4,2.5,2.7 Select methods of communication:5.2 Communicate verbally: 7.3,7.4 Make telephone calls; 3.1,3.2,3.3,3.4 Receive telephone calls 4.1,4.2,4.3,4.6,4.7 Meet and Welcome (2.8) Handle mail (receiving) 3.1,3.4 Meet and welcome: 2.5
Teacher/assessor's signature: A. N. Assessor	Date: 2nd November 2012
Learner's signature: Sheila Learner	Date: 2nd November 2012

Records of questioning

These documents are more associated with verbal questioning rather than written questioning. Written questions automatically create a record, but verbal questions could just happen. The purpose of the document is to provide evidence of what question was asked and the answer given (whether right or wrong). This should then be linked to relevant criteria. Valid questions are those which are related to theory and **underpin** a practical activity.

For example, following the observation above, typical questions might be:

- What would you do if the telephone extension had been busy?
- What would you do if the addressee on the parcel had not been a member of staff?
- Why is it important to use a standard greeting when answering a telephone?
- If a visitor is very early for their appointment, what do you do?

At the end of the record of questioning, it is important that both the teacher and the learner sign to say that the document is, 'a true record of questions and their responses'.

A record of questioning might look like:

Name of Learner:		Date:
Qualification:		Level:
Unit/Assessment:		
Question		Response given by learner
Teacher/assessor's signature:		Date:
Learner's signature:		Date:

Assignment front sheets

The purpose of an assignment front sheet is to provide a standardised method of briefing learners on components of the assignment. As seen in previous planning document (page 295), it will list the tasks to be completed and target dates; it will identify any key/basic or functional skills that are derived from the assessment; it will state the criteria for gaining pass, merit or distinction grades; and usually provide a space for teachers to give feedback on the work. It is customary that the person who designs the tasks should submit the brief to the Internal Quality Assurer for approval before launching it with their group. This ensures consistency within the organisation and a double check before issuing the assignment to learners.

A further example of an assignment front sheet to include feedback might look like:

Qualification Title:	
Unit Title and Number:	
Launch Date:	Submission Date:
Task	Criteria reference Including links to Functional Skills
Feedback	
Grade Achieved:	
Teacher/assessor signature:	Date:

Decisions

Following an assessment, there is a requirement to give feedback. This has already been covered earlier (see Chapter 12). The content of that feedback will form the basis of the assessment judgement. Therefore, the procedures determining assessment decisions and judgements are associated with assessing to the Units of Assessment, marking schemes, grading criteria and hand-in dates. These must always be clearly stated before the assessment. It might be a good idea to double check these during the planning processes. Finally, the outcomes of the assessment should be recorded on tracking sheets, both in the learner's portfolio and the teacher's records.

Marking schemes

These add clarity to the assessment, particularly in relation to the more subjective assessment methods, for example essays and reports, where there may not be a right or wrong answer. A marking scheme may look like this:

ESSAY TITLE: Describe the importance of communication in a specific retail environment	
Definition of communication	One mark
Definition 'specific' retail environment	One mark
Theories associated with communication	Two marks
Links between communication and retail environment	Four marks
Stated factors of importance	Four marks
Coherence of expression	Two marks
Accuracy of spelling and grammar	Two marks
Structure of essay	Two marks
Bibliography, referencing and accuracy of citation	Two marks
Total marks available	20

In this example it is quite clear from the **weighting** of the marks (60 per cent) where the emphasis of the work should be. Yet marks can be lost, for example if the skills associated with essay writing (40 per cent) are not met. There may also be a stated requirement to achieve a pass standard – for example 10 out of 20.

Grading criteria relate to the quality and depth of the work. For example you will see grids written into many of qualification guides that specify what learners have to do to achieve a pass, merit and distinction grades. The information contained within the **grading grids** enables the teacher to challenge learners to aspire to a level greater than that which may be predicted or expected. It helps the learners to clarify what is expected of them in their assessment and hopefully stretch themselves.

EXAMPLE

To achieve a pass grade, learners must achieve all of the pass criteria. To achieve a merit grade, the learners must achieve all of the pass criteria and all of the merit criteria. To achieve a distinction grade, the learner must achieve all of the pass and merit criteria and all of the distinction criteria.

The processes involved in stating and achieving hand-in dates are going to be very specific to each qualification and/or organisation. Some will notionally suggest dates by which work should be submitted, probably using the individual learning plan to negotiate these; other qualifications may specify an absolute and non-compliance means a sanction-type of situation. You and your learners should be fully conversant with which applies and what, if any, sanctions are administered if pertinent.

Tracking sheets

These are the forms that record progress during a qualification. In this context the teacher uses a tracker to show progress of learners. It may be used in a way that the teacher can plot achievement of tasks within an assignment, units or modules within a qualification or framework or completion of homework/class-work activities. It is usual to record the date the unit/task/activity is completed. Best practice models include the date commenced and who assessed the work, with a space to date and initial if the work is internally quality assured. A similar document can be used to plan internal quality assurance (QA) strategies – i.e. identify which part of the qualification and which learners' work are to be sampled.

A tracking sheet might look like:

Qualification title:									
	Unit, Task or Activity								
Name	1	2	3	4	5	6	7	8	ETC
Learner A									
Learner B									
Learner C									
Etc.									

To be effective and meaningful, you should devise a simple marking code to visualise the progress. For example:

- / means a learner has started on the unit/module.
- X means they have completed the unit/module.
- Always add a date when completed, together with teacher/ assessor's initials.
- If QA'd the verifier could date and initial maybe in a different colour pen.

Reporting progress

Reporting progress (or tracking as it is commonly known) is part of the record keeping process. The keeping of records is about organisation, transparency and accountability but recording progress is the part of the process concerned with sharing those records with others in order to initiate a development. This is the move discussed earlier: record keeping is associated with 'assessment OF learning', progress reporting is concerned with 'assessment FOR learning'. As we have already seen, the benefits to the learner when the focus of assessment is changed from measurement to development impacts significantly on the learner's achievement.

Why does progress need to be reported?

Quite simply, because common sense (and current research) says it is the best way to develop potential. If the teacher tells the learner how they are doing, they can engage in a discussion to move forward, rectify mistakes and build on their strengths. It is highly motivational for the learner to be told how well they are progressing. Equally, with constructive feedback, it is valuable to know what isn't going so well, and, maybe through motivational interviewing, you will come up with strategies to overcome this.

The teacher will have to report progress to stakeholders (see Figure 5D). There are three stakeholders directly involved in the assessment process: the learner; their parents or guardians if under 18; their employer if employed.

Parents are also interested to know how their child is performing in the classroom. It is increasingly important that the learning ethos is shared between home and the learning organisation. If additional work is being set to complete at home, it is good to know that parents are helping to ensure it is done.

Employers are interested because they have identified training needs in their employees and have contracted with learning organisations to realise those goals. They need to know that their employees are getting value for money and that they are attending and contributing to learning.

How and when is progress reported?

- One-to-one reviews – informally and formally at regular intervals throughout the programme
- Feedback – after assessments and with all marked work
- Reports – once or twice a year as a summary to parents or employers
- Employer forums – to develop partnerships and collaborative activities
- Parent's evening – to formalise learner development – this is more common in the 14–19 sector.

The timing of reporting is only a suggestion; it will be determined by cost and availability of resources and staff. It is hoped that informal chats will ensure that progress is summarised and reported frequently with more formal monitoring and stakeholder reporting targeted at specific periods throughout the training period.

 ACTIVITY 1

Learner progress

Why do these learners need to know how they are progressing?

Case study 1

From a younger learner's perspective ...

Being aged between 14 and 19 is very exciting; the social life is getting better and relationships are being made and broken in a regular cycle; getting paid for work or through a grant or bursary is great – oh yes – there is that classroom stuff but so long as it is interesting and we get plenty of breaks and it doesn't get boring it is not too bad! However, along come teachers and parents who want us teenagers to gain a qualification and then talk about us as though we care, life is for now, not the future. There's plenty of time for that.

Case study 2

From a mature learner's perspective ...

I am doing this because I want to, I need to change jobs/get a qualification/earn more money/update my skills and I want the teacher's undivided attention to enable that to happen. I am motivated and want challenge, but I also want to come away from sessions with loads of notes, ideas and things to do. I want reassurances that I can do the things I have to, because it's been quite a while since I was last in study.

Key words you might want to consider in your answers:

Focus, motivation, confidence, goals, independence, support, stretch and challenge.

Glossary of terms

Achievement meeting learning goals

Chronological in date order

Competence the knowledge of or ability to do something

Eligibility satisfying entry conditions (of organisation, qualification or funding partner)

Grading Grids tables to determine the level of achievement

Inspectorate e.g. Ofsted, Ofqual

QA Quality Assurance, an official system to establish the quality of something

Registration an official list of entrants on a qualification

Stakeholder a person, either directly or indirectly, associated or interested in the learner or organisation

Underpin support or form the basis of

Weighting adjustment to take account of special factors which
   may distort if not considered

 SUMMARY

In this chapter we set out to achieve the following outcomes:

- To state the importance of record keeping during and after assessment.
- To describe the purpose of assessment in terms of measuring achievement and progress.
- To describe the need for record keeping at individual and organisational level.
- To specify procedures and documents relevant in the planning, implementation and decision making processes of assessments.
- To recognise some simple designs for basic record keeping documents.
- To describe how and why progress is reported, to whom and about whom.

Your personal development

Having been guided to review Chapter 8 which describes methods of measuring learner progress, you have been introduced to the notion of the importance of record keeping both in recording judgements and their part in reporting progress to stakeholders.

You have investigated procedures of planning, implementing and decision making in assessment and can explain them, giving examples of relevant documentation to be used during record keeping. You have looked at some examples of recording documents and are able to critically evaluate how they are fit for purpose.

Regarding recording and reporting progress, you are able to justify why these processes are essential to business practices and developing a learner's potential. You have developed an awareness of the need for marking grids, and how to use grading criteria in order to challenge and motivate learners as well as preparing for assessment.

Finally, your learning is consolidated by engaging in a case study activity to explore why particular groups, albeit stereotypical formats, need to engage in progress development activities.

CHAPTER 14

Enabling learning through assessment

LEARNING OBJECTIVES

The measurable outcomes that you will achieve by reading this chapter and completing the activities are:

....

- To develop the insight gained about inclusive practice and apply that knowledge to assessment practice
- To describe ways of matching assessment to the needs of learners and the curriculum
- To link theoretical concepts of learning and assessment to assessment practice

In Part 6 you will establish what inclusion means and how to create inclusive teaching and learning sessions to meet the needs of all of your learners. You will discover that inclusive practice enhances motivation, and impacts on all aspects of teaching and learning (Part 3), from planning, (Part 2) through delivery and resourcing (Part 4) to supporting learning. In this chapter we will explore this process relating to assessment. Further theories to support learning, motivation, communication and assessment are noted in Part 7.

Purposes of assessment

Assessment is a key function in teaching and learning; it informs the reasons for teaching and collects information regarding the results of that teaching; this makes assessment integral to the process of learning. In their research, Black and Wiliam (1998) suggest that assessment together with constructive feedback will bring about raised levels of achievement. This has reformed the way assessment is perceived in the classroom, bringing about a subtle change from 'assessment *of* learning to 'assessment *for* learning (Assessment Reform Group 2002, Craig and Fieschi 2007).

EXAMPLES OF RELATIONSHIPS TO THEORY – ASSESSMENT FOR LEARNING

A four-year study, commissioned by the Assessment Reform Group (funded by the Nuffield Foundation) to review the research available on classroom assessment. Their finding was that informal assessment in the classroom, with constructive feedback, raises achievement. The associated reports are:

Inside the Black Box, Prof. Paul Black and Dr. Dylan Wiliam (1998) and Assessment For Learning: Beyond the Black Box (1999), University of Cambridge, School of Education

Subsequent research suggested that increasing the amount of assessment does not enhance learning; rather it is using assessment effectively that raises achievement and potential. It recommended strategic and political changes to implement the change from assessment of learning, designed for grading and reporting processes, to assessment for learning, designed for development and progress.

Budge (2005), citing Black and Wiliam (1998), summarises the research and writes:

What works:

- regular classroom testing and the use of results to adjust teaching and learning rather than competitive grading;
- enhanced feedback between teacher and pupil which may be oral or written;
- the active involvement of all pupils;
- careful attention to pupil's motivation and help in building their self-belief;
- self- or peer-assessment by pupils, discussion in groups and dialogue between teacher and pupils.

… and what doesn't

- tests that encourage rote and superficial learning;
- over-emphasis on the giving of marks and grades at the expense of useful advice to learners;
- competitive teaching approaches that de-motivate some pupils;
- feedback, testing and record keeping that serve a managerial function rather than a learning one.

David Budge, TES, Tasting the assessment soup. 18th February 2005.

Any close scrutiny of Ofsted's guidance on what constitutes excellence in teaching will see a clear link between the theory and the recommended methods of working, especially in relation to stretch and challenge and maximising learner potential.

The Association for Achievement and Improvement through Assessment (AAIA), sets out ten principles, devised by the Assessment Reform Group (ARG), as:

Assessment:

1 is part of effective planning
2 focuses on how students learn
3 is central to classroom practices

4 is a key professional skill

5 is sensitive and constructive

6 fosters motivation

7 promotes understanding of goals and criteria

8 helps learners know how to improve

9 develops the capacity for self-assessment

10 recognises all educational achievement.

www.aaia.org.uk/pdf/AFL_10principlesARG.pdf (accessed 30.09.07)

Hattie (1999, 2003) investigated the effect of feedback on achievement and concluded that learners will develop and achieve better with feedback than with grades.

These principles advocate the assessment *for* learning instead of assessment *of* learning. Managers require teachers to measure performance in terms of success, i.e. collecting data about outcomes (assessment of learning). This requires teachers to prove their performance in terms of targets, arguing that learner's performance, whilst born through nurture and tutoring (assessment for learning), is a contributory factor to the final result. Current research and trends seem to argue that it should be the leading role and are therefore pushing for significant policy changes (ARG 2002).

Much is written about assessment; in many of the key texts that you will read, assessment is defined as:

[to] judge a learner's performance against identified criteria.

Fawbert 2003: 247

The process of obtaining information about how much the student knows.

Reece and Walker 2006:35

Assessment equates to testing: if a learner is being assessed, then he or she is being tested.

Tummons 2007: 4

There are three stages of assessment, which associate with learning and its purpose:

1 Obtaining information

2 Forming judgements

3 Making decisions.

The first part, obtaining information, refers to the various methods of collecting the information, but more importantly, the teacher should ask 'why do we collect information?'

You can gather information that relates to:

- learners' progress
- levels of motivation
- perceived and actual levels of attainment
- the effectiveness of teaching methods and practices
- diagnosing the needs of learners
- identification of the support needs of learners
- the confirmation of acquired learning outcomes
- start and end points of learning
- the amount and level of feedback needed to progress learning
- previous learning, experience or qualifications.

This collection of information enables you to make a judgement (assessment) about ability, competence or levels of knowledge and understanding. These judgements can, of course, be made before, during or at the end of learning. You can also use these outcomes to ascertain the effectiveness of your teaching. Assessment should be the tool to celebrate achievement and identify development. Teachers should work hard to promote this notion as all too often assessment has been experienced as a negative tool to criticise poor achievement or failing standards and, therefore, it is very often seen in a threatening way, because we all fear failure.

Inclusion and assessment

Inclusion simply means 'available to all'. Inclusion begins when you first hear about your learners, even before you meet them, and we will discover that the routines you practise will not end until after your learners have left your care towards the next stages of their development, be that further education, training, higher education or employment.

A lot of the focus associated with inclusion centres on planning for differentiation, i.e. meeting the needs of individuals. This starts during initial and diagnostic assessment, the results of which are used in the classroom when you prepare outcomes to suit your learners whilst remembering that the curriculum should also be covered. It therefore follows that checking that those outcomes have been met will vary according to the type and depth of knowledge or skill learned. Hence it is easy to see that assessment must suit both individual needs and the curriculum. Some useful words to remember are:

- Varied – adds interest and meets all needs, known or unknown
- Differentiated – inclusive, relevant, motivational
- Balanced – never too much of one type, so meets varied preferences.

Assessment like learning must be differentiated. Each method of assessment has the ability to be modified (to a lesser or greater degree) to suit the needs of learners. This might be informally or formally.

EXAMPLES OF RELATIONSHIPS TO THEORY – ASSESSMENT

Kolb's (1984) learning cycle states that assessment is a factor that is necessary to keep the cycle a circle. Something is done: a concrete experience which can be thought about (self-assessment). Try to understand it (questioning) and experiment with solutions (observation, peer assessment, more questions and an evaluation) which leads to … another concrete experience and the cycle begins again. Further reading in Chapters 10, 15 and 25.

Bloom's taxonomies (1956–1967, 2001) which can be used to differentiate the learning outcomes which will indicate the types of assessment methods. Low order cognitive skills suit multiple choice questions, high order cognitive skills and affective domain skills suit essays and short answer questions, psychomotor skills suit observations. Further reading in Chapters 5, 18 and 30.

Differentiating formative assessment

It is far easier to adjust assessments for formative purposes than for summative assessment. This is because generally formative assessment is devised by the teacher and therefore it is more able to be controlled.

Differentiation in this case is all about planning and preparation. If we know our learners we can enable them to access their assessment, however learners do not have to disclose their requirements. We should be watchful for their needs.

Some ideas of differentiating formative assessments:

- Nominated questioning at the beginning and end of the session to check progress.
- Progress indicators – to make a demonstrable indication of where a learner starts and where they are following teaching.
- Written question sheets with a mixture of short answer and multiple-choice questions.
- Varying degrees of gapped worksheets.
- Group activities resulting in collective decisions.
- Tutorials or 1:1 progress reviews.
- Self-assessment questionnaires.
- Peer assessment following presentations.
- Different command words used in homework or session activities.
- Varied font type, size, paper colour.
- Ask learners if they need assistance.
- Touring rooms during group activities.

Differentiating summative assessment

Differentiating for summative assessment is more difficult than for formative assessment. This is because you will probably need special permission from Awarding Organisations to deviate from the agreed type of assessment. Difficult, yes, because these things have to be agreed in writing prior to the events, but not impossible. Awarding Organisations will always accommodate those with specific needs: however, they respond to needs, not wants!

You are advised to seek help from examinations administrators, support staff and external moderators (EM) or verifiers (EV). This is essential as you will need the following support in order to differentiate:

- From support tutors you will need professional statements declaring the need and specific allowances that should be made.
- From the examinations office you will need to confirm special arrangements and they will arrange/organise resources, accommodation and invigilation.
- From the EM/EV you will need their written consent, so that they are aware of what is occurring and therefore will expect different assessment products at their visit.

Under no circumstances should you modify a test date or time, or permit additional resources in an examination room without prior, written consent. Your organisation will have been inspected with regards to its ability to conduct controlled assessments or examinations. (JCQ is an organisation linked to the main providers of externally tested qualifications and sets down the guidelines for administering and storing examination papers and scripts)

Variations to summative assessment are usually only applicable to those with a specific need or disability. The learner who always has to do the school run will have to amend their day to cope with an exam that starts at 09.00, whereas the learner who has difficulty in writing due to disability will be allowed extra time. In a formative assessment you may differentiate to cope with the *wants* of individuals, but in a summative assessment only *needs* are addressed.

Under the Equality Act, 2010, if a learner has enrolled to complete their programme of study or course they must be able to access assessment. Organisations must make 'reasonable' adjustments to ensure that learners can access assessment.

Some of the specialist arrangements include:

- Signers or lip readers
- Scribes (writers)
- Speakers/readers
- Viva (oral examination)
- Time – related to time allowed or date of test
- Location
- Specialist equipment and software
- Supporting bi- and multi-linguistic learners.

These formal recommendations will be advised by support tutors or professionals, and are based on extensive assessment of need; typically these are those with physical or mental needs, hearing or sight impairment or dyslexia.

More informally, a teacher can support summative assessment by helping learners to prepare for their exams, tests, questions etc. This can include teaching study skills: note-taking, reading, researching, essay preparation, presenting work or referencing. You may talk through what will happen during observations or examinations, and perhaps use classroom role play or video/DVD to help learners prepare for their assessment.

Differentiating for peer and self-assessment

By its very title, self-assessment will be differentiated as it is an individual assessment, but only if it is different to the self-assessment that everyone else in the session is doing. Peer assessment also needs managing so that it does not set up less confident learners to be dominated by those who are happier to express themselves.

Some ideas to include differentiated self- and peer-assessment in teaching and learning:

- *Learner presentations* – at the end of the presentation ask observers and presenters to assess themselves against some criteria – for example, content, communication, contribution and professionalism. Modify the terminology to suit individuals or use learning support assistants to work with those who may not understand the complexity of the wording.

- *Micro-teach sessions* – as presentations, but ask observers to comment on whether the teaching appealed to their learning style and if they learned anything. This will provide feedback to demonstrate whether or not individual learning preferences and requirements have been met.

- *Tutorials* – specific questions such as which part of the course/assignment was the most difficult? How do your functional skills sessions support your main qualification? Set SMART targets for all academic and pastoral aspects of the learner's programme. Use tutorial planners to ensure that learners have the opportunity to cover things that are important to them.

- *Profiles* – ask learners to describe their abilities against occupational or academic standards, or at the end of the course ask them to describe the key things they have learned and where their development now lies.

EXAMPLES OF RELATIONSHIPS TO THEORY – SELF ASSESSMENT

Kolb (1984). His learning cycle relies heavily on concepts of reflection – which involves self-assessment.

Schön (1983). Reflective practices in-action and on-action rely on self-assessment to influence changes in behaviour.

Boud (1995). Expressed his beliefs that learning and development will not occur without self-assessment and reflection.

Further reading in Chapters 10, 15 and 25.

Finally, as a means of summarising the purpose of assessment, the links between outcome and purpose of assessment and the timeliness of assessment may not be absolutely clear. The following table attempts to make that link explicit.

	Pre-enrolment	Initial assessment	Diagnostic assessment	Formative assessment	Summative assessment
Increasing the motivation of learners	✓			✓	
Diagnosis of functional skills needs			✓		
Establishing understanding of topic				✓	✓
Demonstrating ability			✓	✓	✓
Identifying support needs	✓	✓	✓		
Assessment of unit or module outcomes					✓
Statement of competence					✓
Previous attainment	✓	✓			
Forward planning				✓	
Effectiveness of teaching and learning				✓	

Glossary of terms

Academic relating to education, schools or scholarships

Data facts and statistics used for analysis

Differentiation catering for the needs of all learners to reduce barriers to learning

Inclusion finding opportunities to integrate all learners

Invigilation supervision of examination candidates

JCQ Joint Council for Qualifications

Nurture development of characteristics, beliefs or attitudes

Pastoral concerned with the well-being of learners

Rote teaching by repetition e.g. learning multiplication tables

Success recognition of achievement

Tutoring one-to-one coaching and support for assigned individuals

 # SUMMARY

In this chapter we set out to achieve the following outcomes:

- To develop the insight gained about inclusive practice and apply that knowledge to assessment practice.
- To describe ways of matching assessment to the needs of learners and the curriculum.
- To link theoretical concepts of learning and assessment to assessment practice.

Your personal development

You have discovered the difference between assessment *of* learning and assessment *for* learning and are able to describe the subtle difference between the two concepts. You can explain theories associated with Black and Wiliam, Budge and Hattie to describe the differences.

You can recognise and describe terms associated with development of learning through assessment. You have considered inclusion through differentiated assessment at both formative and summative levels. You have reviewed ideas about how to differentiate assessment to suit needs and strategies to support special assessment needs in summative assessment.

You can link these ideas to theories by Kolb, Bloom, Schön and Boud and the Equality Act.

CHAPTER 15
Quality assurance of assessment

LEARNING OBJECTIVES

The measurable outcomes that you will achieve by reading this chapter and completing the activities are:

....

- To outline the importance of quality assurance and the role of independent assessment in assessment processes
- To explain the meaning of standardisation, verification and moderation and apply them in relation to programmes you assess
- To list the main policies and procedures associated with quality assurance of assessment
- To describe the process of dealing with disputes and appeals against assessment outcomes

What is quality assurance?

Quality assurance (QA) increases the levels of confidence in the value of assessment and the decisions made during assessment; they are mechanisms or policies for ensuring reliable, effective assessment, i.e. guarantees of quality (see also Chapter 29). The purpose of QA is to assure the integrity of the product nationally, to set entry and exit standards that are equal so that all stakeholders know, regardless of where the qualification was achieved, the standards are equal. This is one of the main differences between qualifications and un-validated company training. Qualifications have to be seen to be of a specific standard, whereas company training is designed to meet the unique requirements of a particular organisation. Both assure quality of provision, but company training certificates are less transferable between other sectors because the training is being designed around individual company practices.

Quality Assurance is a process which ensures that assessment decisions are accurate and transparent. In order to provide clarity of this process you will find policies within the organisation to outline expectations and what to do if things go wrong. To meet Awarding Organisations' guidance the following would be expected:

- Assessment policy and/or procedure – outlines assessment procedure, guidance on special assessment requirements, strategy for QA, process for dealing with fails and referrals and general guidance for teams.
- Assessment malpractice policy and/or procedure – guidance on how an organisation ensures consistency and integrity of assessment, including how the organisation will deal with cheating, plagiarism, collusion, falsifying records either by staff or learners.
- Appeals policy and/or procedure – guidance on how the organisation will deal with complaints, disputes and appeals against assessment decisions.
- QA, Verification or Moderation policy and/or procedure – guidance on how the organisation proposes to quality assure the qualifications. It should contain statements relating to frequency and sampling.

- **Approval** policy or procedure – guidance on how an organisation can seek permission to run particular programmes, under the guidance of an Awarding Organisation. Awarding Organisations, who **certificate** the programmes, are required to meet stringent audits by Ofqual, to ensure their quality assurance practices are sound. This procedure would guide an organisation as a means of self-assessing their ability to offer qualifications.

Internal quality assurance

Organisational QA is seen in two parts, both very similar, but directed by different bodies. Internal QA, is, as intimated, controlled from within the approved centre. External QA is initiated by the Awarding Organisation. Within every training and assessment provider, there will be people appointed to check the work of teacher/assessors. Again, terminology will vary here, but most commonly you will see the role of Internal Quality Assurance (IQA). These people are tasked with the remit of quality assuring the assessment process. Each stage of assessment is subject to quality assurance strategies. Those stages include planning, delivering, making judgements, providing feedback and record keeping.

For example:

- IQAs will call meetings to ensure that all teacher/assessors are working to the same set of principles. This is called 'standardisation'. Teacher/assessors may be tasked to review a piece of work and collectively agree the judgement. Alternatively, they may be required to each bring in some examples and share these with colleagues – again – to ensure consistency.
- IQAs will cross check a number of pieces of evidence to confirm that an accurate judgement has been made. The amount of evidence checked will depend upon the experience of the teacher/assessor. This is known as a **risk-based** approach to QA.
- IQAs will co-observe assessments in the workplace to verify the observation process.

- IQAs will check records of assessment to check accuracy of completeness and check that signatures are *bona fide*. They will look at dates to ensure that learners are registered in a timely manner, that evidence matches dates on recording documents and that assessment activities are carried out regularly. This is a compliance approach to QA.

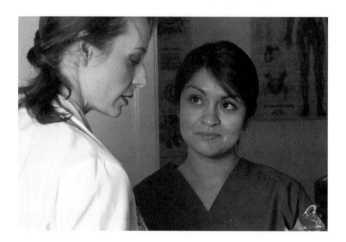

Independent assessment

The basic duties of teachers as assessors and moderator/verifiers have been clearly stated in Part 1, but when it comes to quality assurance, you may find other personnel or functions are involved in assessment. For example, most teachers are also the people that make assessment decisions about their learners; however, this can be seen as too subjective. Therefore, some organisations advocate the requirement to use independent assessors, that is, an in-built system to make some assessment decisions to counter accusations of less than objective decisions. Whilst this may suggest that teachers could be less professional if given both the role of the teacher and assessor, it does give an external air of confidence. By building another tier into the assessment, the quality of the assessment decisions is made more robust. Independent assessment usually means that a particular component must be assessed by someone not previously involved in the training, learning or assessment process. It is not validation of an assessment decision as this remains the role of the verifier or moderator.

Advantages:

- Teachers are protected from accusations of unreliability by using a third party to make certain assessment decisions
- Learners are guaranteed unbiased judgements.

Disadvantages:

- Another tier of assessment means additional costs.

Quality management processes are described in Chapter 29.

Standardisation

Standardisation relates to the consistency and agreement of expected standards or content. It can occur before assessment to set unified expectations or afterwards to agree the standard of marking.

This is a process which is aimed at ensuring all assessment decisions are equal. It ensures that teachers are fully conversant with assessment requirements and consistently make the correct decisions. Periodically, the quality assurance team will convene meetings where everyone involved in the programme meets to discuss the assessment process, identify good practice and support new or weak teacher/assessors. Some examples of typical activities would be:

- Every teacher brings one refer, pass, merit and distinction piece of work. They justify to the group why they have marked to that level.
- Teachers submit an unmarked piece of work prior to the event, which is marked by the IQA. Then at the meeting everyone marks the same piece of work, the outcome being that everyone should award the same mark or grade.
- Every teacher involved in a particular unit or module brings ideas or samples of assignments etc., to the meeting to establish the expected standard for that unit or module, which is then implemented by all teachers.
- The team collectively writes marking grids or *pro formas*.

Second (or third) marking refers to a process similar to standardisation, when one piece of work is independently marked by another person to (hopefully) get the same result.

Verification or moderation

QA has two components: moderation refers to checking the marks and grades awarded by the assessment team. Verification relates to checking that assessment processes are reliable.

This is the main quality assurance process, often called internal verification (IV). It aims to ensure that assessments meet validity (relevant to what is being assessed), reliability (consistently marked) and sufficiency (covers everything) requirements. It does this by sampling assessments. Over the period of the qualification, the work of every teacher and every learner at every location should be sampled. The amount of sampling will depend on the experience of the teacher, the age of the qualification, and the number of learners. This is called a risk-based strategy. The risk is determined at organisation level and approved by the Awarding Organisation. Behind every organisational policy and procedure, every programme should state how they implement the procedure by documenting its QA strategy. Whilst this is generally limited to sampling, it can cover all aspects of QA activity.

For example, a strategy to demonstrate best practice in sampling might state:

An experienced teacher/assessor using an established qualification with a reasonable caseload would have about 10 per cent of their work verified.

An experienced teacher/assessor using a new qualification may increase the sample to 25–50 per cent.

A new teacher/assessor with an existing qualification might be 70 per cent plus rising to 100 per cent for a new teacher/assessor without a new qualification.

Some of the strategies used to quality assure decisions made by teacher/assessors include:

- Observing the teacher/assessor whilst carrying out a workplace observation.
- Observing the teacher/assessor giving feedback to a learner about an assessment.
- Interviewing teacher/assessors.
- Interviewing learners.
- Reviewing product evidence.
- Looking at records of assessment.
- Conducting an audit trail of dates.

Every organisation will have their own verification or moderation strategy, which will depend on resources. Internal verification or moderation (IV) should be part of the process of assessment rather than a product of assessment. This means verifying judgements as they occur. The worst-case scenario in terms of IV is that at the end of a learner's qualification some inaccuracies are discovered, which causes a lack of confidence in all of the judgements. If this were to happen, the organisation and the teachers would lose their reputation and if this is discovered at external verification the centre is at risk of having sanctions imposed on it. Failure to comply may eventually result in a centre being closed.

One of the quality assurance roles of the Awarding Organisation is to comment on the effectiveness of the internal verification/moderation, and it measures its confidence in the organisation accordingly. Organisations will strive for 'direct claims' which means that Awarding Organisations are confident that they are able to quality assure with integrity, and they are authorised to apply for registrations and certificates without constantly seeking approval from external moderators and verifiers.

Further reading in terms of internal verification can be found on Awarding Organisation websites.

Disputes and appeals

These are two terms which broadly mean the same thing, however they can be defined as:

Appeal: A request to reconsider a judgement made.

Dispute: A difference in opinion in an outcome.

There are two very key words associated with the process – fairness, consistency. These must be kept in mind through the whole of the disputes and appeals process.

There may be occasions when a learner disputes the judgement made about the evidence presented by them. At this point teachers need to recognise that a learner has the right of appeal against judgements. Appeals are likely to be either against the process – i.e. a learner believes that part of the planning, delivery or feedback was unfair, or against the outcome – i.e. the learner believes that the judgement should have been different to that recorded.

In either instance, the learner should be allowed to discuss the disputed decision without fear of recrimination. During the learner's induction, they will have been made aware of the process to follow in the case of a dispute or appeal. It would usually commence with an informal, verbal alert to a learner's dissatisfaction. The teacher and the learner would discuss the issue and, hopefully, either the learner will understand more fully the rationale behind the outcome, or the teacher will review the evidence again and over ride the original decision. Even though informal and resolved, there should still be a record of the appeal.

An example of a record for informal appeals:

Learner Name	
Qualification	
Date of Appeal	
Record of Informal Appeal	

Was the appeal/dispute logged verbally or in writing?	
Did a meeting occur to discuss the appeal/dispute?	
Date of meeting: .... Persons present:　　Teacher/Assessor: 　　　　　　　　　Learner: 　　　　　　　　　Others (state)	
Outline the nature of the appeal or dispute?	
Was the appeal/dispute resolved?	

YES	What actions result from the meeting:	
	Appeal lost: Learner agreed with original decision following explanation, judgement stands.	
	Appeal upheld: assessment decision amended in the light of review of evidence or policy	
	Implications for assessment practice: Complete and return this form to Internal Quality Assurer	
NO	The teacher/assessor and the learner failed to agree and wish to enter a formal appeal process Learner signature: Teacher/assessor signature:	
	Complete and return this form to Internal Quality Assurer	
	Date appeal/dispute forwarded to Internal Quality Assurer	

Irrespective of the potential outcome of the appeal, the Internal Quality Assurer must be aware that an appeal is in progress. However, they should not request detail during the early stages in order to remain impartial should a formal stage be entered. An appeal or dispute conversation is a confidential discussion. If this is discussed with others before an outcome is agreed, then the learner may have a justified complaint that the appeal was not held in a manner to minimise bias.

 **ACTIVITY 1**

Dealing with disputes and appeals

Collect a copy of your organisation's Disputes and Appeals policy and procedure and ensure you are familiar with its content. Prepare a briefing session/information sheet about the process to use with learners during induction.

A failure to agree at the informal stage will advance the process to the formal stage.

It is important to clearly express the formal process by which learners can appeal against assessment decisions. This transparency is equally important to the learner, teacher and organisation. An organisation will commit to the addressing of learners' disputes and appeals through a policy and or procedure. The process should state the organisation's commitment to high standards of equality and be applied consistently throughout the organisation.

A policy will define what the organisation's viewpoint is. It ensures that its stakeholders are aware of its commitment to those who wish to appeal or dispute some aspect if its work. For example:

> '...aims to ensure that all of its assessments and assessment results are fair, consistent and based on valid judgements. However, it recognises that there may be occasions when a centre or a candidate may wish to question a decision made'

> *City & Guilds – Enquiries and Appeals policy (August 2008)*

A procedure will define the process a complainant will need to follow in order to make an appeal or log a dispute. It will define the circumstances within which an appeal or dispute is allowed, the time parameters (deadlines) and make assurances regarding confidentiality, impartiality and transparency.

Whilst every organisation will have a variant on their policy and procedure, it should always default to the Awarding Organisation's guidance on appeals and disputes. In essence the process will follow a system similar to:

Stage One In the first instance, the learner refers to the teacher to log an appeal or dispute. They will discuss, clarify and review the assessment and hopefully agree an outcome. Whether the appeal is upheld or lost, the assessment team should review its assessment processes to identify training needs, support for staff, or confirm and rectify any resultant errors to ensure rigour is maintained. This is usually the informal process – described above. Where there is a failure to agree, then the next stage of the process is entered.

Stage Two The learner will formally state their grounds for appeal or dispute, usually within a specified timeframe to the internal quality assurer or designated person. The quality assurer will consider the appeal, which may include a re-assessment of the evidence, another observation or interviews with all relevant parties. A decision will be made and notified to the complainant – again within a specified timeframe. If the appeal or dispute is still not resolved, then the next stage is entered.

Stage Three This stage is broadly similar to the previous stage although the complainant is referred to the Awarding Organisation, who will allocate a representative to investigate the complaint; this is usually the centre's external quality assurer. Their decision is final, although a learner would have the right to appeal directly to the Awarding Organisation.

All stages of the process should be documented and stored securely in line with organisation policy. The Awarding Organisation will want to see records relating to appeals whether upheld or lost.

Glossary of terms

Accurate correct in all aspects

Appeal a request to reconsider a judgement made

Approval permission to deliver qualifications on behalf of an Awarding Organisation

Awarding Organisation a body approved by Ofqual to create and certificate qualifications (AO)

Certificate a recognised outcome of a programme of study

Compliance to meet or agree recognised rules and standards

Consistency unchanging, evenly applied

Dispute a difference in opinion in an outcome

IV Internal Verifier

Malpractice improper or negligent actions

Moderation to check marks and grades awarded by the assessment team

Policy a course of action by an organisation; a statement of intent

Procedure a way of working

Risk-based a strategy of sampling used to minimise the danger of inexperience

Sample a representative of the whole to show trends

Second (or third) marking a marking process in which work is marked by two or more people to confirm a standardised approach

Standardisation a process to confirm decisions and create norms

Transparent overt, clear in meaning

Verification to check assessment processes are reliable

 SUMMARY

In this chapter we set out to achieve the following outcomes:

- To outline the importance of quality assurance and the role of independent assessment in assessment processes.
- To explain the meaning of standardisation, verification and moderation and apply them in relation to programmes you assess.
- To list the main policies and procedures associated with quality assurance of assessment.
- To describe the process of dealing with disputes and appeals against assessment outcomes.

Your personal development

In terms of quality assurance you are now able to express the purpose of QA in assessment and describe some of the terminology. You are able to describe the function of quality assurance and the ways that IQAs will review the teacher/assessor's work in order to guarantee accuracy and completeness.

You are familiar with your organisation's policies and procedures relating to QA, and participate in the process with confidence. You can describe the purpose of standardisation and internal verification or moderation and identify some sampling strategies.

You are able to summarise the responsibilities of the teacher/assessor in dealing with disputes and appeals and are confident in knowing when to refer an appeal to the internal quality assurer.

Part six

Delivering inclusive learning

....

This part and chapters relate to the learning outcomes in the following Units of Assessment:

● Understanding and using inclusive teaching and learning approaches in education and training.

● Delivering education and training.

● Teaching, learning and assessment in education and training.

● Developing teaching, learning and assessment in education and training.

The learning outcomes relating to evaluation, reflection and professional/personal development are dealt with in Part 8 and the learning outcomes relating to your development of the minimum core are in Part 9.

You should also read this part in conjunction with:

Part 2 – Planning to meet the needs of learners;

Part 3 – Facilitating Learning;

Part 4 – Resources; and,

Part 5 – Assessment.

This part develops the learning outcomes of those parts by considering how you would adapt your practice to meet the needs of all learners.

CHAPTER 16
Understanding inclusion

LEARNING OBJECTIVES

The measurable outcomes that you will achieve by reading this chapter and completing the activities are:

....

- To explain the key drivers for an effective inclusive learning environment
- To explain the terms inclusion, equality and diversity
- To describe how inclusive learning enthuses learners and supports success
- To explain the key theories and strategies to develop motivation
- To identify challenges, barriers and attitudes to learning in some key areas of specialist need
- To consider the main factors of inclusion and how they influence teaching, learning and assessment methodology

Establishing and maintaining inclusive learning environments

Providing opportunities for everyone in the community is not a new idea; equality of opportunity appeared in the 1970s and Helena Kennedy QC wrote about widening participation in 1996 (Further Education Funding Council 1996). Several revisions, in the format of legislation and government reports, have culminated in the current notion (or label) of inclusivity. In this context, we are looking at educational inclusion, specifically in post-compulsory education, rather than social inclusion.

Organisations have to plan strategically to deliver equality, diversity and inclusion and are being inspected against their ability to provide opportunities. This has resulted in active marketing towards groups that would not normally enter education and training. In the wider context of inclusion, it means that all learners are allowed to engage in learning, irrespective of social, behavioural, personal traits or ability. At the classroom level, every teacher has a responsibility to ensure that everyone is included.

The opposite of inclusion is exclusion; not something that happens regularly or without a great deal of anxiety, but in education and training one of the changes recently introduced is the delivery of learning to those who have been excluded from compulsory education.

In a report initiated by the Scottish Funding Council (2006: 4), one senior manager in a GFE college said:

> There are people here who would not have been here five years ago. Their circumstances have not changed. They are still living difficult lives; still living in poverty; still have a serious disability or health issue. We can't change these things but we can adapt what we do to help them get here, turn up, feel okay about what they are learning, and leave with what they aspired to.

He continued:

> Good learning does not reinforce previous negative experiences and may remove many barriers.

Therefore inclusion is about meeting the needs of individuals and groups: those needs may be: personal, social, cultural, cognitive, physical or sensory. All have different 'needs', some may also have 'wants'. A teacher who knows and understands their learners will be able to establish the difference. 'Needs' are a given adjustment, 'wants' are appeased if appropriate and convenient.

When inclusion is effective it will:

● Enable achievement and success

● Motivate by celebrating success and inspiring learners

● Develop and maintain positive attitudes

● Foster interest

● Encourage reflection

● Offer small chunks of learning with progressively more challenging goals

● Create positive relationships between teachers and learners

● Create an effective transition towards employment or relevance to further study

● Use individual learning plans to plan and record progress

● Offer a wide range of provision, delivered at times and locations to meet learners' needs.

When inclusion is not effective, it will:

● Disadvantage learners in achieving their learning goals

● Provide poor use of modern technologies to enhance learning

● Offer a narrow range of teaching approaches

● Have insufficient assessment of learning or lack effective feedback

● Withhold development of functional (basic) skills

● Lack adequate methods to collect data or feedback to develop learners or provision.

Inclusion, therefore, is about creating interesting, varied and inspiring learning opportunities for *all* learners; ensuring all learners contribute and are never disadvantaged by behaviours, methods, language or resources. This is described in other ways such as differentiation or 'meeting individual needs': both of these terms tend to refer to the mechanics of inclusion.

ACTIVITY 1

Reflective practice

How do you ensure an **inclusive** learning environment for your learners?

Think about the actions you currently take in planning, delivery, support and assessment. The basics of these stages are discussed in Parts 1, 2, 3 and 5.

Discuss with your mentor the strategies used in the context of your specific group of learners.

The table below explains how the laws relating to equal opportunities are developed into an inclusive strategy.

Equality	Diversity	Inclusion
Concentrates on removing discrimination	Maximises learner potential	Stimulates interest
Can be an issue for disadvantaged or minority groups	Respects all learners	Involves all in learning
Relies on positive action by managers and the organisation as a whole	Relies on implementing policies and practices in context	Relies on applying strategies in the learning environment

Adapted from Kandola and Fullerton (1994: 49)

The key to successful inclusion strategies is knowing your learners and this will start from the moment you meet them.

Inclusive practice concerns the necessity of differentiating to meet individual need. To a certain extent this will increase the motivation and therefore make the learning session more rewarding for learners. It is not, however, a rule. As the teacher, you may have devised various activities, resources and assessment tools to meet everyone's needs, but notice that there is still something missing. So what is it? Well, it is likely to be that you have overlooked the fact that people have characters; they have moods, distractions and emotions. Whilst you may be able to deal with changes in these if they are on going, if they emerge during your session, it relies upon you to 'think on your feet'. It may or may not be possible to sort out the issue or modify your session, and in my experience when you can get around to dealing with it – i.e. for the next session, everything has changed anyway! Younger learners in particular do have quite sudden changes in their behaviour as a result of mood swings and adults may be concerned about other facets of their lives, for example work or family, which temporarily distract them. So the advice is that you need to understand what motivates and remember the importance of knowing your learners.

Types of learners – some expressions you may hear:

- VAK/VARK – visual, auditory (read and write) and kinaesthetic learners – different ways/preferences learners like to learn.
- Disaffected learners – no longer satisfied with the learning environment.
- Disengaged learners – detached or not involved in learning.
- Dysfunctional – unable to deal with normal social behaviours.
- Dyslexia/Dyscalculia – a difficulty in interpreting words/numbers.
- Gifted and talented learners – highly skilled or adept in particular things.
- SEN – special educational needs.
- ADHD – attention deficit hyperactivity disorder.
- Minority groups – learners whose age, gender, ethnicity, disability, etc., is different to that of the majority of the learners in a group.

We will look at the different needs of these types of learners later.

Motivating and enthusing learners

There are many theories relating to motivation; all describe ways of trying to find out why someone wants to learn and how best to make it happen. Further theories are discussed in Part 7.

One of the simplest theories associated with motivation that can be applied to learning is the work of Abraham Maslow (1954, 1970). He focused on needs, arguing that basic needs must be met before a learner can enter a state of mind in which to learn. In 1954 he investigated the motivation of workers and this is frequently applied to learners. In order for a worker (or learner in our profession) to achieve their goals and aspirations, they need to go through a development of basic needs, e.g. comfort, safety, belonging and self-esteem. This is Maslow's Hierarchy of Needs. The chart is usually presented as a pyramid, with the pinnacle or goal being self-actualisation, but I would like to look at it in reverse, that is, starting at the beginning ...

Let us consider the effects of this theory on the learner. In order to be receptive to learning, Maslow's theory (see Figure 6A) suggests that a learner needs to address:

Figure 6A	Maslow's Hierarchy of Needs 1954 interpreted to reflect learner needs: The Back to Basics model.
Physical comfort	The basics of hunger, thirst and sleep are met. The environment is adequately lit and heated, making the surroundings comfortable
Safety and shelter	Working in an environment that has clear boundaries and rules to ensure fairness, safety and developing a confidential, trusting rapport and well-being
Love and belonging	Working in a friendly, caring environment, interacting and communicating, having a good rapport with others
Self-esteem	Feelings of pride, respect, achievement, independence, dignity, encouraged through feedback and praise
Self-actualisation	Feelings of fulfilment, encouragement, optimism, and able to transfer skills and knowledge

In the classroom this is applied usually without any conscious decisions, especially at the lower level. As teachers we talk to learners, create rules, encourage respect and value others' opinions. Our learners respond (i.e. become motivated) by doing what should be considered natural in polite society. It could therefore be argued that failure to comply with acceptable standards of behaviour could (and usually does) affect motivation and subsequent learning. Motivation is simply learners wanting to learn.

Intrinsic and extrinsic motivators

Everyone is driven by either intrinsic or extrinsic motivators. Those said to be intrinsically motivated are developing because they want to; they have an inbuilt desire to progress and want to learn because they can; they are inspired by learning for its own sake, or they just want to do something, almost for their own enjoyment. Those who are extrinsically motivated are developing because somebody or something wants them to or they need to. Maybe they have the offer of financial reward or better job prospects; they might need to learn something in order to do something else. Whatever the reason for the motivation, it is necessary and it is crucial that the teacher knows what their motivational driver is. If, for example, someone is extrinsically motivated they will improve their motivation if their work is displayed on the wall, or other similar outward expression of their achievement: equally, someone intrinsically motivated will get satisfaction from study time to research a topic. Once again, the teacher should play to the strengths of the learner when trying to raise enthusiasm in learning.

This reinforces the fact that by knowing your learners you will have an idea of why they are there, and that will result in different motivational strategies. Someone who is intrinsically motivated already has the desire to achieve, whereas the extrinsically motivated learner needs more praise in order to create the desire to continue.

Intrinsic	Extrinsic
● Recreational learners	● Needs a qualification
● Career learners	● Needs a job
● Self-directed progression	● Needs more money

ACTIVITY 2

Motivation

Why are you doing your teaching qualification?

List the reasons and decide whether you are intrinsically or extrinsically motivated.

What would help you to become more motivated?

Why does reflecting on your own levels of motivation enable development?

Discuss your answers with another member of the course or record your feelings in your reflective learning log.

Medals and mission

This is a goal-oriented theory, based on the desire to be rewarded for achievement. A learner is given a clear direction or task and when it is reached there is a reward. The reward may be money, for example a pay rise on gaining a qualification, it may be a certificate, which could be proudly displayed or it could be acknowledgment from a colleague or teacher in a statement indicating 'well done'. The 'mission' can be a series of small targets or a single target, depending on the preferences of the learners. The 'medal' may also be phased.

Vicious and virtuous circles

As the name suggests, this focuses on the fact that when things start to happen (positively or negatively) a learner enters a circle. The vicious circle is spiralling downwards; conversely, the virtuous circle is spiralling upwards. In motivational terms, if you start to achieve things you are more likely to want to continue. A learner enters a Can Do – Will Do mind-set.

Turner (1990) promoted a model demonstrating the need for praise to promote a better standard of performance (see Figure 6B):

Motivation in training

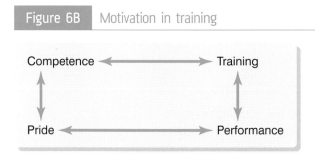

Petty then adopted Turner's model to show how success forms the motivator to further achievement, creating a virtuous circle (see Figure 6C); this is the upward spiral. Conversely in the vicious circle, the statements are in the negative and so the motivation lessens because as a learner fails they are not inclined to progress or do more work.

The virtuous circle (Petty 2004: 47)

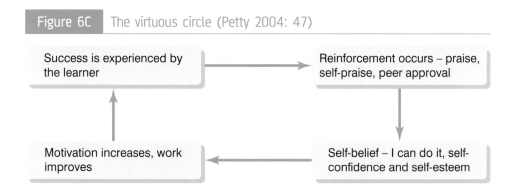

Bandura and self-efficacy

Albert Bandura (1994) suggested that an individual's belief in themselves and their ability is related to what they can achieve. The mind-set here is 'if I believe I can, then I must be able to'. This is self-efficacy, which in this context means that belief in yourself will aid motivation. In the classroom it concerns the strategies you apply and how you address the learner who says 'I can't do this'. This learner needs to be encouraged to try, you will re-explain the topic and through coaching and reassurance you will enable that learner to achieve.

Example conversation:

I hate maths! I can't do it!

– Teacher replies: 'I know, it is difficult isn't it!'

Try: 'which part of this activity are you finding most difficult?' or 'OK, let's break this down into smaller chunks.'

Herzberg's satisfaction theory

Frederick Herzberg (1959) was one of the early writers on motivation. This was originally associated with the workplace, but again, can easily be attributed to learning. He suggested that people need personal growth and interest (recognition, promotion, responsibility) to motivate and that whilst a person's level of satisfaction in their surroundings (hygiene factors) is important, they are not key motivators. Both aspects impact on how motivated they are. This is a 'needs' model in that everyone needs the right conditions, status and security in order to develop.

Example conversation:

Why do I have to do this?

– Teacher replies

a) Because it is part of your course
b) Because you will earn more if you pass
c) Because you will get more promotion opportunities
d) Because it will give you the skills to complete your assignment

a and b are hygiene factors and will motivate less than c and d

Discuss this and why that is so.

Positive and negative reinforcement

These ideas come from the behaviourist theories originally suggested in research on animal behaviour (Pavlov's dog responding by salivating). In learning terms this is about offering positive or negative rewards to motivate. The motivation has a value. Positive reinforcement is rooted in the desire to seek a reward for achievement or good work. Negative reinforcement works on the threat or fear factor of not doing well.

Example conversation:

Both phrases below suggest the same outcome, but the method of delivering is totally different. Which is more positive –

'If you complete the work you may go to break' or

'If you don't complete your work, you can't have a break.'

Discuss in pairs why this is so.

 **ACTIVITY 3**

Thinking about motivation

How to learn about motivation – discussion initiators

One activity you may try centres on the personalities of TV and film characters. Some video/DVD scenes you may want to think about are:

David Brent's management style in *The Office*

Julia Roberts' persistence in *Erin Brockovich*

Basil Fawlty and Manuel in *Fawlty Towers*

Caine and Walters' relationship in *Educating Rita*

Social beliefs in *Slumdog Millionaire*

How does each of these people motivate their staff or protégés or challenge expectations?

List the positive and negative methods each uses and relate those ideas to motivational theory. What can you learn by these examples?

The teacher should consider the advantages of using positive reinforcement as a motivator. Remember, though, that what you offer (or threaten) must be carried out, or it becomes empty reinforcement.

Further reading

Further information and useful online resources

http://tip.psychology.org/motivate.html

http://www.businessballs.com/maslow.htm

http://webspace.ship.edu/cgboer/maslow.html

http://changingminds.org/explanations/theories/

http://www.geoffpetty.com/downloads/WORD/reinforcement.doc

A simple search through a search engine using the following key words will reveal a lot of information: motivation, Maslow, intrinsic, extrinsic, Herzberg, Petty.

Specialist areas of motivational need

There are groups of learners who have particular issues. Whilst not wishing to stereotype needs, a teacher should be mindful of the support these groups may need to offer to improve motivation. If you follow your own rule of assuming nothing, yet seek to find out how individuals access useful learning strategies, you will create an inclusive environment. Some learners may have pre-existing conditions and may already have a statement written by a professional (Learning Difficulty

Assessments (LDAs) conducted under section 139A of the Learning and Skills Act 2000.) which describes preferred or suitable adaptions to ensure they are able to engage fully in learning.

Attention deficit hyperactivity disorder (ADHD)

Some learners may be diagnosed with ADHD. If you have such a learner in your session you should seek advice on their particular needs, but in general learners need to be in a position where they cannot be distracted or distract and see positive role models around them. You should not play to their need to gain your attention, but remember that they easily lose focus and their attention span is poor, so planning is essential when preparing sessions to meet their needs.

In sessions, try to:

- prepare material that is of interest
- create responsibility for their own learning
- initiate peer support systems
- design short, sharp activities
- give feedback promptly
- use plenty of varied activities
- maintain a routine in the classroom
- create clear concise hand-outs
- offer reminders and praise.

Disaffected, disengaged and dysfunctional learners

This group of learners each have their special learning needs and whilst slightly different their characteristics will impact on participation in the classroom. In essence, disaffected learners are no longer satisfied with the learning environment; disengaged learners appear detached or not involved in learning and dysfunctional learners are unable to deal with normal social behaviours. The learners may be disruptive and demonstrate some very challenging behaviour and are more likely to have attendance problems.

Ofsted defined the factors which are most successful in helping these learners to enjoy learning. These include:

- a commitment from all staff to meeting the learners' needs.
- effective monitoring systems to identify learners at risk.
- close collaboration between primary and secondary schools to prevent learners' disengagement at transition.
- the involvement of a wide variety of adults within the school and the community to support the learners.
- regular and effective communication with parents and carers, including involving them closely in determining the strategies to be used to support their children.
- modifying the curriculum and drawing on educational providers beyond the school.
- close working relationships with local agencies responsible for supporting children and young people.

Source: Ofsted, Good practice in re-engaging disaffected and reluctant students in secondary schools (2008) Ref: 070255. http://www.ofsted .gov.uk/resources/good-practice-re-engaging-disaffected-and-reluctant-students-secondary-schools (accessed October 2012)

So, some effective strategies for the teacher might include: monitoring progress diligently, role-modelling acceptable behaviour, being consistent, valuing contributions (focus on positive behaviour), a calm and relaxing learning environment, maybe with background music and softened lighting, using mood boards/traffic light cards to express emotion, adopting buddying and/or mentoring to support learners.

Gifted and talented learners

These are a group of learners who need to be motivated in the same way as every other learner, although it is tempting to 'assume' that because they are able and usually intrinsically motivated they are OK left to their own devices. This group is at risk of becoming bored by learning that lacks challenge in the same way that any other learner lacks motivation; the teacher needs to respond and act upon it by differentiated teaching.

'Gifted' refers to those learners who excel in core subjects, whereas 'talented' usually refers to those skilled in more practical or artistic subjects. More recently 'gifted and talented' has become a general term for those learners who demonstrate high abilities in a number of areas.

Characteristics of gifted and talented learners:

- Quick thinking
- Methodical
- Creative
- Flexible
- Communicative
- Dexterous
- Team players.

Strategies to challenge the group:

- Offering opportunities to investigate and research.
- Setting high order objectives (Bloom, Chapter 5, 18).
- Using open questions to seek opinion or argument.
- Question opinions and ask what if … ? questions.
- Providing opportunities to negotiate own targets.
- Develop learner and learning autonomy.

Specific language needs groups

There are groups for whom education is needed to support the ability to either become employed in the UK or work effectively in the UK. These are groups who are not native English speakers. They may struggle to comprehend the language and it must not be assumed that they possess some specific educational need. There are differences in academic ability as with any group of learners; their need is for language support to enable the groups to participate fully in education. The groups that come into this category include asylum seekers, English as a foreign language (EFL) and English for speakers of other languages (ESOL).

Bilingualism and multilingualism is now common. 17.5 per cent of primary and 12.9 per cent of secondary children speak a first language other than English. This continues the trend in year on year increase of about 1 per cent. Over 300 language categories are reported as spoken in the UK; this does not include dialects.

Source: Annual School Census 2010, Department for Children, Schools and Families. Annual School Census 2011, Department for Education http://www.cilt.org.uk/home/research_and_statistics/statistics/ languages_in_the_population/annual_school_census.aspx (accessed March 2011) http://www.education.gov.uk/researchandstatistics/statistics/ allstatistics/a00209478/dfe-schools-pupils-and-their-characteristics-january- 2012 (accessed September 2012)

Further, there is a promotion of the notion that '…bilingualism in a child or adult is an advantage and does not cause communication disorders'. The Royal College of Speech and Language Therapists (2006).

Teachers are required to ensure that the language of the qualification or framework is accessible and comprehended by all and appropriate strategies are in place to support those learners. The motivation for this group will come from activities in the classroom that are appropriate to their academic level, yet mindful of their ability to understand the concept in a different language.

In sessions, try to:

- prepare material that relates to hobbies or the learner's vocational area
- create responsibility for their own learning
- initiate peer support systems
- maintain a routine in the classroom language
- create clear concise hand-outs, using images
- use personal dictionaries.

Motivation and generating enthusiasm are the most challenging tasks that a teacher is faced with. My suggestion is always to go back to basics: assume nothing and find out what makes your learners tick. Remember that things happen around us and that will change how learners feel about their surroundings, targets and aspirations. Respond logically, encourage and remember that although it is easier to criticise than praise; we all like a 'well done' or 'thank you'.

Key principles for inclusion

The first stage is to identify the need. This can be through a wide variety of early interventions, for example: interviewing and disclosures, initial assessment, diagnostic assessment, references, induction activities or one-to-one reviews. A teacher should be mindful that not all learners are happy to disclose their needs; maybe they think that to do so will impact on their perceived suitability for the course, or that they just do not understand how you can overcome barriers their differences may present. So, keep your eyes and ears open and if you are concerned, either take advice from a more experienced teacher, or raise the issue with the learner, their tutor or your manager.

For the teacher inclusion broadly means that teaching, learning and assessment methodologies are adapted to suit those identified needs, through ensuring behaviours, language, hand-outs and other learning materials are free from bias, and that inappropriate comments are challenged and excluded from the classroom.

When advertising courses and delivering learning, a teacher should not stereotype or in any way disadvantage groups of learners. The environment and all support structures should enable access and include facilities to meet all learners' needs and preferences. You can anticipate inclusive learning strategies, but should never assume. 'Political correctness' is a commonly used term at the moment, and is used to ensure that expressions do not cause offence to any particular group of people.

Let us look at some examples of inclusive learning strategies:

Material	Inclusive suggestions
Hand-outs	Be cautious about the use of 'he' or 'she'. Try to use 'they' or 'their'. Be prepared to photocopy large print versions of text if necessary.
Language	Never use words like 'manpower', 'craftsman'. Challenge inappropriate behaviours, e.g. racism, sexism, homophobia – even if said as a 'joke'. Relate learning to experiences to aid understanding (anecdotes, analogy). Use examples that appeal across cultures and raise interest and values in those cultures that are not the majority within the learning establishment.
Advertising/ course leaflets	Do not stereotype. All courses should be accessible and open to all.
Written and spoken text	Use clear language, without **jargon** and explain technical terms. If the subject contains jargon, ensure that it is explained sufficiently to make meaning clear. Use dictionaries and vocabulary books to aid understanding of terms.
Visual aids	Consider colours and their effectiveness. Red and green are not always clear to all learners, especially those who have colour-blindness. Write clearly in a legible style of writing, avoid writing in capital letters. Use expressions such as wipe-board rather than whiteboard and if you still use them – chalkboard as opposed to blackboard.

Material	Inclusive suggestions
Learning aids	Offer alternative formats, i.e. electronic, paper, large print, Braille, whenever possible. Think about the font type and use more easily read types like comic sans. Use coloured paper to aid readability for dyslexic learners – yellow, pink, pale blue and green are most often recommended following dyslexia assessments.
Use of font style	American research has suggested that key facts are learned more efficiently if font styles are varied (type and style). Consider using emboldened, italics or underlining to stress a key learning point or write in a different font style. http://web.princeton.edu/sites/opplab/papers/Diemand-Yauman_Oppenheimer_2010.pdf
Space	Ensure coats, bags, etc. are not left around the room, ensure there is sufficient space for moving around the classroom. Arrange furniture to enable those with mobility problems to move around the room easily.
Support	Ensure that learners' needs are addressed, which may involve using a specialist team of physical and educational support workers.
Behaviours	Ensure that any offensive behaviours are challenged, including those used innocently or naïvely.

Approaches to teaching and learning

Teaching and learning strategies will vary according to what you want to get out of the session, what the learners are able to achieve within the time allowed, what materials and resources are available to you, the subject matter you are delivering, the needs of the learners and your personal style.

The choice of method will depend on whether you wish to deliver a formal teaching session in which all learners are working on the same topic at the same time, a learner-centred session, where learners are working on the same broad topic but using different methods and resources, or finally a self-study style where learners are working on different aspects of a topic or even different topics, using their own style of learning (Petty 2004: 430).

Factors that influence teaching:

- How learners learn and their preferred learning style
- What the teacher wants to achieve
- The subject matter
- What the learners are capable of achieving
- Time constraints
- Resource implications
- What the learners want to get out of the session
- Where you will teach
- How dependent your learners are.

All learners come to your sessions with preferred ways of learning. As the teacher we can deal with this by creating a number of different activities in each session. It is worth noting here that there is alternative thinking in the research by Frank Coffield (Should we be using learning styles?: 2004) which suggests that there is little evidence to prove that meeting preferences directly raises achievement and submits that it merely addresses variety, which in turn motivates learners. Source: http://itslifejimbutnotasweknowit.org.uk/files/LSRC_ LearningStyles.pdf

Irrespective of your views, you should separate teaching from learning in order to understand these influences. In short, teaching is what we do; learning is what your learners will do. In the following chapter we will look at how to implement inclusivity in the learning environment.

Glossary of terms

ADHD attention deficit hyperactivity disorder

Autonomy independence in the ability to learn

Communication a means of sending and receiving information to share or exchange ideas

Concept an idea

Diagnostic assessment assessment occurring early in the learner journey to establish starting points or identify capability or skill level, particularly in relation to functional skills

Differentiation catering for the needs of all learners to reduce barriers to learning

Dyscalculia associated with difficulties in making sense of numbers and calculations

Dyslexia associated with a difficulty in reading or interpreting words and symbols

Equality of opportunity legislation and focus on gender, age, culture, etc.

Extrinsic motivation motivation derived from the outside of the person

GFE General Further Education

Gifted and talented highly skilled or adept

Inclusion finding opportunities to integrate all learners

Inclusive not excluding any individual or group of learners (adj)

Intrinsic motivation motivation from within the person: natural desire

Jargon language, words or expressions of a specialist occupation

Learning to gain knowledge or a skill; what the learners do during the session

Reflection a considered opinion expressed in speech or writing; thoughts or considerations, developing ideas and thoughts

VAK/VARK visual, auditory (read/write) and kinaesthetic learning preferences – different ways learners like to learn

 SUMMARY

In this chapter we set out to achieve the following outcomes:

- To explain the key drivers for an effective inclusive learning environment.
- To explain the terms inclusion, equality and diversity.
- To describe how inclusive learning enthuses learners and supports success.
- To explain the key theories and strategies to develop motivation.
- To identify challenges, barriers and attitudes to learning in some key areas of specialist need.
- To consider the main factors of inclusion and how they influence teaching, learning and assessment methodology.

Your personal development

You can describe the importance of creating an inclusive learning environment and the historical factors that have led to the notion of inclusion. You are clear about the meaning of equality, diversity and inclusion.

You can describe how theorists suggest that motivation can be improved and relate these suggestions to your own learning environment. You can state a number of ways in which motivation can be improved. You have considered how you are personally motivated to achieve your own teaching qualification.

You can describe the character traits of a number of groups of learners and make suggestions about how to ensure they are able to participate fully in learning.

You can suggest ways of modifying your teaching and learning strategies to ensure that all learners have the opportunity to participate in your sessions. You may have sought advice from your mentor to analyse how you interact with your group of learners.

CHAPTER 17

Using inclusive strategies

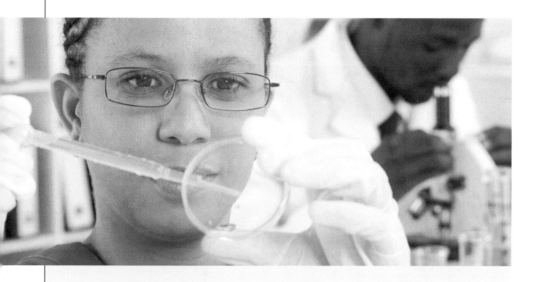

LEARNING OBJECTIVES

The measurable outcomes that you will achieve by reading this chapter and completing the activities are:

- To establish methods of identifying need in order to create an inclusive learning environment
- To identify learning activities and list factors that can motivate learners to engage in learning
- To select appropriate teaching and learning strategies
- To identify and select relevant resources and suggest ways of modifying them to meet individual needs of learners
- To state the importance of the environment in relation to learning
- To explain ways of creating successful learning environments through effective management of the classroom

Creating a first impression

You only have one opportunity to do this. In the first few minutes of meeting someone, we all make a decision about them. Whether this is an accurate impression or not remains subjective; it is human nature! As learners walk in to the classroom, they survey their surroundings, look at the teacher and look at each other. This can be managed so that it has a positive effect by:

- Being on time
- Smiling
- Welcoming learners
- Greeting and seating learners
- Looking clean and presentable
- Being prepared
- Looking calm and organised
- Being confident
- Making sure the room is prepared for the learners
- Friendly introductions.

Think about how you would feel if, when you arrived, there was no-one in the room, it was untidy, and then the teacher arrived mumbling about being busy and the photocopier not working: then the session started and you had no idea of the teacher's name or even the name of the person sitting next to you. Are you even in the right room? Would you feel valued? Would you have confidence in the teacher? Would you expect the course to be any good? Would you come back next week?

It seems obvious when presented like this, but because the first impression counts for so much, you should be particularly aware of it during the first session. When learners don't attend the second session, the teacher should always consider the impact they made during the first session.

A lot of the work of teachers is undertaken on the telephone or by email – so consider how the messages and ways that these communication tools are used and demonstrate good customer service and create a professional first impression.

Telephone etiquette:

- Answer the telephone with your name and department.
- Do not use your personal number for work-related issues, or be very cautious in doing so.
- Collect your telephone messages frequently.
- Take telephone numbers etc. accurately, repeat back to caller to confirm.
- Do not give out contact details of others, however demanding the request. Take the caller's number and let the third party call them.
- Ensure that you follow up/complete promises or actions made.

Email etiquette:

- Ensure salutations and conversations are professional.
- Do not use personal email for work-related issues (or *vice versa*).
- Avoid forwarding emails without checking previous emails in chain.
- Think about how many people are copied in to the email and why you feel they need to be copied.
- Don't forget to attach the promised attachment before sending.
- Think before pressing send – could the email be misinterpreted; email tone is very different to the spoken tones, try 'sleeping' on some emails before sending.

 **ACTIVITY 1**

Learning experiences

Think about a good learning experience. Write down what you liked about it that made it a good experience:

Now think about a bad experience. Again, write down things that made you feel uncomfortable or unhappy with that experience:

Conclude this by listing all of the positive actions that you are going to include in your own teaching sessions. These are your values or principles: things that are so important to you that you will not accept second best.

Ice-breakers

During the first meeting with your learners it is important to find out what they want from the course. Usually entrants to vocational courses will be interviewed to assess their suitability, but in some instances, learners just enrol and the first time the teacher has an opportunity to check suitability is the first session. Whichever route, when you meet learners for the first time, you should find out about your learners, their needs, their learning preferences, their concerns and apprehensions, and gradually introduce them to the rest of the group and their new environment. This type of activity is generally seen as an induction and will usually include an ice-breaking activity.

I	Introduce yourself
C	Create a comfortable setting
E	Encourage communication
B	Break down barriers
R	Reveal concerns
E	Encourage team spirit
A	Ascertain needs
K	Know your learners
E	Establish rules
R	Re-visit previous learning

Different ice-breakers will be used for different things, but a successful ice-breaker is fun, useful and not intimidating. You should remember that learners do not usually like to draw attention to themselves at the first meeting. If you are sensitive to this, then the ice-breaker will do what it says it will do, i.e. break the ice. If you, the teacher, start the activity, maybe by introducing yourself and answering the ice-breaker questions, that will help to relax the learners and make an activity that is interesting and rewarding.

Some ideas:

1. In pairs, interview each other to find out names, an interesting fact about each other and maybe a favourite film or game. Then each person introduces their fellow learner.

What this does. During the introductions, the teacher can write down the names of the group as a table plan, so that immediately the teacher can recall names: learners like to be recognised by name. The teacher can start to create a rapport. For example, next week you can ask how the children are, or if they enjoyed a particular leisure activity. This type of information creates a positive relationship because learners know that you care and are interested in them. Knowing about learners' favourite things reveals the type of things that interest them. This can tell you a little about them. For example, are they thoughtful, active, extrovert or introvert? If you have a confident group, you might also try the, 'If you were an animal, what kind would you be, and why?' type of question. That question can usually be quite enlightening as well as very funny.

2. Devise a little questionnaire, probably written to find out what learners already know about the subject. You can then invite learners to discuss what they've written and what is concerning them.

What this does. In a quiet group, this type of activity will help to settle the learners. Be careful to include some questions that are quite easy in order to reassure the learner. The difficult questions can be off-putting, so remember to assure learners that they will be able to do these things soon. On a recreational course it will tell you about your learners. It introduces the course and can be revisited regularly so that learners can track their progress. It will help you to design a programme of study that meets the group's needs.

3. Split the group into smaller groups of about four or five people and ask them to build something. (For example, build a freestanding bridge using newspaper, using only a set amount of string and sticky tape.). This could be modified to an individual working in a group, by asking the learners to produce a colourful name card that reflects their personality – they are allowed to chatter whilst completing the activity – to gain ideas or explain their choices.

What this does. It develops a team spirit. By getting feedback after the activity it initiates discussion and the teacher can identify the roles learners take when working within groups – leaders, followers, doers, thinkers, artistic tendencies, etc. This can link to the completion of a learning preferences questionnaire, for example VAK, because it has already established that everyone is different.

4. Shield Activity. Each learner has an image of a shield on A3 paper and a supply of coloured pencils, felt-tip pens and/or paints. The shield is divided into four sections and in each quarter, the learner has to draw an image of things that are important to them. For example this might be a match-stick family, a football club logo, a bar of chocolate and a pet; anything goes! Artistic skills are not essential, but can bring some hilarity to the activity. In their table groups they can discuss their shields and how it represents their psyche.

5. Coin in the pocket. Ask each learner to take a coin from their purse or pocket (maybe have a supply of pennies just in case). Ask them to look at the year and tell the group a fact about that year or something they were doing in that year. Learners are allowed to 'Google' a fact, which can help introduce the rule about appropriate use of telephones and mobile equipment in the session or give an indication of confidence in using the equipment.

Can you see the connections between ice-breakers and the concepts of first impression and learning preferences? There are balances to be made – are your first impressions still the same after the ice-breaker? Do the answers to the ice-breaker bear any resemblance to their learning preferences and goals? These first activities are pieces of a jigsaw that will gradually fit together to make a picture, but remember that some of the pieces you put in might have to be moved if they are not quite right!

Teaching and learning activities

Each activity in the classroom will consist of teaching and learning activities. These should be balanced to meet the different learning preferences of your learners (see Part 3) and to develop motivation.

Modern technology allows for a blended learning style which incorporates traditional and computer-based methods. This is often referred to as information learning technology (ILT) or information communication technology (ICT). The use of computer-based technology to enhance teaching methods and resources or develop learner autonomy is widely promoted.

The table considers some of the most frequently used approaches and compares them in the context of teaching and learning activities.

Activity	Value to teacher	Value to learner
Lecture (verbal exposition)	High focus on teacher activity Excellent knowledge base required Uses verbal exposition to impart a lot of information in a short time Clarity and tone of voice needs to be clear, interesting and unambiguous Can be used to deliver to large groups easily Is enhanced by visual aids	Requires good listening and note-taking skills Passive learning Limited opportunities to clarify understanding Appeals to auditory learners
Demonstration	Needs to be well organised before session Explains difficult parts of the task when verbal exposition is not suitable Teacher-centred Links theory and practice	Opportunities to see, hear and smell Allows a task to be broken down into smaller chunks Limited hands-on experiences Appeals to visual learners (ensure everyone can see!)
Group work *See also part 3*	Less teacher-focused Teacher needs to monitor progress to keep on task	Suits kinaesthetic learners Weak and strong learners work collectively

▶

Activity	Value to teacher	Value to learner
	Takes a long time to extract key points	
	Several different ways of working: buzz, snowball (pyramid), jigsaw group activities	
Discussion and debates	Free exchange of ideas on a given topic	Allows ideas to be shared and is an opportunity to value other learners' opinions
	Needs careful management to ensure range of ideas and to keep on task	Suits auditory learners
	Can be used to support other teaching methods	Balanced teacher/learner input
	Develops deeper understanding	
Questioning (Q&A) *See also 6.3*	Different styles of technique: can be call-out or nominated in style	Call-out style is not intimidating
	Collects ideas which can be recorded on board	Challenges learners to think
	Need to ensure everyone participates	Can develop note-taking skills and increase accuracy of learners' notes
	Good way of introducing or summarising a topic	Nominated style will ensure everyone is included in activity
	Assesses understanding of topic	Instant feedback on response
		Appeals to kinaesthetic and auditory learners
Experiential	Teacher does not control the learning, thus developing autonomy	Learners develop their own methods of gaining information
	Teacher is a facilitator	Highly learner-centred
	Can develop personal skills in communication, number and IT	Can stimulate higher ability learners and motivate less able learners

Activity	Value to teacher	Value to learner
	May allow loss of focus	Ideal for kinaesthetic learners Ideal for autonomous learners
Presentations and seminars	Similar to lectures with added dimension of learner activity Key information presented, then deeper understanding acquired through gathering of further information Highly motivational	Able to gather key information and build upon it through their own research Learners investigate their topics and present back to their peers Develops individual styles Balance of teacher and learner activities Suits all learning preferences
Simulation, role-play and practical work	Simulation used for expensive or dangerous activities Builds on previously demonstrated skills Mirrors work place practice Can be costly and time-consuming to organise; needs sufficient resources for all Needs to be carefully managed to ensure skill is practised accurately Some learners may feel self-conscious Will promote and develop safe and healthy practice	Opportunity to practise skills Ideal for kinaesthetic and visual learners Can experience emotions, feel, taste and smell Reinforces previous learning Can learn from teachers, support workers or peers
Games/ quizzes	Develops competitive spirit Can be used to open or close a topic	Fun activity Suits kinaesthetic learners

▶

Activity	Value to teacher	Value to learner
	Useful to keep as a contingency plan 'if time allows' or 'if you work well'	
Research-style activities	Teacher is a facilitator or resource rather than leader of learning Promotes independence in learners	Suits visual and kinaesthetic learners
Case study	Develops higher levels of understanding of a topic Develops problem-solving capabilities Develops critical thinking	Enables learners to develop opinions and ideas from a given set of facts 'Safe' analysis which may impact on later application

Your second rule of teaching should be VARIETY

Variety in teaching and learning will ensure that your sessions are meeting individuals' preferences and needs and are addressing different spans of attention, as well as being interesting for you and your learners. Variety in methodology will also have the effect of helping to differentiate learning. By using a balance of teacher- and learner-centred activities you spread the responsibility of learning. Too many new teachers believe that they should 'perform' for the entire session; all they do is exhaust themselves to a usually passive (and possibly bored) group of learners. In the same way that you would integrate theory and practice whenever possible, intersperse passive and active learning activities – so that everyone benefits from a rest during the session!

The basic strategy for every session should be a beginning, middle and an end. This will form the structure, and will also help when you come to plan and prepare for your sessions. By following this structure you will be demonstrating an organised approach to teaching and learning. This should be the basis of role modelling for your learners; indirectly it will organise them and this will also help in managing the classroom atmosphere. Adhering to the boundaries and rules that you and your learners create as acceptable behaviours will strengthen the structure of your session.

Simple structures

	WHY	WHAT	HOW
Beginning	The introduction Explain what is going to happen in the session Setting the scene	For example: Verbal exposition (VE) Questioning – to check previous knowledge	Teacher-centred intro. Aims on board and spoken (auditory/visual) Collect any homework. Prompt and organised start, set any rules now Use a starter activity to engage learners immediately
Middle	The content Move from the known to the unknown Give clear instruction on how the activity will progress/ time allowed	For example: Demonstration + practical Verbal Exposition + discussion + game E-clip + activity Group and individual activities	Balance of teacher/ learner activity. Learner-dominated activities. Meet Auditory, visual and kinaesthetic needs Maintain discipline and appropriate behaviours
End	Assessment of what has been learned Conclusions and summary	For example: Discussion/ evaluation Quiz or Q&A	Learner-centred. Opportunity to complete notes Corrections provide future notes

▶

WHY	WHAT	HOW
Consolidation Future development Bridge to next session.	Ending in VE – prep or bridge to next session.	Some teacher-centred aspects to conclude. Use a plenary activity to measure progress Issue homework or VLE activities Feedback on learning acquisition, praise good behaviour

Meeting learner preferences

In order to ensure that you are meeting individuals' preferences and needs you need to create variety. This variety will also provide opportunities to meet your learners' learning preferences. Given that learners like to learn either by listening, looking or doing, by including visual, auditory and kinaesthetic teaching and learning strategies (see also Parts 2 and 3), you will automatically create some variety and therefore interest. The lists detail some ideas about how you can modify your teaching sessions, to add variety and meet learner preferences:

Learning techniques suited to those who prefer to learn visually

- Use cards, posters and prompt sheets
- Display session tasks on board
- Write key words on board
- Collate ideas from group activities on board or flip chart
- Supplement verbal exposition with pictures and diagrams

- Ask questions which exploit visual imagination: 'What would it look like?'
- Encourage learners to 'see' words/concepts in their mind
- Use highlighter pens to annotate work
- Use a glossary of terms in a vocabulary book or poster
- Vary colour, font style/size in visual aids in learners' hand-outs
- Use mnemonics
- Number sentences or bullet points

Learning techniques suited to those who learn by listening and speaking

- Listen to learners (teacher and peers)
- Talk through ideas on posters, boards, hand-outs
- Ask questions which exploit auditory skills: 'What does it sound like?'
- Introduce new words through language games
- Give thinking time in group activities
- Use musical connections to words (sing alphabet, use rhyme)

Learning techniques suited to learners preferring movement (kinaesthetic)

- Use breaks/pauses to get learners moving, even within the room
- Locate different activities in different parts of the room
- Use role play or practical activities
- Put words on cards to be sorted into types
- Write letters on cards to make words
- Use Post-It™ notes to record questions in lectures or demonstrations
- Ask questions which exploit kinaesthetic skills: 'What did it feel like?'
- Provide opportunities for learners to do things

The learning environment

The learning environment is any area in which teaching and learning takes place. This may be a classroom, a workshop, a lecture theatre or the workplace. The learning environment is not just limited to a space and equipment; it includes the atmosphere that creates a suitable learning setting. Teachers and learners will have experienced a variety of previous situations; those that are traditional in nature, full of teacher-led activities and learners taught in rows. The opposite, and more favourable route, is that of an engaging environment, i.e. that which is less formal, modern and interactive. The table compares these two environments.

Comparison of traditional and engaging learning environments	
Traditional learning environment	*Engaging learning environment*
Passive learners	Active learners
Learners absorb information	Learners interact with information
Insular learning style	Collaborative learning style
Same ability groups	Mixed ability groups
Teacher-centred	Learner-centred
Isolated themes	Integrated themes
Routine and predictable teaching	Innovative and exciting teaching
Discrete provision	Differentiated provision

The learning environment is within the power of the teacher to control. By choosing teaching and learning activities that empower learners to learn, a teacher will motivate learners and as a result they will achieve. Some of these factors are forced upon us due to funding and economic reasons. For example, the need to keep labour costs low results in different ability levels within the session groups, hence the need to meet individual needs in a group. Some factors arise from changes in thinking and technological developments. A teacher needs to accept these challenges and not create their own barriers to teaching (and learning).

The learning environment should meet the needs of individuals and of the chosen teaching strategies. Before the session starts the teacher should consider how they are going to teach during the session and arrange the furniture in an appropriate manner. Some of the options available for a 'taught' session are:

Desks or tables in rows

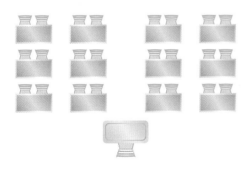

A very traditional arrangement. Suitable for lecture-style presentations, when learners need to focus on the front of the room. Not suited to any session where interaction between learners is needed. When learners enter the room, they usually head for the back row, which may cause problems when delivering a session.

Desks or tables in a U shape

A modern arrangement although not very good utilisation of space. Suitable when learners need to see the front but also need to engage in discussion with others. The teacher can easily reach learners to support

activities although the tables may still form a barrier. The teacher should be mindful that learners sitting towards the open ends of the 'u' may be in peripheral vision and therefore may be forgotten!

Desks or tables in a central block (boardroom style)

Ideal for group work, or when learners need space to arrange large pieces of work or games. Learners become the focus because the teacher is outside of the group, unless they sit down at the same table and become part of the group.

Desks or tables in small clusters (cabaret style)

Ideal for small group activities, such as discussion or jigsaw sessions, or as a way of arranging different activities within a single room space. Seating position may be uncomfortable if learners have backs to the front of the room.

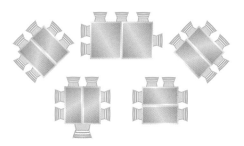

Chairs in a U shape

Ideal for group discussions. Suits very informal sessions, such as those in counselling-type discussions. The teacher either forms part of the group or sits outside of the group as an observer. The teacher can refocus the group by using equipment at the front of the room and the absence of tables removes barriers.

Chairs in rows (theatre style)

Very formal in style. Ideal for presentations and lectures where note-taking and discussion is not required. If questions from the floor are allowed, the teacher will have to repeat questions or use a microphone to ensure everyone can hear.

Chairs around the edge of the room (open style)

Ideal when space is required for role play or active learning strategies. Small groups can perform in front of peers.

In all of the room arrangements, the teacher should remember the health and safety of themselves and others. Tables can be heavy to shift around without the help of others, and there is always the matter of what to do with spare furniture when rearranging a room. You should always put the furniture back to its original position at the end of the session, so some teaching time will be lost in the session. Also, the teacher should consider where learners are to put their coats and bags, how learners will move safely around the room and how those with mobility problems will cope. You should also remember that those with visual impairment may have learnt the room layout and changes will disorientate them. Whilst changing a layout has advantages and health and safety issues can be overcome, always prepare learners for a change. You can either tell them that the room will look differently next week because … or get them involved in the change, explaining why it is necessary. Do not underestimate the feelings of learners.

The size and shape of the room will impact on how the room can be arranged and the types of learning activity that can be undertaken. Rooms are usually allocated by others in your organisation, but if your learner numbers increase beyond what is acceptable, or the room is not suitable for the teaching activities or resources you need, it is worth asking to change rooms, even if only on a temporary basis.

A learning environment should be suitable for learning. Learning will only occur in relaxed and familiar surroundings. The teacher must also consider factors such as temperature and light (Maslow). In a hot room, learners will become sluggish and tire easily. In a cold room, they will be concentrating on trying to get warm. Find out where the thermostat is, or where the remote control for the air conditioning is, or how the windows open. The amount of light needed will vary according to activity. A beauty treatment salon may need muted light, but the artist needs plenty of natural light. You might need to dim the lights to make visual aids more visible or add light to write notes. Where is the light switch?

CASE STUDY EXAMPLE

For many weeks the learners have been attending their session in a particular room, and they will probably have claimed their seat. It will be next to their friend and certainly in a comfortable position. They will always sit there. It is their space!

Move the room around before they arrive and just watch. What do you see?

What you might see is the panic in their faces! They are uncomfortable and do not like it. They will be suspicious and reluctant to participate. If it is an examination period, they will immediately lose any self-confidence they had.

Carefully chosen teaching strategies with good resources in a comfortable environment are the key ingredients to a successful and effective teaching and learning session.

Strategies to motivate learners

Don't smile till Easter!

This was once believed to be the absolute motivator; fair, firm and focused sessions without deviation. However, this is not the 1960s and the current thinking in the education and training sector is empathy, understanding and negotiation. Irrespective of your opinions with regard to these two strategies, the teacher remains the initiator of learning and to do this you need a willing and receptive audience, i.e. learners who are motivated, be that either intrinsically or extrinsically. You the teacher, also need to be motivated; motivated to make a difference in someone's life. Motivation is concerned with the learner's desire (or need) to participate in the learning process (see previous chapter on motivation theories and concepts). The easiest motivator a teacher has in their repertoire is the ability to communicate. This might be in informal words of encouragement or full blown constructive feedback on performance – or any stage in between; it might be a quiet pep talk or a disciplinary, but the power of communication as a motivator should never be underestimated.

To improve motivation, the teacher should:

- Ensure that the learning environment is comfortable (temperature, light, furniture), safe and business-like.
- Ensure that breaks are regular to allow food and refreshments to be consumed. It may be worth noting here that parental support may be needed to encourage younger learners to get enough sleep and eat breakfast before commencing their learning day. Note also that some foods and drinks have been proven to have a detrimental effect on learning and behaviour.
- Create a good rapport with learners. Learning is a shared responsibility in so far as the learner will allow it to be so.
- Devise classroom rules for attendance, behaviour, conduct and assessment, etc.
- Know your learners. Devise teaching strategies which are of interest to them and are learner-centred.

- Explain the purpose of the session, creating an organised and structured learning environment.
- Plan for variety.
- Create short-term targets which are achievable. Consider incentives to reward achievement.
- Consider the assumptions you make and be prepared to challenge them.
- Ensure learners are ready to learn.
- Be prepared to help learners with 'how to learn' skills.
- Support those who are struggling; offer challenges to those who are more able. Keep everyone busy.
- Praise success.
- Give interim feedback in a constructive manner.
- Encourage learners to identify their own goals and have ownership of their own development.
- Recognise that motivation may cause anxiety and that will also need to be dealt with.

By creating a motivational culture, the art of teaching is made easier. However, you must also expect occasional lapses. These barriers are explained in detail in Part 3, but in summary may typically occur when learners are influenced by:

- Peer pressure and group dynamics.
- Hormonal imbalance/physical health.
- Changes in personal or domestic surroundings.
- Work/life imbalance.

Participation and engagement in learning

Participation and engagement is essential in the inclusive classroom. Every teacher should question the extent to which *all* learners commit to contributing in sessions.

Some ideas about how to ensure full and equal participation are:

Differentiated outcomes To ensure that every learner progresses to the maximum in a session, you will need to vary the extent to which you plan learning. In terms of outcomes you may find that in every session you have a number of learning outcomes that everyone will achieve (irrespective of their ability, but related to the learning outcomes of their qualification or goal). However, a number may be able to extend this to slightly deeper knowledge and a few will work to really high-order skills (see Bloom, Parts 2 and 7). This is expressed as: by the end of the session, all learners will be able to…, most learners will be able to…, and some learners will be able to…

Nominated questioning This is teacher-led questioning and aims to ensure that everyone has the opportunity to answer questions. It uses a technique of posing a question, pausing, whilst learners think of the answer, and finally nominating a learner to offer the answer. To ensure that you remember to ask everyone a question, try things like learners' names in a hat (a hard hat in a construction session, a chef's hat in catering) or names on lolly sticks. Or collect your learners name badges and pick them randomly; this is a good way to check they have them with them without a ritualistic 'have you got your ID?' Online sites such as Triptico (www.triptico.co.uk) offer resources to aid learner interaction (some free resources, subscription required for full use) and random name selection.

Differentiated tasks To ensure each learner can succeed and achieve to the best of their ability. Vary the type of task according to the level of support, stretch and challenge the learner requires.

Jigsaw, snowball (pyramid) group work Different types of activities to encourage everyone to contribute to a discussion point and be listened to. Jigsaw activities are those where different groups have different questions, the teacher then consolidates the discussion and findings to ensure everyone is aware of concepts. Snowball (also known as pyramid) is a group activity which starts in individual thought; shared with a partner; shared with another pair, until a group consensus is formed.

Buzz groups These activities are used to consolidate individual thoughts which are transcribed, usually by the teacher, onto a board. Use a 'play or pass' strategy with learners each contributing one thought from their list until their lists (thoughts) are exhausted. You could try variations such as a 'graffiti wall', where learners write their ideas on sections of plain wallpaper which is fastened to the wall – they may use words or pictures to express their thoughts. Or try drawing a brick on an A4 sheet and photocopying it, then issue it to learners so that they can write their thoughts onto the bricks. They can then be fastened to the wipe-board as a wall of ideas and discussed by the group.

Gapped hand-outs and worksheets Instead of just stuffing a hand-out into a file, a learner has to **interact** with it. This helps personal note-taking skills which helps with retention of knowledge. Different types or levels of hand-out can be designed to differentiate between learner needs.

Quizzes and games A fun way of learning. Scrabble is good for spelling and competitiveness can be introduced by organising team Scrabble with extra points for a specialist word. Word-searches, crosswords and Sudoku are good as starter activities, plenaries or while waiting for others to catch-up, and to help development of functional skills. A paper dice can be made to initiate questions as recap or session summaries, and is far more interesting than a test.

ACTIVITY 2

Learner interaction

Ask a colleague or your mentor to analyse your interactions with learners.

A simple mark (/) chart next to a learner's seating position will record the number of times a learner contributes to the session, either by comment, answering a question or asking a question (See Figure 6D).

For example:

| Figure 6D | Interacting with your learners |

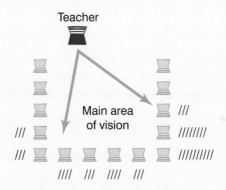

Look at the contact within the main area of vision

Reflection:
What did the results tell you?
How will you modify your practice in light of the results?

Some of the watch points will be:

- Those seated in direct eye contact will participate more than those on the periphery of your vision – so make conscious decisions to include those seated on the edges or hiding in the back row by using nominated questioning or by direct intervention when organising groups.

- Less confident or lazy learners will soon realise that keeping their heads down will not create eye contact and that there is always someone eager to answer questions.
- Reduce the number of 'open to group' questions and develop nominated questions (i.e., pose the question, pause for a few seconds, then nominate your chosen learner to respond).

Delivering inclusive learning

In terms of teaching and learning, this is where we are empowered to most effect. We can control what we do and to a certain extent what our learners do and can achieve. In the previous sections, we have considered how to make our sessions more inclusive, but we can also modify our teaching style and methods, our resources and our assessment techniques either as the programme or session progresses or to become routinely inclusive. Some general inclusive learning strategies that you can try are:

Teaching and learning preferences Ensure that every session includes methods that appeal to visual, auditory and kinaesthetic learning preferences. Follow a structured style – introduction, middle and an end, with a balanced amount of teacher talk and plenty of things to look at and do. Look out for who is making the contributions in the session and make a conscious effort to ensure that all learners take part in the session. Support your less able learners and stretch the imagination of the gifted ones. Vary activities and make learning fun! Use different outcomes and/or assessment activities to differentiate need.

Resources – paper-based learning aids If you have to do a lot of talking, create a hand-out for your visual learners to follow. Better still; make it interactive for your kinaesthetic learners by requiring words to be inserted or questions to be considered. Try an interactive PowerPoint presentation – the teacher's presentation includes all of the facts, but the learners' printed hand-outs have a modified copy with words, numbers, etc. missed out, so although they are following teacher talk, supported by PowerPoint, they also have something to do – therefore meeting all VAK types. Other paper-based activities include self-study packs that provide either catch-up, extra help for those that need help or those that can extend learning or revision uses. Resources to use as starters, fillers or plenary activities include word search, crossword or quiz-word or matching games.

Resources – font type and presentation Use at least a 14 point font, larger in display formats such as PowerPoint. Use a clear font style such as Arial, Tahoma or *Comic Sans*. These plain *sans serif* styles are good. Fonts such as Harrington, *handwriting styles*, or Old English are not very legible, because they are too fussy. I particularly like fonts that represent the letter a as 'a', because I think it is easier on the eyes. Whilst on the subject, blue print on pale yellow paper is quite easy on the eyes – but I appreciate that photocopiers are not generally set up for this, so you may wish to experiment, especially if a learner is suffering from eye strain. Avoid a justified text as it distributes words unevenly across the page. When developing study skills with your learners you should also advocate a similar set of rules for when your learners present their word processed work to you for marking – it helps your eyes as well!

The Royal Institute for the Blind publishes a Clear Print Guideline, which is very informative and is available at http://www.rnib.org.uk/xpedio/ groups/public/documents/publicwebsite/public_printdesign.hcsp.

Accommodation Prepare the room for the activities to be completed in the session, think about what you will be doing and what your learners are expected to do. Different types of group work require alterations to the room layout. You may need to include provision for wheelchair users – which could be height adjustable benches, tables or workstations, or just space to move around safely in the classroom.

Support There are two main providers of support in the classroom; those initiated by the teacher and those delivered directly by the teacher. (See also Part 1). Differentiation is not just the ability to provide support in the form of a Learning Support Assistant, but can include documents to support study. The most common types are assignment frames, writing frames or research frames. Each of these 'frames' has the ability to set questions which will help focus learners' ideas and structure work. They are especially useful when supporting independent learners.

Initiated by the teacher	Delivered by the teacher
Use of Learning Support Assistants (LSAs) to support individuals and/or groups Learning Mentors LRC (Library) Assistive technology Examination support	Modified teaching, learning and assessment methods Modified resources Study aids Use of VLE Homework activities

Assessment In the same way that teaching and learning is differentiated to meet everyone's needs it follows that assessment must also do so. It is too easy to forget that this is also something which needs to be considered, especially as many assessments are prescribed or pre-set by the Awarding Organisations. Any learner receiving learning support can usually apply for special arrangements in any kind of test or timed examination.

Some further ideas include:

● Verbal questioning can be differentiated using nominated styles.
● Written question sheets can include a mixture of multiple-choice questions, yes/no type and short answer type in the same test.
● Homework and class-work assessments could be varied to include things for all learner types:
  – *Visual learners* like to write in bullet points and use images; labelling things; making posters or booklets.
  – *Auditory learners* like to verbalise their answers; write essays; do research.
  – *Kinaesthetic learners* like to make things; do role play; presentations.

See Part 5 for additional notes on differentiating assessment.

In summary, delivering an inclusive learning package means considering what is appropriate and needed. It is a balance of activities, using support staff and guidance to ensure that everyone who wants to access learning can do so, and those who do not usually feel comfortable in accessing learning are confident that your organisation will meet their needs and aspirations.

Managing the learning environment

The teacher is the person in charge of the classroom

This may seem obvious, but you would be surprised to see how often it does not seem to be so. Enabling learners to learn in a safe environment is one of Maslow's themes. Thinking more widely than Health and Safety requirements, managing learning can also be associated with behaviour and is therefore referred to when dealing with younger (i.e. under 19-years-old) learners, although not limited to younger learners. However, managing the learning environment is broader than safety and behaviour; it is about creating a climate conducive to learning. As well as the mechanics of teaching and learning, this will include the classroom rules, the layout, the rapport between teacher and learners, the atmosphere and dynamics. Whereas the teacher can easily manage the former, the latter is less easy to control. It is the point at which teaching stops being a science and becomes an art!

Remembering our rule about assumption, all learners are entitled to and will always demand a well-managed environment. The teacher is the one who, as well as teaching in a well prepared, varied, inspirational and exciting manner, addressing the needs of every individual in their group:

- Keeps control of learners
- Maintains the immediate cleanliness and tidiness of the room
- Cleans the boards
- Reports broken or dangerous equipment or furniture

- Ensures a safe and secure learning environment
- Prepares for any/all eventualities
- Is a role model for acceptable standards of behaviour
- Develops learners
- Sets and secures agreement to codes of conduct
- Ensures security is maintained
- Keeps an eye on the clock
- Determines the frequency and duration of breaks
- Offers guidance, support and counselling services.

If all of this happens, the teacher can consider themselves the 'person in charge'. By putting all of these factors together, the learners will learn in a manner designed to get the best and most efficient learning available. Conversely, try to avoid encouraging a culture of blame and despondency:

'It was a mess when I walked in' or 'It was already broken'. Not the cries of a teenager, but a 'professional' teacher.

'The learners are getting worse' – or are they just unsure of the boundaries and nobody guides them into classroom or learning readiness?

'What time can we have a break?' – usually asked within 30 seconds of the learners entering the classroom, and repeated at two minute intervals.

'The management need to see ...' You might ask yourself exactly what it is you want *them* to see?

And the classic 'I haven't got time to ...'

The main issues in managing a learning environment can be classified into five sections:

1 managing the classroom
2 managing poor behaviour
3 managing punctuality
4 managing the workload and
5 creating learning readiness.

Managing the classroom	
Potential issues	*Possible solutions*
Tables and chairs in a mess	Allow a few minutes at the end of the session to put chairs under tables. Set the standard.
Rubbish everywhere	Insist culprits pick up rubbish and place it in the bin. If the session has created rubbish allow clearing up time at the end.
Writing on board	Clean the board at the end of the session – set an example.
Something broken or damaged	Ensure danger does not impact on your learners and report issues to the site team, admin staff or line manager. Never assume someone has already reported it.
Coats and bags lying around	Identify and instruct learners to place bags etc. in a particular place.
Ambience of room	Display learner work to create a sense of ownership and introduce a colourful area. Change displays regularly. Remove clutter. Keep it tidy and encourage learners to participate in this process.
Promoting respect and independence	Treat learners as individuals. Classroom conversations should be appropriate, and as would be expected in polite society. Encourage listening. Develop thinking skills; give time for reflection. Insist on activities outside of the classroom to develop learning, e.g. homework, LRC, VLE use.

Hint:

Always leave a room as you would wish to find it. Speak to learners as you wish to be spoken to.

Managing poor behaviour
'It's war out there'
'They're out to get you'
Sue Cowley (2003: 52, 83)

Potential issues

- Learners talking at the same time as you
- Confrontational behaviour
- Learners refuse to work
- Learners don't come to sessions ready to work
- Phones/iPods on etc.
- Lack of respect.

Possible solutions

Remember that learners have opted to behave in this way. You can cope!

Keep calm; be clear about what you expect by setting targets; reward good behaviour, ignore bad; be consistent; have plenty of short, varied activities; keep supplies of pens/paper; use silence or counting strategies to gain their attention, identify sanctions and rewards and initiate them when using the 'do or else' speech.

There are two stages to dealing with poor behaviour. First you should try:

1 Patience and nurturing. Setting standards by role modelling and listening to reasons, yet setting and agreeing targets and rewards. For example 'If you write (set amount), you can (listen to music for x minutes/go to break/talk).' You may wish to try peer involvement – getting the group to design and agree the rules and suggest collective responsibility for adhering to them.

2 As a last resort start the 'warning cycle'. Issue a warning, then warn again with what will happen if non-compliant; a repeat means that you should follow through with the sanction (penalty). The level of sanction should reflect the seriousness of the misdemeanour.

Never look scared or argue and never shout or swear. Be assertive not aggressive. Remember 'The Look' – you know the one that says 'beware'. If you still have problems, ask a colleague to observe you and offer suggestions.

Choose your battles wisely – work on the behaviours that will result in success and improvements, and then some of the lesser poor behaviours will follow (see also Chapter 6).

Managing punctuality

Potential issues	Possible solutions
Learners arrive late	First of all consider the impact this has on you, the late learner and the rest of the group. This will influence the action needed.
Do you set a good example by *always* being in the classroom before the time the learners are expected?	Challenge – why are you late?
	Answer – bus, family, doctors, ugh!
Do you permit the latecomer to disrupt the session? Worse still, do you encourage lateness by starting the session again, so they can catch up!	The answer determines the action, but you should do the challenge quickly, and not allow the interruption to impact on the rest of the group. Ask the late learner to settle quickly and ignore it until an appropriate time. Then elicit more info and deal with it appropriately.
	Occasional lateness by someone who quietly enters, says sorry and settles just requires acknowledgement and no further action other than an explanation of what was missed and a target to catch up.
	The ugh! is showing disrespect and if continuous and disruptive you need to follow the warning cycle (a warning, warning and sanction issue, then sanction implementation).

Managing the workload

Potential issues	Possible solutions
Coping with mixed abilities in group sessions	Know your learners and plan for differentiation. (VAK, varied activities and resources, different tasks.)
Time	Prioritise your work and keep a 'to do' list. Set yourself targets and if someone asks you to do something, be realistic in telling

▶

Managing the workload	
	them when it will be done. Better to work like this than be known as unreliable.
Session preparation	Allow time to do photocopying, printing, etc., always have contingency plans in case an electrical/technological piece of equipment doesn't work.
Marking	If you set classwork or homework, you must be prepared to collect it in and mark it promptly with feedback. Try marking work sheets in the session using nominated questioning, swapping papers or issuing answer sheets to prevent the need to take it away from the room.
Disruptive learners or colleagues	You will never change the behaviour of another person, but you can change the way *you* deal with them. Try using strategies like repeat, recap, writing things down, asking for clarification or further explanation. This helps you to take control of the situation.
Organisation	Keep a diary. Note when you promise to do something. Record when marking needs to be returned or sessions must be prepared. List when deadlines are.

Creating readiness to learn	
Potential issues	*Possible solutions*
Learners do not know how to behave in the classroom. Issues around: • attendance, punctuality • meeting targets	The teacher has to teach these skills (in addition to the content of their subject). Much will be done by role modelling, some by spoon-feeding and some by 1:1 tutorials to set targets.

Creating readiness to learn	
• paper and pens • respecting others • being responsible for themselves and others • planning their own learning • handing in work on time • listening • factual comprehension/ retention • independence.	Rules and boundaries are important here to set the standard. You may need to bring a supply of paper and pens to stop the disruption of 'I can't do it because …'. Guide learners into making notes by devising hand-outs with white space. Encourage learners to reflect on what they have achieved at the end of the session and target their own learning in workshops. Support learners to progress to the next stage of their learning journey – e.g. HE, employment, next level.

Glossary of terms

Analysis a detailed examination

Autonomous learner one who requires minimal guidance from the teacher

Blended learning a mixture of traditional and modern/computer-based learning technologies

Buzz group activities small groups interact with the teacher to gather answers

Empowered   given responsibility for something

Engagement connecting with learning; being busy

Facilitator one who supports or stimulates learning

Ice-breaker   an activity used to introduce learners to each other

ICT Information communication technology

ILT Information learning technology

Interact to have an effect on

Intervention an interruption

IT Information technology

Jigsaw group activities small groups discuss different themes within a topic, which are collated by the teacher at the end of the activity

Justified text even distribution of words across the page within fixed margins

Learning preferences the individual's favoured way of learning

Motivation enthusiasm or interest

Participation to take part in

Plenary a conclusion, ending or summary of a period of learning

Rapport a common understanding

Recreational learning a skill for pleasure

Snowball (pyramid) group activities pairs discuss then form gradually larger groups to gain a consensus of opinion on a topic or subject

Starter activity a short activity at the start of sessions to set scene, create learning ethos and engage learners quickly

Teaching to impart knowledge or a skill; what the teacher does during the session

VAK/VARK visual, auditory (read/write) and kinaesthetic learning preferences – different ways learners like to learn

VLE virtual learning environment

Vocational relating to learning the skills of an occupation

 SUMMARY

In this chapter we set out to achieve the following outcomes:

- To establish methods of identifying need in order to create an inclusive learning environment.
- To identify learning activities and list factors that can motivate learners to engage in learning.
- To select appropriate teaching and learning strategies.

- To identify and select relevant resources and suggest ways of modifying them to meet individual needs of learners.
- To state the importance of the environment in relation to learning.
- To explain ways of creating successful learning environments through effective management of the classroom.

Your personal development

You have explored how the teacher needs to manage their environment and considered some strategies which may improve your own classroom management.

You can explain how poor behaviour impacts on the session and describe some potential solutions. You can describe ways in which you will prepare your learners to be ready for learning.

You will have had the opportunity to compare many different types of teaching and learning methods and resources and consider how they will be used in your learning sessions.

You will have understood the need for variety to minimise boredom, increase motivation and meet the different needs of your learners and how your teaching, the environment and your resource choices influence this.

You can now recognise barriers and challenges to learning and devise ways to use teaching and learning methods, resources and personal skills to minimise them, resulting in learners who are eager to learn.

Finally, you have looked around you to check if the area in which you work is suitable for learning and provides an engaging and stimulating environment.

Part seven

Principles and theories

This part and chapters relate to the learning outcomes in the following Units of Assessment:

- Theories, principles and models in education and training.
- Developing teaching, learning and assessment in education and training.

The learning outcomes relating to evaluation, reflection and professional/personal development are dealt with in Part 8 and the learning outcomes relating to your development of the minimum core are in Part 9.

CHAPTER 18

Principles and theories of learning and motivation

LEARNING OBJECTIVES

The measurable outcomes that you will achieve by reading this chapter and completing the activities are:

....

- To state the difference between a principle and a theory
- To list the main schools of learning theory
- To identify the main factors influencing principles and theories
- To establish the links between principles and theories
- To analyse how principles underpin the planning and delivery of learning

Principles and theories

Every time you walk into the classroom you have a set of values and beliefs that you aspire to achieve. These may be as simple as always stating your aims and outcomes at the start of the class, always allowing time at the end of the session to consolidate what has been achieved or maybe you will always give verbal feedback or praise to learners after they complete an activity. These, and many others, are what we call principles. They are the core priorities in your teaching life; you will not deliberately compromise your delivery if it means that your principles cannot be achieved. There are no right or wrong ideas when it comes to values and principles. The detail of the principle will change; the curriculum, the type of learner, the time of day will vary the idea, but generally the main ethos will remain.

There are Principles *for* Learning which relate to accessibility of learning, diversity, inclusion, personalised learning and developmental learning. There are Principles *of* Learning – which are the usual values a teacher takes into the classroom – as described above.

A theory is something which either attempts or has been proven to explain something. Some of the theories we've seen before include Kolb, Maslow and Berne. These will be revisited in this section as they are used to explain some of the principles of learning, and you will be introduced to some new ones. Many of the theories we still find valuable today were developed in the last century, some as long as one hundred years ago. They remain useful to the teacher as a way of developing an understanding of why and how things we do today work. Some teachers do what they do because it seems the right thing to do at the time; they are intuitive, some need to understand the meaning of things to effectively and confidently review their practice. This difference (between the teacher's style), can also be linked to theories, particularly those associated with learning preferences.

In a nutshell therefore, a principle is a value, belief or ethic relating to something you do and the theory is that which explains why it works.

The learning theories

The psychology of learning is very complex, so this overview is simplified for the purpose of trying to compare, contrast and understand the ideas in the context of teaching and learning in today's classrooms. There are three main schools of theory relating to the study of human behaviour, in this case, teachers and learners.

The Behaviourist School

The Cognitivist School

The Humanist School

Others you may come across are:

- Neo-behaviourists – modern theorists advocating behaviourist theories, but adding that the learning must be driven by goals and targets.
- Gestaltists – The main thrust of Gestaltist thinking in terms of learning is that it is based on the notion of insight. The school advocates understanding the whole in order to have a better perception; Gestaltists like to see the big picture in order to assimilate information and therefore like to learn with large or long-term targets. Founded by Wertheimer (1880–1943), Köhler (1887–1967) and Koffka (1886–1941), they are an off-shoot of the Humanist school, totally rejecting behaviourist theories.

Each 'school of thought' attempts to explain why people behave in a particular way. It is not, however, without fuzzy edges. Rarely does one person, teacher or classroom scenario fall completely within one particular school of thought. It is therefore useful to have an overarching awareness of the theories in order to make sense of what is going on in the here and now.

Behaviourist school

This school of thought believes that people respond to things around them. Behaviour is learned from things seen around them or from the environment, or that individuals respond to stimuli and that learning and the ability to learn requires a change in behaviour. Learning is mechanistic. The behaviourist school, however, does not explain things like problem-solving. Other critics also comment that the early research was based on animal behaviour and that humans are not animals, they are more complex. Others criticise the belief that humans just respond, they believe that humans will think. A behaviourist's belief seems to relate to a passive learner who merely reacts to teaching rather than a trait that responds and contributes more actively.

Main exponents of the behaviourist school:

I. P. Pavlov (1849–1936) – a Russian whose research into the digestive system revealed that dogs could associate food with a sound and respond by salivating, thus was initiating the idea of 'classical conditioning'.

S. Freud (1856–1939) – instigated the suggestion of intuitive behaviours and opened up research into personalities and development.

J. B. Watson (1878–1958) – an American who challenged Freud's opinions and produced a further work associated with 'classical conditioning' which stated that people are not born with instincts and will react in a particular way to something through reflex actions. Things that don't work will not be repeated but successful actions will be. He gave rise to the concept of 'trial and error': that human reactions are the result of experiences.

E. L. Thorndike (1874–1949) – produced his 'Law of Effect', which stated that satisfaction serves to strengthen responses to stimuli. He extended the work of Watson and found that animals sought effective outcomes to achieve their goals. He made a significant contribution to the school of behaviourist theories.

Neo-behaviourists include:

B. F. Skinner (1904–1990) – is well known for developing the notion of 'operant conditioning' in which behaviour is a response to previous experience, praise or punishment. Again, this research was carried out with animals and applied to humans. In 1971 he stated the idea that free will is an illusion, it is the stimulus that causes the reaction; or in teaching terms, learners need to be trained to achieve desired or appropriate behaviours. Using Skinner, learning is phased into smaller chunks. He sparked controversy by arguing that cognitive and humanist theories were contributing to the poorer performance in American schools and that 'teachers must learn how to teach' (Skinner 1984). His work was instrumental to the development of programmed learning and it could be argued as a rationale and justification for the emergence of resource-based learning, now more commonly known as e-learning.

A. Bandura (1977) – developed behavioural frameworks and linked behaviour to cognition, moving from the idea of 'trial and error' to 'observation and imitation'. The notion of observation and imitation led into his work concerning influences that shape a person's self-efficacy (effectiveness) and the critical nature of this in terms of self-confidence and motivation.

From our examples of principles, listed in the first paragraph, 'you will always give verbal feedback or praise to learners after they complete an activity', is an example of a principle which would be proven to be effective using behaviourist thinking. This is because the repetition of the task will consistently apply, therefore learners will wait (and expect) the feedback and ultimately will work better at the merest hint of feedback from the teacher, or because they know if they do work hard, they will gain their reward of feedback.

Cognitivist school

The cognitivists believe that learning is a process of acquiring knowledge through thought, senses and experience. This school challenges the behaviourist's beliefs, not just because most of the behaviourist's research was based on animals, but because the cognitivists felt that 'knowledge' was missing in a stimulus model. They

argue that humans have a more complex psyche and that the
behaviourist's research is limited because it assumes that the laboratory
research with animals is able to be automatically attributed to humans,
without further investigation into human idiosyncrasies. Cognitivists
recognise that humans follow mental processes – they think, remember
and process information, and that this information is stored for future
use in both the short- and long-term memories. Sensory models such as
'brain-theory' and 'brain-gym' have emerged from the cognitivist school.
These models attempt to explain the impact that the different sides of
the brain have on learning and how knowing which side of the brain is
dominant can influence learning. The left-brain provides a focus on
logical thinking, analysis, verbal skills and accuracy. The right-brain
provides a focus on perceptions, musicality, aesthetics, feeling and
creativity. There has also been recent analysis on the effects of diet and
hydration on learning (Department of Health, 2005) which concluded
that drinking water has a positive effect on learning.

Main exponents of the cognitivist school:

J. Dewey (1859–1952) – one of the founder philosophers and
psychologists who lived in an era when many were espousing their
beliefs. He believed that learning was borne from reflection and
understanding of surroundings and recognised that people had different
reasons underpinning the desire to learn (early differentiation, circa
1933). He further reinforced the teacher's influence on learning.

W. F. Brewer (in 1972) – who made a comparison between conditioned
responses and co-operation, arguing a more controlled approach to
actions and learning.

J. Piaget (1896–1980) – who is widely known for his work in analysing
the various stages of child development.

E. C. Tolman (1886–1959) – claimed by both neo-behaviourists and
cognitivists. In 1932 he made links between behaviourist and cognitive
schools, by arguing that particular scenarios demand a type of
response which will vary according to the situation, resulting in
purposeful learning and behaviour.

J. Bruner (b. 1916) – stated that there are stages in cognitive behaviours
and learning; first a person gains a piece of information, then learns if it
is transferable to other situations and, finally, checks how useful it is

before storing the information (1966). He stated some rules for instructional teaching.

D. Ausubel (b. 1918) – advocated **discovery learning**. He totally disagrees with rote learning, describing it as inconsequential.

H. Gardner (b.1943) – defined 'multiple intelligences' used to explain learning preferences. He says that teaching and learning should focus on one of seven particular forms – linguistic, logical/mathematical, musical, kinaesthetic, spatial, interpersonal and intrapersonal.

R. W. Sperry (1913–1994) – an American neuro-psychologist famous for split-brain experiments; he developed a greater understanding of left- and right-brain models of understanding cognitive learning. He earned the Nobel Prize in 1981.

C. Hannaford (1985) in the publication *Smart Moves,* initiated the brain gym concept.

From our examples of principles, listed in the first paragraph, 'allowing time at the end of the session to consolidate what has been achieved' is an example of a principle which would be proven to be effective using cognitivist thinking. This is because the act of consolidating the session enables the thinking processes to kick-in. It enables learners to decide where they are going to use or store this information for future use.

Humanist school

This is the most recent area of research and differs from others because it is the one that relates most closely to the varied behaviours of human learning. It is the least scientific of the schools, recognising the complexity and instability in life. Humanist theories argue that people need to search for meanings and need personal goals in order to develop **autonomy**, returning the learner to the centre of learning. There is a lot of focus on motivation, hence many of the theorists are better known to teachers for their work in motivation theory. Humanists put the 'art' into teaching, and advocate a very active, participative style of teaching. Teachers in a humanist school facilitate learning in a conducive learning environment.

Main exponents of the humanist school:

C. Rogers (1902–1987) – a founder of the humanist school who advocated that humans grow and become independent; they like to be accepted for who they are and valued as people. He contributed to the work on experiential learning and considers that the teacher is a facilitator of learning. His approach to learner-centred or 'autonomous' learning is based upon his ideas concerning the concept of the development of the self; that individuals construct a subjective view of what they are like based on their interactions or experiences.

A. H. Maslow (1908–1970) – considers that once basic needs are addressed people will reach their full potential and designs a model of motivational theory which impacts effectively today: Maslow's Hierarchy of Human Needs 1970.

D. Goleman (1995) – Emotional Intelligence. He argues that western learning cultures place an emphasis upon 'intellect' but should also take into consideration a person's emotional characteristics. This can form the basis of current arguments relating to the management of behaviours.

From our examples of principles, listed in the first paragraph, 'always stating your aims and outcomes at the start of the class', is an example of a principle which would be proven to be effective using humanist thinking. In this instance, letting learners know what the whole session is to be about enables them to prepare themselves for learning and feel that they are involved in that process. If they know where they are going, they see the big picture and therefore understand the purpose (Gestaltist theory).

Recommended reading

For further detailed readings about Learning Theories see Child (2004: 124–132), Fawbert (2003: 114–121), Curzon (2003: 35–121).

In the model on the next page (Figure 7A), the three schools of theory are displayed to show how the teaching styles that dominate each area shift from a very teacher-centred methodology within a behaviourist school to a very learner-centred approach in a humanist school of thought. This introduces the relationship between theories, principles and the practice of teaching.

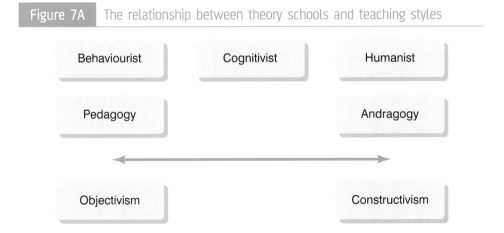

Figure 7A The relationship between theory schools and teaching styles

Factors influencing principles and theories of learning

The factors that influence learning are broadly split into:

- The model of learning (objectivism, constructivism)
- The type of learning (pedagogy, andragogy)
- The level of learning (Bloom, Gagné, surface/deep learning).

Models of learning

In teacher-centred models of learning the content is the focus of the learning. How the teacher is going to impart the subject material will lead to the ways that the content will be delivered. In a learner-centred model the focus of the session is the learner. In this case the learners and how they like or prefer to learn is the key to the chosen methods of delivery. This focal point therefore leads to decisions justifying the selection or choice of models (or styles) of teaching. This may also be influenced by the chosen learning theory (behaviourist, cognitivist, humanist) or approaches preferred by the teacher and learners.

In Figure 7B, the model shows that the content and desired outcomes influence the methods seen in the classroom and the resources that will

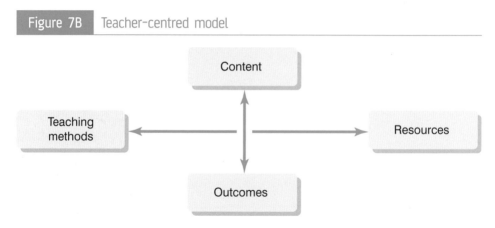

Figure 7B   Teacher-centred model

be used. In this instance the resources are more likely to be teaching aids, in order to consolidate learning. Factors that may influence choice of this method will be time and amount of content.

In the model below, Figure 7C, we see a different approach:

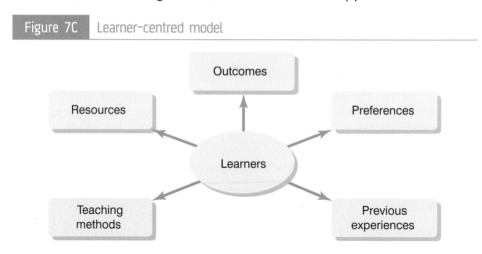

Figure 7C   Learner-centred model

In this model, the learner is at the centre of the session and is the most important person in the learning process. The methods, resources, starting points all consider the learner. It is in this style that you may see experiential and discovery types of learning.

Objectivism This is the name given to the concept that advocates a teacher-centred approach in which the teacher transmits knowledge in the form of rules and seeks for mastery in practical tasks. Rote learning (that of repetitive learning, for example: the alphabet or the times tables, to a point at which they are known automatically) typifies objectivism. The teacher takes the role of an instructor.

Constructivism In the context of teaching, this is a learner-centred method of delivery which focuses on learning that has meaning, explanations and interpretations; it develops through a continual process, modified through experience. The teacher takes on the role of a facilitator. In its truest form, individuals create their own learning; ideas are not given, they are made from experiences. This laissez-faire approach (a non-interference teaching/learning style) is the ultimate learner-centred strategy.

Types of learning

The type of learning will influence and is influenced by the type of teaching and therefore the choice of activities you and your learners do in the classroom or workplace. The choices you make when deciding how to deliver your session are broadly linked to teaching styles and learning preferences.

Pedagogy This is the name given to the skill or ability of teaching. It is predominantly concerned with teacher-centred methods and historically these passive methods of learning have been related to learning being seen as a chore. These previous poor experiences of teaching may still form barriers to learning in current times. Fortunately, most teachers now firmly believe in a more learner-focused strategy, although the name pedagogy is still attributed to teaching, especially that of teaching children. In its purest, but old-fashioned meaning, pedagogy infers an authoritative, autocratic or didactic style of teaching.

Andragogy This term is synonymous with teaching adults, although it can apply to all age groups. It means teaching in a learner-focused style using guided learning techniques and thinking skills (Dewey 1916), which are self-directed. The learning is a very active process in which the learner participates fully with their learning. The two-way shared responsibility of learning models itself on a democratic approach to teaching. It is mid-way between the autocratic and laissez-faire styles previously mentioned.

One of the most significant writers on adult learning is Malcolm Knowles (1913–1997). He made five assumptions:

- Adults move from dependency to autonomy
- Adults gain experience (in life)
- Adults are ready to learn
- Adults move from 'need to learn' to 'want to learn'
- Adults mature and become motivated.

He suggests that adults need to know why they are learning, are very self-directed, responsible, experiential and motivated. Equally, they may be slower at grasping new information or recalling existing facts, more set in their (learning) ways, and display varying levels of self-confidence. Knowles (1984) suggests that teachers 'assist' adults to learn as facilitators rather than 'teachers'. He was influenced by Rogers' humanist school of thought.

The notion of teaching adults raises an interesting debate about when a child becomes an adult. Is it measured by age, maturity or is it a particular point in the lifecycle? Whatever the answer, whilst adults are usually considered to be life experienced, opinionated and generally work autonomously (Knowles 1984), it is also not unknown for them to feel that unless they have been 'taught' and receive lots of materials to put in a folder, that they may not consider that they are making progress.

Levels of learning

The next influencing factor relates to levels of learning and will impact on the planning and delivery of your sessions.

B S Bloom, and a number of other people who worked with his ideas, categorised levels of learning into three distinct areas: Cognitive (thinking skills), Affective (attitudes, beliefs) and Psychomotor (co-ordination skills). He called them Domains. He then sub-divided them into levels, for example, simple recall or imitation type of levels (low order) through to refined, complex and transferable skills (high order). The tables demonstrate how the skills move from being low order to high order and provide some adjectives to describe the depth of learning involved at each level within the domain. See Chapter 5 about how Bloom's theories can be used in planning and differentiating learning.

Cognitive domain These are the thinking skills, at the lowest level based on being able to recall previously taught facts, moving towards thorough understanding leading to considered opinions:

Level	Taxonomy	Learners will be able to:
Low Order Skill	Knowledge	State, list, recognise, draw
	Comprehension	Describe, explain, identify
	Application	Use, apply, construct, solve
	Analysis	List, compare, contrast
	Synthesis	Summarise, argue, explain
High Order Skill	Evaluation	Judge, evaluate, criticise

Based on B.S. Bloom (1956). (Revised in 2001 – see Chapter 5)

Affective domain This relates to the attitudes or behaviours a learner develops. Again it moves from just being aware of a particular belief to a higher level in which the belief is defended and explained in detail:

Level	Taxonomy	Learners will be able to:
Low Order Skill	Receiving (being aware)	Choose, describe, use, select
	Responding (reacting)	Answer, discuss, perform, write
	Valuing (understanding)	Demonstrate, argue, debate, explain
	Organisation and Conceptualisation	Compare, contrast, generalise, modify
High Order Skill	Characterisation (behaviour)	Acts, displays, practises, solves, verifies

Based on Bloom and Krathwohl (1964).

Psychomotor domain The domain looks at the practical or motor skills involved in the learning process. Childhood development is a good example of seeing how actions are developed from copying to automatic reactions:

Level	Taxonomy	Learners will be able to:
Low Order Skill	Imitation	Repeat, copy, follow, replicate
	Manipulation	Re-create, perform, implement
	Precision	Demonstrate, complete, show
	Articulation	Solve, integrate, adapt, modify
High Order Skill	Naturalisation	Design, specify, invent

Based on R. H. Dave (1967).

Bloom argues that there are levels within a task (Taxonomy of Learning) and that the teacher can use this theory to pose questions, set learning outcomes, prepare resources or assess ability which ultimately will recognise that within any group there will be a mixture of learners who grasp the topic at different levels. This is the basic concept of differentiation – or meeting learners' individual needs.

In terms of planning this could mean creating a series of learning outcomes, for example:

- By the end of the session, all learners will be able to …
- By the end of the session, most learners will be able to …
- By the end of the session, some learners will be able to …

In assessment, you will frequently see Bloom demonstrated in the types of verbs used to express outcomes. Some Awarding Organisations use pass, merit and distinction criteria and each one is progressively more complex. For example at pass level you may see words such as explain or describe. At merit you may see analyse and at distinction you may see evaluate. This also links to the depth of knowledge required of a topic.

In questioning you might ask one learner to state a date or particular fact, yet another learner might be required to explain what it means, or another might analyse the effect it has. The questions are posed to learners, whose abilities you are familiar with, to ensure they all contribute to sessions according to their ability or are challenged to stretch or gain higher grades. This leads us to the concepts of surface and deep learning.

Surface learning This is knowledge of a topic or skill which is quite shallow. It is probably based on imitation, repeating or re-writing. There is very little understanding of the topic and usually learners can only repeat what they have been told or shown. They cannot apply the knowledge to different contexts nor argue its value against other ideas or opinions. Rote learning which might be considered surface, due to the repetitive nature of the learning, may be the exception. If I said 'nine times five', there would be a lot of shouts of 45, thus proving the value of those endless chants. The fact that those multiplication tables are then used widely in a number of more complex numerical actions, implies that the depth of knowledge is increased. Surface learning should not be confused with the academic level of learning; it is possible to learn some very complex tasks superficially.

Deep learning This is a phrase used widely to express the notion of a more complete understanding of a topic; the opposite of surface learning. It requires a greater depth of knowledge. Deep learners are usually well read in their topic. They can explain it in many different ways and argue its worth against others' opinions.

Activity 1 provides an opportunity to analyse how teachers learn aspects of their craft at different levels. Hopefully, you will discover that you have a surface learning level in all aspects of teaching, maybe with some depth in one or a few topics. The varied way in which we learn and retain information and the difference in how well we know and understand facts or information within a topic is called a 'spiky' profile. This spiky profile of knowledge is very typical of all learning and knowledge.

 ACTIVITY 1

Surface and deep learning

In this table you will see a number of activities that the teacher engages in; all are part of the curriculum for initial teacher training (ITT).

Using the column titles, analyse the depth of knowledge you have in the areas listed.

	Can recall main points of topic	Can explain many key areas of topic maybe with prompts	Can use topic in a different context or apply in a different situation	Can argue value against others' opinions; well-read/ researched
	Surface ←――――――――――――――→ Deep			
Planning and preparing sessions				
Teaching and learning methods				
Assessment for learning strategies				
Differentiating to meet learner needs				
Embedding equality and diversity				
Codes of conduct for teachers				
Reflection to improve own practice				

Biggs (1987) suggests that we use both deep and surface learning according to how much time we have, the complexity of the task and even the content of the subject. He further suggests that the quality of teaching has a direct impact on the depth of learning.

'Jack of all trades, master of none!'

We do not need (or use) everything there is to know about everything, but we do need to know a little bit about a lot of things and some things we need to know a fair bit more about, hence we all have a 'spiky' profile with regard to what we know and can do.

There is also an idea that in 'profound learning' the learning is so deep that behaviours become intuitive and are used effectively to problem-solve. West-Burnham (2005: 35) describes this as the 'why' level.

Robert Gagné in 1974 added further theories to the concept of levels of learning; however, whereas Bloom created three main divisions, Gagné suggested five main stages, devising a model of progressional learning, relating to different outcomes of learning. Rogers (2002) gave the following explanation of Gagné's work:

> 'motor skills which require practise; verbal information – facts, principles and generalisations which when organised into larger entities become knowledge; intellectual skills – the 'discrimination, concepts and rules' that help in using knowledge; cognitive strategies – the way the individual learns, remembers and thinks, the self-managed skills needed to define and solve problems; and attitudes' (p. 87).

These stages are not as distinctive as Bloom's theory suggests, because Gagné suggests that they are sequential and inter-relate; thus they are the 'conditions of learning' required to result in changes in behaviour. He also suggests that low order skills must be understood before entering his cycle of learning. Gagné follows the neo-behaviourist school's beliefs; Bloom's work links more closely to the cognitivist's views. However, together they form a platform for constructing sessions. This is because both agree and value the stages of learning development:

- move from known to unknown
- simple to complex
- example to principle; and
- concrete to abstract. (Kolb).

In this way learning develops from unnatural or stilted attempts to a natural or automatic behaviour.

The motivation theories

Whichever school of thought (Learning Theory) you are able to relate your teaching incidents to, whatever you advocate as your abiding principle, it is widely recognised that all of them will work better when the learner wants to achieve or succeed, i.e. they are motivated. Increased motivation occurs when the teacher makes a conscious decision to remove all of the barriers to learning that a learner may erect. Teaching, therefore, is a factor that influences motivation. Strategies to improve motivation and the more commonly used theories have already been described in Chapter 16.

These are summarised as:

Maslow (1970) presented his Hierarchy of Needs (see Figure 7D). In this theory he stated that in order for a person to fully achieve their goals they need to satisfy a series of needs; then, and only then, will learners be in a frame of mind which is conducive to learning:

Figure 7D   Maslow's Hierarchy of Needs (1970)

Self-actualisation

Self-esteem

Love and belonging

Safety and shelter

Physical comfort

The arguments and agreements relating to this model are those centred around **intrinsic** and **extrinsic motivation**, i.e. the factors that influence the desire to learn.

 ## ACTIVITY 2

Discussion question – motivation

Learner A

Let us imagine that you are studying for your Diploma because you have to, not because you want to; you are a reluctant learner. You are extrinsically motivated – this is because an external influence (your manager) has told you to do the course, maybe with some kind of sanction if you don't complete it.

Learner B

Let us imagine that you have signed up to complete your Diploma because you love teaching and want to find out everything there is to know about it. You are intrinsically motivated – this is because you have a personal desire to complete and value the benefits of the discussions you have with colleagues about teaching and learning.

According to Maslow, you will be more highly motivated and enthusiastic, especially if you are not hungry or thirsty and you are in comfortable surroundings. This would increase if you knew that your tutors were happy to see you, you felt part of your study or peer group and you felt valued.

Is there a difference in the level of motivation that these two learners would have?

Is Maslow correct or is there more to consider?

Why?

Discuss your feelings about these statements with your peers or in your personal/reflective learning journal.

There are a number of theories associated with rewards. In the earlier chapters you will have looked at a model of 'medal and mission' and 'vicious and virtuous circles' (Chapter 16). In these models there is a belief that if you receive praise and reward when you do well and you have a clear idea of the next goal you will be motivated to continue. Similarly, learners who receive 'positive reinforcement', may be in a behaviourist type of situation, and are motivated to a greater degree than those who constantly receive 'negative reinforcement'.

EXAMPLE

Teachers give points or rewards for good behaviours, hard work, contributions, punctuality, etc. These are collected and traded in for a treat – free coffee in the snack bar, extra printing in the Resource Centre, ten minute pass to play a computer game. This is far more motivational than a disciplinary for repeatedly arriving late for class!

Another theory associated with this type of model of motivation is McGregor's Theory X and Theory Y (1960). In this model, originally researched around the management of a workforce, McGregor argues that the teacher will make one of two assumptions about their learners' motivation levels. The learner (Theory X) will avoid work whenever possible, will need to be persuaded to work and probably has little ambition; the teacher, therefore, acts to de-motivate just by being in the same room as this learner and trying to get him or her to work by controlling and threatening. Alternatively, the learner (Theory Y), wants to learn, is eager to take responsibility for their learning and contributes positively in the classroom. In this case, the teacher acts as a motivator to realise the aspirations of a learner. It could therefore be argued that the teacher's attitudes to learners and motivation are equally as relevant as those of the learners; a teacher's perceptions will influence how they act in the classroom. An example of this is when the teacher assumes that the learners will not do any work, and is not disappointed when they don't. To overcome this, the teacher must not make assumptions (about their level of motivation) and must believe that every learner has the potential to achieve something, albeit to different levels.

There are three models of theory associated with the person which result in motivated learners. The first is Herzberg's Satisfaction Theory. His 'hygiene' factors are the basic requirements on which to build motivational theory. People need status, job security, good working conditions, etc. and then they will be more motivated, especially in conjunction with achievement, recognition, growth and interest. He believed that a learner needs to be satisfied with their work (or learning); that it is in the right environment and that they are confident of the purpose and benefit of the learning. The second is Bandura's 'Self Efficacy' model. In this model, motivation is dependent on the amount of self-belief or confidence a learner has in his or her own ability. It is the belief that a learner will aspire to the level they (the learner) thinks they can achieve, or conversely, if a learner doesn't believe they can do something then the chances are that they won't be able to! Finally, David McClelland argues that those with a need for achievement have a greater level of motivation when they are allowed to solve their own problems, rather than gaining chance results. The learner is in control of their learning and gets a 'buzz' from working out and finding solutions. This is midway between the learner who learns by chance – a gambling type of situation – and the 'conservative' learner who does not participate in any learning opportunity unless the outcome is predictable. McClelland (1988) further suggests that learners with a high need for achievement will attain better results, because they respond well to feedback as they know that this helps them to succeed.

All of these theories have the same result; they broadly mean the same thing, although each advocates a different purpose. Motivation is a desire and that desire is met through:

- Need
- Drive
- Goals
- Satiation.

(Curzon 2003: 225 and Rogers 2002: 95–99)

The link between the classroom and the theory

The learning and motivational theories continually suggest that what happens in the classroom, how the sessions are planned and delivered, impact significantly on the principles that the teacher advocates. In order to make the links between what happens in the classroom and the theories, it might be useful to consider the following:

Experiential learning

Experiential learning is a trial and error model. In its absolute form there is no teacher present in the process. Learning from things that happen and mistakes that are made is promoted by Kolb and Rogers – a humanist school of thought. Dewey, a cognitivist, didn't agree that this type of learning was always effective, referring to it as 'mis-educative'. He thought that sometimes failure is due to poorly chosen methods of learning rather than the inability to learn, although he did advocate that learning is based on experience. Experiential learning will be seen in role-play and case-study activities.

Discovery learning

In a discovery learning model, the learner is allowed to find out things for themselves in order to be able to put them into meaningful patterns. The new information is learned in the context of previous learning. This type of learning therefore is a cognitivist view. Ausubel and Bruner are the main exponents, but with slightly different viewpoints. Ausubel talks about effective experiential learning being meaningful, whereas Bruner argues that not all learning is meaningful, but agrees that learners need to organise their own knowledge and build on things they already know. Discovery learning will be seen in practical situations and research activities.

Sensory learning

In a **sensory learning** model, the teacher recognises and exploits the learner's natural abilities in sight, hearing, touch, etc. Dugan Laird argued that learning is more effective when the senses are stimulated.

75 per cent is learned through seeing

13 per cent is learned through hearing

12 per cent is learned through touch, smell and taste.

Laird (2003: 114)

Sensory learning will be seen in demonstrations, video/DVD studies, and situations where models or artefacts are investigated.

Group learning

Most of the learning that occurs in educational settings will be in large groups. Workplace learning is generally one-to-one or small groups (see also Chapter 7). This is because most learning is funded, either publicly or privately, and cost efficiency demands that groups of learners seeking similar outcomes are collected and taught together. The challenge then for teachers is respecting and valuing the individuals within the group, meeting their needs and creating a cohesive learning environment. **Group learning** is more than just seating people in various combinations; it is about building a team ethos to ensure that group work is shared and learners are willing to work together. There are two theorists associated with group dynamics. Belbin (1993) suggested that people take on a particular role within a group, yet they are all needed to create a team. Again this is derived from the workplace but can be attributed to an educational setting.

- Implementer – does things in the group, turns ideas into actions.
- Team worker – keeps the group together.
- Co-ordinator – organises the team, sets the goals.
- Plant – puts in ideas and suggestions, the creative one.
- Completer – keeps the pace to ensure the job is done.
- Monitor – provides opinions and checks progress.
- Resourcer – brings in the wherewithal to do the job.
- Shaper – directs the team.
- Specialist – provides the knowledge and expertise to do the job.

Belbin (2001) www.belbin.com

Secondly, Tuckman (1965), in Fawbert (2003: 188), identified the stages of team development:

- Forming – the individuals are brought together
- Storming – they jointly consider the task in the context of their abilities
- Norming – they start to work together to develop their objectives
- Performing – they work well together and achieve their aim.

Tuckman later added:

- Adjourning – also described as deforming and mourning, which is when the group recognises and accepts their success and maybe feels a sense of loss as the group disbands.

Group work is not without arguments as individuals offer their ideas and opinions, but hopefully teams will settle. Only when the group is poorly formed ('too many chiefs and not enough Indians') will it implode.

Principles of learning in practice

There are significant relationships between teaching approaches and learning preferences. Many teachers endeavour to meet the needs of their learners, but find it difficult to do so all of the time. This is why the teacher needs principles to underpin and set their own standards.

The teacher's own individuality will impact on the planning, delivery and assessment of learning as will the learner's ability to learn. Personalities, such as:

- extroverts/introverts
- dependency/autonomy
- confidence/timidity.

will influence choices made, but they should not compromise the principles set.

Some principles that may be set:

- I will systematically value the experience my learners bring to their learning.
- I will plan my sessions to include learner-centred activities for all members in the class.
- I will encourage learners to set their own learning goals.
- I will always introduce the session with a clear statement of what is to be achieved during the session.
- My sessions will be structured with an introduction, development of skills/knowledge and a summary of learning.
- I will always assess the learning achieved in the session and give feedback designed to progress the learners.
- I will create an environment conducive to effective learning.
- I will set ground rules for the standards of acceptable behaviour.
- I will value the diversity of learners' backgrounds and challenge instances of discrimination.
- I will structure group work to maximise the potential of the learners.

 ACTIVITY 3

Using principles of learning to think about your practice

Look at the principles that are recorded above. Alternatively list TEN of your own principles.

For each principle:

- identify which learning or motivation theory best applies to your principle
- list the theorists who are commonly associated with the idea
- list three teaching or learning strategies that you will use to ensure you meet your principle
- identify any legislation or codes of conduct that influence your principle.

▶

Collect session plans, resources, etc. which demonstrate your ability to achieve your principles. Save these in your teaching file, discussing them with peers, mentors or tutors.

Extension activity: annotate your plans to show your principles and which learning theories you are using. An example of how to complete this activity is included in Chapter 20.

Reflect on the effectiveness of your ideas.

Glossary of terms

Affective domain concerned with emotions and values

Andragogy how adults learn

Authoritative a self-confident or assertive method of teaching

Autocratic a domineering approach to teaching

Autonomy independence in the ability to learn

Behaviourist a school of thought associated with responses to stimuli

Cognitive domain concerned with thinking skills

Cognitivist a school of thought associated with thinking processes

Constructivism a learner-centred model of learning

Deep learning learning which is memorised and fully understood

Democratic a style of teaching based on negotiation and shared values

Didactic a style of teaching in which teacher projects morals or values

Discovery learning finding things out through research, investigation and discussion

Domain an area or section of learning; a classification

Experiential learning learning by trial and error

Extrinsic motivation motivation derived from the outside of the person

Facilitator one who supports or stimulates learning

Gestaltist a school of thought associated with the whole learning process

Group learning collaborative learning techniques

Humanist a school of thought associated with meeting all human needs

Idiosyncrasies a particular way of behaving

Instructor direct or commanding delivery of information

Intrinsic motivation motivation from within the person; natural desire

Intuitive instinctive; apparently natural behaviour

Laissez-faire a non-interference model of teaching; learner-devised; a laid-back approach

Learner-centred the learner dominates the learning environment

Learning preferences the individual's favoured way of learning

Motivation enthusiasm or interest

Negative reinforcement feedback that inhibits practice and lessens motivation

Neo-behaviourist a school of thought which believes learners are driven by goals

Objectivism a teacher-centred model of learning

Passive learning in which the learners accept teaching with little or no active response

Pedagogy the skill or ability of teaching

Positive reinforcement feedback that enhances practice and improves motivation

Principle a set of values or beliefs promoted by the teacher; a rule or moral code

Psyche the human mind or spirit

Psychology the study of the human mind or behaviour

Psychomotor domain concerned with practical skills

Rote teaching by repetition, e.g. learning multiplication tables

Sensory learning learning which relies on the five senses

Spiky profile mixed levels of learning within topic

Surface learning shallow understanding of topic

Taxonomy a classification

Teacher-centred the teacher dominates the learning environment

Theory an explanation or proof of an idea

 # SUMMARY

In this chapter we set out to achieve the following outcomes:

- To state the difference between a principle and a theory.
- To list the main schools of learning theory.
- To identify the main factors influencing principles and theories.
- To establish the links between principles and theories.
- To analyse how principles underpin the planning and delivery of learning.

Your personal development

Initial paragraphs in the chapter explain the differences between theories and principles and provide sections covering each of the learning theories – behaviourist, cognitivist and humanist. Each section describes the beliefs of the school and the main people associated with the theory.

In Figure 7A, the relationship between the theories and teaching styles is explained.

The factors influencing principles and theories of learning are categorised into three types – models of learning, types of learning and levels of learning, each introducing the main theory and principle exponents.

Activity 1 proves that a learner's understanding of a topic will vary and produce a 'spiky' profile of ability and this will impact on the teaching and learning.

In the section on motivation, which summarises key theories and revises previous learning on the subject, Activity 2 offers an opportunity to explore and evaluate the different emotions involved with motivation, which again impact on teaching and learning.

The choices relating to how learning is planned are categorised into the main types of classroom activity: experiential, discovery, sensory and group learning. Each is described together with reference to theories and activities.

Finally, there is a section which puts all of the ideas learned in the chapter into practice. Activity 3 invites the reader to make the links between principles, theories and teaching and learning strategies, resulting in a thorough understanding of the chapter content. In the next section you will investigate Communication theory and its application in a teaching context.

It is highly beneficial to engage in self-evaluation after reading this chapter. See Chapter 24 for guidance on reflective practice.

CHAPTER 19
Communication theories

LEARNING OBJECTIVES

The measurable outcomes that you will achieve by reading this chapter and completing the activities are:

- To describe the purpose of **effective** communication in a learning environment
- To state the main theoretical ideas surrounding communication models and describe methods that create effective communication
- To express ideas which will enhance communication skills in your learners and yourself
- To state why communication is not always effective and describe the effects this has on learning
- To describe the role and communication lines between the various stakeholders in the education and training process and state the importance of liaison

Communication basics

Teaching is based on an ability to communicate, but you have to remember that it is a two way process. There are times when things interfere with that process, but generally, learning is a result of effective communication. In Chapter 6 you learned about how Barriers to Learning (DELTA) impact on a person's ability to understand a subject and some of these relate to communication.

Are you sure you are communicating with your learners?

Communication is the art of passing a message. If it is to be effective, the person receiving that message must understand it, and be able to respond to it, usually by sending another message. Think back to times when you have played Chinese whispers. Although that was usually a bit of fun, imagine if all communication became muddled during its transmission. Communication is generally in one of three ways, and within each there are different types:

Written	Verbal	Non-verbal
Long-hand	Spoken:	Sometimes called body language.
Shorthand	Direct – face to face,	
Text	Skype, webinar	Dress
Images	Indirect – telephone	Facial Expression
Email		Proximity
Social Networking		Touch

In any communication exchange the teacher should ensure that what has been offered has been understood. The teacher can do this by pausing to summarise things spoken and heard and by asking questions to get feedback from learners to ascertain that they have not only heard, but have understood and comprehended the topic.

Whilst we are on the topic of communication, here are some things to think about:

How much of a piece of writing do we actually read …?

It deosn't mttaer in waht oredr the ltteers in a wrod are, the olny iprmoatnt tihng is taht the frist and lsat ltteer is in the rghit pclae.

Text messaging is a modern language. It is perfectly acceptable for its intended purpose, or even within personal note-taking, but it is not appropriate in formal work, and it certainly does not aid the development of functional skills. Teachers need to create rules for its use. However, teachers should also capitalise on how their learners use technology to communicate, by embracing text speak:

thx 4 ur help 2day ur gr8

(Thank you for your help today, you are great!)

ijwtk y ur l8 ru ok pcme

(I just want to know why you are late; are you okay? Please call me.)

British Sign Language (BSL) is a specialist language for the hearing impaired using hands and fingers to spell and create words. There are significantly fewer words in BSL than in English; sentences are expressed as a whole rather than in a series of words, so ensure that signers in your class receive learning plans and outline scripts in advance of the session.

Makaton is a simplified version of BSL which can be used to support learners with learning difficulties. Unlike BSL it is often accompanied by speech.

Why do people confide in their hairdresser, beautician, doctor, driving instructor?

Answer: because the barrier of proximity/touch is reduced or removed.

Caution: these are managed acceptable instances of touch; society in general has an expectation of space around individuals. If you have to 'invade someone's space' always seek permission. Do you mind if …?

Here are some examples of improving or developing communication skills.

Spellings opener Tell the learners what the words of the session will be. Ask them to spell them onto the board. Ask each learner for one letter (they could nominate who will go next) and operate a play or pass strategy to reduce fear factor.

'Do you understand me' game? Sit learners, in pairs, back to back. Give one a picture or line drawing, and ask them to describe it to their partner, without saying what it is. The partner should make a replica drawing from the instructions given. This enhances skills of description and use of adjectives as well as creating a team spirit and is good fun!

Bridging the gap

In this activity the teacher prepares a list of the words to be used in the next session. In order to keep the learning momentum, the learners are asked to look up or research the words before the next class. Then the opening activity of the class is to review the words. Hey Presto!

The silent class

In this activity the teacher is feigning a lost voice. All of the instructions must be non-verbal – although learners are allowed to speak. They have to take the class. You'll be surprised the effect this has on learners.

It starts with an empathy for the lost voice, but becomes very empowering. Unfortunately, you can't do it regularly.

Barriers to effective communication

Jargon, specialist terminology Demystify expressions by writing specialist or **jargon** words on the board (non-permanent) or why not start a 'new words' chart/poster (semi-permanent and visible) or use vocabulary or personal dictionaries (permanent but not always visible).

Level of language Maturity develops vocabulary. Younger learners haven't learnt the same number of words as more mature learners, nor do they use and understand 'big words'. Be mindful of this when creating hand-outs or using reference material. You can also watch for it in completed written work – a clear indicator of Internet 'cut and paste' if this is not the learner's normal standard of vocabulary.

Language and accent Each country or region of a country has its own pattern of words or accent. Some are more easily understood than others. Speak clearly and slowly until learners become familiar with your voice. Illness may also affect the tone and pitch of your voice.

Noise Background noise can be distracting. Computers, extraction units and machinery all give off a constant noise, which to some gradually disappears, but not all have this ability to cut out noise. Those with hearing impairments also have different tolerances to background noise.

Listening and writing Some learners can't do both at the same time. People with hearing impairment cannot lip-read and make notes. Add note-taking time to classroom or workshop activities. Some sessions include writing time and use music as a background … when the music stops, teaching starts.

Talking and listening Speech should be at a speed which can be understood and you may also need to allow thinking time. This time is valuable for learners to understand and comprehend – in their own words – between speaking time.

Beware of speaking when your back is turned, for example when writing on the board. Eye contact is important to effective communication. When to speak (and stop speaking) is very often determined by eyes, pauses and tone of voice.

Summarise Go over what you have said regularly; use your voice to stress key points and pauses to allow thinking time. Tone of voice also adds interest to speech.

Remember our first rule of teaching
ASSUME NOTHING

Communication theories

In this section, you will find an overview of communication theory. Communication is the act of passing a message from one person to another; effective communication ensures that the message is understood. Communication is a basic skill. It involves listening, responding, speaking, writing and comprehending. As well as these overt methods, there is also the importance of non-verbal communication – the secret messages relayed by the body which help the communication process.

Communication scaffolds many educational initiatives; it is the key to outstanding teaching. Teaching requires communication to be appropriate, relevant and respectful to the individuals or groups concerned.

A definition of communication is: An interaction between one or more people.

The theories

Transmission types include linear models, the most frequently cited being: the Shannon and Weaver Model (1949); David Berlo's SMCR Model

(1960); the Lasswell Formula (by Harold Lasswell, 1976). A circular model is suggested by Osgood and Schramm (1993). The most commonly used theory is Eric Berne's Transactional Analysis (1950s), although this described the process rather than expressing a communication model.

Shannon and Weaver model

One easy to understand model of communication was suggested by Shannon and Weaver in 1949 (see Figure 7E). This is a basic model in which they say that all communication needs:

- An encoder – the means of sending the message (speaking/writing)
- A message – something to say
- A channel – a way of sending the message
- A decoder – a means of receiving the message (listening/reading)
- A receiver – the person to send the message to.

They further add that communication is hindered by noise.

This model is satisfactory in so far that it explains how communication is transmitted; however, it does not suggest how messages need to be understood in order to be effective. Nor does it address how individuals put their own interpretation on messages and that those interpretations sometimes confuse the issue.

This is a transmission type of communication and is effective as a means of sending a message from one person to another. Whilst it

Figure 7E   Communication model – Claude Shannon and Warren Weaver 1949/ David Berlo (1960)

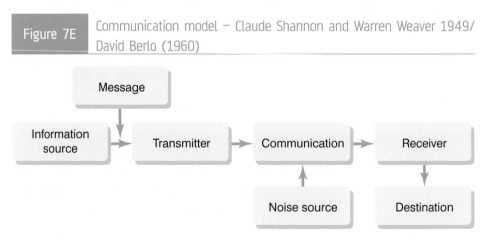

recognises that there may be factors that cause the message to be confused, it is presented in a linear style and therefore infers a one-way process. It is a method of passing information, therefore in a teaching context you would use this style of communication to express facts, to lecture or deliver content using verbal exposition. It does not allow for any measurement of understanding.

David Berlo's SMCR Model (1960) is another transmission type, also linear in style. This is based on the Shannon and Weaver model. In an SMCR model:

$$\text{Source} \rightarrow \text{Message} \rightarrow \text{Channel} \rightarrow \text{Receiver}$$

the source, also described as the 'encoder', sends a message (information, facts, etc.) using a channel (communication method) to the receiver, described as the 'decoder'. The main communication channels used by the encoder are speaking and writing, whilst the decoder uses listening and reading skills. Berlo adds 'thought and reasoning' which he says is 'crucial' to the communication.

The Lasswell Formula (by Harold Lasswell, 1976) is very similar to the Shannon/Weaver and Berlo models although his wording is different. Lasswell's adaptation to the model is the inclusion of 'an effect'. This is starting to recognise that unless the message is understood it cannot be assumed that it has been correctly received.

Osgood and Schramm, in McQuail and Windahl (1993) provide us with a circular model in order to add 'interpretation' to the communication process. They further confirm that transmission types are teacher-centred whereas a circular model allows for more application and feedback.

Transactional analysis

Eric Berne developed his theories of Transactional Analysis in the 1950s; they are more associated with relationships than the actual process of communicating, which offers another perspective. He was inspired by

Freud and the scientific developments of the era. His theories are widely accepted today, but are being modified to meet the modern environment. You will find that they are applied in a wide variety of contexts including medical research, personality analysis and management development as well as communication theory. Not surprisingly, he ascertained that communication was at the centre of human relationships and that communication was natural. He argues that it is a stimulus: thus, we will always speak when spoken to. He does quantify this by saying that those responses will vary according to our 'alter ego states'. Each person is made up of three alter ego states: parent, adult and child.

Parent ego state: This is our voice of authority, very often typified by tried and tested statements, learned from our parents. For example the parent would say: 'under no circumstances', 'always', and advocate values such as don't lie, cheat, etc. The body language may show impatience and the verbal language includes patronising expressions.

Child ego state: This is our dependent state. This is typified by us seeking assurances, or at its worst displaying immature behaviours. It may display temper tantrums, whining voices, baby talk, excuses and big words used incorrectly.

Adult ego state: This is our independent state; the ability to think and act responsibly and maturely. The physical appearance is attentive and non-threatening. Sentences include reasons and negotiated styles.

The styles are not limited to words and also include non-verbal expressions.

Berne states that effective communication is when the states are equal. For example, when someone in the parent state talks to someone in the child state, it is only effective if it is returned in the same style, i.e. the child accepts they are communicating with a parent. Thus the dialogue with younger learners who may be seeking guidance and reassurance as they enter post-compulsory education is usually a parent–child type. As learners mature you are more likely to see adult to adult communications. In short, Berne argues that effective communication is more about relationships than the act of sending and receiving messages.

In the first example, the person sending the messages is doing so in an adult style. This adult-adult situation is ideal; both are equals, which

Berne says is the best scenario. However if it is an adult conversing with a parent or child, then the recipient of the information is not a peer. In both adult–parent and adult–child scenarios the recipient of the information is not matched; the parent wants the controlling role and may rebel against being instructed, and the child is too passive and compliant to respond appropriately. The teaching of adults (andragogy) is an example of adult-adult communication working in practice. Adult–adult leads to effective communication because both are equal and therefore will respond appropriately.

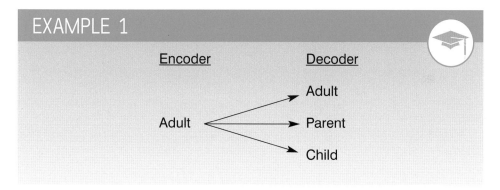

EXAMPLE 1

Encoder   Decoder

Adult

Adult   Parent

Child

In the second example the parent is leading the communication. In this situation the parent will dominate the adult who wants a negotiating role; two parent styles would respect each other and the parent would domineer the child. In some teaching situations, the parent–child scenario is required, for example, when teaching younger learners who need to learn how to communicate, so initially the teacher takes on a parent role in order to nurture their learners. Sometimes, when one teacher is required to lead in a particular situation – for example a target setting mode or a disciplinary, the parent state is useful in moving the situation forward. Once the hierarchy or respect has been established, then it may be possible to enter an adult–adult state.

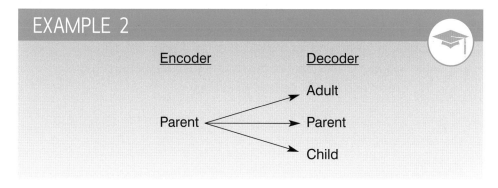

EXAMPLE 2

Encoder   Decoder

Adult

Parent   Parent

Child

In the final example the child is initiating the communication. This is the least effective scenario, because the child does not have the maturity to cope with the role. The only time when this would be effective is a child–child match; again, because they are equals the communication would work. This would be the relationship of two young learners discussing a topic in the classroom. In the worst situations it is seen in 'poor behaviour battle-grounds' when the teacher has lost control of a situation.

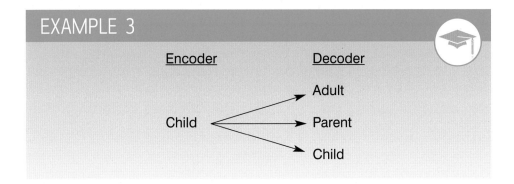

EXAMPLE 3

Encoder   Decoder

                      Adult

Child ←——→ Parent

                      Child

Berne's model can explain some of the teaching dialogues and show how like ego states are the best method of achieving sensible, effective communication.

In the final part of this section, to review and develop your communication style, consider this:

ACTIVITY 1

Scenario

It is the beginning of a new term and the inexperienced teacher is working with a group of 14-year-olds in a vocational setting. Communication is failing and as a result creates a poor behaviour management situation. The teacher thinks that they cannot teach or manage this group and becomes confrontational.

Using Berne's theories of Transactional Analysis, explain the underlying causes of this communication problem. How could the teacher improve this scenario?

The teacher probably made the assumption that the learners wanted to learn the subject, would be motivated and probably enjoy an environment different to that of the methods seen in schools. Using Berne's theory, you may be likely to see the teacher initially trying to communicate in an adult–child position. Unfortunately, this was the first mistake. Younger learners have to learn how to communicate in an adult way. From the day they were born, they (the learners) have communicated in parent–child positions and this is mirrored in schools. In a confrontational situation a child–child position emerges and usually goes nowhere! It is part of the transition between compulsory and post-compulsory education that a parent–child style is maintained and as trust and maturity develop, then a more adult–adult position can be adopted.

 ACTIVITY 2

Effective communication

List the ways that a teacher can improve communication to ensure that it is effective:

-
-
-
-
-

-
-
-
-
-

Now list the ways you communicate with your learners:

-
-
-
-
-

-
-
-
-
-

Following this activity, and the theories previously discussed, identify four improvements that you will make to your communication strategy and how these will develop your principles of learning.

-
-
-
-

Applying communication in teaching

Communication, to a greater or lesser degree, occurs in every teaching and learning interaction. However, just because we have said or written something, it does not mean that it has been received and understood. This leads us to consider the many skills required when communicating.

- *Listening* – The ability to hear what is being said.
- *Comprehension* – The ability to understand what is being said.
- *Speaking* – The ability to express thoughts and messages clearly.
- *Writing* – The ability to express thoughts and messages legibly.
- *Negotiating* – The ability to agree or compromise with others in discussions.
- *Reading* – The ability to understand written text.
- *Empathising* – The ability to understand and share feelings and emotions.
- *Using numeracy* – The ability to use numbers to express ideas.
- *Persuading* – The ability to reason or argue your beliefs in discussion.
- *Networking* – The ability to work in a group to share ideas.
- *Assertiveness* – The ability to be forceful and confident.
- *Sharing information* – The ability to contribute to or take part in discussions.
- *Speaking and writing in a foreign language* – The ability to express ideas to those whose language is different to your own.

This is critical to:

- Workplace harmony
- Effective teaching and learning
- Productivity.

Some of the teaching and learning methods that focus heavily on communication skills include:

- *A presentation* – speaking, listening, reading and writing occur in the preparation and delivery of every presentation. Both learners and teacher present information during their programme.
- *Assignments* – learners will communicate to you through their writing and they will have engaged in communication throughout the gathering of information. The ability to express themselves accurately in their written work is essential to language development.
- *Questioning* – either verbal or written; teachers and learners have to speak or write and listen or read in order to understand and respond to the question.
- *Verbal exposition* – teachers are offering information, learners are listening, comprehending and hopefully rephrasing into their own notes. Accuracy in spelling, grammar and punctuation is essential to ensure meaning and correct interpretation.
- *Feedback* – teachers and learners need to be able to communicate effectively in order to support learning.

Modern communication channels

Teaching and learning is being modernised as communication develops and evolves using modern technologies. We email each other frequently, our learners text us to let us know they will be late, we can receive and mark work online, learning programmes can be 'taught' remotely using distance learning and self-study packs, possibly linked to virtual learning environments (VLEs). Increasingly we blog and chat about things in our lives and participate in forums to ask questions and discuss issues. We need not attend meetings (or sessions!) if we can use video conferencing, webcams and conference calls. Our learners might even catch up with missed sessions by downloading a webcast or podcast! Whilst these technologies continue to improve and become more interactive, there is nothing which beats a blended approach to learning. So don't get too carried away yet, there is still considerable value in communicating face to face and of course, we should not disadvantage those learners who are technophobes or simply do not have access to such resources.

Authenticity – In communicating with learners and other stakeholders it is essential to validate the authenticity of what is spoken and written. Whilst it is easy to identify whose thoughts are being expressed when using direct assessment methods such as observation and questioning, it is not so easy through some of the other assessment methods, for example assignments and essays. Unfortunately, whilst the Internet is valuable for research, it is also easy to express other people's ideas and claim them as your own. This is plagiarism.

Improving communication

REVISION

There are numerous reasons for communication not to work. Using DELTA (disability, emotional, language, technology and ability) classifications (see Chapter 6) and considering language, tone and style you are able to modify your teaching to overcome such barriers.

Negotiating is one of the keys to effective communication. Finding out why learners want to do something (or not), and establishing compromise is when and how a more favourable environment will emerge; a more adult relationship. This will not occur overnight, just because a 16-year-old has started college and thinks they are grown up, it does not necessarily follow that they are adult. This maturity may take up to six months (or longer) to develop before that 16-year-old starts to understand the needs, language and behaviours associated with post-compulsory education. Try not to give up too soon!

Communication is essential in the learning environment and it becomes more effective when enhanced by active learning strategies:

Oral skills can be developed by talking in class, discussions and questioning. By offering learners time to 'solo free write' you are giving all of them time to consider their answers, and this will develop how they participate in constructive talking by increasing their confidence in speaking. Similarly, allowing pair time or small group time to discuss issues and then a feedback slot improves knowledge and thus confidence.

Writing skills can be enhanced by note-taking, class and homework exercises, and written assessments. In any activity that you do you should encourage writing skills, even if the writing is in note form. It could be a hand-out where the learner has to complete missing words, or ideas expressed in writing using note, report and essay formats.

Listening skills can be enhanced by discussion groups, role play activities and teacher talk sessions. These sessions develop listening skills by creating opportunities during which learners have to listen to other ideas; those ideas can be consolidated into their own evaluative work. Asking learners to present mini seminars about a subject will result in them responding to questions posed by others in the group, which results in comprehension activities. ICT skills may also be developed if presenting information using software packages.

Reading skills can be enhanced by paraphrasing, case studies and comprehension activities. By giving a learner something to read and asking them to do something as a result, it demonstrates their understanding of the subject.

These active learning ideas both develop the basics of communication as well as creating lively things to do in class. Even the most passive activity of listening can be enlivened by asking learners to do something with the information just received. The responses from learners will confirm the effectiveness of your communication – that is: is the message received and understood?

How do you know if communication is effective?

There are some simple watch points:

- Facial expressions
- Loss of attention

- Noise level rises
- Leaning back on seats.

There are some simple checks:

- Ask open questions
- Gather feedback
- Recap asking for explanations
- Listen to conversations in group activities.

By watching out for change you will soon pick up vibes about effectiveness.

 ## ACTIVITY 3

Effective communication

Ask a peer to observe a teaching session using the checklist below. Then discuss the outcome and devise strategies to improve communication.

CHECKLIST FOR COMMUNICATION EFFECTIVENESS	
Language used was clear and used tone and expression to create mood	
Technical words and jargon terms were explained	
Learners' body language demonstrated interest in the speaker	
Facilities created for writing, listening and effective recording of information	
Questions were relevant and were open in style (demanding answer – not yes/no response)	
Clarification was sought if unsure about intended meanings – by teacher, by learner, by support assistants	
Feedback was unambiguous	
Activity and learning summaries were clear and highlighted key issues	

Suitable communication strategies were used to ensure all learners participated	
Background noise is minimised	

Communication assessment

How was communication effectiveness assessed?

By self, peers, learners, tutors, other: _____

Reflections about how communication can be improved:

Barriers to learning

Petty explains communication as a chain of events, in which a message is developed, transmitted, heard and comprehended. He expresses this as:

> What I mean → what I say → what they hear → what they understand.

(Petty 2004: 38)

He refers to the game of Chinese whispers as a means of proving that communication as a messaging system can sometimes go a little awry. This, however, is a linear model, a one-way process: effective communication is formed from a two-way process. That is, there needs to be some form of check to ensure that what is said has been understood.

Just because you are a good teacher and everything around you is conducive to learning, it does not necessarily follow that your learners will be able to learn. Sometimes, their previous experiences in learning will form a barrier which will prevent learning occurring; with widening participation in learning comes a variety of behaviours which, if inappropriate, can interrupt or constrain the learning process, resulting in disengaged learners and problems with attendance and punctuality.

Additionally, staff may be reluctant to meet the new challenges in the curriculum, and be expected to cope with learners who bring their many characteristics and individualities. These obstacles must be managed.

Some of the main issues that you will see in learners are: lack of confidence; lack of vocational/basic skills; lack of understanding about expectations and ineffective transition from the previous to the current learning programme. These can be overcome by:

- Access to preparatory courses
- Learning at a level/pace relevant to need
- Modes of attendance to meet need
- Negotiated learning
- Targeted learning
- Supported learning
- Structured tutorials.

Increasingly, the principle of putting the learners first when designing programmes is being demonstrated in schemes and learning plans. This can be achieved by:

- Delivering topics practically before underpinning with theory.
- Designing the curriculum to meet learner needs rather than staffing wants.
- Addressing deficiencies on functional skills by differentiating, discrete provision, flexible learning materials, learning support, but always embedding the skills and supporting the development of learners.
- Using holistic learning strategies to minimise repetition in programmes.
- Preparing learners for learning.
- Spreading out assessment over duration of the course.
- Assessing with consideration of other commitments of learners.

Equally, you might not be good at getting the message across, in which case you need to review your methods and adapt your strategies accordingly. Why not build reflection into your scheme of work – an odd week here and there to discuss the learning acquired. The teacher can then react to learners' requests for re-teaching, time to practise and apply knowledge, catch-up with notes and filing or simply just breathing space to assimilate the learning.

Liaising with learners, peers and other stakeholders

Liaising means to co-operate. It is important that everyone in the educational context is working to the same outcome, even if they are motivated by different drivers. Let us consider the various people (the stakeholders) involved:

The learner

The learner wants to achieve their learning aim or ambition. There are sometimes periods when this is not their primary goal (other factors may influence their progress), but generally they are enrolled to reach a specific goal. They will liaise with their teachers and employers – or if under 18, their parents.

The learners' parents or guardians

Learners aged below 18 remain the responsibility of their parents or guardians. As such they care about the progress of their wards and may contribute to that process (to varying degrees). They will liaise with teachers and learners, through parent and carer events or by accessing their child's online progress recording systems.

Other teachers or tutors

They are involved in the process of helping their learners develop. They will be a team of people, each responsible for a specific part of their curriculum. They will liaise with learners, parents or employers (dependent upon age of learner), other teaching staff and managers.

Management teams

They oversee the work of teachers and undertake quality assurance arrangements. They will liaise with teachers, governors and funding bodies.

Governors/board of directors

They have overall responsibility for the running of the organisation. They will liaise with the management team and funding bodies.

Employers

Employers will either send their staff for training or receive people at the end of their training and education. They want to ensure that training offered in either case is relevant to their needs and is up to date. They liaise with learners and teachers and funding bodies.

Funding bodies

They provide the money to pay for courses and training and therefore want assurances that the monies are well spent. Funding may be from public or private sources. They will liaise with employers, managers and the governorship or directorate.

Other people in the process are:

- Corporate services (finance, personnel, admissions)
- Careers, employment agencies
- Awarding Organisations, regulatory bodies
- Inspectorates
- Government bodies, and
- Care and support services.

Whilst each has a valuable role, their contact is usually restricted to one of the group of primary stakeholders, listed above.

The co-operation between all of these groups of people is vital to the smooth running of the organisation. Communication between the parties ensures that learners receive the most efficient and effective learning that can possibly be provided. The learner is at the hub. Without learners, teachers wouldn't have anyone to teach, parents and employers would not need or be able to promote training as a means of economic survival, funding bodies would not need to support learning and managers and governors would not have organisations to strategically direct. Historically, the learners were very often the smallest voice in educational development. Therefore, it is not surprising that most educational initiatives desire to ensure that strategy is wholly responsive to learner needs; as a result you will hear about 'Learner Voice' strategies being used to listen to learners.

By representing this sequence visually, you will see the possible reason for the learner voice not having a strong impact on how education happens. It may be a cynical viewpoint, but the people who control education have the least dealings with those who participate in it, which means it befalls the teacher, who has a greater role in the liaising between those involved in the process of education, to ensure meaning and value are provided for all stakeholders. So, whilst the learner is the centre of the education, the teacher is the centre of the communication (see Figure 7F).

Figure 7F   Communication channels

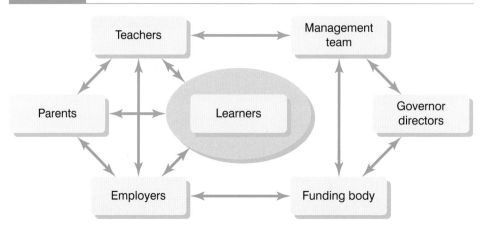

Whilst discussing stakeholders, it may be appropriate to mention 'the learning contract'. It is becoming more and more frequent that learners are asked to sign documents committing to achievement, attendance or compliance to rules.

Argument for:	Argument against:
<ul><li>Learner is clear about expectations</li><li>Learner commits to a learning agenda.</li></ul>	<ul><li>Value to learner or organisation</li><li>Legal requirement or moral value.</li></ul>

It is quite acceptable that these documents are used; however, how binding they are remains an issue.

Glossary of terms

Body language using conscious or unconscious gesture to express feelings

Communication a means of sending and receiving information to share or exchange ideas

Context the setting in which learning occurs

Disengaged uninvolved with learning

Effective to produce the intended or desired result or outcome

Efficient productive working without waste

Ego self-importance or personal identity

Holistic the big picture; the whole qualification or curriculum

Hub the centre

Jargon language, words or expressions of a specialist occupation

Linear in communication, a message following a direct line

Negotiating agreement and compromise towards outcome

Transmission type in communication, a message passing from
    one to another

 SUMMARY

In this chapter we set out to achieve the following outcomes:

- To describe the purpose of effective communication in a learning environment.
- To state the main theoretical ideas surrounding communication models and describe methods that create effective communication.
- To express ideas which will enhance communication skills in your learners and yourself.
- To state why communication is not always effective and describe the effects this has on learning.
- To describe the role and communication lines between the various stakeholders in the education and training process and state the importance of liaison.

Your personal development

You have established the basics of communication and are able to describe different ways of communicating and describe the main methods of communication. You have considered some approaches to developing communication skills between you and your learners. Your raised awareness on the subject of communication will enhance your development of personal skills and can be used to demonstrate outcomes of the Minimum Core (see also Part 9).

You will have looked at theories of communication and seen how they can be applied to the dialogue between teacher and learner. You can summarise the key theories and have revised previous learning of what constitutes barriers to learning.

You will be more familiar with how effective communication will be achieved using the models suggested. In Activity 1 you considered the ego states referred to in Berne's Transactional Analysis and how they influence classroom communication.

You have considered ways that communication can be made more effective and the impact that effective communication has on the learning process. In Activity 2 you are asked to review your communication methods and how these could be developed in the hope that this knowledge will help you to achieve some of the principles and values you set yourself. This was developed in Activity 3 by the reflection of your own communication style with a subsequent identification of personal development strategies.

Finally, you have reviewed the roles of people associated with learning and identified how they must liaise with each other to improve the learning environment and how the teacher communicates has a direct impact on learning.

In completing this you should be able to demonstrate:

- Effective communication in the classroom.
- Active learning to develop communication.
- Efficient liaison between stakeholders.
- Application of communication theory in your classroom principles.

CHAPTER 20

Applying principles of learning and communication

LEARNING OBJECTIVES

The measurable outcomes that you will achieve by reading this chapter and completing the activities are:

- To justify teaching and learning strategies in the context of theories and principles
- To demonstrate justifications in your planning documentation

Applying the theories

In this chapter we shall think about the principles and theories and consider how this is evidenced in your teaching role. Most of the practical application of the theory will be observed by your tutor or mentor in the way you deliver your session, but we can look at the documents to support your rationale. In order to set this chapter into context, you should read an explanation of the difference between a principle and a theory and a summary of the main theories in the previous chapters.

The table below attempts to link why we need to be aware of what goes on behind the teaching. You would not be alone in thinking: 'why do I need to know about theories?' I concede that some of you do what you do in the learning environment because it seems right, but it does help to confirm your confidence if you understand why that was a good idea. As part of your Initial Teacher Training you are required to 'justify' your actions to prove you are not only a successful teacher but that you realise the consequence of your actions and how they impact on others.

The links between principles and theories and teaching practice

Summary of previous chapter:		Impact on practice
Principles	These are your personal values and the professional values advocated by LLUK and Education and Training Foundation. They may also include codes of conduct set by your organisation to address legislation	Behaviour codes Dress codes Attitudes Relationships Personal actions Planning and delivery

Summary of previous chapter:			Impact on practice
Theories	*Learning:*	*Communication:*	Initial assessment
			Diagnostic test
	Behaviourist	Transmission	Tutorials
	Cognitivist	Relationship	Planning and
	Humanist		preparation
			Support strategies
	Models of learning		Referral systems
	Types of learning		Delivery of sessions
	Levels of learning		
	Motivation		
Teaching methods	Experiential		Choice of activities
	Discovery		Resources selected
	Sensory		Assessment methods
	Group		Modern technologies
			Delivery of sessions

On the left of the table you will see the principles and theories covered in the previous chapters and the right hand column links to things that you will do with your learners as part of your teaching role. It is not an absolute classification in that many things could apply across all teaching and learning activities carried out in the education and training sector; it lists the main impacts that the particular values and theories will have.

In the previous chapter (page 423), we listed some principles which defined our values in the learning environment. Using some of these, I will explain the links and the practical application, noting some of the potential changes that could impact on practice and therefore change the session focus; these may be considered areas for development.

The ten suggested ideas are:

- I will systematically value the experience my learners bring to their learning.
- I will plan my sessions to include learner-centred activities for all members in the class.
- I will encourage learners to set their own learning goals.
- I will always introduce the session with a clear statement of what is to be achieved during the session.
- My sessions will be structured with an introduction, development of skills/knowledge and a summary of learning.
- I will always assess the learning achieved in the session and give feedback designed to progress the learners.
- I will create an environment conducive to effective learning.
- I will set ground rules for the standards of acceptable behaviour.
- I will value the diversity of learners' backgrounds and challenge instances of discrimination.
- I will structure group work to maximise the potential of the learners.

Principle: *I will set ground rules for the standards of acceptable behaviour*

Theories: This principle is embedded in a *behaviourist* school, because it is very mechanistic and demands an automatic type of response. If I say x – you do x – without question – or else. It is *autocratic*. It relies on the belief that learners will follow good examples. The motivation factor meets *Maslow's* suggestion that learners will ultimately feel safe and confident in their environment and therefore will become more motivated; it is *extrinsic* motivation. In terms of communication it tends to exact the *linear models* and would be a *parent–child* relationship within Berne's Transactional Analysis. The principle is a *pedagogic* approach due to the teacher-led approach. Dave Vizard (www.behaviourmatters.com) offers practical solutions to managing challenging behaviour.

Development: By involving the learners in the decision about what is and is not acceptable behaviour, you could move it towards a democratic humanist approach. This more intrinsically motivated approach with a shared responsibility is developing a mature learning environment and moves younger learners towards an adult way of learning and acting.

Principle: *I will plan my sessions to include learner-centred activities for all members in the class*

Theories: This principle relates to a *cognitivist* approach because it is creating opportunities for learners to consolidate and compartmentalise their learning, developing their knowledge. It can also follow Humanist (Rogerian) theory concerning autonomy in learning. It is a *democratic* approach because the teacher remains in control of the environment but includes and probably values the learner's abilities to find out things for themselves. It follows a *constructivist* model of learning in which the learner is considered first, allowing the teacher to become a *facilitator* of learning rather than an initiator. The inclusion of the word ALL in the principle means that the teacher will be differentiating learning to address different levels of ability in the group, and would probably use *Bloom's taxonomy* to state the different outcomes. Motivation theory is *McGregor's Theory Y,* because of the teacher's beliefs in the learners.

Development: This can become a humanist approach by ensuring the learners understand the purpose of the activities in the context of their whole learning programme. This is a Gestaltist way of thinking. By ensuring that the activities are designed to apply to or analyse previous learning, you would be encouraging high-order learning which will create a deeper understanding of the topic. These developments may optimise the learning for intrinsic learners.

 ACTIVITY 1

Look at the principles advocated in the example below and identify relevant theories in the same way as suggested above. There are two versions according to how confident you are in analysing theories and relating them to principles …

Version A:

Principle: I will always introduce the session with a clear statement of what is to be achieved during the session

Theories:

Principle: My sessions will be structured with an introduction, development of skills/knowledge and a summary of learning

Theories:

Version B: hints and prompts …

Principle: I will always introduce the session with a clear statement of what is to be achieved during the session

Theories:

This principle is Behaviourist/Cognitivist/Humanist because …

The teaching style used to create this principle is Autocratic/Democratic/Laissez-faire, which would make the type of learning pedagogic/andragogic and the learning teacher/learner-centred. The session could be differentiated using ……….'s theories to create surface/deep learning. The principle is an example of developing motivation by … [describe] …, re-creating ………'s theories of motivation. Communication is linear/circular and follows B....'s theory of T...... A..... using ..../......... ego states to describe the relationship between the teacher and the learner.

Principle: My sessions will be structured with an introduction, development of skills/knowledge and a summary of learning

Theories:

This principle is Behaviourist/Cognitivist/Humanist because …

The teaching style used to create this principle is Autocratic/Democratic/Laissez-faire, which would make the type of learning pedagogic/andragogic and the learning teacher/learner-centred. The session could be differentiated using ……….'s theories to create surface/deep learning. The principle is an example of developing motivation by … [describe] …, re-creating ………'s theories of motivation. Communication is linear/circular and follows B....'s theory of T...... A..... using ..../......... ego states to describe the relationship between the teacher and the learner.

As a further example, in the next activity we will look at when we use these theories and principles. The main document that you use in teaching which would demonstrate how you apply principles and use the theories is your planning document – the Learning Plan. The Learning Plan below has been annotated to show where the theories appear and where principles are advocated. You may wish to complete a similar activity using your learning planning form and include it in your teaching file:

Learning Plan

Programme: BTEC ED in Uniformed Public Services (Year One)

Module: Understanding Discipline in the Uniformed Public Services

Subject: Intro to authority and discipline

Class size: 17   **Age of Learners:** 16–18   **Class layout:** group tables

---

Lecturer: **   **Date:** ** November 20**   **Time Allocated:** two × two hour sessions (Wed/Thur)

Aim: To introduce ideas of discipline and authority and consider how and why they impact on UPS

P1 – the need for and role of discipline in UPS, M1 – analyse need, D1 – evaluate impact

P6 – explain nature of authority in UPS, M4 – explain importance and consequences of lack of

Principle: I will always set the context of the learning within the bigger picture – Humanist Theory. Progression from low to high order cognitive skills – Bloom's Taxonomy

---

Outcomes of the session: *Principle: I will ensure that the learning outcomes meet every learner's ability. Theory – motivate by providing opportunities for achievement (virtuous cycle). Outcomes are developmental – Bloom.*

All learners will be able to:

- define the specific terms associated with this unit (discipline, self-discipline, authority, obedience, conformity and compliance)
- describe the purpose of discipline in the context of a public service sector
- identify the rank system of a chosen UPS

Most learners will be able to:

- apply research into a poster recording levels of authority
- commence an investigation into the nature of authority in a chosen uniformed public service

Some learners will be able to:

- link the rank systems to the need to create discipline and authority in UPS
- evaluate the importance of discipline and authority

SESSION PLAN DETAIL Introduction/recap; Development; Assessment; Conclusion (recap on objectives); Homework (prep for next session)	PROPOSED METHOD OF DELIVERY/ LEARNING	POSSIBLE RESOURCES
Introduction: Share outcomes. (*Principle: I will always tell learners what session is going to be about*) Discipline plays an important role in the public services; it affects effectiveness and efficiency. Discipline is usually part of a hierarchical command system. 5mins	Verbal Exposition (VE) *Teacher-centred pedagogy* *Cognitive school* *Principle: Although essential to pass key information I will keep teacher-centred activities to a minimum.*	Text books: GRAY and CULLINGWORTH www specific service *Principle: I will strengthen learners' ability to learn by preparing them for learning and developing study skills.*
Six terms associated with discipline: • DISCIPLINE • SELF-DISCIPLINE • CONFORMITY • COMPLIANCE • AUTHORITY • OBEDIENCE 15mins intro + 35mins activity *Learner-centred pedagogy, words are known.*	Write each word on board; ask learners to thought shower words or expressions associated with each. Split group into six (friendship gp) – give each a piece of flipchart paper and ask them to define one of the terms. Nominee to share and explain, with examples, the definition with other groups, put sheets on wall for reference. Text book research *Humanist in activity – teacher = facilitator*	Note taking sheets Spare pens Wipe-board/Pens Electronic board (if available) Give handout to support notes at end of activity

▶

Hierarchy of Public Services Discuss what 'hierarchy' means. Discuss 'rank system' Impact of discipline/authority in ranks of UPS 15mins intro + 45mins activity + 5mins summary *Development from known to unknown*	Nominate a sector, e.g.: Armed Services, Police, Fire and Rescue, etc. Get into those groups. Investigate the rank structure in your chosen service. Devise a poster showing the rank insignia in ascending order and explaining authority and levels of command. Start preparing the poster. Internet research *Constructivist – Discovery learning*	May need to re-arrange room or sub-split large groups. A4 and A3 size paper to facilitate photocopying for each learner's file. Poster materials box – pens, crayons, felts, coloured paper, card, rulers
Session Two		
Recap work in previous session five mins	Nominated Questioning – learners to say one short thing about the words explained yesterday (DSCCAO).	
Why do we need rules? Why do people need to follow orders? What happens if people don't follow orders?	VE Intro *(Autocratic – teacher centred)* Group activity – about four–five in each group then nominated group response to teacher *(Changed to democratic – learner-centred – discovery and group learning)*	Board/pens – spider diagrams Note making sheets/pens Split D level learners within groups
Ten mins intro + 15mins group work + 20mins feedback and consolidation	Extend Q give each member a sub-question: *(Bloom – High order skills to challenge distinction level learners)*	

Humanist thinking – developing learners' ideas and opinions	Give THREE rules that you have to abide by in college or work – who issued them, why do you think it is a rule, do you conform? What punishment could you expect if you are found to be disobedient?	
Continue with the poster project (assignment task 1) 45mins Ensure that spelling and grammar used is correct and cite all sources of information	Tour classroom – feedback and comment *Facilitator role – Feedback develops self-esteem – Maslow/Bandura* Extend Q: analyse how rank systems help discipline and authority *(Bloom)*	Poster materials box Dictionaries Harvard Ref sheet
Summary Review flipcharts used to create definitions 5mins Ask each group who is lowest/highest rank in their chosen service Issue question sheet – collect in and keep in assignment file 20mins	Questions – Why does the person in the lowest rank need to receive his orders? Why does he obey them? Who does the person in the highest rank receive his orders from? Extend Q – why is respect important?	Question sheets

Details of Differentiation (meeting the needs of individuals):

Learners progressed from BTEC first should have an awareness of rank systems from last year so nominate them to lead discussions *(Principle: I will always value the experience that some learners bring to the group)*

W, X, Y, Z working towards Distinction criteria – split between groups. Nominate questioning to mirror p, m and d criteria as relevant *(Principle: I will strive to provide challenging opportunities for learners who aspire to high levels of achievement)*

Assessment of learning outcomes:

Observation of performance in session – behaviour, content development, outcome

Question sheet

A, B need extra support – no support assistant available on Wed; keep a close eye – team A with X. Split C, D, E – need to keep focused Support Assistant (Thu) – Work with A. Help to make notes and file in folder. Help to keep focused by rephrasing q repeatedly *(Principle: I will provide support for those learners that need the extra help)* 1:1 in group activities *(Principle: I will provide opportunities to develop team building skills by devising group activities)*	Work contributes to summative assessment by assignment *Principle: I will always check that learners have met session outcomes.* *Motivation Theory – sense of achievement aids learning. Praise and reward.* *Humanist school – aware of own learning*

You will notice that the session does not include one particular style of teaching throughout the session. This is because as the teacher **differentiates** and includes variety into sessions so the style of teaching will change. It is important to make these adjustments: it reduces boredom and adds interest; it shows how you respond to your learners; and creates a learning environment based on respect and shared responsibility. You may also find that something occurs in the session that requires you to be responsive to learner needs, which sees you having to change your teaching style or methods. As we already know, it is perfectly acceptable to change your plan during a session – the evaluation will explain the justification (or rationale) behind the change. The important factor is that the change should not compromise your principles.

Glossary of terms

Code of conduct a set of standards governing professional values

Differentiate catering for the needs of all learners to reduce barriers to learning

Impact an effect; an influence

Justify explain or prove something

Learning environment general term for where learning occurs

LLUK Lifelong Learning (UK) Sector Skills Council

LSIS Learning and Skills Improvement Service (disbanded July 2013)

Principle a set of values or beliefs promoted by the teacher; a rule or moral code

Rationale the reasons for an action

Theory an explanation or proof of an idea

Value something which is important

Verbal exposition teacher-talk

 # SUMMARY

In this chapter we set out to achieve the following outcomes:

- To justify teaching and learning strategies in the context of theories and principles.
- To demonstrate justifications in your planning documentation.

Your personal development

This chapter is demonstrating that what occurs in the classroom, usually quite naturally, has got a theoretical justification. This means that our actions can be explained by theory.

First, there is an overview of the main theories of learning and communication and instances in teaching and learning where they may occur.

Second, there is a list of ten principles which you may advocate in your role and two of them are explained, again, using the theories seen in previous chapters. This is followed by an activity in which the reader is invited to carry out a similar exercise on two further suggested principles.

Finally, a session plan is used to further explain the links between theory and practice. It is hoped that this final example consolidates the theories, principles and how the teacher uses them in their everyday teaching life.

CHAPTER 21
Curriculum in context

LEARNING OBJECTIVES

The measurable outcomes that you will achieve by reading this chapter and completing the activities are:

....

- To describe the evolution of curriculum in the UK
- To identify factors affecting strategies in delivering a curriculum model

The history of curriculum change

As you can imagine in this era of continuous change, the curriculum has also had its own developments, some as a result of legislation, and others as a result of reports by respected individuals. Listed below are some of the highlights.

1870	First Education Act (Forster) set compulsory education for 5 to 13-year-olds, which became free in 1891
1880	Attendance Officers enforce schooling for 5 to 10-year-olds
1899	Leaving age raised to 12 years old
1902	Education Act (Balfour) established Local Education Authorities
1918	School leaving age was raised to 14 years old
1944	The Education Act (Butler), formalised primary, secondary and FE agendas. School leaving age was raised to 15 years old – implemented 1947
1951	GCEs introduced
1959	Crowther Report recommended FE for 15 to 18-year-olds
1965	CSE introduced in Secondary Modern Schools, replacing School Leaving Certificate and a parallel qualification to the Grammar School GCE
1972	Leaving age raised to 16 years old
1973	Manpower Services Commission (MSC) set up
1978	Youth Opportunities Programmes (YOPs) introduced Warnock Report on Special Educational Needs
1980	White Paper 'A new training initiative: a programme for action' paved the way for YTS and TVEI initiatives

▶

1983	Technical and Vocational Educational Initiative (TVEI)
	Youth Training Scheme – one year scheme (YTS) replaced YOPs
1985	FE Act – allowed colleges to self-fund some of its provision
	Green Paper 'Education and Training for Young People' expanded YTS to a two-year programme
	Certificate in Pre-Vocational Education (CPVE) introduced
1987	National Vocational Qualifications (NVQs) introduced, overseen by National Council for Vocational Qualifications (NCVQ)
1988	Education Reform Act (Baker), replaced GCEs and CSEs with GCSEs and introduced the National Curriculum to schools
	MSC became known as Training Commission
1989	Youth Training (YT) replaced YTS
1990	'Core skills' became collective name for literacy and numeracy
1991	White Paper 'Education and Training for the 21st century', saw FE colleges removed from Local Education Authority control, resulting in 'Incorporation' in 1993
1992	FE and Training Bill (Further and Higher Education Act, 1992) – the FEFC was formed to fund all school/university academic education (about £11 billion), resulting in control being taken away from LEAs
	General National Vocational Qualifications (GNVQ) introduced as an academic equivalent to NVQs
	Ofsted established to inspect schools
1993	Adult Learning Inspectorate (ALI) formed to inspect publicly funded work-based learning for over 16s
1995	Modern Apprenticeships introduced
1996	J. Tomlinson Report – inquiry on behalf of the FEFC into FE provision for learners with disabilities and/or learning difficulties – identified a need for a more inclusive curriculum

	Ron Dearing's Review of Qualifications (16 to 19-year-olds) commissioned by School Curriculum and Assessment Authority (SCAA). It was largely ignored
1997	Helena Kennedy reports on poor participation of minority groups in FE which resulted in Widening Participation themes
	NCVQ and SCAA amalgamated to become Qualifications and Curriculum Authority (QCA)
1999	Moser Report on literacy and numeracy resulted in targets for achievement of these basic skills
2000	Curriculum 2000 (Blunkett), saw the introduction of AS/A2 and AVCE qualifications in a bid to assimilate level 3 provision
	Learning and Skills Act
	Learning and Skills Council formed
2001	FE Teachers' Qualifications (England) Regulations rationalised teaching qualifications and introduced mandatory acquisition of a qualification
	New Deal introduced – qualifications for the long-term unemployed
	Offenders' Learning and Skills Unit (OLSU) formed
	FEFC closed (resulting from recommendation in Learning and Skills Act – replaced by Learning and Skills Council (LSC)
2002	Green Paper, '14–19, Extending Opportunities: Raising Standards' (DfES)
2003	Green Paper, 'Every Child Matters' resulted in the 2004 Children Act
2004	M. Tomlinson Report suggested reforms in 14–19 year curriculum, which was also largely ignored although did result in the 2005 White Paper, 'Education and Skills'
	OLSU's responsibility extended to policy and funding
2005	Merger of Ofsted and ALI announced
2006	White Paper, 'FE: Raising skills, improving life chances'
	Leitch Report, Prosperity for all in the Global Economy: World Class

	Skills Personalising FE: Developing a vision for the future (DfES) 2020 Vision: Report of the Teaching and Learning in 2020 Review group
2007	World Class Skills: implementing the Leitch review of skills in England Announcement of School leaving age to be raised to 18 ITT Reforms – IfL registrations – CPD requirement – QTLS/ATLS DfES split to become Dept. for Innovation, Universities and Skills (DIUS) and Dept. for Children, Schools and Families (DCSF)
2008	Education and Skills Bill New Diplomas introduced Joint letter from John Denham and Ed Balls outlining key challenges for the time QCF Framework introduced with a collection of new qualifications. Regulated by Ofqual (England), DCELLS (Wales) and CCEA (Northern Ireland). Implemented from 2008–09 academic year with qualifications coming into use from September 2009
2009	DIUS and DCSF closed following government reform. Department for Business, Innovation and Skills (BIS) and Dept. for Education replace the former departments
2010	Academies Act White Paper: The Importance of Teaching recommends strategies for managing behaviour, changes in Inspection regime and to free schools from bureaucracy. Change will be implemented in new Education Act LSC closed following a chequered life. Replaced by Skills Funding Agency (SFA) and Young People's Learning Agency (YPLA)
2011	Education Act. The Act saw the dissolution of a number of quangos (GTC, TDA, QCDA). Lifelong Learning (UK) LLUK was dissolved with their responsibilities transferred to Learning and Skills Improvement Service (LSIS) White Paper: New challenges, new chances

2012	Lingfield Report on Teaching Qualifications
	Revised Ofsted framework for inspecting learning and skills providers
	Review of GCSE in favour of return to old O Level type examinations
	YPLA disbanded. Education Funding Agency (EFA) replaced it
2013	School leaving age to be raised to 17 years old
	New revised teaching qualifications for post-compulsory education. Draft De-regulation Bill published
	LSIS work completed and organisation disbanded. Employer related aspects of their work transferred to Education and Training Foundation, employee aspects to IfL
2015	School leaving age to be raised to 18 years old

Based on Gillard (2007), Neary (2002)

Although curriculum will be defined more fully later in the chapter, a basic definition might be useful here. A curriculum is a way of delivering learning. It is more than delivering a qualification; it is about the socio-economic needs of the community, the intricacies of that qualification, the aspects of the course that enhance the value of the qualification and the softer skills that are developed. Curriculum models are a political agenda and the sector has seen much change – and will continue to do so.

Change in curriculum is necessary to respond to weaknesses in the current curricula. Policy change is usually as a result of political, economic, sociological, or technological changes. Effective curriculum must be responsive to the needs of learners and employers and by reflecting upon the needs of society, it provides teachers with the agenda for change and improvement. The policy changes in curriculum filter down to the 'chalk-face' as adaptations and amendments to the subjects taught, and so the teacher is required to change or modify what or how they teach.

As we discovered in Part 1, the scope of the education and training sector is huge. 11 per cent of Higher Education and 42 per cent of all

16-19 learning is delivered in the further education system, all of it primarily supported through public funding. Three million learners are funded, costing taxpayers £3.6 billion; as much again is received through other contributions and course fees. £3 billion is spent on apprenticeship training with £698 million used for apprentices aged between 19 years and 24 years. (BIS, 2012) In the current austere times, the public purse is being reduced necessitating change in the sector. Questions about the reliability of qualification grades will lead to more change. These are just two current themes, suffice to say that the education and training sector will be subjected to change and also desire change to improve and develop.

The number of changes in curriculum will cause frustration in the teaching and learning sector. It seems that initiatives alter strategy constantly; this means that teachers and trainers are always having to keep up with the changes in their working practices or updating skills and knowledge through their continuing personal and professional development. The professional teacher or trainer now has to accept the inevitable modifications and be proactive in implementing changes. It is a natural evolution.

Why change?

- To develop to meet needs
- To correct previous errors
- To pre-empt future needs

- To reflect opinion
- For change's sake?

The curriculum choices in the sector are now largely influenced by funding and that funding is now demand led. The funding bodies research the local labour market information to identify what the economy needs to fulfil employment and social need. They will only fund that which is essential; employers must fund their training needs and individuals must pay for their own development. Coffield (2008: 44) raises an argument in which he questions 'who is making the demand?', and suggests that not everything 'demanded' can be afforded. In essence, we are working at a time of rapid change; that change is our challenge. The 'curriculum choice' or options available are depicted in Figure 7G which consolidates all of the structures, models and routes in the contexts of the education and training sector.

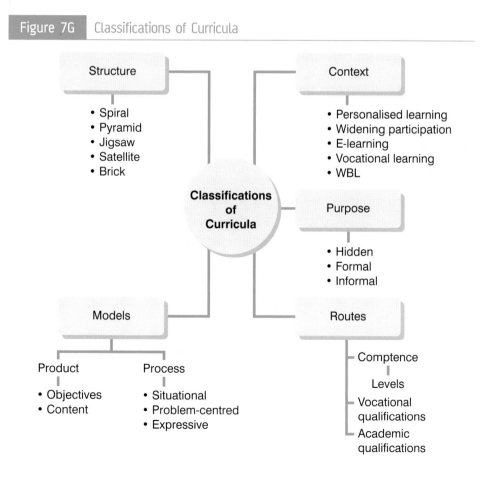

Figure 7G Classifications of Curricula

Investigating the curriculum

PEST is a way of thinking about the external and internal factors that affect something. It is used extensively in the business sector, but it can also be applied to almost any aspect of teaching.

P	Political
E	Economic
S	Social
T	Technological

You may also see the analysis tool explained as 'STEP', it means exactly the same. PEST/STEP = political, economic, social, technological. Some more recent models have added additional letters:

PESTLE = adds legal and environmental.

Additional reading on PEST

http://www.businessballs.com/pestanalysisfreetemplate.htm
http://tutor2u.net/business/strategy/PEST_analysis.htm
http://marketingteacher.com/Lessons/lesson_PEST.htm

 ## ACTIVITY 1

PEST analysis

Consider the current curriculum that you deliver. In recent years how has it changed, what is impacting on it at the moment and what does the future hold? Identify what is influencing those changes from the ideas given.

For example:

How did your curriculum planning change with the introduction of the QCF Framework?

What is the impact on the cessation of funding for large employers?

How do the government priorities impact on the content of your curriculum?

How do the funding priorities influence curriculum?

How are you altering your teaching to meet the requirements of 'outstanding' – as defined by Ofsted.

Extension Exercise: consider legal and environmental issues in your PEST analysis (see Figure 7H).

Figure 7H A curriculum PEST Analysis

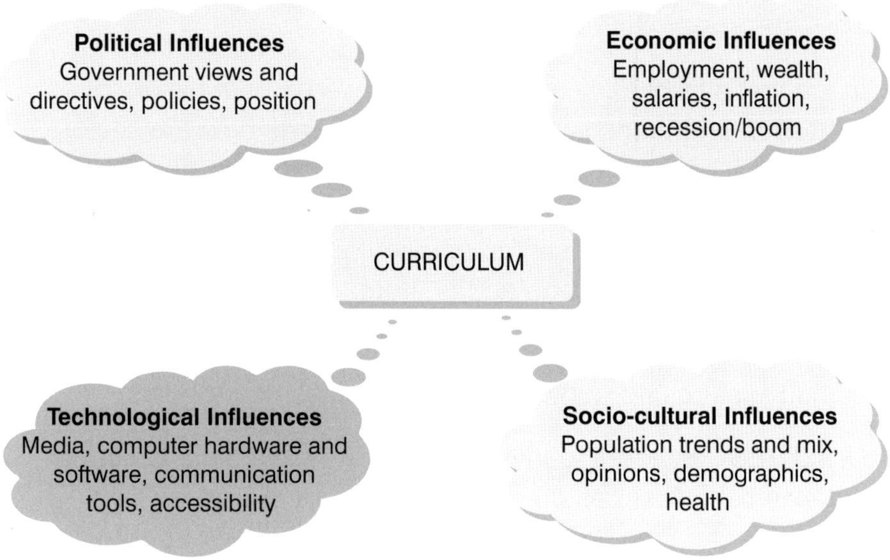

Political Influences
Government views and
directives, policies, position

Economic Influences
Employment, wealth,
salaries, inflation,
recession/boom

CURRICULUM

Technological Influences
Media, computer hardware and
software, communication
tools, accessibility

Socio-cultural Influences
Population trends and mix,
opinions, demographics,
health

Glossary of terms

Demand led prioritised funding

Effective to produce the intended or desired result or outcome

Evolution a gradual development

PEST an analysis tool to identify political, economic, social and technological influences

 SUMMARY

....

In this chapter we set out to achieve the following outcomes:

• To describe the evolution of curriculum in the UK.

• To identify factors affecting strategies in delivering a curriculum model.

Your personal development

In the first part of this chapter, we reviewed a brief history of education and curriculum. It is possible to see how the sector has evolved and responded to various reports and pieces of legislation that have been published. We also considered why the changes are necessary to ensure that 'UK plc' has the education system it needs and is proud of.

Figure 7G showed an overview of the main classifications of curricula; structure; context; purpose; routes and models.

Using PEST as a tool to investigate change, we have looked at the external influences on education and the Education and training sector. The first activity caused you to think about your own curriculum and attempt to map its own history and potential development. In Figure 7H some suggestions about what influences curricula are established.

CHAPTER 22

Theories, principles and models of curriculum

LEARNING OBJECTIVES

The measurable outcomes that you will achieve by reading this chapter and completing the activities are:

- To state the main models and theories associated with curriculum design
- To establish the link between theories and principles of curriculum
- To describe the routes and context concerning curriculum
- To identify key factors in planning and designing curriculum

The curriculum context

Curriculum in its widest **context** isn't just about preparing or designing courses for your groups on a scheme of work. Of course you will consider the content, but you have to do that considering how your department or organisation works, and within policy or strategic constraints. There are several interpretations of curriculum; these are influenced by the context and are clearly linked to things in the political and funding agendas.

Firstly, the basics, let's look at the main contexts that you may be involved in.

Work-based learning (WBL) In this curriculum the needs of employers are the major priority. The curriculum addresses the requirements of employers and aims to raise a learner's ability to gain employment.

Key words are: employability skills, employer engagement, apprenticeships, work experience.

Vocational learning This is a curriculum type that addresses a number of stakeholders. It meets the learners' needs to have employment skills, the academic need to provide qualifications and the employers' needs to fill its vacancies with qualified staff.

Key words are: QCF, Diploma, Foundation Degree.

Personal development In this curriculum the needs of the individual are paramount. The curriculum is designed to address personal need, aspirational need, progression and transfer of skills and knowledge. This sector includes training courses to meet individual and organisational needs.

Key words are: personalised learning, enrichment, coaching, tutorials, cpd.

Widening participation In this style of curriculum the needs of groups are considered. There will be socio-economic benefits. Including all people in the local community is the first priority. In some cases education is taken to the community so that venues are non-traditional locations, rather than the more traditional attendance at a local college of further education. Curriculum may be designed to suit a specific group of learners or specific issues relating to a group of learners.

Key words are: **inclusion**, adult and community learning.

E-learning In an **e-learning** context the curriculum is designed to be shared online to support self-study (see Figure 7l). This might complement other provision or be the sole strategy for learning.

Key words are: blended learning, virtual learning environment (VLE).

Figure 7l   The contexts of curriculum

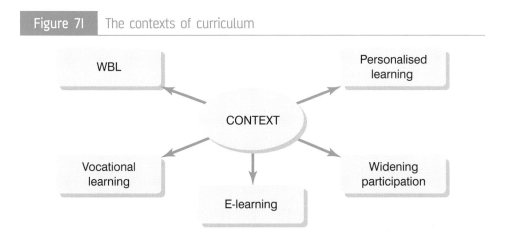

Models and theories of curriculum

Curriculum models are approaches or procedures for implementing a curriculum. Different **theorists** have opinions on the most effective way, which is dependent on the *context* of the learning. It is through curriculum models that concepts and theories move into practice, i.e. into teaching.

This section will focus on the main models of curriculum and note the main protagonists of each of them. Whilst many try to label curriculum in a particular style, it is more common that the teaching undertaken in the education and training sector will not wholly be in any one style. Several variants are noted; commonly, **curricula** are described as 'product' or 'process'. In its simplest of definitions, curriculum as a product depends on the setting of objectives which are the learning goals and the means by which learning is measured. A process model focuses on the relationship between learner and teacher and therefore looks at the delivery of learning, the methods by which the delivery is completed and the distance a learner travels; these are indicators of success.

Models of Curriculum PRODUCT MODELS A prescriptive type	
Objectives Model	*Content Model*
Tyler (1949) Bloom (1956) Davies (1976)	Hirst (1974)

PROCESS MODELS Stenhouse (1975)		
Situational Model	*Problem-Centred Model*	*Expressive Model*
Grundy (1987) Skilbeck (1976) Lawton (1983)	Boud (1991) Bruner (1966)	Eisner (1985)

The curriculum model chosen will determine the choices made in terms of teaching and assessment strategies; they will be influenced and in some cases predetermined by awarding bodies, organisational constraints, funding bodies and political initiatives.

Objectives model

Summary

- Behaviourist in style
- Defines learning outcomes

- Establishes learning
- Organises learning
- Measures learning
- Prescriptive model.

In this model, the curriculum driver is what the learner needs to know. Outcomes are specified in terms of what the learner will be able to do at the end of a given period of learning. It is focused on the dissemination of facts, techniques and information to address those outcomes and may become a little authoritative in style. Assessment will always be against the specified outcomes, with teaching adapted to ensure that outcomes are met. Much vocational training is of this style and so the teacher will need to show how these learning chunks build to create the learners' goals; this will prevent any concerns a few learners may have about the purpose of the learning.

The main criticism of the model is that it may have a tendency to provide shallow learning over a wide range of topics. Although many expect this organised style of delivery, some may feel as though they do not control their learning. In the worst (and very rare) reactions, learners may become de-motivated and show a lack of commitment. The advantages of this style come from the way that it can be standardised, both internally and externally, so that teachers are confident, clearly guided and able to network with colleagues about issues as well as share resources and ideas.

The model can be easily adapted to fully address the needs of learners by differentiating outcomes for different learners:

By the end of the session, *all* learners will be able to …

By the end of the session, *most* learners will be able to …

By the end of the session, *some* learners will be able to …

This strategy is useful:

- when linked to pass, merit and distinction levels of achievement
- when teaching different ability levels in sessions
- when delivering roll-on, roll-off modular sessions
- when working with learners with special educational needs
- when managing workshop sessions
- when coping with inconsistent attendance patterns.

Davies (1976) identifies verbs used in defining outcomes. He suggests that there are two types of verb used; those that are open to interpretation – for example: to know, to understand, to appreciate or to believe; and those that are clear in their meaning: to write, to identify, to solve, to construct, to list, etc. (see also Part 2). His suggestion is widely advocated amongst teachers and inspectors who agree that the verbs in the first list are not easily measured and are very broad, thus making the second list preferable. The verbs 'know' and 'understand' are more commonly associated with aims rather than measurable outcomes.

Bloom's Taxonomy of Learning, discussed previously, is used widely in an objectives model in order to define outcomes of learning.

Ralph Tyler is one of the main theorists of product- or objectives-based curriculum. In designing curriculum, he suggests (1949: 1) that teachers should question:

- The purpose of education.
- The experiences likely to provide those purposes or outcomes.
- The organisation required.
- The measurement of the attainment of the purpose.

This is a very systematic approach; to be effective the curriculum must be measurable otherwise you will not know if the goals are reached. Those goals may be:

  FORMAL – what a learner needs to know to pass their course

INFORMAL – what is nice to know, but not essential to pass their course

HIDDEN – what is learned beyond the formal and informal aspects.

One of the criticisms of a product curriculum is that it leans towards behaviourist and cognitivist learning values, yet a rounder, wider curriculum would meet a more humanistic view. Current funding methods also encourage a product-centred model. The product model can, therefore, be insular. In its favour, is the fact that an objective-based curriculum is more reliable in that stakeholders are aware of the scope of the curriculum as it is easier to create a national standard, whereas process models can be more subjective.

Content model

Summary

- Transmits existing knowledge
- Focus on intellectual development
- Defined by a syllabus
- Does not consider how.

The outcomes in this model are unspecified; it is an open rationale where learning follows ideas and concepts. It develops intellect based on scientific, philosophical, moral or artistic values. Assessment is around opinions and the use of theories rather than the recall of facts; the assessor marks around the exploration of the idea rather than a right or wrong statement. The teaching is aimed at initiating, searching and discovering ideas and cognitive values.

Process model

Summary

- Content defined in cognitive terms
- Focus on learning how to learn
- Descriptive model.

As its name suggests this over-arching model of curriculum is concerned with content, i.e. the key components which make up the knowledge required of a specific topic.

A process model is concerned with all aspects of the topic – the content and its wider effects. It has its roots firmly grounded within humanist values. Curriculum planned in this way considers the individual learner and how they like to learn and how they need to apply their learning. Stenhouse (1975: 95) recognises that this model does not encourage a standardised approach to the delivery of learning or the outcomes of teaching and learning.

Situational model

Summary

- Emphasis in context, culture, society
- Hidden curriculum
- Considers the learner's experience.

This model defines curriculum by the influences which impact upon it. This makes this a responsive model. In a situational model of curriculum, writers consider external and internal factors in order to create a curriculum that is 'fit for purpose'. Every stage of the design is analysed and must be appropriate to the purpose – from both the teachers' and learners' points of view.

Problem-centred model

Summary

- Application of knowledge
- Discovery learning
- Reflective
- Active learning.

This curriculum model develops around the notion that learners need to be able to apply their knowledge to solve problems and create opportunities in order to move forward in their learning. Bruner's spiral model (1966) is one theory associated with problem-centred curriculum, saying that new ideas are a result of previous learning.

In problem-centred activities, the facts and theories explored are generally restricted to those that have an impact on the issue at hand; the problem helps to consolidate and apply the learning. The problem may be devised by the teacher, in which case the learning outcomes can be pre-empted, or they can be devised by the learner, in which case the learning is more *ad hoc*. At any one time learners can be working on different areas of the topic or field of learning. The teaching is a discovery model and follows the development of reflection (Kolb, Schön) in order to bring about the learning. This type of curriculum develops higher or deeper levels of learning. Assessment tends to be a mixture of checking understanding of key facts and underpinning them by concurring with opinions and reflections.

One downside to this style is that curriculum may not be fully covered and 'additional' problems will have to be set in order to complete the learning; this is more of a problem when combining an outcome-based assessment curriculum, with a delivery model following a problem-solving learning curriculum.

Weyers (2006) made some suggestions for active learning strategies to enhance learner engagement when following these more open activities:

1 Organise information
2 Highlight important information
3 Make information meaningful
4 Check and refine learners' understanding of topic
5 Promote transfer of information and 'generalisability'.

Quite simply, this means that the learning must not be so random that it is difficult to assimilate into the context of the learning, and it should always be checked to ensure that learners understand what they are finding out and are able to put it into their own words or situations.

Expressive model

Summary

- Personal goals
- Experiential learning.

This curriculum is concerned with personalised and/or experiential types of learning. Learners explore issues of their own desire or interest; they are intrinsically motivated. This model suits those who are well prepared or experienced in learning. Skills for learning how to learn will have already been acquired, or will be being delivered alongside, probably through an instructional or objective-based method of curriculum. Teaching this type of curriculum will be facilitative. Assessment is more about the journey than the specific learning outcomes. Art curricula frequently exploit the expressive abilities of its learners to develop their attitudes to the subject.

Curriculum routes

The competence model

Competence models are derived from an outcomes model of curriculum. The competences are a set of performance standards that a learner is able to know, understand or demonstrate by the time they complete their learning. Modern qualifications, particularly vocational qualifications, are written as competence models (see Figure 7J). Some NVQs remain as work-based qualifications. They are offered at all levels of the QCF Framework.

Levels of competence

The original NQF Framework (forerunner of the QCF) established some descriptors to show how the levels of a qualification change as they progress through the levels. The QCF Framework is described in more detail in Chapter 10. The descriptors below describe the five levels of the old NQF, but remain a useful indicator to guide readers through the

Figure 7| Competence model

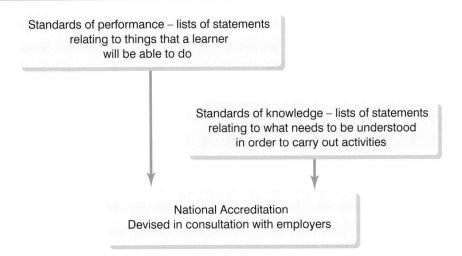

Standards of performance – lists of statements relating to things that a learner will be able to do

Standards of knowledge – lists of statements relating to what needs to be understood in order to carry out activities

National Accreditation Devised in consultation with employers

levels of qualification. The list compares the NQF with the QCF. One of the main differences between the two frameworks are the number of levels, so these descriptors show both frameworks; the original five levels of the NQF and the modified 8 levels of the QCF.

The levels below are used to determine the stage someone is at in terms of their ability, or the level a qualification is awarded at, or to provide an aspirational goal for learning.

QCF entry level/pre-entry A basic level of competence indicative of skills and knowledge at below GCSE pass level.

NQF/QCF level one Competence which involves the application of knowledge in the performance of a range of varied work activities, most of which are routine and predictable. Indicative of skills and knowledge equivalent to GCSE grades D to G.

NQF/QCF level two Competence which involves the application of knowledge in a significant range of work activities, performed in a variety of contexts. Some of these activities are complex or non-routine and there is some individual responsibility or autonomy. Collaboration with others, perhaps through membership of work group or team, is often a requirement. Indicative of skills and knowledge equivalent to GCSE grades A* to C.

NQF/QCF level three Competence which involves the application of knowledge in a broad range of varied work activities performed in a wide variety of contexts, most of which are complex and non-routine. There is considerable responsibility and autonomy, and control or guidance of others is often required. Supervision of others is emerging. Indicative of skills and knowledge equivalent to A level passes.

NQF level four/QCF level four, five and six Competence that involves the application of knowledge in a broad range of complex, technical or professional work activities performed in a variety of contexts and with a substantial degree of personal responsibility and autonomy. Responsibility for the work of others and the allocation of resources is often present.

The QCF framework divides this level of autonomy with qualifications at Level 4, 5 and 6, i.e. under-graduate and graduate levels

NQF level five/QCF level seven and eight Competence that involves the application of a range of fundamental principles, across a wide and often unpredictable variety of contexts. Very substantial autonomy and often significant responsibility for the work of others and for the allocation of substantial resources feature strongly, as do personal accountabilities for analysis, diagnosis, design, planning, execution and evaluation.

The QCF framework divides this level of autonomy with qualifications at Level 7 and 8, i.e. the post-graduate qualifications of Masters and Doctorate levels.

Source: QCA (2004), Ofqual 2009

The vocational model

Sometimes called Vocationally Relevant Qualifications (VRQs), the qualifications have a different focus to the work-related NVQs, although they are still designed to be relevant to subject employability. This means that they can be delivered in a learning environment, whereas the NVQs are/were a training tool. Very often there is a link to the world of work through work experience, visiting speakers or work activities. In apprenticeships there is very often a VRQ delivered as the 'technical certificate' which is used to form the basis of learning before embarking on the NVQ component. Qualifications are offered at most levels of the QCF Framework as Awards, Certificates or Diplomas. Edexcel also offer Extended Diplomas at level 3.

The academic model

These are routes based on theoretical knowledge of the subject, although many will contextualise the learning. Commonly, some subjects within the National Curriculum (GCSE/A levels) and Higher Education provision fall into this category. Recent curriculum initiatives have sought to offer alternatives to academic study, especially within the choices offered to 14-year-old pupils.

The links between principles and curriculum design

Now let's put all this together in a way that demonstrates the connections between the theory and what is done in the classroom.

Principle: I structure my teaching to meet my learners' needs

Practice

- Ensure that there is a balance between curriculum and learning reflected in teaching methods and assessment strategies used.
- Avoid 'teaching' – focus on 'learning'. This is where the sessions always consider what the learner needs to get out of the session, i.e. seeing learning from the learners' perspective. Brilliant teaching does not always equate to effective learning.
- Explain to learners what is going to happen. This might be through course handbooks, stating aims and outcomes or negotiating individual targets.

- Integrate easy and hard facts evenly and mindfully through group work, discussion groups and role plays to create opportunities for everyone to develop ideas and concepts.

Theory

- Objectives model (if outcomes defined).
- Process or expressive models (if negotiated outcomes).
- Jigsaw or pyramid structure of curriculum (see Chapter 23).

Principle: I always move from the known to the unknown when delivering topics

Practice When delivering the curriculum, use a variety of strategies to identify what learners already know. This may be on many different levels:

- Checking qualifications required pre-entry – for example, an Extended Diploma applicant needs between three and five GCSEs at A* to C in order to enter the programme.
- Tests to determine suitability – for example, competence checks to ascertain levels or diagnostic tests to check literacy levels, etc.
- Discussions to find out about background – for example, advice, guidance or interviews prior to enrolment sessions or before a learner progresses to the next level.
- Recap activities at beginning of sessions – for example, to refresh the mind of last week's session, or, check understanding before moving on within the topic.
- Task analysis or formative assessment during topic – for example, checking that the learner knows the basics before extending or developing a topic. Learning to drive is a good example of how a topic develops in complexity.
- Integrated tasks – for example, assignments that consolidate learning from a variety of subject areas taught.

Theory

- Objectives model.
- Problem-solving model – in latter part of programme.
- Brick or pyramid structure of curriculum.

Principle: I deliver my sessions in order to develop deeper learning

....

Practice This involves developing learning so that a fuller understanding is retained; a more holistic strategy. This is particularly important in order to be able to apply a basic skill in different contexts. This development of 'critical thinking' is based on a learner's ability to apply or analyse information and use it in different ways. This will be commensurate with the levels of learning; you wouldn't expect the same analytical abilities in level one and level three learners, but it can still be present. This 'constructive alignment' means the balance between your teaching and assessment strategies matching the levels of learning and curriculum outcomes.

One of the main things we do in sessions to develop deeper learning is to teach basic skills or study skills to learners. With these basic *building blocks* they are able to 'hang' additional information and achieve in their studies. Another strategy commonly seen is the '*must know, should know and could know*' style of deciding on topics to be taught. In this style, the specified topics are taught as a priority and according to time constraints or how quick learners grasp the ideas, additional information is added which might be slightly outside of the syllabus. There is a danger associated with this strategy; and that is the tendency to teach to exams or assignments without even covering all of the required outcomes, which is demonstrating neither deep nor shallow learning. Although there are not many teachers who, in the last few weeks of a module, are not concentrating on getting those last few pass criteria out of learners!

Theory

- Bloom's Taxonomy, Biggs.
- Problem-centred model.
- Spiral structure of curriculum.

Principle: I endeavour to deliver the curriculum in an efficient way

....

Practice Whilst not a primary consideration for the teacher, working within the constraints of the funding methodology will impact on the delivery. Those managing the curriculum will make demands of the teacher which seem to be of lesser importance than the teacher's primary role of imparting knowledge, but nevertheless the teacher must take into consideration:

- Statistics – current performance measured against required performance.
- Rules – number of learners required in the room, utilisation of staffing hours, number of guided learning hours (GLH) required to deliver the topic.
- Environment – accommodation, equipment.
- Market – research, intelligence, competitors.
- Costs – funding source, learners' contributions, remitted fees, full cost provision.
- Staffing – skills, availability.

Theory

- Coffield (2008).
- Objectives model – related to funding.
- Jigsaw structure of curriculum.

Glossary of terms

Authoritative a self-confident or assertive method of teaching

Context the setting in which learning occurs

Curricula plural of curriculum

Curriculum a programme or model of study

E-learning learning using electronic systems or equipment

Inclusion finding opportunities to integrate all learners

Process curriculum focuses on the delivery of learning

Product curriculum focuses on the outcome of learning

Theorist someone who creates an idea or explanation of something

VRQ vocationally related qualifications

 SUMMARY

In this chapter we set out to achieve the following outcomes:

- To state the main models and theories associated with curriculum design.
- To establish the link between theories and principles of curriculum.
- To describe the routes and context concerning curriculum.
- To identify key factors in planning and designing curriculum.

Your personal development

In the first part of this chapter, we have looked at the two main types of curriculum: product and process and the divisions resulting from the work and ideas of a number of theorists.

Then, in the next section, we have reviewed the various routes available to learners and the competence framework designated by Ofqual for current use in determining the level a qualification is awarded at.

In the next section, we looked at linking the ideas learned. That is, the principles by which we set our standards, how practice is directed to achieve those standards and how the models of curriculum influence or position us. This section is linking the intrinsic values of the teacher to the extrinsic values impacting upon the teacher.

Finally, in the last part, we looked at the basics of planning and designing a curriculum and the principles, practice and theory that need to be considered.

CHAPTER 23
Designing the inclusive curriculum

LEARNING OBJECTIVES

The measurable outcomes that you will achieve by reading this chapter and completing the activities are:

....

- To define the meaning of curriculum in the education and training sector
- To describe the context of curriculum in current educational strategy
- To analyse the structure of the curriculum in the education and training sector
- To identify how equality, diversity and inclusion are met in curriculum design

The curriculum vision

In 2005, in a White Paper and in 2011, under the auspices of the Education Act, the Department for Education and Skills (DfES)/ Department for Business Innovation and Skills (BIS) gave their vision for curriculum change. They announced curriculum reform to increase the number of learning routes available through qualifications which are:

'tailored to the talents and aspirations of individuals, better preparing young people for further study and/or skilled employment'.

DfES (2005)

This has set the current agenda for teaching, tutoring and training in the education and training sector, namely employability.

Curriculum in the education and training sector is largely determined by:

● Ofqual (a regulatory body set up to coordinate qualifications)
● Awarding Organisations (organisations that write and accredit qualifications)
● Ofsted (an inspectoral organisation)
● SFA/EFA (the public funding contractors).

All strive to ensure that the learners' experience of education and training is of very high quality, value for money and meets their aspirational and career needs.

Defining curriculum

To many, a curriculum is a course, something bigger than a single module or qualification. In reality, curriculum is more than a course; it is the way the course is delivered, the content, the learning environment, the external and internal influences; it is the 'learning experience' (Smith 2002).

This publication defines curriculum as: a programme or model of study. The struggle to define the term is made all the more difficult due to different perceptions and beliefs. Albert Einstein wrote:

'I never teach my pupils; I only attempt to provide the conditions in which they can learn.'

This adage reinforces the importance of the learners rather than the struggle to create an all-encompassing definition.

In practice, when defining curriculum, you need to consider:

- The knowledge that teachers impart – the syllabus.
- The process of teaching – the pedagogy.
- The product of teaching – the assessment.
- The style of delivery – the praxis.

Some definitions you may see include:

'All the learning which is planned and guided by the school, whether it is carried on in groups or individually, inside or outside the school.'

John Kerr in Kelly (1983: 10)

'A programme of activities designed so that pupils will attain so far as possible certain educational and other schooling ends or objectives.'

Grundy (1987: 11)

'On the one hand curriculum is seen as an intention, plan or prescription … on the other, it is seen as the existing state of affairs in schools.'

Stenhouse (1975)

'The formulation and implementation of an educational proposal'.

Jenkins and Shipman in Neary (2002: 40)

'The curriculum is all too simply whatever course we happen to be teaching at the time!'

Dunnill in Armitage (2003: 192)

'A curriculum usually contains a statement of aims and of specific objectives; it indicates some selection and organisation of content; it either implies or manifests certain patterns of learning and teaching, whether because the objectives demand them or because the content organisation requires them. Finally, it includes a programme of evaluation of the outcomes.'

Taba in Curzon (2004: 185)

 ## ACTIVITY 1

Classroom recap activity

This activity is to consolidate your prior understanding.

Define the word 'curriculum'.

Each individual should write their definition on a Post-It™ note.

Use a pyramid activity – individual thoughts, shared and agreed with a partner, shared and agreed with another pair, and so on until one definition has been agreed by the whole group.

Some of the definitions seen before have included:

- A plan to specify the intended learning
- A group of modules to create a qualification
- What the teachers do with their learners
- The government's instruction about what to teach
- The choices offered to create learning programmes
- A list of objectives to create an 'education'
- A philosophy of ideal learning.

How do your definitions compare?

Have you created the ultimate definition?

Designing the curriculum

Curriculum design is the planning and delivery of knowledge and experiences in a transparent, effective manner. The key words used here are:

- *Transparent* – the purpose both in educational and sociological terms must be clear to all.
- *Effective* – easily understood with the ability to be applied by teachers and learners in a measurable way.

Many teachers will not need to know how to plan and design their own curriculum, given that most of the work is already within established frameworks. However, if you are given the opportunity to influence the shape of a curriculum it is worth knowing where to start. One strategy which encourages thought on the subject is to note external influences – the macro-environment. By jotting down ideas you will be able to be proactive in creating ideas, solutions or answers to the issues that impact on how the curriculum is planned and designed.

Once the major external influences have led you to plan and design your curriculum framework – it will probably lead you to a particular model – then the next series of influences need to be addressed. These are more associated with internal influences. Finally you will consider the advantages and disadvantages of the current and proposed models, trying to ensure that it complies with everything everyone is asking you to meet. A tough challenge!

With any type of curriculum model there are basic ideas which steer the process of learning:

> Learning is PLANNED – ideas introduced, links to previous and future teaching.
>
> Learning is DELIVERED – teaching techniques, management of the classroom and assessment for learning.
>
> Learning is EXPERIENCED – by the learners, recommended by learners and employers.

All three parts must be right for any curriculum to be effective. One idea for putting all of these ideas together in order to analyse them, is to do a SWOT analysis:

Strengths

> What is good about the current model?
>
> Does it meet the needs of learners and employers?
>
> What are the good parts of the programme – staffing, resources?
>
> What is the potential?

Opportunities

> Are new employers moving into the area?
>
> What policies and practices would benefit from the development?

Is it going to lead to more efficient processes?

Is there a market?

Weaknesses

Why is the current curriculum model not working?

Which areas of the teaching and learning are not providing what you want?

Do you need a different skill-set to deliver the change?

Threats

What might prevent a successful implantation of a new model – staff, resources?

Is it affordable?

Is it achievable?

Are your competitors ahead of you?

Once you have done all of the research you will have an idea of the 'how', 'when', 'why', 'what' and 'where' possibilities. This will shape your curriculum.

Primary and secondary curriculum

In some contexts one curriculum model is used wholly when delivering learning. This is the primary route – which in my experience tends to be outcome-related, if only because success can easily be measured and standardised and so becomes the main way of writing qualifications. However, as teachers we are individuals, we are encouraged to meet learners' needs as individuals and we like doing things our own way and sometimes that means amending our curriculum, through modifying our teaching methods. The amendments should not compromise the way we (need to) deliver our topic, thus we may use more than one curriculum model – hence secondary curriculum.

ACTIVITY 2

Reflecting on the curriculum

Reflect on a recent activity – something related to your teaching that you have thought about recently. Examples might be:

- Why a particular resource worked well.
- Why a session for one group worked well, but when repeated with a different group was unsuccessful
- Why *are* Monday mornings so difficult?
- Why the chat to X worked to improve commitment.

Now think about the basic teaching skills (planning, methods, assessment, resources) you have learned so far and establish a link between those basics and how you have modified the skills to make them work for you.

Idea/recent reflection:

_____

Skills/knowledge applied:

_____   _____

_____   _____

_____   _____

_____   _____

How did you modify your practice to overcome a problem?

_____

_____

_____

_____

This activity works to stimulate ideas about the links between objective and problem-centred models of curriculum. It can also serve as a reflective activity to develop own practice.

You have just completed an activity in which you have related information learned from an outcome-based curriculum model – planning techniques, teaching and learning methods, assessment strategies, managing your classroom; and used those basic skills in a different context to solve a problem. This is an example of how the ideals of two models can be integrated successfully, or how the curriculum content spirals to develop deeper understanding. It is quite normal to see a different approach to learning being used to create deeper learning required in higher level programmes. A word of warning though, changing models half way through a programme can be confusing, and you will probably still be constrained by parameters of the primary curriculum.

 ACTIVITY 3

Primary and secondary curriculum

Consider your own curriculum:

Is it purely one curriculum style or a bit of a mixture? Identify the primary and (if applicable) the secondary curricula you apply in your teaching.

Primary:

Secondary:

Your interpretation of these curricula will show in your scheme of work and learning plans.

Annotate your scheme of work to show curriculum styles.

The hidden curriculum

The hidden curriculum is defined as:

That which a learner learns that is not planned as part of their main syllabus.

Wilson, 2008

A teacher should always consider the positive aspects of a hidden curriculum. Some of the things which may be described as hidden are very beneficial. The wider social and personal development aspects of learning can be covered easily under this heading. For example: encouraging learners to turn up on time will help them keep a job when they complete their study, yet is a common example of one of the things a teacher does to develop learners which does not get recorded on the scheme of work.

Is the hidden curriculum a valid method of developing autonomy and responsibility?

Very often the 'hidden curriculum' is not hidden to the teacher; it is a valuable component of the academic or vocational specifications. It may be that some developments are hidden to make them more palatable to reluctant learners. The whole notion of the 'readiness agenda' means that many of the skills required to develop to the next stage and often taught are not included in the scheme of work. They should be included to give them their true acknowledgement within the learning experience.

 ## ACTIVITY 4

Hidden curriculum

List aspects of your curriculum which occur but are not planned as part of the main syllabus.

Describe the positive and negative effects of each aspect of your hidden curriculum. Evaluate the importance of the hidden curriculum.

Positive aspects of the hidden curriculum	Negative aspects of the hidden curriculum

Consider how the planned and hidden curriculum you design can influence learners' readiness to develop. You might want to consider the extent to which a curriculum helps to prepare learners for the next stage of their development. This is known as the Readiness Agenda:

Confident, skilled learners are always ready for the next stage of their development:

Classroom	Learning	Higher Education
Role	Work	Job
Success	Return	Independence

(Lewisham College 2002, www.lewisham.ac.uk)

The structure of curriculum

There are many different ways of structuring a curriculum (see Figure 7K). According to Butcher (2006) and Neary (2002), there are five shapes:

Figure 7K   The structures of curriculum

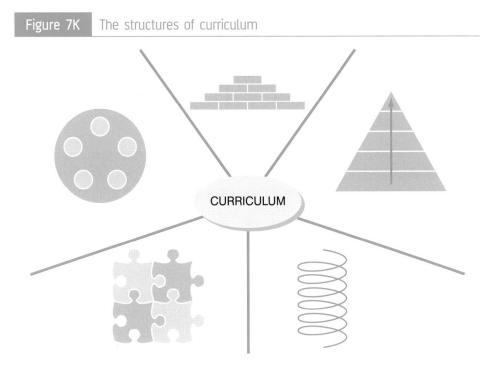

A brick design is where the subjects build upon each other and collectively create the final goal. It is a **linear** design of curriculum. A linear curriculum is based on the assumption that learning goes forward without being influenced on the way; one piece of learning leads to the next, etc. This model of curriculum could be described as 'a production line', in which learners enter education, follow their course and exit with quite a narrow development. In the current era of inclusivity, e-learning, skills for employment, this type of model seems inappropriate, because it does not consider that people are different; people come into education and training from a range of backgrounds and experiences; people want different things from their learning.

A satellite or subject-based curriculum is where subjects are independent and not related to each other; however they do collectively make a very broad topic. An example of this might be in a programme called Catering, which might include subjects such as Food Preparation, Restaurant Service and Housekeeping.

A jigsaw or co-ordinated curriculum is where each section is a topic in its own right and when collected together makes an overall goal. This might be seen in any modular course or maybe in an NVQ or QCF qualification in which the units make the qualification, but can be accredited as stand-alone qualifications. It is popular in vocational training.

A pyramid or integrated curriculum is where several different themes with a common goal link to make a final topic. They may increase in complexity before reaching a goal. This type of curriculum is common in vocational programmes in which the basics are underpinned by functional or study skills.

A spiral curriculum model continually re-visits topic areas in increasingly more complex situations, requiring transferable skills. An example might be a teaching qualification. The main concepts, say teaching methods, are revisited in the context of meeting learners' needs, developing autonomy, inclusive learning; and in each you have to understand and apply knowledge in a different way. Jerome Bruner advocated a spiral curriculum in which the topic themes constantly run through the learning, which gets broader as knowledge and skills develop. He argues that this makes the transfer of learning into other contexts easier. His theory is based on a Piaget style of development in which 'practice makes perfect'.

Credit accumulation and transfer scheme

Commonly known as CATS, this is a way of creating values on qualifications. The current QCF framework follows this strategy of credits.

According to criteria implemented by Awarding Organisations, every Unit of Assessment, a subsection of learning, is given a point score, based on its level, size and learning outcomes. Qualifications, therefore, get a value which helps learners understand how they fit into single qualifications and how they compare with other maybe similar sounding qualifications. The 'transfer' part of it allows a certain number of points gained in one qualification to be used towards another. This is visible in some qualifications, where subsequent qualifications allow for previously gained Units of Assessment to be included.

In the Initial Teacher Training (ITT) qualification framework, each Unit of Assessment is given a value. Qualifications, consisting of a number of Units of Assessment are then written, which must comply with the credit values and be approved by Ofqual. Qualifications are offered by many Awarding Organisations and universities; whilst the credits values and rules of combination must be complied with, the Awarding Organisation can re-name its modules and qualification titles. Hence you may find courses called Diploma in Education and Training; DTLLS; the Certificate in Education (Cert Ed) or the Post-graduate Cert Ed (PGCE). A university PGCE will contain some higher level units – typically at Level 7 – to acquire the post-graduate status. Entry to a PGCE is usually limited to those with a first degree.

In modular curriculum models, the units or modules with their values are clustered to make qualifications. Each module has its own learning outcomes and can be accredited individually or in the qualification cluster. Again, using ITT qualifications as an example, you see similarities in the Units of Assessment in both the Award and the Certificate and to a certain extent, in the Diploma. Similarly, in vocational programmes, units such as Health and Safety are common across broad curriculum areas.

Equality, diversity and inclusion in the curriculum

Firstly, inclusive practice is a requirement of anti-discrimination laws. Amongst others, the Equality Act 2010 requires every education provider to have a policy about diversity and challenging racism. Disability Discrimination laws also gave rise to statements about how an organisation addresses inclusion. It is not an optional way of teaching and designing learning (see Part 6). As a teacher you should think of it as an entitlement of learners rather than something that needs to be done when an instance occurs. It must be proactive and not reactive and turn reactions into positive promotion of diversity. It is concerned with approaches to teaching and methods of assessing learning. In the curriculum, it is a way of improving diversity by reflecting and mirroring the social picture. Diversity and curriculum synergy leads to enhanced learning and the raising of awareness and high levels of respect.

By establishing and rectifying anomalies in equality a greater level of inclusion will be achieved. This might be by recognising under-representation or under-achievement in specific groups and creating strategies to address the imbalance.

> An inclusive curriculum is one in which all staff and learners feel valued, irrespective of age, gender, race and disability, sexual orientation, religious or personal beliefs, background or personal circumstances. It is also one to which all staff and learners need to be committed.
>
> *Talbot (2004)*

Two documents, by the University and College Union (UCU) make some useful suggestions to advise teachers, with some helpful and thought provoking case studies.

It suggests that 'the curriculum may provide space to promote Equal Opportunities' and offers ideas:

● Audit curriculum for instances of inequality and examples of celebrating diversity.

- Ensure language used is inclusive, non-discriminatory, being careful to make a good balance between political correctness and inclusion.
- Inclusive practices don't occur overnight; it takes time to make a systematic change, but don't devolve responsibility waiting for someone else to implement the change.
- Don't make assumptions about needs based on stereotype – always ask. For example: assuming the blind learner needs their work in Braille, assuming the dyslexic learner wants hand-outs on coloured paper. Anticipate but don't predict.
- Consider tasks carefully – when you set the homework to research this, download that – Can everyone access it? – It may be more than access to the equipment; there may be implications for the visually impaired.
- When using dictionaries, don't limit them to English dictionaries, provide translation from English into foreign language types.
- Allow time in your planning to modify materials.
- Reduce anxiety by providing detailed information about the course.
- Remember that not everyone will disclose their needs.

To ensure an inclusive curriculum, consider the following:

- Language
- Tone and voice
- Image
- Dress
- Ethics
- Connections
- Examples and role models
- Global perspectives
- Knowledge
- Teaching methods and resources
- Assessment and feedback
- Counselling and support
- Access.

Recommended reading

The University and College Union website at http://www.ucu.org.uk

See also Part 6 – Delivering inclusive learning

A useful website which notes cultural events, celebrations, holidays and even lunar phases is http://www.earthcalendar.net and can provide interesting facts to add to sessions.

Ensuring that the curriculum and all aspects of your teaching are inclusive is important; the learning environment that is created must be suitable and accessible to all. More importantly, try to avoid the 'box ticking' approach to equality by embedding it into the curriculum; ensure that you meet the needs of all learners and create a respectful learning environment.

SENDA

SENDA stands for the Special Education Needs and Disability Act (2001) and links strongly with the Disability Discrimination Act (1995) to such an extent that SENDA has become Part 4 of the DDA. This means that educational establishments must not treat a disabled person less favourably than anyone else. This applies not only to accommodation but equally to the services it provides. (See http://www.techdis.ac.uk/index.php?p=3_12_21.)

Implementing a curriculum

Having established the curriculum model that you are going to use (see theories), you then need to make it happen. Implementing the curriculum means making sure that all aspects of the teaching and learning match up with the chosen model.

Using a mind map (see Figure 7L) to consider the relationship between curriculum and teaching and learning, you quickly realise that they are intrinsically linked, each affects the other. The curriculum model you choose will impact on the way the topic is taught and assessed. The availability of resources, physical and human, and the needs of the learners will impact on how the topic needs to be modelled.

If curriculum is defined as the planning and delivery of knowledge and experience in a transparent, effective manner, then the teacher has a responsibility to create that effectiveness and transparency in the way they deliver the subject:

TRANSPARENCY. The curriculum must be clear: learners, teachers, employers and other stakeholders must be able to understand the purpose. The purpose will have an educational justification as well as meeting and responding to political, economic, social and technological requirements.

EFFECTIVE. The curriculum must be easily understood and be able to be applied by teachers and learners in a measurable way. If it does not meet its purpose (defined above) then it is not effective. Educational institutions will also add value for money into this category.

Figure 7L Curriculum mind-map

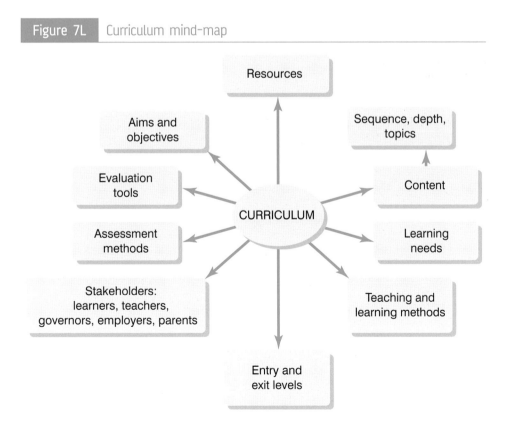

Analysing and evaluating the curriculum

Who makes decisions about what *you* teach?

In this section there are a number of questions to make you think about your curriculum and who or what is impacting on it. You might not be able to change things significantly, but this analysis might indicate the extent to which you can contribute to ensuring what you have is fit for purpose.

 ACTIVITY 5

Your curriculum models

How much say do you have in:

- The content you deliver?
- The order you deliver your topics in?
- The depth of understanding you provide?
- The range of topics included in the wider aspects of the programme – the core subject, functional skills, enrichment or complementary studies?

How do you know that your topics have been 'received' and 'understood'?

Does your curriculum follow a product or process model?

Are there plans to modify the curriculum?

How does your curriculum address equality, diversity and inclusion?

What additional factors emerge from your curriculum, e.g. study skills, personal development, improvement in timekeeping, preparing learners for HE or work?

It is both good practice and a management requirement that the curriculum is evaluated. Rarely, however, do the likes of you and I get the opportunity to evaluate curriculum *per se*; we are more likely to evaluate our interpretation and implementation of the curriculum within our own organisation. It is important to review the provision against quality and performance standards, for example Ofsted requirements.

When evaluating the curriculum we are trying to establish the answers to the question: does my curriculum choice (to include teaching and learning methodology) lead to successful learners and how does that balance the political and organisational targets of an organisation? These two indicators very often cause a conflict; which is more important? Coffield (2008: 1) considers the imbalance between these two aspects and advocates a return to putting learners first. He suggests that the tide needs to turn:

> 'We are familiar with current practice: ritual genuflection is made to the central importance of learning, but the sermon swiftly becomes a litany of what the government considers to be the really key elements of transformation – priorities, targets, inspection grades and funding – and the topics of teaching and learning disappear from sight ...'

He suggests that maybe we are losing focus on our priorities; is the way to improve the quality within the sector to concentrate on the teaching and learning, or is quality driven upwards by business processes and measuring performance against grades and targets? This may be, according to some, tongue-in-cheek research, but it is nevertheless thought provoking.

The funding bodies consider learners by demanding that organisations who accept monies to fund provision ensure its quality and achievement effectively and efficiently, and the way they check this is by numbers – how many succeeded in achieving their target qualification? The only sanction they then have is to refuse to fund organisations that don't perform to their standards. That means that data, stats and more stats (and checks to make sure that the data and stats are correct!) is a primary tool for evaluating the curriculum. This is why you are always being asked to report figures for attendance, achievement, quality audits and the like.

In order to balance these opinions on successful curriculum, it is important that we analyse the provision both by numbers (quantitatively) and by learner voice (qualitatively) and make decisions about improvement based both on opinion and performance.

Therefore any document used to analyse the curriculum must include both facets. Whichever method of evaluation you use, the most important part of the process is 'closing the loop'. Having identified what is good and not so good about the provision, it is essential to devise a plan to build on the strengths and provide opportunities to develop where necessary.

The usual reflective tools can be used to make personal and professional improvements and develop practice. In the following activity you are asked to look at a number of familiar scenarios and decide what you might do to improve the situations. You will carry out this type of activity as part of your own personal development strategies.

 **ACTIVITY 6**

Case studies

How would you suggest the teacher improves or deals with the following?

1 Retention of learners in a Level 2 vocational qualification is below the national average for the sector. There are usually good enrolments but after a few months learners start to miss sessions and then some don't turn up at all. When the teacher rang one learner she said that she had got a job, so that was alright wasn't it?

2 Learners seem quite stressed around the end of the first semester. Each module, which is delivered by a different teacher, has an assessment which means several assignments are handed in together. When learners ask about this they are told that 'We [the teachers] have to check that all of the outcomes are met in each of the assignments, so they [the learners] should keep up to date with work to prevent it all needing to be done at the same time'.

3 The learners in a secure environment are told that they must do basic skills sessions. They are tested as they enter the establishment, some being transferred from other places. They do not see the point of the sessions. On occasions they refuse to work and can become aggressive. They rarely display these poor levels of motivation in their vocational subjects.

4 The exercise class in the village hall has been going for years. It is successful and learners return year after year. Newcomers join the

class and follow the routines by watching the teacher or the more experienced members of the group. The learners are always complimentary of the teacher, proven by their continued attendance. They are quite annoyed at the thought of the fees going up next term and have written to complain.

When answering the case studies above, try to analyse the curriculum module being used and the teaching and learning methods being used. Can the teaching team change their working methods to improve these situations? Possible solutions are at the end of the chapter.

Curriculum is about what we teach, influenced by a number of factors and managed and controlled by a number of others, ourselves included. It is very often difficult to understand how a teacher can influence curriculum; they cannot at national level – even in this democratic society. They can, however, contribute to consultations at organisational level, and manipulate the implementation – i.e. at the classroom or training level. It is at this level that the teacher has the ultimate level of control and influence. Of course we must work within the constraints but flair, inspiration and passion are what the learners see, not the bureaucracy, and nor should they!

Glossary of terms

Autonomy independence in the ability to learn

CATS Credit Accumulation and Transfer Scheme

Curriculum a programme or model of study

Employability in a position or suitable to be employed

Enrichment activities added to the curriculum or course to make a better learning experience

Inclusive not excluding any individual or group of learners (adj.)

Linear in curriculum – single dimensional

Mind map a visual representation of ideas

Model a description or example to represent an idea

Modular a curriculum or programme made up from several modules or units

Pedagogy the skill or ability of teaching

Praxis practical skills as opposed to theoretical skills

Rules of combination an Ofqual term referring to how Units of Assessment can be put together to make a qualification

SWOT an analysis tool to identify strengths, weaknesses, opportunities and threats; used to assess current practice

Syllabus the structure of a qualification

Transferable something learned in one context used and applied to another

Transparency overt, clear in meaning

Units of assessment (UoA) statements of knowledge and/or competence which describe the learning and assessment outcomes of a unit, clustered to make a qualification

SUMMARY

In this chapter we set out to achieve the following outcomes:

- To define the meaning of curriculum in the education and training sector.
- To describe the context of curriculum in current educational strategy.
- To analyse the structure of the curriculum in the education and training sector.
- To identify how equality, diversity and inclusion are met in curriculum design.

Your personal development

In the first part of this chapter, we reviewed the recent drivers moving curriculum strategy forward. This considered the national picture and the impact this has at regional and organisational level.

In defining the term 'curriculum' we sought to find an over-arching statement. This is made difficult due to interpretation, but in a classroom exercise, you engaged in an activity to consider and justify your interpretations. We also have considered issues around primary, secondary and hidden curricula.

The context of the education and training sector was explained in terms of learner types in order to further identify the link between national, regional and personal opinions. With a further classification, the curriculum was explained in terms of structure, which offers ideas on how the curriculum fits together. Having established the macro-environment we looked closer to home to consider how pedagogy influences and is influenced by curriculum. We concluded that irrespective of the chosen curriculum, we need to be transparent and effective in our duties.

Following on from the ideas around curriculum structure, we consider how the different components are given values (CATS) and interact to make the learning experiences seen in the sector.

The subjects of equality, diversity and inclusion were explored and how curriculum must meet the demands of everyone: learners, employers, teachers, awarding bodies and other stakeholders. This section focused on the issues within the power of the teacher, namely: the impact of creating an inclusive curriculum.

Whilst analysing the curriculum we sought to find out how much influence the teacher has in promoting the curriculum to learners, parents and employers. We also reviewed the parallel – how much the curriculum influences teaching.

Finally, we considered how curriculum is evaluated. In this instance we restricted the evaluation to that which we can control – namely, at organisational level looking at the quality systems locally available and deciding upon their effectiveness.

In Activity 6, in order to consolidate all aspects of the curriculum chapters you examined some typical problems. You were asked to identify the curriculum model used and how it could be developed to overcome the problems the teacher was having. This brought together everything you have learned so far about models and pedagogy and created a deeper learning by asking you to apply that knowledge in a different context.

Possible solutions and discussion topics for the case studies in Activity 6.

Scenario 1

Teachers should consider how they manage attendance in classes and how they monitor progress; they may consider target setting to raise aspirations. In some situations learners may be able to be transferred into work-based learning programmes so that they can continue to study whilst working.

Scenario 2

The teaching team should consider a more holistic approach to the setting of assignments, either by linking common criteria or by pacing the hand-in dates. The teaching staff might also consider how to support time-management skills by including workshops or catch-up activities into their schemes of work.

Scenario 3

Teaching teams should embed as many functional skills into the vocational curriculum as possible and make top-up activities interesting, contextualised and relevant. Where learners are being transferred into the establishment, a fuller history should be passed to the new teams.

Scenario 4

It seems here that the sessions are becoming more of a club so the teacher needs to turn it back to a learning environment. By tracking progress of skills learned and demonstrated in the routines and expressing these to learners it will revise their focus. A teacher should also stand back and watch the experienced learners, maybe setting advanced skills to challenge them or allowing them to peer mentor newer members. Unfortunately the funding changes mean higher fees, this should be sensitively explained to learners.

Part eight

Wider professional practice and development

This part and chapters relate to the learning outcomes in the following Units of Assessment:

- Wider professional practice and development in education and training.

The learning outcomes relating to evaluation, reflection and professional/personal development are dealt with in Part 8 and the learning outcomes relating to your development of the minimum core are in Part 9.

This section, whilst containing a stand-alone Unit of Assessment is also inherent in many other units containing assessment criteria relating to reflective practice.

Other aspects of the education and training sector which contain reference to the development of personal and professional practice through reflection include:

Part 2 Planning learning

Part 3 Facilitate learning

Part 4 Resources

Part 5 Assessment

Part 6 Delivering inclusive learning

Part 7 Principles and theories.

CHAPTER 24

The reflective practitioner

LEARNING OBJECTIVES

The measurable outcomes that you will achieve by reading this chapter and completing the activities are:

....

- To explain the terms reflection and reflective practice
- To explain the general term continuing professional development (CPD)
- To explain the effects of reflective practice
- To describe personal development and how this can benefit the teacher
- To describe the purpose of CPD
- To review the main methods of engaging in CPPD

Defining the terms

First of all, let us list the terms that will be used in this section:

- Reflection
- Reflective Practice
- Continuing Professional Development – aka CPD
- Continuing Personal and Professional Development – aka CPPD

Reflection is an expression used to describe the act of thinking about occurrences, which for the teacher is their teaching role; it should be an essential part of their responsibility. It is more than analysis which is the expression used for collecting and understanding information; it is more than evaluation which is concerned with creating meaning from the information gathered. Reflection is the next stage – questioning the meanings. Reflective practice is the skill of being reflective.

Continuing professional development (CPD) is a collective term used to describe the many ways you can develop and improve your practice. Continuing professional development is not just going on courses, it is any activity which results in a change in practice. In summary, reflection is the process used to identify if and when development is required; CPD is the vehicle to provide that development. Reflecting again, then ensures that the development is effectively used to raise performance. CPPD infers that development is broader than that required to develop professionally, in that personal skills can also be developed.

Reflection and reflective practice

Is reflection a benefit or a chore?

Reflection means learning from experience, mistakes and success. It is a process of self-awareness, through critical analysis, leading to informed decisions about development. The ability to reflect must be learned; a teacher must learn to be honest, constructive and remain impartial when reflecting. It may not be a systematic, intuitive personal skill. If it is too critical, too congratulatory, too shy, or too confident it will not answer the key question when reflecting: 'How was it for you?'

When analysing yourself or receiving feedback from a colleague, it is important not to feel threatened. All judgements are made for a purpose, and for you, the recipient, the purpose is to improve, develop and become a better teacher. A reflective practitioner does not operate in a blame culture; they wonder about the impact of their actions and what they can do or change to make things easier, better, more efficient and more effective. The important emotions are not concerned with failure but with how to regard each experience as a learning opportunity.

It is important to remember on what and why a teacher reflects, and that is the core business value: the learning process.

What can be reflected upon?

- Sessions – methods, resources, assessment, etc.
- Communication
- Behaviour: learners' and teacher's
- Success and attainment
- Self: skills and knowledge
- Learners' views.

In fact any event or occurrence is worth reflection.

How does reflection occur?

- Questioning
- Discussions and chats
- Questionnaires
- Interviews
- Observation: formal and informal
- Observing
- Feedback.

When does reflection occur?

Always or never. That seems an odd answer, I hear you say. Reflection is something that good teachers engage with and coasting teachers don't bother about. The choice is yours! The argument here is the nature–nurture debate. Is good teaching natural or is it developed?

> ## REFLECTION
>
> ### The way to ensure that what worked yesterday will work today.

Whilst it is easy to blame learners for poor teaching, the blame should lie with the teacher's inability to adjust and modify their skills to meet their learners' needs. Unfortunately, the plan used for the session last year cannot be wheeled out indefinitely without adjustment. The reflective practitioner has the confidence to take the good and bad outcomes on the chin and deal with them. Experience in teaching makes things easier; you'll build up a set of tried and tested ways of working and use peer and mentor support to share the highs and lows.

Figure 8A explains the various stages of the reflective process, which starts with the teacher trying to analyse information about their performance and ends with them undertaking activities in order to improve their working practices.

Reflection challenges the teacher to get out of their comfort zone and be receptive to change. It does, however, need skills which have to be learned or developed.

The skills required to reflect are:

- Description
- Observation
- Critical analysis
- Evaluation
- Objectivity

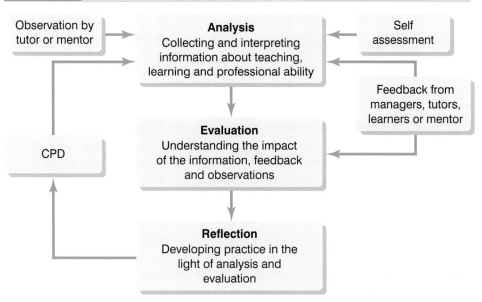

Figure 8A   The reflective process

- Open mindedness
- Rational thinking.

According to Bain (1999), in order to reflect effectively, the teacher needs to fully understand what has occurred and have the ability to make conclusions and recommendations based on experience, advice and hind sight in a non-defensive manner. Atherton (2005: 1) suggests that 'real reflective practice needs another person as a mentor or professional supervisor, who can ask appropriate questions to ensure that the reflection goes somewhere and does not get bogged down in self-justification, self-indulgence or self-pity'. Finally, Moon (1999: 63), states that reflection is 'a set of abilities and skills to indicate the taking of a critical stance'.

Effective reflection is formed from several stages: question, analysis, evaluation and reflection. Using an extract from a checklist for a post session evaluation to explore this:

Preparation and planning	Did I set outcomes for the session?
	Did I share those outcomes with learners?

The answers to these types of questions are usually YES or NO responses (i.e. closed questions). Therefore, there is no analysis. To analyse this preparation and planning section, you must ask the questions above, but then ask yourself a 'so what?' question or create an open question.

For example:

Did you set outcomes for the session? Answer *YES*

So what? *Because I shared the outcomes with my learners they were clear about the focus of the session and what they needed to do.*

OR

What was the effect of preparing measurable outcomes for the session?

It meant that my learners knew what the session was about.

Reflection can then occur. Reflection is about trying to improve things or understand cause and effect, i.e. to improve your practice. Taking our previous example, a reflective teacher might say, *'and next time I will write them on the board and re-visit them at the end of the session to prove how much they've learnt in the session'.*

EXAMPLE

The stages of reflection

Question	Did you test that learners had learnt something in your session?
Analysis	The evidence: The question sheet at the end of the session enabled me to check that learning had occurred
Evaluation	Because/So what? The question sheet was effective in checking learning because the questions were focused

	and aimed at the different abilities in the group, so that I could check the depth of learning
Reflection	Impact/future actions The question sheet was effective and showed that all learners had grasped point A. The second point, however, was not understood by all and I need to recap this in detail next time

 ACTIVITY 1

Reflective task

In a style similar to the table above, reflect on an issue concerning teaching and learning. An example is given in the question, but you can alter it to make it more relevant to your practice.

Question	**How well did I differentiate learning today? Did I engage all learners?**
Analysis	
Evaluation	
Reflection	

In summary, reflection is a process. It isn't easy; it won't just happen, but the results of effective reflection are long lasting. It *is* worth the energy!

Proactive personal development

It is suggested that there are links between theories associated with reflection and those of motivation; a teacher must have the desire to develop themselves. This can be demonstrated as a development model, in which the teaching life is mapped.

A non-reflective practitioner will follow an open cycle (see Figure 8B) represented as:

Figure 8B   Model showing decline resulting from lack of development

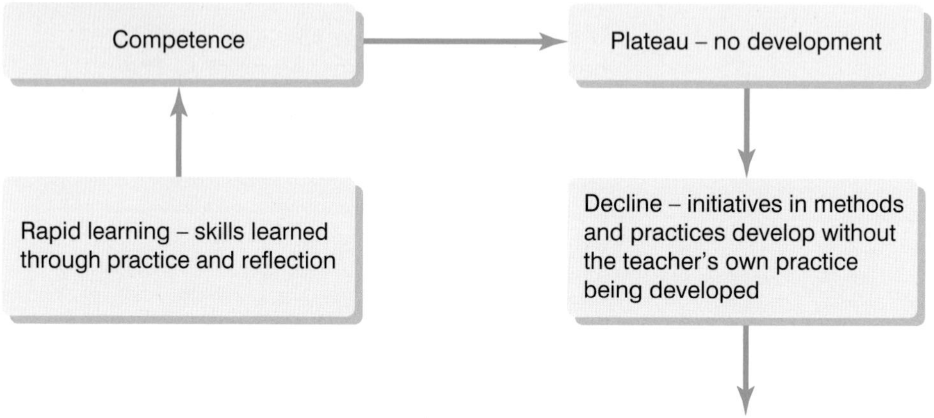

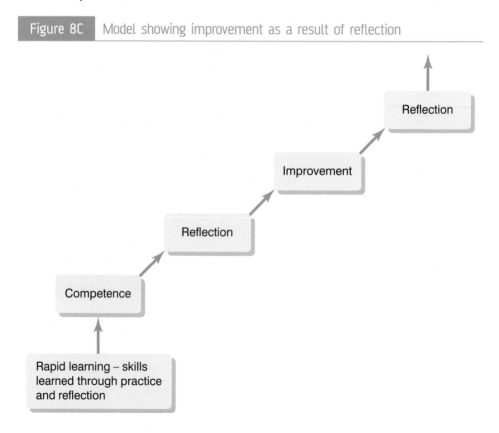

Alternatively, in the second model (Figure 8C), it shows how someone enters into constant improvement and development, thus keeping up-to-date with everything around the sector, through engagement with reflective practices.

Figure 8C   Model showing improvement as a result of reflection

This reinforces the point that development is determined by the individual teacher: thus it is within the power of the teacher to state when that development will occur. Does the teacher wait until they need to develop or do they develop to prepare themselves for what is to come? To a certain extent, this decision is usually taken out of the hands of the teacher by the teacher's line manager, but a reflective practitioner will always be ahead of their manager; always seeking to do better.

What constitutes personal development?

The simplest answer to that is: anything which develops the person. That can be:

- Teaching skills to make a better teacher.
- Functional skills to support and enhance literacy, numeracy and ICT skills.
- Study skills to enable efficient learning.
- IT skills to enhance skills in using computers, e-learning and e-communication.
- Tutor skills to support learners' development.
- Assessment skills to improve the reliability of judgements.
- Theoretical skills to improve understanding of roles.
- Character skills, time/stress/relaxation, to support the teacher under pressure.
- Legislation updates to ensure compliance.
- Research skills to maintain up-to-date practice and knowledge.

There are many other categories. In short, development = progress.

Progress will then lead to efficient and effective teachers, which in turn will lead to a successful learning environment – which is our key priority.

Recommended reading

Hillier, Y. (2005) *Reflective teaching in further and adult education.* London: Continuum.

Continuing personal and professional development

Continuing professional development, or more commonly CPD, is one of those terms that runs frequently from people's tongues, is very meaningful, but is rarely analysed to understand exactly what is meant by the expression. There are many definitions of CPD but first let us look at the phrase itself.

- Continuing means that it never ends; it is a continuous process.
- Professional means that it is focused on a specific role.
- Development means that it is goal-orientated.

Strathclyde University define CPD as: '[a] continuous process of personal growth, to improve the capability and realise the full potential of professional people at work' (www.cll.strath.ac.uk/). Another definition from Scotland is, 'anything undertaken to progress, assist or enhance a teacher's professionalism' (www.scotland.gov.uk/).

Training

Knowledge, competencies
professional development
teaching of vocational or prac
practical skills provides the b
- On-the-job training tak
- Off-the-job training aw

Continuing professional development is not unique to the teaching profession. In 2002, a report to review performance measures in the construction industry in order to create an ethos of sustainability and professionalism, led to the publication of the 'Accelerating Change' report, in which it is advocated that CPD is a 'holistic commitment to structured skills enhancement and personal or professional competence' (Sir John Egan, 2002).

In September 2007, The Further Education Teachers' Continuing Professional Development and Registration (England) Regulations (SI No 2007/2116) were launched. In 2012 they were repealed. This meant that teachers no longer needed to register with the Institute for Learning (IfL) and engage in a set number of CPD hours each year in order to maintain their registration and licence to practice. This removed a mandate for teachers to engage in CPD which, it could be argued, effectively forced CPD on teachers. The many who engage in CPD positively, fully aware of the benefits, did not change their practice during this period, because they valued the professionalism that CPD brings to their role.

Continuing Professional Development (CPD) and reflective practice are intrinsically linked. Quite simply, CPD is the act of gaining new skills and knowledge; reflection is making sure that the new skills and knowledge have an impact.

Different types of people teach; there is no particular type of person that will make a good teacher. In some trades and professions, experience leads to mastery; this is not true of the teaching profession, probably due to the main variable – the learner. Consequently, the teacher needs to constantly refine their skills. There are times when it feels like you need 'to run in order to keep up' with the sector.

Why do we need to engage in CPD?

The outcomes of CPD are gained by all: the teacher, the teaching team and the organisation. The impact of the CPD benefits the learners because they are faced with professional, knowledgeable and committed staff.

The main benefits are:

- To increase credibility
- To build personal confidence
- To provide career development
- To enhance earnings
- To keep up to date with facts, technology and skills
- To maintain professional (IfL) membership
- To motivate and improve effectiveness
- To cope with change.

For the organisation you work for, CPD:

- Maximises staff potential
- Updates skills to reflect changing business needs
- Responds to change
- Improves morale
- Develops teams
- Raises efficiency.

Investing in staff in the form of CPD is expensive yet is a necessary business requirement. There is no specific formula for calculating the budget for CPD as it will be dependent on need and funding availability, but not all CPD has a direct financial cost; most involves a time commitment.

Continuing personal and professional development (CPPD) is a process designed to improve performance. The most effective CPPD is that which is engaged in positively and thoughtfully. Chapter 26 looks at working examples and the ways that you can put CPPD into practice, this section gives an overview of the methods.

Approaches to CPPD

Continuing personal and professional development is the outcome of a reflective process in which current levels of performance are analysed and evaluated to identify where you need to be. Again, it is worth noting what reflection really means:

To practitioners, reflection means creating opportunities to pause and think about how effectively learning is taking place.

You can reflect on positive or negative experiences (both provide the opportunity to identify good and bad bits) and try and analyse why they are good or bad. You can learn from mistakes and successes. CPPD is the means to initiate improvement. Incidentally, our learners also need time to reflect. For them reflection means thinking time and pauses in sessions in order to consolidate learning, so it is equally important to create reflective moments for our learners.

Your ability to reflect and identify your development will depend upon:

● How you like to learn

● How urgent the change is required

● How much time you have available

● Your perception of your existing skills.

Most reflective practice occurs after what is described in many texts as a 'critical incident'. However, the use of the word 'critical' can be misconstrued. Although not intended, this appears to indicate something that has gone wrong, because one meaning of the word critical is 'a crisis point'; somebody in a critical condition is considered to 'be seriously or gravely ill'. In the context of reflection, critical is meant more positively, meaning 'identifying the merits and faults of something'. A more expressive offering could be 'noteworthy event'. Whichever terminology you prefer, the key is to reflect on both the good and bad things that occur. It is equally as important to understand why something worked well as it is to understand why it didn't.

People perceive CPPD in different ways according to their opinion and the value they place on the situation. If the CPPD is compulsory, the teacher probably rebels against the purpose, however well meaning; those events that are voluntary offer more empowerment and therefore, are received in a more positive way. There are several approaches to CPPD in which you reflect on events and activities.

Action research – identifying areas of development and using the training cycle (identify, plan, implement, evaluate) to fine tune practice aiming for improved teaching. Action research may involve considering theory and comparing or developing your teaching according to reading and acquired knowledge.

Peer observation and review – pairs or small groups observe each other and investigate collective issues to identify and share good practice.

Action learning – problem-solving from real situations. Individuals and small groups reflect on elements of a session and set out to learn from their mistakes and successes. Action learning can also describe the 'tweaks' made during a session to respond to what is going on around you. This type of learning is 'thinking on your feet'.

Learning logs – critical incidents or noteworthy events are recorded, analysed and evaluated to establish the reasons behind effective and ineffective strategies. The teacher writes a descriptive piece about a teaching scenario and asks him- or herself why it worked or did not work. The reflection will also include strategies to address future modifications.

Dialogue – informal chats in the staffroom or over a coffee; in fact anytime the conversation turns to teaching and learning. The sharing of good ideas or strategies that work in a specific situation, a good resource found, the address of a useful Internet site or how they dealt with a particular learner.

Mentoring – using a critical friend or specialist teacher to discuss teaching, gain new ideas or fine tune practice. It is usually a confidential relationship, based on trust when two people can share challenges, successes and worries and together plan for better practice. Mentoring is based on an experienced member of staff supporting a colleague.

Coaching – often confused with mentoring, but very different. In coaching the recipient is guided to develop solutions to issues concerning them. Together the colleagues explore ideas, critically evaluating noteworthy events. A coach does not offer answers, but aids the coachee to consider their actions and come up with new goals or answers to issues.

Case studies – written scenarios which lead individuals or groups to identify best practice or suggest ways of improving a given situation. This is a safe way of making suggestions prior to trying things out 'for real'.

Reading and research – topics are investigated using published materials. The individual reads many different strategies and analyses their preferred ways of working. By working in this way, some teachers feel more confident or safe to develop their practice knowing that they have investigated thoroughly.

Networking – attending meetings or conferences, working for related organisations, acting on committees or working parties brings a wealth of new ideas into a department, which can be shared with colleagues.

TES (and archived Teacher's TV) – an extensive collection of teaching resources from all parts of the education sector: http://www.tes.co.uk /teaching-resources/ Teachers are encouraged to share resources using the 'free to register' site.

Glossary of terms

Attainment reaching the goal or qualification aim

CPD the abbreviation for continuing professional development

CPPD the abbreviation for continuing personal and professional development

Critical analysis a detailed examination resulting in an opinion or argument

Critical incidents events that have a significant effect

Intrinsic motivation from within the person; natural desire

Mastery comprehensive ability

Reflection a considered opinion expressed in speech or writing; thoughts or considerations, developing ideas and thoughts

Reflective practice thoughtful practice to develop skills

Research an investigation

 SUMMARY

In this chapter we set out to achieve the following outcomes:

- To explain the terms reflection and reflective practice.
- To explain the general term continuing professional development (CPD).
- To explain the effects of reflective practice.
- To describe personal development and how this can benefit the teacher.
- To describe the purpose of CPD.
- To review the main methods of engaging in CPPD.

Your personal development

Initially we defined some key terms and explained what reflection and CPD means both to the teacher and the organisation. By providing some previously published opinions it offers the reader some suggestions for definitions. You will have considered what reflection is and how to use it to develop your own practice.

You are now able to describe the process of identifying current strengths and weaknesses and show how improvement provides continuous opportunities for development using a range of methodologies introduced in this chapter. These approaches to CPPD will be developed in later chapters.

You should be confident in explaining how and why you should evaluate and reflect on your performance and, following your teaching sessions, will demonstrate an ability to make reflections and prepare your development plans, in order to improve your practice.

CHAPTER 25

Theories and principles of reflection and CPPD

LEARNING OBJECTIVES

The measurable outcomes that you will achieve by reading this chapter and completing the activities are:

....

- To describe the main theories and principles of reflective practice
- To review how theories underpin the learning process and are important in reflection
- To identify key stages of the reflective process
- To evaluate your own practice against theories and principles of learning and communication
- To identify ways of adapting and improving own practice
- To develop an action plan to meet development needs

Theories associated with reflective practice

As with any other part of teaching, there are a number of models, created by **philosophers** and research, which help to explain the process of reflection and the reasons why it is important.

John Dewey wrote about reflective thinking in 1933. He suggested a five-stage model that takes someone through a problem to a solution. Simplified, it broadly follows a route of:

● Identifying the problem

● Thinking about answers, and

● Experimenting with solutions.

In this version, it expresses the notion of 'thinking about answers' in order to create the reflection, and thus identify a solution.

One theorist, David Kolb (1984), is used frequently to explain learning processes. He describes how people learn from their experiences, using trial and error (see Figure 8D). In this way, he explains how reflective practice builds upon things that happen (concrete experience) and develop through understanding why into a 'have another go' scenario. This, he suggests, is a logical cycle of development which constantly (through repetition) leads to better practice.

| Figure 8D | Kolb's learning cycle (1984) |

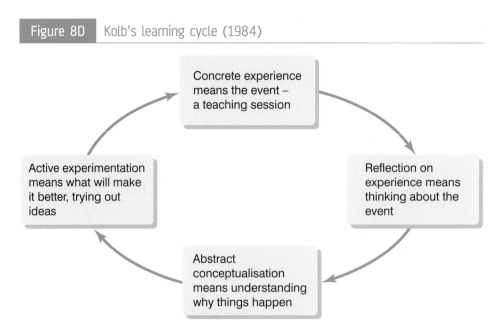

Concrete experience means the event – a teaching session

Reflection on experience means thinking about the event

Abstract conceptualisation means understanding why things happen

Active experimentation means what will make it better, trying out ideas

The year before this, Donald Schön (1983) had categorised theory i: two types:

1 Official theory – tried and tested strategies, passed down through the ages.
2 Unofficial theory – personal ideas used to problem-solve.

This was developed further when he considered reflection and suggested that reflection also occurred in one of two ways:

1 In-action – when thoughts (reflections) are made immediately and adjustments are made which react quickly to a problem. That is, those which could be described as thinking on your feet or, more cruelly, winging it!
2 On-action – when considerations (reflections) are made after the event. This is a more analytical and thought-out process in which future practice is amended. This is very similar to Kolb's opinions.

In 1985, Stephen Brookfield added his contributions to the beliefs of others. In his theory, Critical Lenses, he thinks about how we respond to assumptions. He states that what we are told can work (in theory), but that it may differ in practice. The analysis of this reminds us that a teacher's development is influenced by that which is around us, by the assumptions we make and by the events we experience. Do we always see what is in front of us?

More recently, David Boud (1995) adds to the theories, suggesting a clear link between self-assessment and reflection; learning only occurs as a result of both processes. This is similar to the thoughts of motivation theorist Bandura (1994) (see also Chapter 18), who said that in order to develop, someone must want to do so.

Applying this back to Boud, in order to learn (and improve), you have to be sufficiently motivated to want to analyse your own performance and spend time thinking about improving.

The theories of reflection as a learning tool

Learning and CPD are linked and this is particularly noticeable when looking at theories and models. The use of models to justify the practice of engaging with CPD is as important as the reverse; i.e. the development of models in the light of changing practices.

Most of the theories relating to reflection are derived from models associated with describing learning. It therefore has to be accepted that in the context of the theory, reflection is an experimental process to identify developments and CPD is the act of improvement or modification; both are therefore perceived as part of a learning process.

In the 1930s, Dewey (from the cognitivist school) first challenged traditional learning methods by talking about learning by experience. His notion of 'reflective action' was based on the idea that people constantly check their own performance and seek to develop but in order to learn they need to reflect (think about) their actions.

David Kolb's learning cycle (1984), previously shown in Figure 8D, is a model that explains how learning occurs. It is represented as a circle although there is not a particular starting point; dependent upon whether you are a 'thinker' or a 'doer' you will enter at different places in the cycle. The cycle is useful as an explanation of training, experiential learning and reflection. Kolb expanded this to suggest the characteristics of people within the cycle and how that influences how they respond to the learning process. More recently, Peter Honey and Alan Mumford (1992) used this model as a means of explaining that people like to learn in different ways – as pragmatists, theorists, activists or reflectors, although it must be remembered that these are labels – and very general ones at that.

In the illustration, Figure 8E, you will see the three very similar models described as follows are super imposed into one diagram. Whilst you will see, in this instance, three models, there could be an argument that they all say similar things, so the different models are not necessary.

In one of the represented models, Kolb's experiential learning cycle, he demonstrates the basic process of:

- *concrete experience* – undertaking an activity, feeling the emotion of the experience
- *reflective observation* – analysing it, watching oneself and considering what is going on around them

| Figure 8E | Kolb's experiential learning cycle |

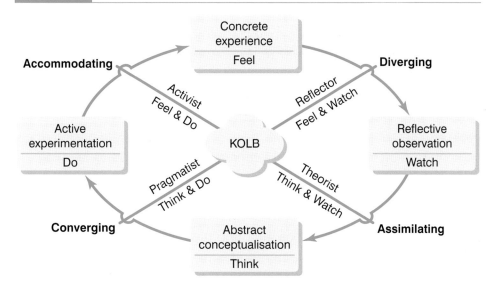

- *abstract conceptualisation* – thinking about why it happened, trying to understand why, and
- *active experimentation* – having another go at the activity, trial and error.

In another of his models, represented in Figure 8E, Kolb talks about the characteristics or preferences that people have during experiential activities:

- *Diverging* – those who avoid making assumptions
- *Assimilating* – those who absorb information
- *Converging* – those who follow patterns, and
- *Accommodating* – those who find ways to deal with issues, sometimes without a plan.

In the final representation it shows Honey and Mumford's model, a questionnaire devised to identify the preferred learning styles classifications, based on Kolb's models and expressed as four categories:

- *Reflectors* – who like to consider why things happen in the way that they do; they like to feel (experience) and see (watching).
- *Theorists* – who must identify every possible eventuality to ensure they make the correct decisions; they think and watch what goes on around them.

- *Pragmatists* – who will have a 'controlled' go, to test ideas and suggestions; they think and do.
- *Activists* – the people who do; they enjoy the experience and aren't frightened to try out new ideas.

Putting all of these models together it is easy to see the link between Kolb's and Honey and Mumford's views. All believe that in order to develop you need to follow a process; different people will enter the cycle at different points but all will follow it around the circle back to their beginning. Although experiential learning is clearly linked to learning preferences, Rogers (2002: 111) states that all of the learning styles are needed in order to develop practice, reminding us that the learning styles are preferences and not rules and that most people demonstrate multiple learning characteristics although they may be dominant in one particular style. The reference here to learning styles/preferences is to recognise that if people learn differently, then they will also use that learning in different ways and so a 'one size fits all' CPD strategy will not work. In reflective scenarios, teachers should also review the activity and the way they need to gain new skills and recognise and value differences.

It is also noteworthy, that Coffield (2004, 2008) is challenging current thinking and strategy and provides an alternative opinion on learning preferences. Although some say he is being mischievous in his publications, others feel that he is verbalising unsaid beliefs. He has listed 70 different learner preference theories and analysed 13 in detail. He argues against the widespread adoption of a particular style, particularly by managers and inspectorates. He does not dispute that people are different and like to learn in different ways, but he is against a generalised 'pigeonholing' to influence teaching styles.

Phil Race (2005) disagrees with the cyclical nature of Kolb's model. He finds the theories too wordy and perplexing. With a more modern view, he believes that learning starts with an issue and radiates out to encompass the change and development. He suggests, metaphorically, that it occurs in the same way that throwing a pebble into a pond starts the water rippling (Figure 8F). His theory therefore is known as 'Ripples'. In the shift from learning to reflection, he introduces the idea that there are five factors involved in successful learning and development:

- Wanting to learn
- Needing to learn
- Learning by doing
- Learning through feedback
- Making sense of things.

Commencing with the desire (need or want) to learn, a ripple effect is sent through the model with each stage having an effect on the next. The final stage of feedback may cause the ripples to return towards the middle again. The model is representative of a trial and error model when the teacher constantly reviews what is going on, modifying when necessary, and moving forward to achieve the desired result. The idea, presented by Race (2005) is shown in Figure 8F.

Figure 8F Race's ripples (2005, pp. 26–29)

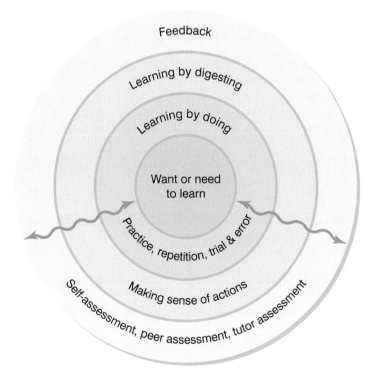

A model that you may find useful when thinking about development is that of Brookfield's Lenses. Brookfield (2007) suggests that sometimes we only see what we want to see and should look beyond our own beliefs and expectations. He suggests that reflective practitioners might want to look at problems through the eyes of others in order to get a bigger picture. He says: 'best teaching is critically reflective – constant scrutiny of assumptions about teaching' (2007: 2).

Let us consider the example in the following activity:

 **ACTIVITY 1**

Perspectives of relection

Look at the following statement:

'A TEACHER SHOULD DESIGN DIFFERENTIATED ACTIVITIES IN EVERY SESSION'

What do *you* think? Try to give your personal opinion, not someone else's or something that you've heard.

Response . . . .

What comments do you think your immediate supervisor would make to this statement?

What comments do you think your learners would make to this statement?

What comments do you think a lesson observer or inspector would make to this statement?

What comments do you think the parents, carers or employers of your learners would make to this statement?

Has your original opinion altered? In what way is your opinion influenced by other's responses?

Another study relates to the work of Donald Schön (1930–1997), who worked with Chris Argyris (1923–), concerning a model of 'theories of action'. Firstly, they expressed their opinions about learning and reflection. Very simply, they argued that people create their own theories in order to make sense of their actions, hence 'theory in action' (1974). In further work they describe learning as 'loops' (1978). In 'single-loop' learning if something goes wrong, a person thinks of another way and revises the action. In 'double-loop' learning, if something goes wrong the person asks themselves why and thinks of alternatives before having another go at the task. The double-loop idea is nearer the concepts of reflection in which the teacher would always question their performance in a bid to improve. However, whilst the idea challenges Kolb's opinion of learning being a cyclical process, this simplistic linear process does not recognise that sometimes in modifying the first situation you might also identify other necessary improvements, in which case a circular approach is more relevant.

Schön's (1983) second model is an effective suggestion for how reflection occurs. He suggests that there are two types of reflection. There are the reflections that occur which necessitate immediate response (reflection-in-action) and there are those reflections that occur after the event (reflection-on-action).

Reflection-in-action is the type of reflection that you and I might commonly describe as 'thinking on your feet'. It is an immediate response to something that happens in the classroom, for example, when touring the room following the launch of an activity you repeatedly hear from the groups that an important fact has either been misinterpreted or misunderstood, so you stop the activity and go over the fact again before re-commencing the activity. This is you reacting in favour of your learners by changing your learning plan to meet their needs. This is why a learning plan is a 'plan' and not a 'tablet of stone', so that you can be responsive.

Reflection-on-action is a more systematic, analytical approach to reflection. The reflection occurs after the event, rather than as it is happening. It is when you consciously evaluate your sessions with the aim of checking what went well and what needs to be modified next time you deliver a similar session. This is achieved through the writing of journals or post-session evaluation documents.

Bain (1999) *et al.* discuss levels of reflection, putting forward the notion that the ability to reflect improves with practice. They suggest that reflection is a spiral, broadly based on Kolb's Experiential Learning

Cycle, but in which reflective ability increases with experience. This is also not unlike Bloom (1956) who also suggested that levels of learning move from low to high order skills.

At its lowest level, by an inexperienced teacher or student teacher, reflection is personal and generally descriptive. At the next level a (student) teacher will ask questions of themselves. In the next stage the teacher is able to relate the incident to previous experiences or current discussions. At the fourth level, the teacher is trying to understand why things happen. Finally, the teacher fully understands what has occurred and has the ability to make conclusions and recommendations to improve their practice.

Finally, a teacher may wish to look at a practice model.

'Teaching Squares' is a process of linking with colleagues to share experiences, observe practice and engage in dialogue about teaching and learning. The partnership approach is non-threatening.

Reciprocity and shared responsibility Assumes that partners in the process have different roles and therefore share risks	*Appreciation* Aids development in a positive way
Self-referential reflection Aids identification of own learning points and therefore becomes non-critical of others	*Mutual respect* Aids empathy and respect of others in the partnership

Wessely (2002) Teaching Squares

In teaching squares a group of four people, preferably from different disciplines, observe each other and engage in shared reflections. This is a good way of engaging in peer observations, which is undoubtedly an excellent method of improving performance and sharing best practice.

There have been many contributors to the field of reflection, less so for CPD, although the main contributors to CPD are the thousands of people who participate in it each year. Most of the work around reflection argues its worth as a means of improving individuals to cope with the demands of their profession. CPD is an outcome, but it can also be an initiator of further development. If CPD were to occur without any reflection, then it would be meaningless.

Developing own practice in the context of the theories and principles of learning and communication

Evaluating your current practice

In any evaluation it is necessary in the first instance to know where you are now. Although you have this new knowledge of the theories, you have always had principles (see Part 7) in respect of your teaching standards – although they may not have had the label 'principle'. Remember, there are no right or wrong answers.

 ACTIVITY 2

Devising principles

This first activity requires you to think about what those principles are. By using a self-assessment questionnaire to identify your current beliefs and then a few questions which require an honest critique of your practice you will be able to reflect on the answers.

In the left hand column you will see questions which are designed to help you think about four basic principles – one around planning, one relating to the structure, another about differentiating activities and finally, one looking at assessment. In the right hand column are some suggested responses. They may not be exact, but the exercise is to prompt ideas from which you will be able to design your own statements.

▶

Question	Is your response?
How does planning and preparation help you in your teaching role?	As I know my subject inside out I don't feel I need to do learning plans, but I know what I'm doing.
	I have an idea of what I'll do and make sure I've got copies of hand-outs etc., so that I've got everything I need to deliver the topic.
	I have to write a script, if I don't then I don't feel in control.
	I feel my learning plan gives me confidence and ensures I appear professional.
	Other:
What is the usual structure of one of your sessions?	I tend to 'go with the flow'; I take my lead from my learners.
	It is structured with 'military precision'.
	I have a beginning where I introduce the topic, a middle where we add new stuff and an ending in which I summarise what's happened.
	I start with what I know my learners know, and build on it from their experiences and ideas.
	Other:
How do you vary your sessions according to the different learners you have?	I am meticulous in making sure that everyone has an individual learning plan and is set goals for the session.
	Each session includes a variety of activities so I guess that

	everyone will find something to their liking.
	I've done a learning preferences questionnaire, so I make sure that every session has the potential to meet those needs.
	To keep things interesting I vary each session, with catch up sessions every so often.
	Other:
How do you know that your learners have learned the topic you've taught?	I do a test at the end of every session.
	The sessions build up so that they have the necessary information for their coursework.
	They'll tell me if they don't understand something.
	Discussion, group and practical activities demonstrate their abilities and I respond to that.
	Other:

You may of course wish to modify one or more of the answers to make it more representative of your teaching – you can. This activity is to help you identify *your* principles not inflict principles on you!

From your answers, can you identify what your underlying principles are for:

● planning sessions?
● structuring sessions?
● meeting learners' needs?
● assessing learning?

Each principle will generally start with 'I will always …'

You should now have four principles, relating to planning, structure, differentiation and assessment; these are the values that you currently take into your learning environment.

You now need to analyse each one:

- Is it accurate in terms of *all* the sessions you run?
- Do you adhere to all of them without compromise?
- Is that what you want, or is it a 'best shot' ideal?

The ultimate test of your principle is …

How would you defend your principle if challenged about it by a colleague?

To answer this you need to think about the theories you explored in the first part of this chapter. Whatever your principle, it will be correct if you can justify it against the theory. If other people don't agree, it is probably because they are exponents of different theories, not that they are necessarily correct.

 ACTIVITY 3

Justifying principles against theory

(HINT: Review Part 7 before progressing to this activity)

- Is your principle supported by a behaviourist, cognitivist or humanist school of thought?
- Does it advocate a teacher-centred (objectivist) or learner-centred (constructivist) model of learning?
- Do you use a style of teaching based on pedagogy or andragogy?
- How do you develop the levels of learning – Bloom, Biggs or Gagné?
- Which motivation theory do you follow?
- Is the learning effective due to your methods of communication?

In completing this activity, you have created the opportunity to investigate a few of your principles and start to think about whether or not they are principles or whether they are hopes and wishes. Usually if your principle is not consistent practice or you can't justify it against theory then it may be a hope rather than a principle.

Alternatively, when listening to others justify their principles you may realise that there are alternative ways of doing something. In these cases you may feel the need to develop your principles.

Identifying changes in your practice

As with many other teaching and learning activities, time and experience will mean that you re-think what you do in the learning environment and why you do things in a particular way. Reflection is the key to this development. Whether it is a deliberate act of reviewing your practice or an *ad hoc* decision based on experience (Schön, 1983 and Kolb, 1984), either will result in identifying things that you want to do differently. Being receptive to the need to develop is the key to successful reflective practice. A couple of good questions to ask at this point are:

- What principles would you *like* to be able to advocate?
- What principles do your lesson observers say you *should* develop?

What is the reason behind you not having these principles now – is it inexperience, inability or that you don't have the time or skills to develop them?

Identifying the change is sometimes the easy part. You will have your own ideas, and we all know somebody that tells us 'if I were you ...' However, sometimes you may not know what to do to change, in which case you may benefit from seeking advice from managers, peers or mentors, listening to feedback from learners, or simply listening or asking questions in the staffroom, i.e. engaging in a CPPD opportunity.

Implementing change

Having analysed your current practice and considered the developments you wish to make you will finally be able to start thinking about how to make the changes.

The people who can help are:

- Your *tutor* on the teacher training programme. They will have observed you and given you ideas. During the discussions in sessions you may have ideas of your own.
- *Peers* on your training programme will often share ideas and experiences.
- Your *mentor* is an experienced practitioner in the same teaching area as yourself. They will be familiar with the curriculum and the learners so may have ideas they can share. Your organisation may also employ generic mentors who can help with wide-ranging teaching skills.
- Subject learning/specialist *coaches* are trained in supporting the staff teaching within curriculum areas and have access to an extensive range of material, so may be able to coach you towards implementing your ideas.
- Other members of the *team* will have experience of delivering a similar subject and will certainly know the learners, although they may not have experience of sharing their knowledge or the time to spend lots of time with colleagues.
- Your *manager* will usually be quite experienced in terms of delivering learning and assuming you feel comfortable working with him or her,

will be able to share with you the organisation's values which may help you understand your own principles.

The strategies that can help are collectively known as continuing professional development (CPD) activities; the following will help you to learn of new ideas, suggest ways of implementing changes and provide the theory to support your ideas.

- researching using text books or the Internet
- professional discussions with colleagues
- attending in-service training events
- personal study
- problem-solving activities
- trial-and-error practice
- action research
- reflective journals or diary logs

One of the most difficult yet important parts of implementing a change in practice is having the idea in the first place. So take the advice, be receptive to new ideas and become a reflective practitioner. Whether it works or not is sometimes immaterial. Many things that occur in your teaching seem like a good idea at the time, you should only feel pressured to change if things are not working or you are convinced that there is a better way of working. If your principles are resulting in your learners achieving in a timely manner and all of the necessary pieces of teacher administration are complete, then chances are there's nothing much wrong, you may only wish to get more efficient.

You may find it helpful to document the changes you wish to make in an action plan. This will help you to prioritise your actions, keep focused on the developments and monitor success on the way. In the next chapter you will learn about the many different ways to help you to develop. A suggested format for an action plan might be:

What change or modification do I need to make?	Why?	Who can I ask to help me?	What cpd strategies will I need to engage in?	When does this need to be achieved. Indicate when done ✓ or ✗	How will I know when the change is successful?
Example:					
One of the principles I wish to include in future sessions is to provide feedback to learners on how they are progressing in my sessions.	Theory suggests that it improves motivation. I want my learners to succeed.	My recent lesson observation stated that feedback was 'inconsistent' and that I should use 'constructive' feedback to learners following activities. Ask my mentor for ideas. Is there a corporate document that I should use?	Book appointment with mentor/tutor. Investigate the expression 'constructive'. www, text books. Ask if there is any guidance on Intranet. Check cpd plan for any events or workshops (attend if and when).	date	ALL learners will be clear about what they have to do to improve their practical skills and coursework.

ACTIVITY 4

Action planning

From the information in this chapter, identify at least one development need that you have. Consider how you are going to implement this change and what you perceive the benefits to be. Use the suggested grid above to give you some ideas and check your answers after reading the next chapter.

Recommended reading

Wessely, A. (2002) Teaching Squares: a handbook for participants. National Training Forum – www.ntlf.com/html/lib/suppmat/ts/tsparticipanthandbok/pdf

Pollard, A. (2005) *Reflective Teaching: Evidence Informed Professional Practice,* London: Continuum

Glossary of terms

Ad hoc random, unplanned action

Critique detailed analysis

Develop advance or improve ability

Evaluation to form an idea about something, to measure its effectiveness

Identify to determine or recognise something

Justify explain and prove something

Learning preferences the individual's favoured way of learning

Models a description or example to represent an idea

Philosopher someone who studies theories, attitudes or beliefs

Self-assessment **(an individual)** a method of confirming own ability

 SUMMARY

In this chapter we set out to achieve the following outcomes:

- To describe the main theories and principles of reflective practice.

- To review how theories underpin the learning process and are important in reflection.

- To identify key stages of the reflective process.
- To evaluate your own practice against theories and principles of learning and communication.
- To identify ways of adapting and improving own practice.
- To develop an action plan to meet development needs.

Your personal development

The chapter commences providing an opportunity to review the links between learning and reflection, which are noticeable when you look at the work done in theoretical research, providing many similarities in approach.

The main theories discussed were those of Dewey, Kolb, Honey and Mumford, Race, Brookfield, Schön and Bain. Each theorist describes their opinion of reflection although they are broadly similar; they conclude that reflection is effective as a means of development. The activity around Brookfield's theory provides the chance to think a little wider than personal viewpoints, aiming to change preconceived ideas and increase the significance that a teacher may attribute to CPD.

In the next part of the chapter you identified and evaluated your current principles of learning and communication. In the activities you selected relevant or close principles in relation to planning, structure, differentiation and assessment. You then used these to fine tune your own principles and in the second activity, you justified them against previously learned theoretical models. This gave an opportunity to review your principles and practice against perceptions of best practice, theory and advice offered. You then considered areas for improvement and change.

Finally, using a reflective model you have decided if change is necessary and how you would initiate any changes that were needed. You then considered how any resultant actions could be recorded in an action plan, together with an idea of how your action plan can be achieved.

CHAPTER 26
Improving practice

LEARNING OBJECTIVES

The measurable outcomes that you will achieve by reading this chapter and completing the activities are:

....

- To identify and select your own approach to continuing personal and professional development (CPPD)
- To evaluate formal and informal processes which lead to personal development
- To use reflection and feedback to plan your development and learning needs
- To describe direct and indirect strategies for acquiring feedback
- Identify how you can use assessment outcomes to develop the way you work in the future
- Analyse the effectiveness of your teaching strategies and identify opportunities to improve practice to 'outstanding'
- Inform your personal development plan
- To record the outcomes of CPPD activities and the impact they have on individuals, teams and organisations

Recognition that your performance can be improved is accepting that whatever does (or does not) happen in the classroom is in the hands of the teacher. The teacher can, by changing their own actions, influence the behaviours of others. In order to be able to improve your practice, you have got to be able to analyse and evaluate it. This is asking you to really break down what has occurred and check critically if things went well or not (see Chapter 25). Only when this analysis is complete can the teacher move to development and improvement.

Identifying development needs

Continuing professional development (CPD) is any activity that is undertaken in order to help or develop a teacher's professionalism. The additional 'P' in CPPD stands for 'personal' recognising that a teacher may need to develop skills other than those deemed for professional development.

What constitutes CPD/CPPD?

- Development of functional skills – e.g. literacy, mathematics, ICT.
- Development of personal skills – time management, problem-solving, etc.
- Development of professional skills – e.g. subject specific updating.
- Development of study skills – note taking, researching, etc.
- Development of teaching skills – differentiating, planning, ILT, etc.
- Development of legislative changes – copyright, health/safety, equality, etc.
- Development of support skills – special educational needs, learner support.
- Development of skills to embed functional skills into sessions.
- Awareness of imminent changes in policy or practice.
- Awareness of new management information systems.
- Awareness of organisational processes and procedures.
- Refreshing teaching skills.

Signposts to successful CPD include:

- Identify the starting point – what do you already know, what do you specifically want to find out.

- Don't expect a quick fix – a one-hour awareness or training session on a topic is unlikely to be the answer. You may need to go back to the classroom and practise the skills, fine-tuning them for you and your learners.

- Different activities work for different people – some learn from books, some learn by watching, some listen to experienced practitioners; you'll need to find out what suits you – try a learning preferences questionnaire to help discover your preferred way.

- Listen to the experts – they've probably had the same professional and emotional development as you, they will have empathy with your situation and will be happy to guide, but they may only prompt the motivation to try things out, they may not have all the answers.

- You are not alone – however foolish you feel, you are not the only person that is trying to tackle a problem – be it planning, behaviour, assessing, admin or whatever – always seek support.

- Think wider than going on courses, sometimes the answer is closer to home than you think.

- Take responsibility for your CPPD, empower yourself.

Initial (self) assessment

Initial assessment starts with an assessment of current strengths and areas for development. The things that are identified will depend on some variables:

- Your experience
- Your environment
- Your organisation
- Your learners

This is what makes your teaching unique. Others may have similar developments identified, but the context in which you make those developments is personal to you. The self-assessment will be your planning process. It may be useful to start your CPPD planning with a modified form of SWOT analysis.

ACTIVITY 1

CPPD SWOT analysis

You should complete the activity with the following documents to hand:

- Your job description and person specification
- Your department's most recent self-assessment report
- Your department's quality improvement plan
- Your CV
- Your most recent appraisal and lesson observation/micro-teach report
- Your Individual Learning Plan – from ITT course.

Evaluate:

Personal strengths	Skills required to carry out your job
Skills possessed but not used	Personal weaknesses

Keep a copy of your self-assessment in your folder, together with any resulting action plans.

Self-assessing is by far the most prolific and influential way of developing your practice. Only you honestly know what goes on in your sessions, the emotions you feel and the confidence and abilities you possess. Others may periodically enter your domain and make comment – which you may or may not eagerly grab – but only you know the whole truth!

Feedback resulting from self-assessment is a way of analysing the thoughts you have either at the time or later: it may be a very informal process. It may be that on the journey home at the end of the day you wonder why Learner X reacted like that in the session, or wondered how you could have delivered that bit of information in a better way, because it was clear that it wasn't fully understood, or how you could improve your use of a particular resource to make it more interactive – lots of things may go through your mind. It is important to realise, however, that you did what you did because it seemed right at the time, but with hindsight you could have…. It may be that you did what you did because that's all you knew; you may not know what else you could do.

The use of Professional Development Planners (PDPs) is a means of recording your development and learning, but may tell you about what else you need to do. For example:

Activity	Learning outcome	Future development
19 May 2013 Attended event in B149, to learn how to access data about how many learners pass their course. Organised by MIS team. two hours cpd.	Learned how to use the management information system to find out how many learners started, stayed and completed course. I now understand the importance of completing forms and responding to requests about numbers.	Found out that retention was not very good, especially for learners who start late on their programmes. Need to work with team to create an online induction to support late starters and ensure through tutorial and initial assessment that they settle into their course. Discuss at team meeting next week. Talk to lead tutor and Learner Services.

From this chart several things can be noted:

- Events attended
- Number of continuing professional development (CPD) hours

- What you got out of the development activity
- What further training is required.

The **feedback** in this instance is concerned with the teacher finding out that there is a retention issue on the course; probably during the course the trainers were able to give ideas about why and this enabled the teacher to plan some more development to overcome this secondary discovery.

Using feedback and reflection to identify development needs

Feedback comes to the teacher in many ways (see Figure 8G), and it is not always expected! Feedback, however derived, should be the starting point for a reflection and any resultant action, through CPPD or direct action.

Feedback will come from a variety of sources:

Direct:

- Self-assessment
- Peer assessment
- Performance assessment
- Learner feedback.

Indirect:

- Diaries and logs
- Action research
- Professional development planners.

Figure 8G Feedback-based improvement model

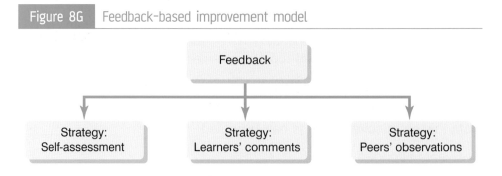

Post-session evaluation

An evaluation might be written after each session or a series of sessions or maybe in the form of a log or diary. Alternatively, a checklist is a simple method of starting the process of reflection or improvement.

The main parts of the session that you should reflect on are:

- Planning and preparation
- Teaching methods, participation and differentiation
- Assessment methods and questioning
- Learner progress
- Communication
- Resources.

You may also wish to reflect on:

- Tutorials
- Meetings
- Assignments (yours and theirs)
- Reading and research.

Post session evaluation is considered essential when teaching. More formally during your training you will be required to complete a post session evaluation checklist following many of the sessions used in your teaching practice evidence. As an experienced or qualified teacher this becomes less ritualistic and more informal. It is more likely that the post session evaluation will occur verbally or within the confines of your own mind. Obviously for future reference and evidence of development, these personal or verbal reflections are not as valuable as a CPPD strategy, but never discount the 'conversation' that you have with yourself when returning to the staffroom, or indeed the chat with the person sitting at the next desk.

Here is a suggestion for a self-assessment checklist to use after a session, with some ideas on how to complete it.

POST SESSION EVALUATION

Session:

Date:	Time:

Group:

Planning and preparation
Documentation, outcomes, variety, timing

Comment here about the quality and effectiveness of your documentation (SOW and LP), planned and actual outcomes, justification of (the planned variety of) teaching and learning strategies, proposed pace and timing of session.

Did the session go to plan?

To what extent does your plan demonstrate that your proposed session will meet the needs of all learners?

What effect did your planning have on your preparation, confidence and focus?

Delivery
Methods, differentiation, resources, balance, structure

Comment here about the quality and effectiveness of the methods, including traditional and modern methods you used in the session, the differentiated strategies used, your resources, balance of teaching and learning activities, structure of session (beginning, middle and end), how your teaching strategies supported weaker learners and challenged more able learners and promoted independence.

You may also wish to reflect on how you made your sessions inclusive, advocating equality of opportunity and celebrating diversity.

Learning
Engagement, participation, motivation

Comment here about the quality and effectiveness of how learners engaged with you and the content, the level of learners' participation, how you raised motivation and enjoyment in the topic.

Note strategies used to ensure safe working; learners who enjoy and succeed; skills relevant to employability or preparations for the next level/stage of learning.

Learning is the most important factor of teaching. If learning does not happen then teaching is inadequate. How can you ensure learning occurs? How do you know that your learners are making progress?

Environment
Room layout, safety, temperature, facilities, equipment

Comment here about the quality and effectiveness of the room layout, health and safety factors, impact that temperature had on learning, the facilities available and how you used them. Note any malfunctioning equipment to report later.

If an incident occurred, who do you need to report it to? (Sites or security, health and safety officer, line manager)

Rapport
Communication, behaviour, discipline, attendance

Comment here about the quality and effectiveness of your communication strategies (verbal, non-verbal and written), the learners' behaviour, how you dealt with any discipline issues, the effect of punctuality and attendance on learning.

Do you need to plan top-up activities for learners who missed this session?

Do you need to create a list of jargon used in sessions?

Do you need to follow up on any incidents in the session?

Assessment
Variety, achievement of outcomes, Q&A style, homework

Comment here about the quality and effectiveness of the different assessment methods used, the variety of methods chosen, whether or not learners achieved the planned outcomes, the style of Q&A used, and any homework set.

How well did you consolidate one chunk of learning before moving onto the next?

How do you KNOW that your learners have learned something in this session?

Can you identify exactly what each and every one of them achieved in the session?

Overall comments

What worked well? Why did it work well?

What was not successful? Why not?

How would you deliver this session again if you needed to?

What actions do you need to take – amending resources, addressing classroom management issues, etc.?

DOES THIS SESSION REFLECTION RAISE CPD ISSUES?

It is important also to mention at this stage, that you never stop learning and developing your teaching. Your teaching qualification is a bit like your driving test; the real learning starts afterwards. I have yet to meet the most experienced teacher who doesn't have a session they would rather forget and feel glad that they were not observed in. Equally, there is nothing like the feeling you have when you know that the session you've just delivered was fantastic! The important thing to remember is to chat about both scenarios to try and find out why.

Remember that checklists like this are to remind you about events; they will aid later reflections and enable adaptations for future sessions. The example is mainly descriptive with some analysis. Look at how this might be completed:

Session:

Date: February	Time: 10 – 12

Group: ED Second Year Level 3

Planning and preparation
Documentation, outcomes, variety, timing

I had a written copy of my plan on the desk. I found it useful there because at one point I forgot where I was, and had to refer to it to get me back on track. The timings were mixed, I allowed too much time to introduce the topic but when we went into the discussion group it was longer than I expected. Never imagined that the feedback would be so detailed, everyone wanted their say, even though others had said the same things. My writing of outcomes is much better now; I need to move now to differentiated ones for some students.

Delivery
Methods, differentiation, resources, balance, structure

I followed the advice of my tutor and used a very structured approach (had a beginning, a middle and an ending). In the main body of the session I introduced the topic with teacher talk and I didn't really do another teacher bit until the end. The middle was a mix of group activities using pyramid and jigsaw group strategies. The pyramid got a little manic; I don't think I managed it very well, especially as the groups got bigger. I remembered to photocopy my notes for AB, but then others wanted them - I think they may want them to prevent making notes themselves. Must speak to their tutor - do they know how to take notes? My ending was not good, because I had run out of time.

Learning
Engagement, participation, motivation

They seemed to like this way of learning, plenty of time to think about answers to problems. I think everyone joined in, but can't be sure.

Environment
Room layout, safety, temperature, facilities

I'm used to this room now, so I know what it's got and how to use everything. Wasted time setting out room when learners were in, I could have got in earlier (it is empty during the break). Didn't put it back when I'd finished cos I'd run out of time - should I? Noticed the iWB pen is missing.

Rapport
Communication, behaviour, discipline, attendance

Some good discussions going on, this must be useful in their communications session. I asked them to write key words in their personal dictionaries. No problems with behaviour this week - was that because I did more group work? Archie was off again today.

Assessment
Variety, achievement of outcomes, Q&A style, homework

Didn't really assess today, I listened and I think that they all met the outcomes because they took part in the discussion groups and we all got the same information from the groups. Do I know if they all progressed?

Overall comments

I was happy with the session, although the timing was still not right. Need to copy notes in case Archie is in next week. Group work was good.

ACTIVITY 2

Session evaluation

If this was your session evaluation, what reflections would you make?

How would you change the session if you had to repeat it?

What feedback would you give to the teacher if you had observed this session?

Diaries, logs and journals

These are means of recording events. They are used with a self-assessment process to help you to remember what happened. Although an indirect form of feedback, it creates the opportunity for feedback through records. The feedback comes when you re-read the logs. One of the advantages of keeping logs, particularly about critical incidents (noteworthy events), is that the reasons for things happening may not be explained until much later. If a student is playing up in your session, you may think at the time 'oh, that's unusual', but carry on nevertheless. It may not be until weeks later that you find out about something that happened in that learner's life that caused the unusual outburst. The reflection may be that next time you might initiate an 'are you OK' discussion (at an appropriate time). Just remember that they may say 'Yes', which wouldn't move anything forward at the time.

A typical journal page might look like this:

REFLECTIVE LOG
Incident Describe the incident or event on which you want to reflect
Questions What questions or issues does this raise?
Actions What thoughts do you have to overcome/build on this experience? Who will help you?
Reflection Reconsider the experience and any actions taken. What is the impact? Is the situation worse, same or better?

Learning to be a reflective practitioner is one of the key development areas for a teacher. It is hard to see things objectively, and it is equally hard to criticise your own practice without making excuses for occurrences. Seek the advice of your tutors, mentors and colleagues and learn to accept feedback as a genuine desire for self-improvement rather than a threat.

To develop your performance using self-assessment and reflection, especially in the more informal style described above, it is important that you move towards a more formal style in order to make it more valuable. To do this, it is better to write things down so that you can look at them later, in the cold light of day, perhaps with someone. List the facts, be descriptive, write down your immediate thoughts, feelings, reactions (i.e. start the evaluation) and then close the book until later.

In a more formal self-assessment process, you may decide to consider each part of your session systematically. You will certainly be asked to do this frequently as a student teacher or newly qualified teacher (NQT). It is part of the way you will learn teaching skills.

You may wish to engage in some detailed action research, i.e. a detailed investigation into something. It is when you undertake a systematic trial of a new or different strategy and analyse the effects – thus giving you feedback on future development. A good way of getting feedback following action research is to seek the views of your colleagues, i.e. peer review.

Peer assessment/review

Another method is to seek comments from a peer. Any feedback about a session is valuable. If your peer observes you they will see things you don't or give you an idea for an alternative method of doing something.

Feedback in peer assessment is an effective tool. It will be used during the early parts of your teacher training to support micro-teaching sessions. In this case you will deliver a small teaching session to your peers and ask for their comments. According to what they write or say, you will make decisions about future practice. As you develop as a teacher, you will initiate support and comments from other teachers, or mentors.

The chances are that they will use a document similar to the one used for self-assessment and together you will discuss the things that emerge. You may ask someone to come in and help you because you are struggling with a particular issue, or it may be part of your organisation's procedures that colleagues engage in peer assessment in order to initiate useful conversations about teaching and learning. It may be part of your development that you work with a mentor who is an experienced peer specifically assigned to support peer development. Peer review is an excellent vehicle for sharing good practice, either in conversation or e-forums.

The conversation that follows a peer observation, which is not judgemental, is a version of feedback. It is no different to the feedback you give to your learners to develop their skills and knowledge. The feedback itself should consist of comments, personal opinions, advice and suggestions. As with all feedback, it is up to you what you do with the suggestions and advice. Hopefully, it will give you ideas, but good feedback will 'listen' to your justifications and together develop ideas for improvement.

There are two things that you can do with feedback from peers: use it or lose it!

A peer might be:

- Colleagues informally making comments on your teaching in response to staffroom conversations.
- Colleagues formally making comments on your teaching through a peer mentoring system.
- Subject learning coaches sharing good ideas and resources.
- Teacher training tutors making assessments about your teaching.
- Mentors offering advice on techniques seen in sessions and other teacher activities.

More formal peers include:

- Managers making comments during annual performance and development reviews.
- Lesson observation teams making judgements about your teaching and the impact it has on learning.
- Internal verifiers/quality assurance staff validating decisions made during an assessment.

Good feedback will always start with sentences aimed at highlighting strengths seen. Constructive feedback continues with observations and discussions regarding development areas. Good feedback allows you to develop your own ideas, rather than receive imposed strategies. Effective feedback ends with the notion of an agreed plan for development. Contribute to the feedback by questioning or challenging statements to ensure you fully understand. Feedback should not be an instruction; it is a method of coaching to success.

How the development ideas are expressed will vary according to the formality of the feedback activity. In a mentoring situation you may hear:

> You need to …
>
> If I were you …
>
> You must/should…
>
> Have you ever tried …?
>
> Try this…

In a coaching situation, you may hear:

> Have you considered …?
>
> I wish I could …
>
> How could you do that differently…?
>
> Can I use …?
>
> Did you know …?

Your receptiveness to feedback from peers will depend upon:

- Who those peers are
- Whether the feedback is positive or negative
- Whether or not you respect the peer
- If it is what you want to hear
- If there are further anticipated effects following the feedback.

The important thing here is to listen, decide what you want or can do and reflect on how any identified improvements can be achieved or how the best practice can be shared.

Learners' views

Feedback and opinions increasingly comes from learners. Feedback from learners is one of the most valuable, yet least used feedback tools. Who better to ask about the quality of the teaching than those in receipt of it? Feedback from learners can be gathered through questionnaires or interviews, formally and informally.

You may, for example, ask learners periodically, 'What is the best bit of my session?' or 'What was the bit you least enjoyed?' Hopefully the answer to the first question is not 'the end' and the answer to the second question 'the start'. If it is, then you will need to become reflective and quickly seek advice from your mentor! The important thing is that the teacher gets into the habit of reflection.

You will probably find that your organisation undertakes surveys. These are generally quite specific and focused on the general learning experience. You may (or may not) see the full surveys, but the corridors are probably full of 'you said this … and we did … ' types of posters. These are great to show learners and visitors that you listen to views and comments, but for this feedback to be effective for you, you need something a little more specific. This might be in the form of a 'Classroom Critical Incident Questionnaire' (Brookfield 2007).

Ask your learners:

- At what moment in the session did you feel most engaged with what was happening?
- At what moment in the session did you feel most distanced from what was happening?
- What action (by teacher or student) was most helpful?
- What action (by teacher or student) was most puzzling?

The answers to these questions should be able to tell you which of your teaching strategies are most effective. You should make sure, however, to question enough learners to get a sufficient response. You will find that learners have different preferences when learning and this will impact on their replies. This method can also be used when you want to try something new. Don't be frightened to say 'I'm giving this a go and at the end of the session I'll ask you about it'. Learner Involvement is a high profile activity and reflects the change towards a customer focused business model.

ACTIVITY 3

Learner feedback

List the ways you do/could collect information from learners about:

- The teaching
- Their course or programme
- The learning environment
- The support they receive.

ACTIVITY 4

Learner questionnaire

1 Devise a questionnaire to use with a group of learners to find out if they enjoy and learn in your sessions. Note in your journal when you issued it, and undertake a self-assessment of the session.

2 Analyse the results of the questionnaire, writing the results in your journal.

3 Compare your self-assessment with the analysis of the student questionnaire.

4 Complete a table like this:

Main self-assessment outcomes: List the main points you thought were good/bad in the session.	Main student questionnaire outcomes: List the main points your learners thought were good/ bad in the session.

State the similarities between your self-assessment and the student questionnaire

State any differences between your self-assessment and the student questionnaire

Comment on the perceptions of your learners' experiences and compare them to your own

Reflection:

5 Justify why any differing opinions have occurred. Make suggestions about how your performance could be modified in the light of these findings.

Acquiring and responding to learners' feedback

There are a number of informal and formal methods of collecting views of students. Learner responsiveness or learner involvement is a proven strategy to develop practice and is common in many facets of the organisation. Our concern will be limited to using learner feedback to raise standards of teaching and learning.

At its simplest, the Post-It™ note, for example, means that learners can make a comment at the time it becomes apparent, without interrupting the flow of the session (things like 'I don't understand that' will be written on the Post-It™). The use of flash cards (usually using traffic light colours) provides the teacher with immediate feedback about levels of understanding. End of session discussion groups are effective in establishing the extent to which learners have achieved the desired learning outcomes. Focus groups are slightly more managed events and the interviewer has a clear idea of what they are trying to find out and will lead questioning in that direction.

Informal	Formal
Post-It™ notes	Surveys
Discussion groups	Evaluation sheets

▶

Informal	Formal
Verbal Q&A	Questionnaires
Flash Cards	Focus groups
Covert feedback: Attendance Behaviour	Tutorials Complaints cards

Most organisations delivering training use 'happy sheets' to capture the first reactions to the course or training activity. They are useful to a certain degree. (Did the course match its publicity? Did you achieve your planned objectives? How do you propose to use the learning gained?). However, in terms of evaluating the effectiveness of the learning it comes too soon: learners have not had the opportunity to use the learning or discuss it with anyone. Surveys are another frequently used strategy to establish student satisfaction. There are companies that carry this task out for an organisation and then match performance to other organisations it works with; this helps to benchmark performance against other providers.

Whatever the method of collecting information, it is of no use and would be a waste of time unless something is done about what is gathered from the information. You must close the loop.

You may collect information for a number of reasons:

1 To confirm that learners are happy on their chosen programme of study
2 To audit that processes have occurred, for example: induction paperwork completed, assessment processes are completed
3 To find out if learners' own objectives have been met
4 To check that differentiated learning methods are suitable
5 To inform quality assurance processes – course review, self-assessment, internal verification, satisfaction surveys
6 To confirm understanding

The final stage of collecting information and receiving feedback from learners is to use it to the benefit of the organisation, the teacher or the learners.

 **ACTIVITY 5**

Responding to learner comments

Look at the following results from learner feedback strategies. What would you do if this came to your attention?

- You find out from session Post-It™ notes that three learners did not understand a key theory you were trying to explain.
- The induction review form shows that not all learners received copies of the Student Charter.
- The course evaluations from today's course confirmed that many learners thought the course would give them ideas to use when they returned to their own establishment.

And using indirect feedback:

- The annual student survey said that 37 per cent of learners felt that the prices in the café were too expensive, 87 per cent would recommend their programme to someone else and 67 per cent said that they thought the staff delivering on their programme were helpful and friendly.
- The attendance during Miss B's session is rarely above 40 per cent. Other teachers of that programme have attendance averages of 80–100 per cent. Are learners 'voting with their feet?'

Assessment outcomes

The results of assessment will obviously tell us how well our learners are progressing in their programme or how much information they have understood; it may tell us how well they can transfer knowledge or skills into different situations. It is essential that we look at assessment outcomes and try to analyse what they are telling us. This evaluation will open up issues which can then be addressed. Tummons starts this process off by saying:

> Evaluation of the assessment is about judging the extent to which the assessment does what it is supposed to do.

Tummons 2007: 87

A reflective practitioner will take this one stage further and comment about what those results mean to them and endeavour to improve their own performance. For example:

 **ACTIVITY 6**

Case study: extract from a reflective diary

I set some short answer questions to do as part of the summary of the session. There were five questions collectively covering the learning outcomes I set at the beginning of the session, with a question about some 'nice to know' information that I covered immediately after break. I put the 'nice to know' question in to challenge the learners and I'm really pleased that they all answered it very well. In fact they all did very well in the test, mostly getting four out of five. When I looked in more detail I found out that a lot of them (six learners out of 17) generally went wrong on the same question.

I looked at my teaching notes later and checked that I had covered the topic; it was done by talking it through in some detail. I told the group to take notes and checked that they were writing, so I really can't understand why the question was poorly answered. In fact, I distinctly remember that it was just before break and that straight after break I covered the 'nice to know' bit which they did well in.

QUESTION: If you were reflecting on this event, what conclusions would you make?

Evaluation – suggested conclusions:

In this situation the teacher has not made the link between the teaching style used, the time within the session that the topic was covered and the outcome of the test question. Perhaps there is also a link between those that got the question wrong and their learning style; the topic was ideal for auditory and kinaesthetic learners, but not good for visual learners. Add to this that it was just before break and things like tiredness and low attention spans may have an impact on the learners' ability to retain information. The topic may have been one of those parts of the subject that is quite complicated and so has to be explained in detail to be understood. The teacher may have believed that the information was important so had to be delivered by verbal exposition, but that can be boring, because it is a passive activity.

Reflection

What would you do next time if you were the teacher?

DISCUSS this in groups and make notes in your own reflective journal.

What can assessment tell us?

Progress. A test can reveal how well, or not, a learner is progressing. This information can be used in tutorials to offer additional help in the topic, perhaps by directing attention to self-study packs or by advice to attend support workshops. It could be that the learner needs additional training in the skill before attempting another practical test. Do you need to arrange additional sessions, more practice or support?

Effectiveness of teaching. As in the reflective practice exercise above, if it was clear that a large number of learners had not grasped a topic, that topic should be revisited. It also reinforces the need to ensure that the questions or observations cover as much of the topic or curriculum as possible. If you don't ask the question, you won't know the answer! Do you need to change the way you teach a particular topic?

Effectiveness of assessment. Were all of the questions valid and reliable (see Part 5). Did the questions produce the expected answers? Were you able to mark them objectively? Was there a good coverage of topics/syllabus? These questions will establish how good your questions were in testing knowledge. If you were observing performance, you need to think about how useful this activity is in generating evidence for what is being assessed. Do you need to redesign certain aspects of the assessment? Look at the self-assessment checklist below and use the right-hand column to comment upon whether or not the assessments you use follow the rules.

ACTIVITY 7

Evaluate assessment techniques

Think of an assessment activity you have done recently. It could be something you've done at the end of the session to check learning, a module assignment, a unit task or programme end test.

Using the checklist below, answer the questions as fully as you can. The more detailed the answer, the better your analysis will be.

Validity ● How do the questions or tasks relate to material covered in sessions or in syllabus requirements? ● State how the assessments are balanced to reflect the (importance/significance of the) topics. ● Is the language or expression clear, unambiguous and understood? ● How do learners know what is expected of them?	
Reliability ● Describe the purpose of the marking guide or sample answer sheet. ● Describe how consistency in marking is to be achieved.	

- Describe the format of the assessment. Is this the most effective way of gathering evidence (proof of competence)?

Sufficiency

- How does the assessment cover aspects of the syllabus:
- In its entirety?
- Over a number of assessments?

Authenticity

- How do you guarantee that it is the learners' own work?

Relevance

- Describe how the assessments fit into the overall programme.
- Describe how they are related to industry/commercial standards.

Recording

State how the outcomes of the assessment are reported and recorded:

- To other tutors
- To learners
- To stakeholders.

Review how all aspects of the assessment were effective:

- Were there hard bits?
- Were the tasks successfully achieved?
- Were there tasks suited to all learners?
- Do the results show an even distribution of correct responses/ competence?

What do you think were the key strengths of the assessment?

What do you think were the key weaknesses in the assessment?

Administering the tests. Sometimes the answers can reveal how well we carried out the assessment. Things like: too little time to complete fully; classroom activity could not guarantee that everyone completed it independently; homework activity was not completed by everyone; proximity of learners meant that copying occurred; similar question/s not being answered or answered incorrectly. Do you need to review the timing or resources?

Statistics and outcomes. What do the results show? You can look at average scores to identify how easy or difficult the test was, and if there are similarities or trends between correctly and incorrectly answered questions. What does it tell you about the way you wrote the test, delivered the topic or distributed easy and hard questions?

The evaluation is 'How well have you taught?' If you consider that imparting knowledge is a key role and the measure is the recall, application or **mastery** of knowledge and skills, then you have to ask yourself, 'If the measure is not achieved, do I assume that the teaching is poor?' Not necessarily: it tends to mean that you have not taught in a way the learner can learn. In summary, teaching in a differentiated way is known to support the needs of everyone in your session, and therefore, assessment results will confirm the effectiveness of your differentiation.

Assessment and emotions

Assessment brings about many different feelings. The teacher can alleviate these emotions and thus help learners to do their best in assessments.

 **ACTIVITY 8**

Assessment emotions

Reflection

Think about the last time you were assessed. What were the emotions you experienced? How did your teacher prepare you for the assessment?

Consider:

- O/A Levels, GCSE exams
- Driving test
- Job interview
- University or college tests – dissertation, exams, assignments, NVQ observations
- Classwork and homework activities

Describe your emotions in two lists:

1 Positive emotions – for example: excitement, relief, ambition
2 Negative emotions – for example: fear, anxiety, nerves.

How could the teacher overcome the negative emotions?

How has the assessment developed since you did it?

In the activity above you may have discovered that the positive aspects of assessment are fewer than the negative aspects. Some of the things that can be done to help learners prepare for assessment include:

- Explaining what will happen
- Visits to assessment centres or rooms
- Practise tests
- Feedback to support strengths
- Practise form filling
- Imitate style of assessment

- A SWOT– strengths, weaknesses, opportunities, threats – analysis to show collective emotions
- Motivational interviewing.

Evaluating and reflecting on the assessments you use in the classroom and at the end of the programme will facilitate a positive move forward in your own development.

Performance assessments

Feedback from performance assessment is something that will probably occur either as part of your assessment on a teacher training qualification or as part of your organisation's quality assurance processes. Appendix: Top Tips offers some suggestions for successful Teaching Observations. A performance assessment will make a judgement on your abilities.

If it is an observation from your tutor, then the purpose, whilst assessing your competence, will also be to initiate conversations about skills and give developmental feedback. The outcome will probably be 'meets criteria', 'satisfactory' or 'requires improvement' – the wording may vary, but they are the usual outcomes of a teacher training assessment.

If the observation is part of the quality process by an inspection team, then the feedback is probably going to be more of a judgement than feedback. You will be told your particular strengths and weaknesses, from which you should be able to ascertain your grade. The observers are making judgements about the learning experience, to which you contribute, but may not control. Not all observers will tell you your grade and any feedback may either last a few seconds or be detailed.

If your observation is part of your organisation's quality improvement strategy, then you will find that the feedback part of the process will be detailed and enable you to discuss development opportunities or identify aspects of your practice to share with colleagues. There will be the required judgement, in the form of strengths, areas for improvement and a grade, but they are used more to inform the reporting process than the development part.

Whilst feedback varies according to your organisation's process, the grades in this process are likely to follow Ofsted's Common Inspection Framework – given that most of the education and training sector is measured in that way. The grades are therefore likely to be:

- *Grade 1 outstanding.* There are many strengths and few, if any, weaknesses, the teaching is exceptional and promotes an inspirational learning experience for all learners.
- *Grade 2 good.* The strengths outweigh the weaknesses. The learning experience is sound with many examples of good practice. All learners' needs are met and their attainment is greater than would be expected.
- *Grade 3 requires improvement.* There are a balance of strengths and weaknesses, leading to satisfactory learning experiences. The teaching meets most learners' needs and the attainment is as would be expected.
- *Grade 4 inadequate.* The weaknesses outweigh the strengths, resulting in learners who do not succeed in their goals and targets.

These grades are used by internal and external inspection teams to make judgements about the organisation's performance. It is likely that the judgements will be expanded onto some form of criteria grid to inform teachers about what to do to improve as well as providing guidance to observers and standardise practice.

How to become outstanding

Firstly, any observation is making a judgement about the learning experience. However, as the teacher is structuring that experience, there could be an inference that the judgement is attributed to the teacher. A judgement of 'requiring improvement' generally means that you have demonstrated many of the basics required of a teacher to initiate learning. It does mean that you can make both your teaching and your learners' experience better; reflection will help to achieve that – so will the help of an experienced teacher or mentor to initiate the ideas or motivate you into demonstrating them.

> 'There are few/no weaknesses identified in the lesson observation document, what else could I have done to get a grade one?'

This is one of the most frequent questions after an observation. Many teachers are good or better, which means that (in the observed session) the methods and activities they chose enabled learning to occur. It means that all of the learners responded well to activities and the session was well prepared, structured and executed. The observer is measuring the amount of learning and the teacher's role in initiating that process. The 'Handbook for the inspecting of further education and skills', published by Ofsted (2012), gives a very good indication of the rising expectations of the learning experience. The current priorities in terms of outstanding teaching relate to:

- Meeting the needs of all learners (differentiation and inclusion).
- Promoting independence.
- Supporting, stretching and challenging learners to maximise potential.
- Measuring and monitoring progress of learning (assessment for learning).

In this activity you might like to see how you are doing in **aspiring** to that grade of **excellence**: an outstanding session.

 ACTIVITY 9

Self analysis to outstanding

These are some statements, which *together* create the features of an outstanding session. In this activity you should read the statement and decide, using the self-analysis grid, how consistently you meet this standard. The key words highlighted express the quality indicator.

Planning

'*Comprehensive* planning demonstrates *highly effective* use of outcomes of previous assessments and enhances learning by meeting all learner needs.'

I do this always	I do this sometimes	I rarely do this	I need to develop this

Classroom environment

'Teachers promote *exceptional* working relationships that inspire learning.'

I do this always	I do this sometimes	I rarely do this	I need to develop this

Starts

'The session commences with an *air of purpose* and learners are clear about what they are learning'

I do this always	I do this sometimes	I rarely do this	I need to develop this

▶

Recap

'*All* learners are able to develop their skills based on a sound understanding and application of previous learning'

I do this always	I do this sometimes	I rarely do this	I need to develop this

Presentation skills

'Teachers are knowledgeable and *enthusiastic*, and the best are *inspirational,* skilfully imparting *their passion* to students.'

I do this always	I do this sometimes	I rarely do this	I need to develop this

Variety of teaching strategies

'Teachers use a *very wide* range of imaginative teaching strategies. These include revision games, group and pair work, debates and presentations.'

I do this always	I do this sometimes	I rarely do this	I need to develop this

Questioning

'Students are expected to *articulate* answers to questions in some *depth*, and are gently discouraged from monosyllabic responses.'

I do this always	I do this sometimes	I rarely do this	I need to develop this

Integration of functional skills

'Learners make *extremely* effective use of *all* opportunities to improve their functional skills'

I do this always	I do this sometimes	I rarely do this	I need to develop this

Differentiation

'Activities have been devised that meet *all learners' needs* and have the ability to *stretch and challenge* the more able and enable the weaker students to learn *effectively.*'

I do this always	I do this sometimes	I rarely do this	I need to develop this

Promotion of ILT

'Teachers use ILT in a highly *creative* way to promote effective learning both in and *outside* of the classroom'

I do this always	I do this sometimes	I rarely do this	I need to develop this

Assessment and targets

'Marking is *meticulous* and feedback gives students *clear* guidelines on ways to improve their work. Students are set *demanding* minimum performance standards at the start of their course.'

I do this always	I do this sometimes	I rarely do this	I need to develop this

Developing learner skills

'Students learn how to be *critical and analytical* as well as gaining good subject knowledge. Additional skills, such as group work and oral skills, are *well developed* through the teaching and learning methods used in the classroom.'

I do this always	I do this sometimes	I rarely do this	I need to develop this

Summary

'Learning is *constantly* checked throughout the session and *summarised* well at the end of sessions.'

I do this always	I do this sometimes	I rarely do this	I need to develop this

Independent learning

'Learners are *exceptionally* confident to work *independently* and monitor their *own* progress'

I do this always	I do this sometimes	I rarely do this	I need to develop this

The outstanding session has most, if not all of the left hand boxes ticked. Remember that outstanding sessions are not those which tick boxes, they are a collection of inspiring activities and exceptionally high levels of learning; they appear natural not showcased.

HOW DID *YOU* DO?

Identify three things that you are going to develop in order to aspire to that outstanding experience.

1

2

3

Source: Modified from training activity devised and delivered by Bradley Lightbody, College Net (2008).

Planning your CPPD

Planning CPPD, like many other educational processes is a business process, driven by cost/benefits strategy. A typical process in planning CPPD might be:

Organisational targets
(set by government/funding bodies)
↓
Specific strategic values and goals
(expressed in mission statements)
↓
Team targets
(identified through internal quality processes)
↓
Appraisal or performance review processes
↓
individual targets

Whilst identifying targets for an individual, the manager and teacher may agree on the development required in order to achieve those objectives, for example:

- To improve teaching and learning
- To improve success, retention and achievement of learners
- To meet curriculum change (new qualification types etc.)
- To address changes in policy, procedure or processes.

These would be written more specifically than stated here, but the list is offered as generic suggestions.

The next part of the process is the actual cycle of teaching/training. This follows a circular model of identifying training, designing or accessing training, implementing ideas and assessing and evaluating the impact (see Chapter 1). This will probably lead in turn to further identification of development needs.

There are a number of strategies that constitute CPPD, although the list is not exhaustive:

- Self or peer assessment opportunities
- In-service training events
- External events, conferences and seminars
- FE or HE courses
- Functional skill development
- Initial teacher training
- Updates on teaching and learning initiatives
- Committee membership
- Working party policy development groups
- Visits to other organisations
- Visits by other organisations
- Involvement with professional bodies
- Writing journal or magazine articles
- Professional reading or research
- Team or co-operative teaching
- Mentoring or supporting colleagues

- Coaching
- Evaluation resulting from lesson observations
- Participating in secondment or placement opportunities
- Curriculum analysis and review
- Curriculum planning and development
- Working with agencies – e.g. job clubs, careers service, etc.
- Progression or succession development
- Working with stakeholders – e.g. parents, governors, awarding bodies
- Contributing to internal or external quality or audit teams.

When planning CPPD it must be realistic, otherwise it will not be achieved. You may need to prioritise ideas into lists:

Things I must do	Things I should do	Things I could do

These priorities will need to recognise the constraints listed earlier:

- The urgency of demands imposed by self, peer or manager
- How significant the development is
- Time available to undertake the activity
- How enjoyable the activity is (learning preferences).

Just a word of caution here, analyse objectively, trying to avoid a 'cherry-picking' strategy which will ultimately result in inaccurate priorities being identified.

Recording your CPPD

The teacher is required to account for their CPPD activities during annual reviews or appraisals and can be set targets for CPPD achievement by their line manager. Teachers have a professional responsibility to create CPPD goals and to record and evaluate their development. Where a teacher undertakes CPPD activities, and it is considered good professional practice to do so, it is the responsibility of the individual teacher to record it; systems to do so are available in electronic and paper-based formats. There is not a specified recording device, although members of the IfL can access a link to a software programme (REfLECT™) which not only records the activity, but provides a storage area for journals, planning documents and all linked paperwork.

> 'CPD is most effective when practitioners reflect on their professional practice, develop a personal plan based on their identified needs and match this against their organisational context and development plan'.

> *Institute for Learning (2008)*

Recording your CPPD is not just listing the types of activities you've undertaken. The value of CPPD is in how it has impacted on you, your learners, the rest of the teaching team or the organisation you work for. If it does not impact on any of the above, you should question the necessity in the first place. The economic and financial culture at the moment does not support CPPD activities that merely achieve comments such as:

> 'It was good to see that everyone was experiencing the same issue', or
> 'Lunch was good'

There are two main records that you need to keep.

- The CPPD Plan
- The CPPD Record

Both belong to the individual teacher and it is their responsibility to keep it up to date. However, the line manager should agree the Plan (if they haven't contributed to its preparation) and sign off the Record as being an accurate account of developments achieved in the stated period. The documents below are suggestions; you could use either REfLECT™ or your organisation's paper or electronic recording systems.

CONTINUING PERSONAL AND PROFESSIONAL DEVELOPMENT PLAN				
COVERING THE PERIOD FROM: 2012–2013				
Extract from entries:				
Planned CPPD activity and date identified	Aims and desired outcomes of activity	Suggested methods to achieve the planned outcomes	Target date for completion	Actions
Performance Development Review PDR: September 2012 Improve stretch and challenge activities	To identify key implications. To raise awareness of impact of S&C in sessions. To improve value-added by supporting, stretching and challenging to maximise potential	Peer observation Shared good practice ideas from staff forums Attend cppd event	November 2012	Enrol for programme? How? Check with Personnel? Check date of next inset day
	To improve the quality of teaching and learning	Mentor support	July 2013	
Lesson Observation Any identified actions	Questioning techniques Differentiation Managing a workshop session	CPPD events	Easter 2013	Check with manager before embarking on activities requiring funding

Organisation: A N Other Training

Name: Joe Bloggs

I agree to support the Continuing Personal and Professional Development plans identified above.

Manager's signature: Ima Boss   Date: September 2012

Review Date: December 2012

It is likely that a plan will include specific tasks to be achieved and some generic statements to ensure that you can respond to on going issues. The plan should not be entirely management driven. It should include personal aims. It is hoped that both the manager and the member of teaching staff will happily negotiate proposals which meet personal, team and organisational targets, which will allow for aspirational development and career progression, within any budgetary constraints.

CONTINUING PERSONAL AND PROFESSIONAL DEVELOPMENT RECORD				
COVERING THE PERIOD FROM: 2012–2013				
Extract from entries:				
Date of event/hrs	Nature of event	Why?	What did I learn from this	How the organisation, teams and myself have benefited
27/10/12 7 hours cpd	Peer observations x 3	Identified in my PDR. This is becoming high profile and all staff are required to attend	What S+C means, what constitutes stretch, ideas and how it impacts on learners' success	I have been more conscious when planning sessions. I will now use IA more thoroughly and more confidently; my planning seeks to include a wider variety of experiences. In team meetings we discuss how to create more S+C into the curriculum

08/02/13 Three hrs	Managing workshops Research activity	My lesson observation suggested that this could be developed	Using the Internet I found a lot of information about workshops, mostly to do with setting clear learning goals	I ensure that at the start of each workshop I give 2-3 mins to each learner to check/ identify what they wish or need to achieve in the session, I can then check that as I tour the workshop and/or study centre. At the end of the session I have something to measure their achievement against and set further goals for the next session or for their home study. X Ref Workshop planner.doc
TOTAL No CPD HOURS 10 hours	Organisation: A N Other Training Name: Joe Bloggs This document is agreed to be a true record of Continuing Personal and Professional Development undertaken. Manager's signature: Date:			

Good practice suggests that you should always record your CPPD, if only to act as a reminder of your development. It is not always easy to remember to do this systematically, but you should decide whether you are a paper person or an electronic person and stick to that system of recording. Each year, usually in your annual performance review (appraisal) you will be required to review your plan against achievements with your line manager.

Glossary of terms

Analysis a detailed examination

Aspiring one's hopes and ambitions

Assessment to make a judgement about something, measurement of achievement

Benchmark a standard or point of reference to compare performance

CPD continuous professional development

Critical incidents events that have a significant effect

Excellence a grade one indicator meaning to be exceptionally good at teaching

Feedback verbal or written comments about the assessment intended to bring about improvement

IfL Institute for Learning

Imaginative a grade one indicator meaning creative or resourceful

Journal a diary

Justify explain and prove something

Learner Involvement customer service initiative about listening to learner's opinions

Mastery comprehensive ability

LP abbreviation for learning or session plan

NQT newly qualified teacher

Q&A abbreviation for question and answer

PDR (APR) abbreviation for performance development review; annual performance review; appraisal

Peer someone of the same status

REfLECT™ Trade mark software recording system from IfL

Research an investigation

SOW abbreviation for scheme of work

STRATEGY a systematic process

SWOT an analysis tool to identify strengths, weaknesses, opportunities and threats; used to assess current practice

Syllabus the structure of a qualification

 SUMMARY

In this chapter we set out to achieve the following outcomes:

- To identify and select your own approach to continuing personal and professional development (CPPD).
- To evaluate formal and informal processes which lead to personal development.
- To use reflection and feedback to plan your development and learning needs.
- To describe direct and indirect strategies for acquiring feedback.
- Identify how you can use assessment outcomes to develop the way you work in the future.
- Analyse the effectiveness of your teaching strategies and identify opportunities to improve practice to 'outstanding'.
- Inform your personal development plan.
- To record the outcomes of CPPD activities and the impact they have on individuals, teams and organisations.

Your personal development

In the first part of this chapter, you looked at some of the ways that you might engage in CPPD. Each approach was briefly described to give ideas about the different contexts in which they may be used. The discussion around identifying development needs listed several ideas that may need to be addressed, together with some hints to ensuring CPPD is effective. The section on self-assessment was reinforced with an activity to carry out this analysis. The activity was a modified SWOT analysis in which you compared your current strengths and known development needs against the skills required to carry out your job.

In the next part of the chapter you looked at receiving feedback as an initiator of development and how that feedback may be collected. These ideas were progressed to consider how post session evaluation impacts on development. There was a detailed breakdown of how and what to write in an evaluation, with ideas, reflective questions, links to current initiatives and key prompts.

The section continued with information about feedback from learners and peers to improve performance, making suggestions about collecting and using feedback. Three activities around the importance of learner feedback extended your understanding to consider hidden meanings of learner behaviour.

Then you considered how the outcomes of assessment can provide further feedback. You have compared the terms assessment and evaluation and how they apply to your development. You have used your skills learned to date to engage in an activity/case study which requires you to link assessment outcomes with teaching performance.

In a final activity in this section, you have explored the emotions that surround assessment and how you might overcome negative feelings.

You should be able to confidently use ideas and checklists to identify your own strengths and areas of development, with the aim of improving your assessment techniques.

The next part looked at performance assessments and how observations of teaching practice are used in the sector to audit and develop performance. You will understand the grade descriptors that apply to observations and in the final activity in this chapter you engaged in a task to help you aspire to outstanding. The activity, modified from a College Net training session, provides statements of merit and requires the individuals to assess their own performance at this high level and identify gaps. Using words such as inspirational and imaginative it raises the levels of performance.

Finally, we focused on planning and recording CPPD. There is a review of the planning process which links hierarchy and dissemination of organisational needs to the training cycle. The chapter concludes with a suggestion for a paper-based planning and recording system for your CPPD activities.

In summary, this chapter introduced a wide variety of self-assessment tools to question, analyse, evaluate and reflect upon your own teaching, taking views from all of the people involved in the learning process.

CHAPTER 27

Concepts and values of professional practice

LEARNING OBJECTIVES

The measurable outcomes that you will achieve by reading this chapter and completing the activities are:

....

- Describe and analyse key aspects of professionalism
- Reflect on ways in which your professional practice enhances the learner experience
- Explain how your professionalism contributes to the demands of external influences
- Describe your professional values

Defining professionalism: A set of collectively held
norms that regulate teaching according to values
and practices.

Craig and Fieschi (2007: 2)

Professionalism refers to a style of behaviour; it is something that is
deemed appropriate to the job role. There is not a list of professional
behaviours, but LLUK describe professional values (LLUK 2006), and
organisations will create their own codes of conduct. There is also
common sense. Teachers are in control of their own professionalism
and it is the ability to self-regulate that will prevent difficult situations
arising. It is, therefore, a good idea to link new teachers with more
experienced staff to help them through these sometimes unwritten rules.

Professionalism is also determined by the systems in which we work.
The ever changing way in which teaching is planned, delivered,
assessed and monitored, calls for another level of professionalism.
Either through desire or necessity, teachers cope well with the changes
they face; in fact so well that the change itself has become the norm,
and we constantly look for new curriculum ideas, new ways of creating
income, developing provision to meet the requests from employers and
learners. This is what we do; it is the professional within us that leads us
to keep up to date and in tune with what's going on around us.

The move from a vocational occupation into the teaching profession is
usually under-estimated. The education and training sector relies
significantly on the skills and experience of its workforce and their ability
or desire to want to make a difference by passing on those skills to a new
group of learners. The expectations of those entering the profession is
great; however highly qualified in their subject, new teachers are required
to undertake teaching qualifications. The role of a teacher is broader than
that of teaching. A teacher is also an administrator, tutor, assessor, quality
assurer and an analyst. Teaching is a profession, not a job.

The professional approach to work does come at a cost: the
commitment to teaching. Teachers have to balance their home and
workplace activities. The teacher does a significant amount of planning,
preparation and marking at home. This makes for a more 'professional'
approach to teaching, but it conflicts with family life. There do not seem
to be enough hours in the day to do everything that needs to be done;

hence the need to 'take work home'. Even our learners expect this commitment. Students seem quite shocked to see their teacher at the local supermarket and handing in a piece of work on one day and expecting it marked for the following day's session is not unusual (although frustrating when they have left it until the last minute anyway!). It is important to get the work/life balance correct whilst maintaining a professional approach. Alarmingly, according to the University and College Union (UCU 2007), teachers, on average, do 11 hours of unpaid overtime each week. Be careful and sensible with regard to this issue and be realistic in what you can and will do.

Davies (2006), in talking about professionalism in the sector, says that teachers come into teaching from many backgrounds; some are graduates, some are experienced practitioners in their vocational subject. It is this diverse background of the teaching staff that helps to make the education and training sector what it is today. People come into teaching because they want to share their experiences and knowledge with others; they complement their backgrounds with a teaching qualification, either as a personal value or in response to it being a mandatory requirement. The Lingfield Review of 2011 investigated the impact of the 2007 Regulations and concluded that Initial Teacher Training will remain a mandatory requirement for teachers and form part of national government policy until September 2013, at which point the legislation will be revised. A draft De-Regulation Bill has been published (July 2013).

Further reading

The Further Education Teachers' Continuing Professional Development (England) Regulations, 2007

The Further Education Teachers' Qualifications (England) Regulations, 2007

On the Agenda, September edition, IfL, 2012; and http://www.bis.gov.uk/
   assets/biscore/further-education-skills/docs/c/12-706-consultation-
   revocation-further-education-workforce-regulations.pdf)

Teachers have the option to voluntarily register with the Institute for
Learning and be part of an independent, practitioner-led, professional
membership body. They can complete a 'Professional Formation' to
become 'Qualified Teacher Learning and Skills' (QTLS); the Further
Education equivalent to QTS (Qualified Teacher Status) in schools. In
order to maintain a status as a professional, the teacher has to keep up-
to-date through engagement with a CPD process. Formerly by
regulation, but now more likely to be by local agreements, a full-time
lecturer is expected to participate in around 30 hours of continuing
professional practice each year. This amount is usually reduced pro-rata
for fractional or sessional staff, typically to a minimum of six hours.
Teachers are advised to consult their Contracts of Employment or HR
departments for further guidance on expectations.

Professionalism also includes the ability to teach well. Therefore, many of the
standards expected of teachers refer not only to a behaviour and a code of
conduct but also to an ability. It is these abilities that were explained in the
Professional Standards (LLUK 2006) and set a standard to be demonstrated
whilst undertaking teacher training qualifications. Again, the recent changes
and demise of LLUK, in favour of LSIS, their departure in favour of the
Education and Training Foundation and a review of the regulations will
impact on the extent to which these standards are used; nevertheless they
do provide a good basis for scaffolding a professional value.

Professional values, knowledge and practice

The Standards for Teachers, Tutors and Trainers (LLUK 2006) set out
three types of professionalism. The *values* that underpin everything we
do, the *knowledge* necessary to complete tasks well and the application
of *teaching* skills.

The *values* cover topics such as:

- learners' progress and achievement
- equality and inclusion
- teachers' reflection and development

- communication and collaboration
- working within codes of conduct
- quality of teaching and learning
- motivating learners
- integrity of assessment.

You will recognise these as not too dissimilar to the Principles of Learning described in Part 7. The values set out the standards we hope to achieve every time we meet our learners. By working in this way we are deemed to be professional and our managers can measure our performance to confirm competence and therefore confirm our professionalism.

As professionals we are also required to know and understand how to make the values listed above happen. By engaging with your Teacher Training programme and participating in training events within your organisation, your knowledge increases to cope with the changes in the sector. Similarly, there are standards of performance that are required in the classroom and staffrooms. What constitutes professionalism will vary according to the circumstances in which the teaching takes place; the standards of professionalism will always be high.

Baume (2006) identified five elements required in teaching:

- Context – in what setting the teaching is undertaken.
- Goals – what the teaching is intended to achieve.
- Knowledge – what the teacher should know about effective teaching.
- Virtues – what values, principles or codes of practice inform the teaching.
- Competences – what the teacher needs to be able to do in order to teach effectively.

Baume describes these elements in the context of European Higher Education; we are lucky in that the Lifelong Learning UK standards are clearly defined and agreed on a national level. Some of the professional practice standards advocated by LLUK (2006) include:

- Encouraging progression and development
- Promoting equality and inclusivity
- Improving through feedback and evaluation
- Sharing good practice
- Communicate and collaborate

- Conform to statutory and organisational codes
- Establish safe and purposeful learning environments
- Motivate and encourage learners
- Promote and develop autonomy
- Plan and prepare sessions
- Use a variety of methods and resources in sessions
- Assess learners
- Keep up to date in specialism
- Be literate, numerate and technologically up to date.

But what about the assumptions; the things that experience teach us: our common sense. Where do we find out about those? Little things like not knowing the code to the photocopier can seriously affect how we perform; our confidence may be reduced and it may appear as a poor level of professionalism. Our professionalism is also affected by the professionalism of those around us. On your first day in a new organisation, you will be told many things, sometimes to a point of overload; people are trying to be helpful but it is sometimes difficult to take everything in. A piece of advice here: at the end of the first day, make sure you know the name and phone number for your line manager, a mentor (or similarly experienced colleague) and a member of the admin team. With these points of reference there will not be many pieces of information you won't be able to find out – if they don't know the answer to your question, they'll know who to ask!

How do you know what you don't know?

	Detail	Help through ...
The basics	Toilets, rest areas, work rooms Timetable – diary commitments. Breaks, tea kitty arrangements. Security codes: Log-on passwords. Stationery requisition. Emergency procedures. Pay procedures. Staff room etiquette – noise, space, phones, etc.	Induction Line manager Administrative staff Health and Safety Manager Personnel

	Detail	Help through ...
The protocols	Use of IT equipment. Use of reprographic equipment. Policies and procedures. Staff and student Charters. Specialist rooms and equipment.	Mentor. Line Manager Intranet or VLE Advanced Practitioner
The inter-actions	Learner/teacher relationships Dress codes Behaviour code Use of phones/computers for personal use Classroom etiquette and rules	Experienced staff Mentor
Using information	*Pro formas* for learning plans, schemes of work, etc. Forms to record learners' progress and achievement Use of computer-based management information systems (MIS) Applying for funding for development	Intranet or VLE Mentor Experienced staff MIS administrative staff CPD Manager

Ways to improve professionalism

Our professionalism is maintained through continuous development and monitored through processes such as observing teaching and learning activities. Whilst the organisation in which you work will provide opportunities for personal development, the only person empowered to develop your professionalism is yourself. There are a number of activities and tactics that will help:

- Strive to develop your experience from initial teacher training through to advanced practice.
- Professionals in the classroom strive to be inspirational, are enthusiastic and teach with a passion, i.e. become outstanding teachers.

- Participate in CPD activities to keep up to date with initiatives.
- Continually look for new or better ways of working.
- Know what is expected of you.
- Engage positively in feedback sessions from lesson observations and peer observations.
- Set standards for learners to help you manage your time and workload.
- Be realistic when asked to do things; better to do a few things well than loads of things badly.
- Don't be afraid of saying 'no'.
- Undertake a variety of activities to multi-skill and position yourself for future change.
- Influence and promote change and development.
- Set yourself challenges.
- Read publications and journals for teachers.
- Look at TES (http:www.tes.co.uk).
- Highlight useful websites in your 'favourites' box.
- Encourage others to progress.
- Celebrate when things are successful.
- Promote good practice.

The impact of a professional approach

It sounds obvious, but in order to become professional you will need to identify and reinforce existing skills and learn new ones. Professional development is not something that is done to you, it is yours for the taking, and therefore you will need to take a proactive stance. The key word in describing independent or autonomous learning is 'responsibility'. The individual knows what they want, how they want it and when they want it. Teachers improve their professionalism by developing their own autonomy and, equally, improve their learners' ability to develop by increasing theirs too. The more independence and autonomy you have, the more confident and professional you appear; the more autonomy your learners have, the easier your teaching role is, in that you become less of a teacher and more of a facilitator of learning.

The independent teacher/learner has a number of characteristics:

- They like to control the pace of their learning
- They are able to manage and control the direction of their learning
- They work happily without support or require only minimum help
- They have the ability to self-assess objectively
- They have good time management skills
- They are intrinsically motivated
- They are self-directed
- They are aware of their own learning preferences
- They are fully aware of their own needs and how those needs will be met
- They are confident
- They like to learn through experience (Kolb, Schön).

Independence in learning will ensure that the teacher remains aware of, and responsive to, their surroundings and thus maintains their professionalism.

Look at the activity below and find out how you like to develop.

 ACTIVITY 1

....

Are you an independent learner?

Rate yourself:

1 = I strongly agree with the statement
2 = I agree with the statement
3 = I neither agree nor disagree with the statement
4 = I disagree with the statement
5 = I strongly disagree with the statement

▶

Statement:	☺			☹	
	1	2	3	4	5
I can set aside dedicated time to study					
I am able to organise my time well					
I prioritise my workload well					
I know what my goals are					
I know where to get information about a range of topics					
I am confident in reading and referencing material I find in books					
I can use search engines to find information					
I am a good communicator					
I have good levels of study skills					
I am focused when researching and reading					
I am objective when I analyse my strengths and areas for development					
I am highly motivated					
I enjoy learning					
I only require occasional support from tutors					
I am a reflective person					

The Results:

If you have ticked statements mainly in columns 1 and 2, then you are someone who likes to learn independently.

If you have mainly ticked statements in columns 4 and 5, I would suggest you are someone who benefits from attending courses to learn new skills.

If you have ticked mainly in box 3 or ticked unevenly across the table, then you have the potential to become an independent learner; you are able to initiate your own learning, yet like group learning and value your progress being monitored by a tutor.

Create a personal action plan to improve your autonomy as a learner.

Everyone controls their own learning to a certain extent, as we become more confident, experienced and self-aware the autonomy develops so that full independence occurs and the teacher develops and learns with minimal interventions from others. This level of professionalism will help us not only in the teaching aspects of our role. The impact of our professionalism will result in our learners having a better inclusive, learning experience and that is, after all, our primary purpose.

All of your learners will benefit from your professional approach; you will be far more aware of how to ensure they all achieve their goals and develop not only the skills required of their qualification, but skills for life.

By completing a PEST analysis of 'professionalism', you will see how the factors that influence your role will also provide the solutions to those influences.

 **ACTIVITY 2**

Pest analysis of professionalism

Consider the influences on the teaching profession, using a PEST analysis. Then consider how your professional approaches and principles will impact or contribute to those factors. Some key headings are included, but add some detail to those which apply to you:

	political	economic	sociological	technological
External Influences	e.g. government views and directives, policies.	e.g. employment, wealth, salaries, economic climate	e.g. population trends, demographics, health	e.g. computer hardware and software, communication, accessibility

▶

PROFESSIONALISM			
Impact	e.g. compliance with rules, success at Ofsted. How does what you do meet national and local targets?	e.g. meeting funding rules, learner numbers, increased salary How does what you do meet economic targets?	e.g. creating employable learners, opportunities for all groups in society, job satisfaction How does what you do meet social and community needs?	e.g. competent in admin of the role, up to date with own skills. How does what you do match the technological requirements of the era?

Glossary of terms

Code of conduct a set of standards governing professional values

Collaboration work effectively with others on an activity or project

Graduates people who have a degree

Inclusion finding opportunities to integrate all learners

Independent autonomous, working without supervision or dependence on another person

Integrity   having values and principles

Intranet internal computer-based communications network

MIS Management Information Systems, computer-based data storage software

Professional working as an expert within the sector

VLE Virtual Learning Environment

Vocational relating to learning the skills of an occupation

 SUMMARY

In this chapter we set out to achieve the following outcomes:

- To describe and analyse key aspects of professionalism.
- To reflect on ways in which your professional practice enhances the learner experience.
- To explain how your professionalism contributes to the demands of external influences.
- To describe your professional values.

Your personal development

In the opening paragraphs of this chapter we looked at a definition of professionalism, especially in the context of the teacher. We explored aspects of the teaching role and explained various descriptors of professionalism. The section also considered the importance of Lifelong Learning UK's professional standards for teachers, tutors and trainers in the sector and how they are used to indicate a professional approach to teaching.

The chapter progressed with a list of some of the things 'you need to know but, maybe, are too frightened to ask'. It also suggested who might be able to answer those questions for you. The text listed a number of ways that you could demonstrate professionalism.

You reflected upon the importance of developing autonomy as a means of demonstrating a professional approach to work. Whilst in this context it looked at the independence and autonomy of the teacher, it also suggested that developing autonomy in your learners is advantageous. The activity showed a self-assessment questionnaire, which was designed to discover how independent you are and what that means to your own learning preferences and development strategies.

Finally, you considered and had an opportunity to complete an activity, which helped you to link how the external factors that influence teachers can impact on you and how your professionalism will turn these factors into an inclusive learning experience.

CHAPTER 28
Policy and regulation

LEARNING OBJECTIVES

The measurable outcomes that you will achieve by reading this chapter and completing the activities are:

- To analyse the implications for and impact of government policies on practice in the education and training sector
- To analyse ways in which government policies and the requirements of regulatory bodies impact on practice in own specialist area
- To explain the roles of regulatory and funding bodies in the education and training sector

Who determines the policy?

The sector is influenced by many. Each government will set out its vision for the sector, most recently that vision is expressed within the Education and Skills Bill (2008) and the Education Act (2011). Overall management of the sector is under the Department of Education and Department for Business, Innovation and Skills (BIS) and regulations are formed from Bills, White Papers, Acts and other legislative processes. Various government departments are then appointed to oversee, advise, fund and quality assure the sector.

- Ofsted
- Skills Funding Agency/Education Funding Agency
- Ofqual
- Joint Council for Qualifications (JCQ)
- QAA
- LLUK, SVUK – LSIS (until July 2013), Education and Training Foundation
- IfL
- Sector Skills Councils
- Awarding Organisations
- Audit companies.

Ofsted

The Office for Standards in Education is the government department tasked with the role of inspecting quality and standards in education and training organisations. It publishes its findings on its website and thus it creates the opportunity for stakeholders to review quality of provision prior to deciding which educational establishment to attend. It uses a 'Common Inspection Framework' (CIF) to set the performance standards. It makes a judgement about a provider by seeking answers to questions relating to Outcomes for Learners, Quality of Teaching, Learning and Assessment, and Leadership and Management. The questions in the CIF are also answered in the provider/organisation's self-assessment report (SAR), which demonstrates how high quality is achieved, sustained and improvements are ensured. The current framework is applicable to inspections in a four year period from September 2012.

The Common Inspection Framework criteria:

In judging *outcomes for learners*, inspectors evaluate the extent to which:

- all learners achieve and make progress relative to their starting points and learning goals
- achievement gaps are narrowing between different groups of learners
- learners develop personal, social and employability skills
- learners progress to courses leading to higher-level qualifications and into jobs that meet local and national needs.

In judging the *quality of teaching, learning and assessment*, inspectors evaluate the extent to which:

- learners benefit from high expectations, engagement, care, support and motivation from staff
- staff use their skills and expertise to plan and deliver teaching, learning and support to meet each learner's needs
- staff initially assess learners' starting points and monitor their progress, set challenging tasks, and build on and extend learning for all learners
- learners understand how to improve as a result of frequent, detailed and accurate feedback from staff following assessment of their learning
- teaching and learning develop English, mathematics and functional skills, and support the achievement of learning goals and career aims
- appropriate and timely information, advice and guidance support learning effectively
- equality and diversity are promoted through teaching and learning.

Finally, inspectors evaluate the effectiveness of leadership and management, and decide if leaders, managers and governors:

- demonstrate an ambitious vision, have high expectations for what all learners can achieve, and attain high standards of quality and performance
- improve teaching and learning through rigorous performance management and appropriate professional development

- evaluate the quality of the provision through robust self-assessment, taking account of users' views, and use the findings to promote and develop capacity for sustainable improvement
- successfully plan, establish and manage the curriculum and learning programmes to meet the needs and interests of learners, employers and the local and national community
- actively promote equality and diversity, tackle bullying and discrimination, and narrow the achievement gap
- safeguard all learners.

(www.ofsted.gov.uk)

Equivalent organisations:

Wales – Estyn HM Inspectorate for Education and Training in Wales (www.estyn.gov.uk)

Scotland – Education Scotland, formerly HM Inspectorate of Education (www.educationscotland.gov.uk)

Northern Ireland – Department for Education (www.deni.gov.uk)

Eire – Department for Education and Skills (follows European Regulations and Frameworks) (www.education.ei)

Quality assurance agency (QAA)

Established in 1997, the organisation seeks to safeguard and help to improve the academic standards and quality of higher education (HE) in the United Kingdom, so that students have the best possible learning experience. It is funded through subscriptions from universities and project work undertaken for funding bodies.

(source: www.qaa.ac.uk)

They have three roles: the setting and maintaining of threshold academic standards; assuring and enhancing academic quality; and information about higher education provision.

The UK Quality Code for Higher Education (the quality code) sets out the expectations that all providers of UK higher education are required to meet.

It was revised in 2012 to replace the Integrated Quality Enhancement Review (IQER) process. The new process, set for implementation from 2013 is The Review for Higher Education in Further Education (RHEFE).

There are to be four themes by which to establish the provision: standards, quality, enhancement and public information, the main change being far more student engagement. The process starts about 16 weeks before the review visit, when higher education providers are expected to complete a self-evaluation of their provision.

Further reading

www.qaa.ac.uk/assuringstandardsandquality/quality-code.

http://www.qaa.ac.uk/Publications/InformationAndGuidance/Documents/ quality-code-brief-guide.pdf

http://www.qaa.ac.uk/AssuringStandardsAndQuality/quality-code/Pages/ default.aspx (accessed December 2012)

Key Information Sets (KIS) are a series of statements about higher education courses. To standardise the information and enable potential students the opportunity to compare and contrast courses, the HEFCE required providers to produce 'sets' of information about: student satisfaction, outcomes for students, teaching and learning methodology, assessment methodology, fees and finance, accommodation and professional accreditation. All of this information is available at the Unistats website, http://unistats.direct.gov.uk/

Ofqual

In England, the Office of the Qualifications and Examinations Regulator (Ofqual) is bound under **statute** to ensure that Awarding Organisations and their approved centres comply with a set of regulations relating to quality assurance. They are also responsible for vocational qualifications in Northern Ireland. University degrees are regulated by the Qualifications Assurance Agency (QAA).

In respect of Ofqual, the regulations are:

- The statutory regulation of external qualifications in England, Wales and Northern Ireland (2004).
- NVQ Code of Practice (revised 2006).
- Regulatory principles for e-assessment (2007).

- Regulatory Arrangements for the Qualifications and Credit Framework (2008).
- Operating rules for using the term NVQ in a QCF qualification title (2008).
- The Apprenticeship, Skills, Children and Learning Act (2009).

You do not need to be able to recite these, but you should know that they underpin the values of delivering and assessing accredited qualifications. The various regulations aim to meet the needs of learners, maintain standards and comparability, promote public confidence, support equality and diversity and ensure value for money. To this end they specify that Awarding Organisations and approved centres must comply with a set of guidelines.

Ofqual also regulates vocational qualifications in Northern Ireland, with the Council for the Curriculum, Examinations and Assessment (CCEA) which regulates other qualifications in Northern Ireland.

In Scotland, qualifications are regulated by Scottish Qualifications Authority (SQA).

In Wales, the regulatory body is the Department for Children, Education, Lifelong Learning and Skills (DCELLS).

In Eire, the National Qualifications Authority of Ireland (NQAI) has responsibility.

Wilson (2012)

For additional detailed information use the following links to the websites:

Ofqual: http://www.ofqual.gov.uk/

CCEA: http://www.rewardinglearning.org.uk/

SQA: http://www.sqa.org.uk/

DCELLS: http://wales.gov.uk/

NQAI: http://www.nqai.ie/

In addition, Ofqual sets out a framework to categorise qualifications, thus enabling transparency when looking at equivalences in qualifications. Formerly the National Qualifications Framework (published by The Qualifications and Curriculum Authority (QCA) and latterly, Qualifications Credit Framework (2009), the table below provides an overview of the frameworks, including the links to Higher Education qualifications (see also Chapters 10 and 22).

National Qualifications Framework (NQF)	Qualifications Credit Framework (QCF)	Framework for Higher Education Qualifications (FHEQ)
Pre-2009 Levels, e.g.	**2009 onwards levels, e.g.**	**Levels, e.g.**
LEVEL 5 NVQ Level 5 (NQF)	LEVEL 8 Specialist Award Awards, Certs, Dip in Strategic Direction	LEVEL 8 (D) Doctorates
	LEVEL 7 BTEC Professional Dips, Certs or Awards NVQ Level 5 (QCF)	LEVEL 7 (M) Masters Degrees Post Graduate Cert/ Diploma in Education
LEVEL 4 Certs of Higher Education HND, HNC NVQ Level 4 (NQF)	LEVEL 6 BTEC Professional Dips, Certs or Awards	LEVEL 6 (Graduate) Bachelors Degrees Bachelors Degrees with Honours Graduate Certs & Diplomas Professional Graduate Cert in Education
	LEVEL 5 BTEC Professional Dips, Certs or Awards HND	LEVEL 5 Diploma of Higher Education Foundation Degree HND
	LEVEL 4 BTEC Professional Dips, Certs or Awards HNC NVQ Level 4	LEVEL 4 Certs of Higher Education HNC

National Qualifications Framework (NQF)	Qualifications Credit Framework (QCF)	Framework for Higher Education Qualifications (FHEQ)
LEVEL 3 A Levels GCE Applied Subjects International Baccalaureate Key Skills Level 3 NVQ Level 3 (NQF)	LEVEL 3 BTEC Awards, Certs or Diplomas at L3 BTEC Nationals OCR Nationals NVQ Level 3	
LEVEL 2 GCSE A* to C Key/Functional Skills Level 2 NVQ Level 2 (NQF)	LEVEL 2 BTEC Awards, Certs or Diplomas at L2 Functional skills at Level 2 OCR Nationals NVQ Level 2	
LEVEL 1 GCSE Grades D to G BTEC Intro Dip and Cert OCR Nationals Key/Functional Skills Level 1 NVQ Level 1 (NQF)	LEVEL 1 BTEC Awards, Certs or Diplomas at L1 Foundation Learning Tier Pathways NVQ Level 1 Functional Skills at Level 1	
ENTRY LEVEL Entry Level Certificates ESOL Skills For Life Functional skills at Entry Level	ENTRY LEVEL BTEC Awards, Certs or Diplomas at Entry Foundation Learning Functional Skills at Entry Level	

The structure of the QCF, adapted from http://www.qca.org.uk/qca_8150.aspx

Skills funding agency, education funding agency

These are the current agencies (2012) responsible for funding the sector. Together the agencies fund most of the education and training sector including compulsory education. Other agencies include Higher Education Funding Council for England (HEFCE) and Welsh and Scottish departments.

The funding Family Tree:

Each year the departments set out their funding guidance; it is within these parameters that organisations plan and deliver their curriculum. Whilst year on year the funding is lessening, the funding is used to support a broad number of education and training types. This is complemented by contributions made by learners and employers. There are also an increasing number of courses provided under arrangements to fully recover all costs associated with the delivery and assessment of the course.

Agencies directing quality management

Learning and Skills Improvement Service (LSIS) Formerly the Quality Improvement Agency (QIA), it strives to ensure that the sector is known for its excellence and offers itself as a critical friend to organisations in order for them to achieve and perform to their fullest potential. The QIA was initially formed as a governmental response to the White Paper – *Further Education: raising skills, improving life chances* (March 2006). During

2008 the QIA, together with the Centre for Excellence in Leadership (CEL), became known as the Learning and Skills Improvement Service. LSIS is the sector-led body formed to accelerate quality improvement, increase participation and raise standards and achievement in the Further Education and skills sector in England. In 2011 it took over the work of LLUK and had a key role in the development and review of teacher training qualifications. Its work will be ceased in July 2013. The Education and Training Foundation is to take up some of their work.

(Sources: www.qia.org.uk and www.centreforexcellence.org.uk)

Lifelong Learning UK (LLUK) – ceased March 2011

An independent employer-led sector skills council which was responsible for the professional development of staff working in the sector. It supported the work of:

- community learning and development
- further education
- higher education
- libraries, archives and information services, and
- work-based learning.

(Source: www.lluk.org)

Standards Verification UK (SVUK) ceased March 2011.

A subsidiary of LLUK for the verification of Initial Teacher Training and Workforce Development. It worked closely with organisations who offer Initial Teacher Training qualifications in order to standardise and quality assure the delivery.

Its business is now transferred to Institute for Learning and Learning and Skills Improvement Service.

(Source: www.standardsverificationuk.org)

Institute for Learning (IfL) Formed in 2002, the IfL is the professional body for teachers, trainers, tutors, student teachers and assessors in the Further Education and Skills sector. It covers:

- Adult and community learning
- Emergency and Public Services

- FE Colleges
- Ministry of Defence
- Armed Services
- The Voluntary Sector
- Work-based Learning.

The organisation seeks to raise the professional status of teaching professionals. The IfL was elected as the body to confer ATLS/QTLS when the revised regulations for teachers were published in September 2007, resulting from 'Equipping our Teachers for the Future' 2004. In 2012 it returned to a voluntary membership and its status became that of an independent, practitioner-led organisation funded by its professional membership.

Sector Skills Councils (SSC) One of a number of organisations who represent occupational sectors. SSCs cover 90 per cent of the workforce skills and training interests. They represent the employers in small, medium and large businesses, write national occupational standards (NOS) and offer professional services. They used to be called National Training Organisations (NTOs) and help underpin the standards for NVQs and vocational training. LSIS was one of the associate members. There are approximately 20 SSCs representing most of the employment sector.

Source: http://www.sscalliance.org/SectorSkillsCouncils/
AssociateMembers.aspx

The various overarching assessment strategies, written by the SSCs (http://www.ukces.org.uk), define the main protocols for assuring quality for the qualification. Every SSC is required to define its assessment strategy to ensure integrity in assessment. It will cover rules such as assessor experience and competence, quality assurance requirements, specific sector idiosyncrasies and guidance on interpreting and assessing the occupational standards.

The post-compulsory education sector classifies provision into one of 15 subject sector areas (SSAs), thus providing a structure by which to benchmark provision.

SUBJECT SECTOR AREA CATEGORIES

1 Health, Public Services and Care

1.1 Medicine and Dentistry
1.2 Nursing and Subjects and Vocations Allied to Medicine
1.3 Health and Social Care
1.4 Public Services
1.5 Child Development and Well Being.

2 Science and Mathematics

2.1 Science
2.2 Mathematics and Statistics.

3 Agriculture, Horticulture and Animal Care

3.1 Agriculture
3.2 Horticulture and Forestry
3.3 Animal Care and Veterinary Science
3.4 Environmental Conservation.

4 Engineering and Manufacturing Technologies

4.1 Engineering
4.2 Manufacturing Technologies
4.3 Transportation Operations and Maintenance.

5 Construction, Planning and the Built Environment

5.1 Architecture
5.2 Building and Construction
5.3 Urban, Rural and Regional Planning.

6 Information and Communication Technology

6.1 ICT Practitioners
6.2 ICT for Users.

7 Retail and Commercial Enterprise

7.1 Retailing and Wholesaling
7.2 Warehousing and Distribution
7.3 Service Enterprises
7.4 Hospitality and Catering.

8 Leisure, Travel and Tourism

8.1 Sport, Leisure and Recreation
8.2 Travel and Tourism.

9 Arts, Media and Publishing

9.1 Performing Arts
9.2 Crafts, Creative Arts and Design
9.3 Media and Communication
9.4 Publishing and Information Services.

10 History, Philosophy and Theology

10.1 History
10.2 Archaeology and Archaeological Sciences
10.3 Philosophy
10.4 Theology and Religious Studies.

11 Social Sciences	12 Languages, Literature and Culture
11.1 Geography	12.1 Languages, Literature and Culture of the British Isles
11.2 Sociology and Social Policy	
11.3 Politics	12.2 Other Languages, Literature and Culture
11.4 Economics	
11.5 Anthropology.	12.3 Linguistics.

13 Education and Training	14 Preparation for Life and Work
13.1 Teaching and Lecturing	14.1 Foundations for Learning and Life
13.2 Direct Learning Support.	
	14.2 Preparation for Work.

15 Business Administration and Law
15.1 Accounting and Finance
15.2 Administration
15.3 Business Management
15.4 Marketing and Sales
15.5 Law and Legal Services.

(Source: http://www.thedataservice.org.uk/datadictionary/businessdefinitions/SSAs.htm)
Accessed Oct 2.12

Awarding Organisations (AO)

These are the organisations responsible for devising and accrediting qualifications. They are overseen by Ofqual who regulate how they operate. The 'Centre' is the name given to the college or training provider offering the qualifications. They entrust the responsibility for quality assurance to Centres who agree to uphold standards. The AO remains accountable to Ofqual for the integrity of the qualifications.

The external quality assurance system used by Awarding Organisations is called either External Verification or External Moderation. Vocational qualifications such as NVQs tend to be verified, while academic and vocationally related qualifications (VRQs) tend to be moderated. The process is similar; it is a way of ensuring that organisations who deliver qualifications on behalf of an Awarding Organisation do so with rigour and integrity. The process starts with a planned visit (or desk-based activity) during which the nominated representative of the Awarding Organisation (the External Quality Assurer – EQA) looks at work which has been delivered, assessed and internally quality assured within the centre. If everything is satisfactory the Awarding Organisation will authorise the issue of certificates. A visit concludes with a report detailing good practice and areas for development. These can then be transferred to the organisation's Quality Improvement Plan.

The AO also has the ability to restrict activity in centres that do not perform to the required standard. The sanctions, regulated by Ofqual, limit the activity within the Centre dependent upon the degree of non-compliance. At the highest level of sanction the Centre may be closed and risks losing reputation and the ability to deliver qualifications.

Level 0 tariff: the qualification has direct claims status (DCS) without any identified action points.

Level 1 tariff: the qualification has DCS with minor action points which must be addressed before the next visit.

Level 2 tariff: the qualification has DCS withheld or removed. This is either as a result of a serious assessment or verification concern or a previously identified action not being met. EQA has to sign off qualifications before a certification claim can be made.

Level 3a tariff: Registration of new candidates is suspended. The EQA considers that the centre is at risk of not upholding quality standards if more registrations were to be allowed.

Level 3b tariff: Registration and certification is suspended. There are significant serious concerns about the integrity of the assessment and internal quality assurance within the programme.

Level 4 tariff: Suspension of specified qualification. The Awarding Organisation considers that there is an irretrievable breakdown in the management and quality assurance processes which compromise the integrity of the qualification. The Centre must note this on any future applications for course approval.

Level 5 tariff: Suspension of all qualifications. The Awarding Organisation considers that there is an irretrievable breakdown in the management and quality assurance processes which compromise the integrity of all qualifications run at the Centre. The Centre must note this on any future applications for course approval.

Joint Council for Qualifications (JCQ)

Established in 2004, it represents seven major organisations:

AQA – Assessment and Qualifications Alliance

CCEA – Council for the Curriculum, Examinations and Assessment (N Ireland)

WJEC – Welsh Joint Education Committee

Edexcel

City and Guilds

SQA – Scottish Qualification Authority

OCR – Oxford, Cambridge and RSA Examinations.

These main providers of QCSEs and vocational qualifications collaborate through JCQ to share information, create opportunities to inform strategy and jointly respond to national issues. JCQ has a set of agreed principles, codes of conduct and provides a common format for qualification certification. In addition, it devises rules and regulations for the conduct of examinations to ensure security, integrity and clarity. Centres delivering examinable subjects will receive a visit from JCQ as part of the approval process to deliver such qualifications.

Source: http://www.jcq.org.uk/about_us/index.cfm

Audit companies

Building upon the best practices seen in the accountancy sector, auditors are a familiar contributor to quality management. They are used by organisations as consultants and by government agencies as inspectorates. Their role is to validate the accuracy of information. The subsequent reports enable organisations to implement improvement and government agencies can use the outcomes to risk assess the integrity of their providers. Audits regulate the business processes and provide third party assurance of (usually) financial stability.

The 'big five' companies are:

- Pricewaterhouse Coopers
- Ernst and Young
- KPMG
- Deloitte
- Tribal.

ACTIVITY 1

External influences

Now consolidate all of this information by completing the following in respect of each of the qualifications you teach on:

Qualification Title:

SSA:	QCF Level:	SSC:	Type:	Funding stream:

Awarding Organisation:	Status of last EV report:

Inspected by:	Grade at last inspection:

For example:

Qualification Title: *Award in Education and Training*

SSA: One of 1-15 categories of subjects	QCF Level: One of levels Pre-entry to L8 on the QCF	SSC: The body who writes the Occupational Standards and Units of Assessment	Type: FE/HE/ School link/ WFD/ Adult & Community Learning (ACL)	Funding stream: SFA/EFA/ full cost/ County Council/ HEFC etc
Education and Training - 13.1 Teaching and Lecturing	*Level 3*	*The Learning and Skills Improvement Service (LSIS)*	*FE*	*SFA*

Awarding Organisation: The organisation who certificates the qualification	Status of last EV report: Could be DCS or a sanction
City and Guilds	*New, but last External QA report was DCS*
Inspected by: Likely to be Ofsted or QAA	Grade at last inspection: If the subject wasn't inspected, then look at the grade for the learning establishment
Ofsted (Initial Teacher Training)	*Grade 2*

This activity will require you to ask some questions and do some research, but will give you an insight to what influences the programme and staff.

Glossary of terms

Academic Standards agreed level of educational competence

Achievement Gap expression used to focus on the way different groups in society perform against each other, e.g. boys and girls

Audit an official inspection by an independent person

Compliance to meet or agree recognised rules and standards

Direct Claims Status a high level of confidence from an AO, resulting in the ability to claim certification without a visit from an EQA (DCS)

Performance Management interventions and monitoring to maintain high standards

Regulation a rule or directive made by an official organisation

Robust strong approach, highly confident, reliable

Sanction a penalty for disobeying the rules

Statute a written law passed by a legislative body

Sustainable able to be maintained over a period of time

Vision mental image of the desired future

SUMMARY

In this chapter we set out to achieve the following outcomes:

- To analyse the implications for and impact of government policies on practice in the education and training sector.
- To analyse ways in which government policies and the requirements of regulatory bodies impact on practice in own specialist area.
- To explain the roles of regulatory and funding bodies in the education and training sector.

Your personal development

This informative chapter has outlined the key drivers of regulation and policy in the sector. It can be read with Chapter 21 which elaborates on the timeline of many of the organisations. The various organisations have been described, although are subject to change and the reader is advised to regularly review the status of the organisations mentioned.

In the final activity you have consolidated a lot of the information which plays a large part in shaping and developing the qualification or course you teach on.

CHAPTER 29

Quality management

LEARNING OBJECTIVES

The measurable outcomes that you will achieve by reading this chapter and completing the activities are:

....

- To define and state the difference between quality assurance and quality improvement
- To compare and contrast the main quality agencies and systems
- To list and describe ways of assuring and improving quality
- To evaluate the effectiveness of quality management in improving performance

Effective quality assurance

In Chapter 15, we have already looked at the quality assurance initiatives which help to provide a level of confidence in relation to assessment activities. In this chapter we look at quality management in general and how it is used to improve performance.

O'Connell (2005:182) describes the management of quality assurance as 'putting systems in place to ensure that high standards are achieved: as little as possible is left to chance in ensuring "right first time"' He states that by being proactive in the approach to quality assurance (QA) there will be a more productive outcome than relying on a reactive approach, i.e. discovering problems and putting actions into place to resolve them.

Cole and Kelly (2011:332) maintain that quality management (QM) is both proactive and reactive. They agree that 'written procedures, instructions, forms or records help to ensure that everyone is not just "doing his or her own thing" and that the organisation goes about its business in a structured way'.

Effective QA therefore, starts with procedures and systems to describe the correct way. The manager of the QA process will therefore be responsible for ensuring compliance.

Typical procedures seen in the education and training sector are:

- Admissions, enrolment and registration policy and procedures
- Information, advice and guidance policy and procedures
- Support for learners policy and procedures
- Management Information procedures
- Assessment and IQA policies and procedures
- Learner discipline and behaviour policies and procedures
- Human Resource Management policies and procedures
- Equality policy and procedures
- Health and Safety policy and procedures
- Safeguarding policy and procedures.

Any organisation approved to deliver training and education must have effective quality assurance systems in place to ensure high standards.

The systems will be implemented from within the organisation and from time to time will be inspected by external organisations.

The quality process follows a cyclical strategy of planning, implementing, checking and actioning improvement. This is explained in Figure 8H below.

Figure 8H   The quality cycle

PICA: Plan for quality processes, Implement the quality procedures, Check the outcomes, Act on the improvements required, is an acronym designed to help you remember the various stages of the quality cycle. Each relates to a particular aspect of quality assurance procedures and on completion of the cycle there will be an inevitable requirement to recommence the cycle thus ensuring continuous improvement.

Defining the terms

There are a number of expressions that you will come across when talking about quality. Although they have different meanings, you will sometimes come across them being interchanged; they all come under the generic term of Quality Management (QM). QM is initiated at organisational level and monitored in the sector by external agencies.

- Quality Control – checks the integrity of the process
- Quality Assurance – systematic checks to provide confidence
- Quality Improvement – a process to improve the reliability of quality systems.

Quality means doing it right when no-one is looking.

Henry Ford

Much of the discussion in this section is concerned with the quality management relating to the sector in general and provides a basis for understanding why things happen, and thus develops an empathy with the broader aspects of quality. The specific aspects of quality that most teachers will come across are those surrounding:

- Verification and moderation on behalf of Awarding Organisations to validate the certification of achievement.
- Assessment and evaluation processes surrounding inspection by agencies such as Ofsted and IiP.
- Analysis of performance at course level to collect information about learners' achievements.
- Monitoring of poor performance (individuals, courses, departments).
- Judgements about the learner's experience collected through lesson observation.

From a teacher's perspective, quality assurance is related to teaching, learning and assessment monitoring. It is these aspects that they are empowered to influence. Before you embark further in this chapter, consider where you are now in terms of controlling quality within your teaching.

ACTIVITY 1

How good are you?

List five ways you know or can check on how good your teaching is.

1

2

3

4

5

Need a clue?

- Who checks your teaching?
- How do you know if your learners enjoy their sessions?
- What happens after you've marked work?
- How do you know how well you are doing?
- How good is your course?
- How well do your learners achieve, progress and attain their goals?

Quality control

Quality control (QC) is checking the quality of the goods produced or services provided to ensure that bad workmanship is minimised and faulty goods or poor service provision is not passed onto the customer. In the education and training sector the customers are our learners, their employers, parents or carers; the 'goods' are the learning experience and the 'services' are the support and business functions.

The quality control systems that you will find in educational establishments include:

- Course review
- Self-assessment reports
- Observations of teaching and learning
- Learner satisfaction surveys
- Complaints cards
- Internal verification/moderation.

Quality assurance

Quality assurance (QA) derives from a business model. QA is a process that manages quality control systems to reassure managers and other stakeholders that systems are in place to undertake those checks.

Quality assurance ensures that goods and services (i.e. the learning experience) are fit for purpose, value for money, performed to a high standard and meet legal requirements. QA also provides a mechanism to intercept and identify error which can then be corrected. Accurate and effective identification of strengths (and how to build upon them) and areas for development are crucial to the success of an organisation.

The quality assurance systems that you will find in educational and training establishments include:

- Teaching and learning strategies
- Internal review/inspections
- SAR validation boards
- Learner voice processes
- Standardised documentation
- Programme, course or tutoring files and audits.

External quality assurance strategies used to confirm and validate quality include:

- Ofsted inspection
- IiP/Matrix/ISO assessments
- Framework for Excellence assessment
- External verification/moderation.

Quality improvement

Quality improvement (QI) is a strategy to list improvements and record how and when they will be achieved. By then recording the successful completion of the action, the 'loop is closed' and the revisions become the new QC process. Quality improvement is less effective when top-down; it needs to originate from within the organisation, with contributions from everyone.

The quality improvement systems that you will find in educational establishments include:

- Quality Improvement Plans
- Quality Improvement Boards

- Academic Boards
- Course Improvement Meetings
- Annual Assessment Visit
- Standardisation of assessment committees.

Quality management

Quality management (QM) is the driver that plans, implements and monitors the use of systems and procedures to control and assure the quality of goods and services. In the education and training sector our 'goods' are teaching and learning activities; services are things like student services, personnel, finance, administration, MIS, etc. The notion of quality practices has been evolving for a number of years. Some names associated with quality theories are:

Joseph Juran (1904–2008) – acclaimed writer and consultant who investigated a problem and cause system and advocated training and accountability as a major contributory factor to ensuring quality.

Walter A. Shewhart (1891–1967) – who is associated with quality control methods for production systems in order to improve reliability. He initiated the Cycle of Learning and Improvement – Plan–Do–Study–Act.

W. Edwards Deming (1900–1993) – who was inspired by the work of Shewhart and is widely acknowledged for developing processes to control quality, especially in America during WW2 and Japan in the 1950s. He modified Shewhart's Cycle to read Plan–Do–Check–Act which still forms the basis of many quality processes.

Henry Ford (1863–1947) and Karl Friedrich Benz (1844–1929) – associated with developing quality processes in the automotive industries.

Total quality management (TQM)

The motto for TQM principles is an attitude of 'right first time'; it is a 'zero tolerance' to poor quality. Quality is at the heart of the TQM organisation with everyone doing their part to ensure everything hits the highest of standards (see Figure 8l).

Figure 8l	A TQM Model for Education

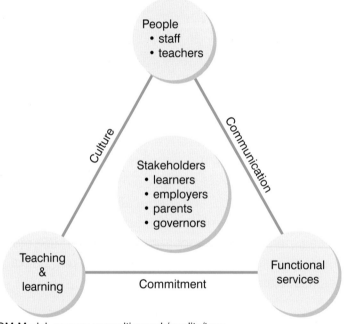

Based on TQM Model, source: www.dti.gov.uk/quality/tqm.

In the diagram, the stakeholders (the learners, employers, parents and governors) are central to the organisation. Surrounding them are the various things they will experience – the people, the support or functional services and of course, the teaching and learning. To maintain quality, the systems and procedures need to be communicated and understood by all, there needs to be a commitment to quality and quality improvement, and ideally, the organisation should be known as one in which quality and improvement are embedded into the culture of the organisation.

ACTIVITY 2

A case study

Joe is an experienced teacher, teaching on the Extended Diploma (ED) in Health and Social Care and the L2 Diploma in Health and Social Care. He also delivers Functional Skills, English and provides support and assessment to learners on the Level 2 NVQ in Care.

He works predominantly in the Care department; functional skills delivery is part of a wider support team, facilitating apprentices on a number of qualifications. Joe is quite confident with the ED programme; he has been teaching on the programme for a number of years. The Level 2 Diploma is brand new. The functional skills aspect of the work is OK; the difficulties arise from lack of motivation from learners, but Joe is quite used to being creative to raise learners' interest. The work on the Care NVQ is also brand new for Joe, and he is finding the transition to these different styles of working challenging.

His manager for the Care department has asked him to comment about the ED course he works on. Although the learners Joe teaches do well on his unit, this is not the same for the qualification overall. His manager is trying to find out what might be the reasons for this.

Joe is being asked to comment on achievement, teaching and learning, learners' enthusiasm and interest, support for learners and leadership of the programme. This is broadly in line with the Common Inspection Framework.

- How will the answers to these questions help Joe's manager to develop the Extended Diploma?
- What other quality initiatives might provide additional information?
- What recommendations might arise from the scenario?

Joe is also about to complete the first part of his course review for the Level 2 Diploma. He feels this is difficult because he has little to compare with what he is doing. What support would you give to Joe?

▶

Joe has just found out that the External Verifier is visiting the training company next month. As Joe is a new member of the team, the verifier is asking to speak to him. He is not looking forward to this, yet doesn't want to let the team down.

- What advice would you give to Joe to help him prepare for the visit?
- What information do you think he will need?
- How does this activity aid quality improvement?

This case study will have caused you to reflect on some of the things that Joe (and you) do in your normal daily routines to ensure that your learners have the best possible experience your organisation can provide.

In the next activity, you are asked to think a little more systematically and list some quality initiatives and their purposes.

 ACTIVITY 3

Quality processes

In your normal teaching life, list the quality processes that you participate in.

List others that you know occur, but do not directly involve you.

Quality Activity	Main aim or purpose of the activity	Frequency

From your list, which quality activity has the biggest influence on you, and why?

_____

_____

_____

_____

Systems to manage quality

1. Common inspection framework (CIF)

Following on from the information about Ofsted as a regulatory body, the Common Inspection Framework provides the standard to be applied to all aspects of the learners' journey. The CIF lists a number of questions (see Chapter 28) and the Handbook for the Inspection of Further Education and Skills, April 2013 also gives detail about the judgements made. So, depending upon the answers to the questions and the evidence supplied to prove the responses, organisations are graded according to their performance and excellence. The grades applied are:

Grade 1	Outstanding
Grade 2	Good
Grade 3	Requires improvement
Grade 4	Inadequate

Sources: http://www.ofsted.gov.uk/resources/how-colleges-improve

http://www.ofsted.gov.uk/resources/handbook-for-inspection-of-further-education-and-skills-september-2012, version April 2013

2. Self-assessment

As well as having a sound theoretical purpose (analysis, evaluation and reflection), self-assessment is also a requirement of funding bodies. A self-assessment report makes a judgement about the performance of the organisation. Ofsted check the accuracy of this self-regulation during the inspection visits. The frequency of the visit is risk-assessed and will vary according to the outcomes of the public data available to Ofsted.

In preparing the self-assessment report, teams gather to evaluate the previous year. The process starts with a course team co-ordinator preparing their annual course review, which is collated into programme area Self-Assessment Reports (SAR), broadly in line with Subject Sector Categories. These are then further collated into an overall SAR which provides the answers to the questions posed in the Common Inspection Framework.

This informs a six-stage process to quality improvement, which fits into the business cycle:

1 New SAR and QIP written
2 SAR and QIP validated
3 Governors and/or HMI during monitoring visits evaluate the SAR
4 Curriculum Planning Review
5 Monitoring of performance
6 Outcomes feed into the new SAR.

3. Framework for excellence

A quality assessment tool, devised by the Learning and Skills Council (LSC) and now managed by LSIS, which aims to improve performance by setting 'clear, unambiguous standards of excellence that all providers will want to achieve, so that they can demonstrate the quality of their provision'.

The Framework comprises three 'dimensions', each with two or three key performance areas (KPAs) and each having Performance Indicators (PIs). Wherever possible it uses information and results from other audit and inspection strategies.

Dimension 1	Dimension 2	Dimension 3
Responsiveness	*Effectiveness*	*Finance*
KPA 1a: Learners	KPA 2a: Quality of Outcomes	KPA 3a: Use of Resources
Performance indicators Learner views Learners' destinations	Performance indicator Success rates	Performance indicators Funding economy Resource efficiency Use of capital
KPA 1b: Employers	KPA 2b: Quality of Provision	KPA 3b: Financial Management and Control
Performance indicators Employer satisfaction survey Amount of bespoke training	Performance indicator Ofsted inspection grade	Performance indicators Accountability Financial planning Internal control Financial monitoring
		KPA 3c: Financial Health
		Performance indicators Solvency Sustainability Status

(Source: http://ffe.lsc.gov.uk/)

The information is made public through the FE Choices website to help future learners and employers make informed decisions about the organisation they, their child or employee will attend. The data is also part of the Ofsted health check in determining the frequency and timing of inspection visits.

http://fechoicesinformation.skillsfundingagency.bis.gov.uk/

4. Programme self-assessment and action document (PSAAD)

This is higher education's equivalent to self-assessment reports for the Education and Training Sector. The document collates information regarding enrolments and achievements, feedback from external examiners and future actions required to improve. It provides an annual commentary on the performance of HE programmes. It is also known as Annual Monitoring. This document is also relevant to those who teach HE in the FE context.

5. Investors in people (IiP)

A set of standards designed to recognise and value the importance of people and their contributions to business improvement. It mirrors the teaching/training cycle in that the standards reflect the planning, implementation and evaluative stages development. The Standards seek to address and confirm the organisation's commitment to training and developing its staff, and IiP assessors gather evidence from both managers and employees. It has ten categories of investigation, split into three parts, reflecting the training cycle:

Plan:

1 Business Strategy
2 Learning and Development Strategy
3 People Management Strategy
4 Leadership and Management Strategy.

Do:

5 Management Effectiveness
6 Recognition and Reward
7 Involvement and Empowerment
8 Learning and Development.

Review:

9 Performance Measurement
10 Continuous improvement.

Source: http://www.investorsinpeople.co.uk/Documents/Branding2009/IIP_framework_ summary09.pdf. Accessed Sep 2012

6. International organisation for standardisation (ISO)

ISO is recognised throughout the world, and due to language differences have adopted ISO as their acronym. Based on the training cycle, it enables organisations to work more efficiently and effectively by checking that the systems and procedures are implemented consistently throughout the organisation. There are over 17 000 different standards covering a wide variety of sectors, disciplines and initiatives. The two most commonly seen in the education and training sector are those associated with quality management and environmental management. The current series for quality management is the ISO 9001 standard and the ISO 14001 is the standard for environmental management. These international standards certify the process rather than the product.

(Source: http://www.iso.org)

7. Matrix assessment

Matrix standards are service standards relating to information, advice and guidance. Assessment looks at the work of those involved in giving assistance to learners as they embark on their post-compulsory learning. There are eight standards:

Delivering the service:	Awareness
	Defining the service
	Access to information
	Support in exploring options.
Managing the service:	Planning and maintaining the service
	Staff competence and support
	Feedback from customers
	QI through evaluation.

(Source: http://www.matrixstandard.com)

8. PQASSO

This stands for Practical Quality Assurance System for Small Organisations. Primarily for the voluntary sector and small businesses, it has wide-ranging criteria covering planning, services, monitoring and evaluating. It is an off-the-shelf QA system, written as a book to describe the system and offering a step-by-step approach for businesses. It covers the following aspects of business:

- Planning
- Governance
- Leadership and management
- User-centred service
- Managing people
- Learning and development
- Managing money
- Managing resources
- Communications and promotion
- Working with others
- Monitoring and evaluation
- Results.

The PQASSO Quality mark also provides users with an accreditation to recognise their quality systems.

(Source: www.ces-vol.org.uk)

9. Customer service excellence

The Customer Service Excellence standard focuses on customer service in the public sector and makes standards for communications and consultation. It ensures people's opinions are heard. It is a quality assurance system to encourage and enable organisations to deliver an understanding of the needs and preferences of their customers and local communities.

(Source: http://www.customerserviceexcellence.uk.com/aboutTheStandardCSE.html)

10. Peer review

This is an effective strategy which looks at initiating collaborative arrangements for similar organisations to review each other. For example: sharing ideas, participating in self-assessment panels, shadowing lesson observers to standardise grading. It builds upon the notion of transparency in quality assurance systems, sharing good practice and seeking advice from objective observers.

11. Quality improvement plan (QIP)

This document, which is written following a review and evaluation of performance, records what needs to be developed and how it will be achieved. A suggested plan is presented on the next page.

If there are a number of areas for development it may be necessary to prioritise the order you address them in. Developments on your plans can be:

- *Essential* – Failure to develop in this area will have significant effects on provision.
- *Desirable* – Systematic developments arise from routine quality processes or in response to initiatives.
- *Aspirational* – Developments which would enhance provision, but which only need to be carried out if time and skills allow.

12. Risk assessment

Assessing risk is both an internal process and one that is undertaken through audit and inspection. In the context of quality management, it checks that an organisation is able to objectively evaluate its ability to improve. The assessment indicates how much risk is associated either with the organisation *per se*, or with individual procedures. Organisational risk assessment provides the audit bodies and Ofsted with an indication of the frequency and intensity of inspection required. Procedural risk assessment provides the organisation with an indication of how effective a department or area is. Risk assessment can also be applied when prioritising improvements which are necessary.

Suggested format for a QIP

QUALITY IMPROVEMENT PLAN

Area for development	Actions required	Success indicator	By whom	By when	Review	Met Y/N
In this section you should write the development point, for example:	In this section you should identify the various activities you need to carry out in order to achieve an improvement	How will you know that your actions have achieved the desired result?	In this section you should identify someone whose responsibility it is to ensure success	In this section you should identify a realistic date by which you can confirm whether or not improvements have been achieved	In this section you can identify a point at which you will check how you are progressing with the actions and therefore check that you are on target to achieve success	
Achievement on Level 2 programme is below national benchmark	Design a course handbook. Include study skills to the programme. Monitor tutorial documentation to confirm effective advice is being given.	Achievement rate increased to match National Average	Course tutor Course Team	July 2013	December 2012 – check handbook issued to learners. October 2012 – check scheme of work includes study skills. December 2012 and March 2013 – audit tutorial records, observe a tutorial	

Risk assessment is a final measure in terms of quality which identifies the amount of risk that failure to implement an action incurs. Organisations should carry out their own business risk assessment.

EXAMPLE

A significant risk to providers of education and training is 'failure to recruit learners'. Every organisation should have a plan to ensure that this doesn't happen, or what it has to do if recruitment is lower than anticipated. Other risks include:

- Failure to secure funding
- Failure to pay suppliers
- Failure to meet targets for success
- Failure to meet needs of learners/local businesses etc.

External bodies will also make a risk assessment on organisations regarding their ability to provide services to learners. For example: Awarding Organisations use their external verification processes to assess the risk of centres in being able to provide rigorous assessment of their qualifications. If the risk is high then centres will be subjected to more careful scrutiny.

The SFA/EFA assess the risks associated with funding training organisations and colleges; if targets for success and financial security are not met then they will not continue to engage with the organisation for learning contracts.

 ACTIVITY 4

Quality initiatives

In this activity you should discover which quality initiatives are implemented in your organisation. A few are listed to give you a start …

Initiative	Last done	Key staff involved	Key purpose	Key outcome
Ofsted Inspection				
Self-Assessment Report				
Quality Improvement Panel				
Annual Assessment Visit				
Awarding Body Verification or moderation				
Investor in People				
Framework for Excellence assessment				
Observation of Teaching and Learning				

Use the information contained in this chapter, but also talk to other members of staff, especially the management team and more experienced teachers. Don't be frightened to ask questions such as:

- Why do we do this?
- What benefits result from these activities?
- How do they improve performance of individuals, teams and the organisation as a whole?

Finally, there is no single QA system which is suitable for all providers in the sector and covers all aspects of the business of learning. Some systems are undertaken voluntarily, others are an accepted requirement. The important thing is to ensure that the outcome of quality initiatives leads to a development and that an organisation can prove it has done so; thus every development identified whether successfully actioned or not, needs to be completed, thus the loop is closed. The purpose of quality management is to ensure organisations are consistently effective and efficient in their work.

 ACTIVITY 5

Quality improvement

Following on from the previous activities, list two things that you are going to do differently or improve upon now that you are more aware of quality standards in your organisation.

Activity	Who can help?	How will you know that you've made an improvement?	When do you hope to have achieved this by?

Recommended reading

Ewans, D. and Watters, K. (2002) *Using quality schemes in adult and community learning: a guide for managers,* Learning and Skills Development Agency.

Ravenhall, M. and Kenway, M. (2003) *Making a difference: leading and managing for quality improvement in adult and community learning,* Learning and Skills Development Agency.

Sallis, E. (2002) *Total Quality Management in Education,* Routledge.

Glossary of terms

Audit an official inspection by an independent person

Learner voice term given to processes which gather feedback from learners

PICA an acronym for remembering the parts of the Quality Cycle: plan, implement, check, act.

Quality Control checks the integrity of the process

Quality Assurance a system of review to confirm that processes are in place and applied to guarantee the quality of the service or product; systematic checks to provide confidence

Quality Improvement a process to improve the reliability of quality systems

Quality Management a statement of policy/cultural values in relation to quality

Self-regulation the ability to check own performance without asking others

Stakeholder a person, either directly or indirectly, associated or interested in the learner or organisation

Standardisation a process to confirm decisions and create norms

TQM Total Quality Management

 SUMMARY

In this chapter we set out to achieve the following outcomes:

- To define and state the difference between quality assurance and quality improvement.
- To compare and contrast the main quality agencies and systems.
- To list and describe ways of assuring and improving quality.
- To evaluate the effectiveness of quality management in improving performance.

Your personal development

The first part of this chapter is concerned with explaining the meaning of quality control, quality assurance, quality improvement and quality management. In the first activity you analyse where you are starting from in terms of awareness of quality initiatives.

You engage in three further activities; one which sets a scenario in the form of a case study and asks you to consider teaching and learning processes and requires you to suggest improvements or advice to the tutor; the second requires you to review current quality initiatives at your organisation; in the third you are required to think more widely about quality events in your organisation, their benefits and the outcomes they achieve. You have also analysed the impact of these initiatives on the organisation, stakeholders as well as yourself.

The middle part of the chapter lists and briefly describes the more common agencies and models used to implement quality management. Some of these are obligatory to the organisation; some are taken up in a more voluntary manner.

The closing part looks at the overall outcome of quality management, namely the improvements necessary to drive the business forward. It also looks briefly at risk assessment and the importance of understanding the implications of failing to have or comply with a quality management strategy.

In the final activity you were required to evaluate an aspect of your own performance and consider how it can be improved. You were asked to consolidate what you have learned so far and link it to your practice. You have identified at least two things that you will do differently and given yourself a CPD plan for improvement.

Following ideas introduced in Chapter 15, you have extended your understanding of QA from that relating to assessment to the more general QA strategies in place and how they are used to improve performance.

Part nine

Minimum core and functional skills

This part relates to the learning outcomes relating to minimum core
contained in other Units of Assessment

CHAPTER 30
Applying the minimum core in context

LEARNING OBJECTIVES

The measurable outcomes that you will achieve by reading this chapter and completing the activities are:

- To raise awareness of functional skills and the minimum core in the education and training sector
- To identify opportunities to deliver functional skills and competences in language, literacy, numeracy and information communication technologies (ICT)
- To develop competence in language, literacy, numeracy and information communication technologies (ICT)
- To identify opportunities to develop your skills and understanding of literacy, language, numeracy and ICT
- To demonstrate your progress through referencing teaching and learning activities and your personal development to the standards

Brief history of functional skills

In 1998, the Moser Report highlighted the poor basic skills in society, saying that one in five people were functionally illiterate. The Leitch Review in 2006 stated that one-third of adults do not have basic school leaving qualifications. **Functional skills** are a key element of the 14–19 reforms as set out in the 14–19 Education and Skills White Paper (DfES 2005), which defines functional skills as:

> Core elements of English, mathematics and ICT that provide an individual with essential knowledge, skills and understanding that will enable them to operate confidently, effectively and independently in life and work.
>
> *14–19 Education and Skills: Implementation Plan (Feb. 2005)*
> *www.dfes.gov.uk*

The Basic Skills Agency (2001) writes:

> The ability to read, write and speak English and to use mathematics at a level necessary to function and progress at work and in society in general.
>
> *http://www.basic-skills.co.uk*

2004   Final report of the Working Group on 14–19 Reform. The report made key recommendations to include functional skills as a key aspect of core learning

2005   14-19 Education and Skills White Paper expressed concerns about the standards in the application of English, mathematics and ICT

2007   Implementing the Leitch Review of Skills in Education said that FS must be part of the employability programme which is aimed at getting the unemployed into work

2007   QCDA created first design of the qualifications – piloted in the sector

2010   Further modifications and a formal pilot of the qualifications announced. The Minister of State for Further Education, Skills and Lifelong Learning issued plans to implement FS fully from 2012

2011   New Challenges, New Chances report indicates that FS will be a mandatory part of training apprenticeships. It further confirms

that it will be part of the core curriculum for 14 to 19-year-olds
and offered as stand-alone qualifications for the over 19s

2012   Amendments to the assessment structure resulting from the
pilot, and in September the qualifications were widely available

2013   The Wolf report into Key Stage 4 National Curriculum is on-
going and may recommend further changes

Functional skills (FS) are a series of qualifications and development
initiatives to standardise qualifications for English, maths and ICT. In the
past and in the present they have been known by several different names:

● Core skills
● Common skills
● Basic skills
● Key skills
● Minimum core.

Irrespective of the name, functional skills refer to the mastery of English/
literacy, maths/numeracy and ICT/information technology. These are the
skills that underpin all learning and without them learners will struggle to
meet the demands of their qualification, the world of work and life skills.
Edexcel refer to the fact that the skills 'equip learners with the basic
practical skills required in everyday life, education and the workplace'.
AQA talk about having, 'better FS skills mean a better future – as
students and as employees'. Each of the names listed relates to a style
or level of qualification; you will still hear them referred to as such in the
staff room. Do not be confused – everyone is talking about the same
broad topic, the range of terminology in use indicates the many
changes in the topic; all are mutations of qualification designed to
improve English, mathematics and ICT skills. For example:

● *Common/core skills* were attached to academic qualifications, such
as General National Vocational Qualifications (GNVQs).
● *Core Skills* (Scotland) is the equivalent qualification in Scotland.
● *Essential Skills* (Wales)is the equivalent qualification in Wales.
● *Basic skills* are an initiative introduced by government, to raise the
standards of literacy and numeracy in the post compulsory sector,
usually assessed by a test.

- *Literacy/Communications and Numeracy/Application of number* are alternative expressions for English and mathematics.

- *Key skills* are basic skills applied to or in the context of a vocational qualification, usually demonstrated by preparing a portfolio of evidence. Towards the end of their 'life' they were assessed partly by portfolio and partly by end test.

- *Minimum core* is what you are addressing, probably at Level 3, in your teacher training qualification. It covers language, literacy, numeracy and ICT. Included within the Minimum Core will be the assessment of personal skills and the ability to deliver functional skills to your learners.

- *Functional skills* introduced formally in 2012 to provide a development post-GCSE, to develop English, mathematics and ICT skills in context, i.e. at a functional level. Abbreviated to FS they are formally tested by a combination of internally marked and externally assessed examinations. Speaking and listening assessments are internally marked and the rest are externally set, with tests offered on-demand to Centres offering the qualifications. From the original ethos, the assessment methods have been amended and currently require that the delivery of FS is expected to be embedded in the core subjects and that the tests are neither embedded nor contextualised; they have a pass/fail outcome.

Functional English qualifications include reading, writing, speaking and listening. Functional mathematics qualifications include representing, analysing and interpreting mathematical information. Functional ICT qualifications include finding and selecting information, entering and developing information and developing presentations. Each level from Entry 1 through to Level 2 has progressively more complex tasks and details required to show competence. There are several sources of information on the worldwide web:

Useful resources and information

....

Resources and teaching information:
http://www.niace.org.uk/
http://www.bbc.co.uk/skillswise

http://www.basic-skills.co.uk/resourcecentre
http://www.learndirect-advice.co.uk/helpwithyourcareer/jobprofiles/

Standards and qualifications:
http://www.city-and-guilds.co.uk
http://www.ocr.org.uk
http://www.edexcel.org.uk

Information:
http://www.edexcel.com/quals/func-skills/Pages/default.aspx
http://store.aqa.org.uk/resourceZone/pdf/functional-skills/AQA-FSK-W-LEAFLET.
   PDF

Self-Assessment Tool:
http://www.move-on.org.uk/

Functional skills development of learners

Whatever the current name, and there will be others, it is bestowed upon the teacher to develop these skills in their learners at every opportunity. It cannot be assumed that learners leaving full-time compulsory education (school) have sufficient skills in English, maths and IT to achieve their qualification. The Government sets the target that a learner leaving school should have, amongst others, English and maths at Level 2 (GCSE grade A* to C), and school performance tables reflect their ability to meet these targets. Most post-compulsory providers undertake diagnostic tests with their learners during induction to confirm the level of competence of their new entrants. Functional skills are available at Entry1 to Level 2; they are mandatory in Apprenticeship frameworks.

Generally, a learner should achieve their Functional Skills at the same level as their main qualification. There will be variants to this to match curriculum specifications, for example, learners on Computer Programming courses may do ICT qualifications at a higher level or hairdressers may do English and maths to an equivalent level of their main qualification and ICT to one level lower. These variants will often be designed by whoever writes the course programme but may also be recommendations from the Awarding Organisation. Within any group of learners there will be those who have already attained the relevant level and those who have not. Whichever, best practice should determine the functional skills required to meet the job role and the results of diagnostic assessment will determine suitability and additional support needs.

Embedding functional skills into teaching and learning activities

Embedding skills means that functional skills are taught within the main subject topic in a seamless way. *Integrating* functional skills into your teaching means that you will set activities which meet the standards; they may or may not be in context. By incorporating functional skills into every activity they will become embedded. Embedded skills are always in context.

Every activity that occurs in a teaching and learning session has the potential to gather information which demonstrates a learner's ability against functional skills – the level of the functional skill will be determined by the complexity of the information. The following table demonstrates some examples of embedded functional skills.

A learner who is *listening to the teacher* at the beginning of a session is listening for and identifying relevant information

In a *question and answer session* the learner will be both listening and speaking, or if it is a written question sheet they will be reading and writing

By *designing a poster* for display in the classroom, in addition to the subject matter the learner will have to:

- calculate the overall size of the poster
- estimate the size of the smaller parts to be attached to the poster
- decide on the ratio and proportion of text, picture and white space
- present information in a visual format
- gather data from a variety of sources – the Internet, books, magazines or people, etc.
- write text (handwritten or word processed)

▶

- read data sources
- interpret and summarise information
- display images or pictures

A catering learner *baking a cake* will have to:

- read the recipe
- interpret the information into a time plan of work
- calculate the time the task will take
- estimate the size and number of bowls required
- measure the ingredients
- talk to the teacher or support worker for advice and listen to their reply
- talk to other learners, hopefully about the cake!
- solve problems relating to the planned activity

In *reading this* book, you are:

- understanding explanatory text
- inferring meaning
- using reading strategies – skimming, scanning or detailed reading
- summarising information

A *visit to a supermarket* will require the learners to:

- write a shopping list
- calculate the cost of two or more items
- compare the price/weight of similar items
- talk to shop assistants/cashiers
- follow basic instructions
- listen to total cost of shopping and give money
- calculate the amount of change needed

A group of learners, *investigating a topic* and *presenting their findings* to the group will:

- respond to extended questions on a range of topics
- speak clearly and confidently using informal and formal language
- design a presentation using IT software
- present information grammatically correct, in a logical order and proofread the work

- present information in graphical format
- contribute within the group, engage in discussion about findings, arguments and opinions
- summarise information from a number of sources

Functional skills are essential; they will help your learners to achieve and succeed in life. By embedding the functional skills into the curriculum both you and your learners can overcome the fear of English and maths, which may have been a barrier to earlier success in the subject. Sometimes giving something a different label, whilst confusing to the teacher, may side track the learner into success.

 ACTIVITY 1

Personal development

Stage One: Take an idea or learning plan to your organisation's Functional Skills Advisor, Teaching and Learning Mentor or your ITT tutor. Sit with them to map the functional skills that emerge from the activity. Ask questions like 'why' and 'how' and don't forget to ask 'how can I develop the activity to include ...' Deliver the session and note any unplanned functional skills that occurred.

Stage Two: Use a copy of or download the relevant functional skills standards from an Awarding Organisation and repeat the task in Stage One above on your own. Take the completed mapping exercise to your Functional Skills Advisor, Teaching and Learning Mentor or ITT Tutor and discuss it. Make any amendments and deliver the session. Note any unplanned functional skills that occurred.

1 Evaluate how many opportunities to embed functional skills there are in your session.

2 Did you set a functional skill learning outcome?

3 How might you modify the session to include more opportunities?

Identifying functional skill abilities of learners

In the post-compulsory sector, we are constantly faced with meeting people struggling with English, mathematics and ICT skills. The reasons behind these levels of ability are varied and subjective, but suffice to say, they are real and may inhibit our learners' abilities to achieve their potential.

People need functional skills for different reasons:

1 Those who need a quick update to get their skills to the required level

2 Those who need minimal support in functional literacy or numeracy

3 Those who need specific targeted help to develop their skills.

There is a fourth group who may need support and that is those whose first language is not English. In this group they may be literate and numerate in their mother tongue but not able to transfer those skills into a second language.

 ACTIVITY 2

Exploring functional skills

In the context of your subject, what functional skills do learners of that subject need in order to be proficient?

It may help to break those skills down:

Literacy:
Speaking
Listening
Writing
Reading.

Mathematics:
Numbers
Measurement and shape
Handling data

Information Communication Technology:
Equipment
Software – use, modify, present information
Save, retrieve, print
Mobile and communication technology.

You should think about the skills required to achieve technical or knowledge abilities AND skills to aid learning.

Identifying appropriate levels of functional skills

Screening The obvious thing to do as part of your enrolment or selection process is to check that your learners have the minimum requirements for entering your programme. For example: entry to an Extended Diploma might require five GCSEs at C or above (or equivalent). It is the 'equivalent' that usually causes problems, but the QCF (see Chapters 10 and 28), guides you to academic and vocational equivalents and a CV will help you decide about the skill levels of mature learners.

Initial assessment The next check is likely to be at induction. You can observe and/or interview your learners. You can look at set pieces of writing and ask questions to identify ability levels. Learners with poor functional skills, especially the more mature ones, are adept at disguising those skills. Some things that may alert you to problems are:

- 'I forgot my glasses, so I can't do it'.
- 'I'm in a rush, can I take it home and do it later?'
- Patchy completion of the enrolment or application form.
- Distracting conversations or behaviours.

Some strategies that help to reassure learners about why you need to do these initial assessments include:

- Talking about improving skills rather than poor skills.
- Raise self-esteem; motivate by looking at values and reasons.

- Explanations.
- Discussing outcomes and support.

Diagnostic assessment. The final method of checking ability is usually either a routine strategy of induction or a response if you suspect that there may be inadequacies in functional skills. There are a range of tests, both paper-based and online, to ascertain the level of ability. Some learners with poor functional skills benefit from computer-aided resources. It is highly likely that learners will have what is called a 'spiky profile'. This means that they are good at some aspects and weaker in others, causing them to be at different levels on the QCF.

Minimum core development of teachers

This section considers the ways in which you (the teacher) can develop your skills of literacy, language, number and information and communication technologies.

One of the first things that should be done as part of your qualification is to find out your current ability in the minimum core themes and then identify how you will develop them. This will probably be done by initially asking you to produce any previous certificates in the subjects, for example, GCSEs, O levels, A levels or adult literacy or numeracy tests. If you do not have such certificates, or can't find them, you may be asked to sit diagnostic assessments to confirm your level of competence. This information will then be transferred to your individual learning plan (ILP). Most providers of teacher training will specify the minimum level of competence required to enter their programmes. Generally, if you do not hold at least a Level 2 qualification in English or literacy, you will struggle to meet the requirements of the assessment of the programme and risk not being confident to teach or assess your learners. You should seek additional support should this be the case.

The minimum core is a set of competences, similar to those of the functional skills qualifications, designed specifically to complement teacher training. They were written by Lifelong Learning UK (LLUK), which became part of LSIS (until they were dissolved in March 2013). As a summary, the LLUK minimum core elements are:

Language and literacy:

● Personal, social and cultural factors influencing language and literacy learning and development.

● Explicit knowledge about language and the four skills: speaking, listening, reading and writing.

● Personal language skills.

Numeracy:

● Personal, social and cultural factors influencing numeracy learning and development.

● Explicit knowledge about numeracy communication and processes.

● Personal numeracy skills.

Information and communication technology (ICT):

● Personal, social and cultural factors influencing ICT learning and development.

● Explicit knowledge about ICT.

● Personal ICT skills.

NOTE: Teachers' qualifications (and the regulation thereof) are under review. This information is accurate at time of writing.

Each section of the minimum core requires you to have both the skills and understanding to develop the functional skills of your learners and your own personal functional skills. Currently, for the Award in Education and Training (AET) there is no requirement to evidence the minimum core, although you may find that it is at this point that your own skills are first analysed. In the L5 Diploma in Education and Training (DET) and in the L4 Certificate in Education and Training (CET), the focus is on the development of personal skills and some Units of Assessment require you to demonstrate how your literacy, language, number and ICT skills are used in the teaching setting. Your programme will include opportunities to develop and demonstrate improving skills either embedded into the programme, as part of your teaching experience, within a continuing professional development programme or as a stand-alone session.

The minimum core is initially assessed through **self-assessment** and action planning. This will be reviewed regularly through your course and targeted developments made. Teachers of literacy and numeracy are required to hold specialist Diplomas in Education and Training and should have Level 3 personal competence on entry to their Diploma course.

Developing literacy and language skills

In the same way that you may be developing your learners' functional skill needs, your own personal skills may benefit from a similar exercise. For the teacher these skills will be development from ideally Level 2 skills (at entry) to Level 3 skills (on exit). These skills are known as the *minimum core*. That means the standard of literacy, language, numeracy and ICT required of teachers. There is still much national development in this subject in so far as it will apply to teachers – are the skills embedded and evidenced through the role or is there a need for testing? It really is watch this space at the moment, but this section concentrates on developing skills as part of the role, rather than attempting to 'teach' Level 3 functional skills in literacy, language, numeracy and ICT.

Listed below are the standards of competence currently required of teachers. They will probably seem complex and confusing at first – it is normal to think that. Your tutor will guide you through the process by creating an individual learning plan to identify exactly what you need to do to develop the skills. This may vary according to the skills you possess as you start the programme and changes in policy and assessment of functional skills.

Source: Addressing literacy, language, numeracy and ICT needs in education and training: Defining the minimum core of teachers' knowledge, understanding and personal skills: A guide for initial teacher education programmes. July 2007 http://www.excellencegateway.org.uk/node/12019. Accessed February 2013.

Note: The coding system used within the standards below is unique to this publication and is used to link the suggested activities with the standards.

Some of the activities listed below are more effective when carried out under the supervision of a literacy, numeracy or ICT specialist. The standards used in the activities below are taken from the document referenced. The minimum core standards are subject to change.

The minimum core standards (literacy)

Part A   Knowledge and understanding

Personal, social and cultural factors influencing language and literacy learning and development:

- The different factors affecting the acquisition and development of language and literacy skills (LAK1).
- The importance of English language and literacy in enabling users to participate in public life, society and the modern economy (LAK2).
- Potential barriers that can hinder development of language skills (LAK3).
- The main learning disabilities and difficulties relating to language learning and skill development (LAK4).
- Multilingualism and the role of the first language in the acquisition of additional languages (LAK5).
- Issues that arise when learning another language or translating from one language to another (LAK6).
- Issues relating to varieties of English, including standard English, dialects and attitudes towards them (LAK7).
- The importance of context in language use and the influence of the communicative situation (LAK8).

Speaking

- Making appropriate choices in oral communication episodes (LAS1).
- Having a knowledge of fluency, accuracy and competence for ESOL learners (LAS2).
- Using spoken English effectively (LAS3).

Listening

- Listening effectively (LAL1).

Reading

- Interpreting written texts (LAR1).
- Knowledge of how textual features support reading (LAR2).
- Understanding the barriers to accessing text (LAR3).

Writing

- Communicating the writing process (LAW1).
- Using genre to develop writing (LAW2).
- Developing spelling and punctuation skills (LAW3).

Part B   Personal language skills

Speaking

- Expressing yourself clearly, using communication techniques to help convey meaning and to enhance the delivery and accessibility of the message (LBS1).
- Showing the ability to use language, style and tone in ways that suit the intended audience, and to recognise their use by others (LBS2).
- Using appropriate techniques to reinforce oral communication, check how well the information is received and support the understanding of those listening (LBS3).
- Using non-verbal communication to assist in conveying meaning and receiving information, and recognising its use by others (LBS4).

Listening

- Listening attentively and responding sensitively to contributions made by others (LBL1).

Reading

- Find, and select from, a range of reference material and sources of information, including the Internet (LBR1).
- Use and reflect on a range of reading strategies to interpret texts and to locate information or meaning (LBR2).
- Identify and record the key information or messages contained within reading material using note-taking techniques (LBR3).

Writing

- Write fluently, accurately and legibly on a range of topics (LBW1).
- Select appropriate format and style of writing for different purposes and different readers (LBW2).
- Use spelling and punctuation accurately in order to make meaning clear (LBW3).
- Understand and use the conventions of grammar (the forms and structures of words, phrases, clauses, sentences and texts) consistently when producing written text (LBW4).

Some activities that will develop your knowledge, understanding and skills:

A case study

Identify an individual or group of individuals and identify their educational and cultural backgrounds, their barriers to learning and any specific learning need relating to literacy (LAK1, LAK2, LAK3, LAK4, LAK7). What are their aspirations and how does literacy form part of their development? (LAK2, LAK8).

The session

Conduct a typical session and map it to the minimum core.

Alternatively, observe a session and comment upon the speaking, listening, reading and writing activities of the teacher and learners (LBS1, LBS2, LBS3, LBS4, LBL1, LBR1, LBR2, LBR3, LBW1, LBW2, LBW3, LBW4).

Reference the objectives or outcomes of the session/s to Functional Skills standards (FS Entry/L1/L2).

This activity is also effective when the analysis is related to learning styles and teaching methods, thus (hopefully) demonstrating a balanced, inclusive style (e.g. visual, auditory, kinaesthetic; active/passive).

Understanding material

Analyse a hand-out, worksheet or assignment task in relation to the complexity of the language, the activities it requires (writing something or reading and comprehending, etc.), and reference it to national standards/core curricula (LAR1, LAR2, LAR3, LAW1, LAW2, LAW3).

Comprehension – research

Interview someone whose first language is not English and find out how they cope with learning and teaching in a second or foreign language. How has their language choice changed and are there external influences on language choice? (LAK2, LAK3, LAK5, LAK6, LAS1, LAS2, LAS3, LAL1, LBS1, LBS2, LBS3, LBS4, LBL1).

An alternative activity is to listen to about five minutes of a person speaking in a foreign language. Then discuss your feelings, and identify if you understood anything through expression or gesture (LAL1, LBL1, LBS4).

Another similar activity is to attempt to decode some text using a different alphabet system, shorthand or Wingdings font (LAR1, LAR2, LAR3, LAW1, LBR2).

Shadow drawing

Two people sit back to back. One person (A) has a simple picture; the other (B) has a blank sheet of paper and a pen. (A) gives instructions to (B) in the hope that (B) will replicate the picture. (B) is allowed to check the instructions, but may not look at the original picture (LBS1, LBS2, LBS3, LBL1).

This same exercise can be achieved using the board game Visionary.

Colour – action research

- Use a range of coloured transparencies/plastic wallets and place over the top of white hand-outs.
- Experiment with coloured pens on boards and overhead transparencies.

- Select a different colour when writing on the interactive board.
- Photocopy hand-outs onto different coloured paper.
- Print hand-outs using a different font colour.

Compare and contrast the clarity of the colours and decide which are more easily read. This strategy of colour clarity is particularly useful in supporting learners with dyslexia (LAK3, LAK4, LAR2, LAR3, LAW1, LAW2, LBR2). It will show that you are aware of barriers which impede language and literacy development.

Everyday activities

Most of the activities you engage in everyday will demonstrate your understanding of literacy and language (and in some cases numeracy) and how it could impact on learning. In writing reports your own skills of reading and writing will be developed, especially in terms of spelling, grammar and punctuation and paraphrasing. (LBW1, LBW2, LBW3, LBW4). When interviewing or speaking to learners to elicit the information, your own oral communication and listening skills are developed (LBS1, LBS2, LBS3, LBS4, LBL1).

Developing mathematical skills

The minimum core standards (numeracy)

Part A   Knowledge and understanding

Personal, social and cultural factors influencing numeracy learning and development:

- The different factors affecting the acquisition and development of numeracy skills (NAK1).
- The importance of numeracy in enabling users to participate in, and gain access to, society and the modern economy (NAK2).

- Potential barriers that can hinder development of numeracy skills (NAK3).
- The main learning difficulties and disabilities relating to numeracy skills learning and development (NAK4).
- The common misconceptions and confusions related to number-associated difficulties (NAK5).

Communication

- Making and using judgements about understanding (NAC1).
- Communication processes and understandings (NAC2).

Processes

- A knowledge of the capacity of numeracy skills to support problem-solving (NAP1).
- Making sense of situations and representing them (NAP2).
- Processing and analysis (NAP3).
- Using numeracy skills and content knowledge (NAP4).
- Interpreting and evaluating results (NAP5).
- Communicating and reflecting on findings (NAP6).

Part B   Personal numeracy skills

Communication

- Communicate with others about numeracy in an open and supportive manner (NBC1).
- Assess your own, and other people's, understanding (NBC2).
- Express yourself clearly and accurately (NBC3).
- Communicate about numeracy in a variety of ways that suit and support the intended audience, and recognise such use by others (NBC4).
- Use appropriate techniques to reinforce oral communication, check how well the information is received and support the understanding of those listening (NBC5).

Processes

- Use strategies to make sense of a situation requiring the application of numeracy (NBP1).

- Process and analyse data (NBP2).
- Use generic content knowledge and skills (NBP3).
- Make decisions concerning content knowledge and skills (NBP4).
- Understand the validity of different methods (NBP5).
- Consider accuracy, efficiency and effectiveness when solving problems and reflect on what has been learnt (NBP6).
- Make sense of data (NBP7).
- Select appropriate format and style for communicating findings (NBP8).

Whereas dyslexia is associated with a difficulty in interpreting words and symbols, dyscalculia is associated with difficulties in making sense of numbers and calculations. Some people just seem to panic when faced with maths, whereas others really enjoy working with numbers. Hence there seems to be emphasis in the numeracy standards on 'supporting' and 'sensitivity'.

A case study

Identify an individual or group of individuals and identify their educational and cultural backgrounds, their barriers to learning and any specific learning need relating to numeracy (NAK1, NAK2, NAK3, NAK4). What are their aspirations, and how does numeracy form part of their development? (NAK2, NAK5).

Data-related activities

Many of the things a teacher is required to do will relate to analysing numbers. How many passed their course (**achievement data/success rate**), how many stayed until the end (**retention**), what is the average pass mark etc. You need to learn how to follow these simple formulas and present your own statistics.

For example, look at the following register:

		Week number										
		1	2	3	4	5	6	7	8	9	10	%
A		/	/	/	/	/	0	0	/	/	/	80
B		/	/	0	0	0	/	/	0	0	0	40
C		/	0	/	/	/	/	/	/	/	/	90
D		/	/	0	/	0	/	0	0	0	0	40
E		0	0	/	/	/	/	0	/	/	/	70

A has attended 8 out of 10 sessions. To calculate the percentage: 8 ÷ 10 × 100. This will give you 80 per cent. The **formula** is always the number of sessions attended, divided by the number of sessions possible, multiplied by 100.

What else does this table tell you?

- The average attendance is 64 per cent.
- There were 60 per cent of learners who completed their course.
- E started late; did this impact on achievement?
- What happened in week 7?
- Is there a link between the absences of B and D?

Analyse the attendance at your sessions in number and percentage format.

What is the average (mean) attendance?

(NBP1, NBP2, NBP4, NBP7, NBP8)

Numeracy ice-breaker

Using five or six random numbers and the basic mathematical signs of add (+), minus (−), divide (÷) and multiply (×), make a given number. You do not have to use every number or sign, but may only use any number once. Give a time limit of 20–30 seconds.

For example:

4, 10, 3, 7, 8. Make 559.

(Based on *Countdown*, Channel 4).

(NBP2, NBP3)

Discussion about how you felt when presented with a calculation should conclude this activity. Did you understand the instructions? What is the link between communication and number?

(NAK3, NAK4, NAK5, NAC2, NBC1, NBC4, NBC5)

Answer: (7 × 8 = 56 × 10 = 560) (4 − 3 = 1). 560 − 1 = 559

Interpreting and evaluating results

Carry out a survey with your learners. Use a questionnaire that responds to questions in a quantitative way. For example, yes/no, strongly agree/agree/disagree/strongly disagree, true/false. Analyse the results and present the findings as 'x per cent of learners agreed that …' etc. What does the information tell you?

(NBP1, NBP2, NBP3, NBP5, NBP7, NBP8)

Minimum core numeracy – averages in assessment

You may be asked to prepare statistical information to record assessment, achievement or progress. You may wish to analyse the results of your own assessments for similar reasons. One way of doing this is to identify norms or standards, either to identify trends or compare data with other sets of data. To do this it is advantageous to present data in percentages or using averages. As part of your personal numeracy development, you need to be clear about the expressions mean, median, mode and range and how these can help you analyse results (see Chapter 17).

The *mean* is the average score; it is the easiest of the averages to calculate. It is done by totalling the scores and dividing by the number of learners.

Learner	Score
Jake	19
Sam	18
Phil	12
Sian	15
Sarah	17
Chloe	19
Adam	20
Rafiq	18
Mo	14

In this example:

The scores total 152 ÷ 9 = 16.8. This means that the average score is just under 17 out of 20. This can be represented as a percentage – the average score is 85 per cent.

The *median* is the exact middle of the data set. Using our example above, first you should write them in ascending or descending order:

12, 14, 15, 17, 18, 18, 19, 19, 20. The median is 18 because there are four figures below and four figures above the middle value.

The *mode* is the number that appears most often. In our example there are two modes: 18 and 19.

The *range* of scores is calculated by taking the lowest score from the highest score. In this example 20 is the highest score and the lowest is 12.

$20 - 12 = 8$. The range therefore is 8.

Developing skills in information communication technologies

The minimum core standards (information and communication technology – ICT)

Part A   Knowledge and understanding

Personal, social and cultural factors influencing ICT learning and development:

- The different factors affecting the acquisition and development of ICT skills (IAK1).
- The importance of ICT in enabling users to participate in, and gain access to, society and the modern economy (IAK2).
- Understanding the range of learners' technological and educational backgrounds (IAK3).
- The main learning disabilities and difficulties relating to ICT learning and skill development (IAK4).
- Potential barriers that inhibit ICT skills development (IAK5).

Communication

- Making and using decisions about understanding (IAC1).
- Communicating processes and understandings (IAC2).

Processes

- Purposeful use of ICT (IAP1).
- Essential characteristics of ICT (IAP2).
- How learners develop ICT skills (IAP3).

Part B   Personal ICT skills

Communication

- Communicate with others with/about ICT in an open and supportive manner (IBC1).
- Assess your own, and other people's, understanding (IBC2).
- Express yourself clearly and accurately (IBC3).
- Communicate about/with ICT in a variety of ways that suit and support the intended audience, and recognise such use by others (IBC4).
- Use appropriate techniques to reinforce oral communication, check how well the information is received and support the understanding of those listening (IBC5).

Processes

- Using ICT systems (IBP1).
- Finding, selecting and exchanging information (IBP2).
- Developing and presenting information (IBP3).

Technology is moving so quickly that it is sometimes difficult to keep up to date, both with equipment and skills. Teaching involves using technology to aid learning. Hand-outs are clearer when freshly printed. Interactive boards can save what you write on them and print off copies for learners. But have you ever 'lost the will to live' in front of a poorly delivered PowerPoint presentation? Using ICT needs to present a balanced approach and therefore every teacher needs to know and develop their skills in ICT.

A case study

Identify an individual or group of individuals and their educational and cultural backgrounds, barriers to learning and any specific learning need relating to ICT (IAK1, IAK2, IAK3, IAK4, IAK5). What are their aspirations and how does ICT form part of their development? (IAK1, IAK2).

The session

Conduct a typical session and map it to the minimum core.

Alternatively, observe a session and comment upon the ICT activities of the teacher and learners (IBC3, IBC4, IBC5, IBP1, IBP2, IBP3).

Group or individual activities or discussion points

List the ways that computers, the Internet and email influence our lives (IAK2).

List the resources that include technology (IAC2, IAP1, IAP2).

How comfortable are you with ICT? (IAK2, IAK5, IAC1, IAC2, IAP1, IAP3).

What is legal and what is not in terms of accessing and using material on the Internet? (IAK1, IBP1, IBP2).

Are learners disadvantaged in any way by the use of ICT? (IAK4, IAK5).

Self-assessment

Can you use: a word processing package, a presentation package, a spreadsheet application, a database package, a publishing package, an email application, a search engine?

For each would you consider that you are proficient, acceptable, OK with the basics, or nor very good?

Can you open, save, print and retrieve documents?

Do you know what all the icons mean and what shortcuts there are?

Do you understand terms like virus, spam, surfing, download, blogging? (IAC1, IBC2, IBP1, IBP2, IBP3)

Recording progress of the minimum core

It is important that you are able to demonstrate your progress against the minimum core standards. It is not sufficient that you 'think' the tutor has done this, so 'it must be covered'. Here are some suggestions about how you may record (sometimes called tracking, referencing or mapping) your progress.

Idea 1

Use this column to either write the standards in full or use a coding system as suggested above for each of the literacy, numeracy and ICT standards	Use this column to explain how you have met the standard
=XAMPL= Part B Personal language skills SPEAKING Expressing yourself clearly, using communication techniques to help convey meaning and to enhance the delivery and accessibility of the message (LBS1)	I communicate to my learners verbally, through hand-outs and through my PowerPoint presentations. I use body language to express my feelings and to interpret theirs. I communicate to my peers and managers using spoken and written formats, which include email. My sessions are structured to have a clear beginning, middle and ending and each session progresses from the previous; I use recap to show explicit progress. Whenever I can, I relate the subject to examples from my own experience and try to engage learners in discussions about their own experiences. I have used visual images in hand-outs and have created models to demonstrate the topic.

Idea 2

....

Standard	Task 1	Task 2	Task 3	Task 4	Task 5	Task 6	Task 7	Task 8	Etc.
	Each task should be described								
Write the standards or use a coding system	Use a ✓ show when done								
LAK1	✓	✓		✓					
LAK2	✓			✓					
LAK3		✓	✓	✓					
LAK4	✓		✓						
LAK5	✓		✓						
etc.									

Sources

....

1 *Addressing literacy, language, numeracy and ICT needs in education and training: defining the minimum core of teachers' knowledge, understanding and personal skills. A guide for teacher education programmes,* June 2007, The Sector Skills Council for Lifelong Learning.

2 *Addressing literacy, language, numeracy and ICT needs in education and training: defining the minimum core of teachers' knowledge, understanding and personal skills. A guide for teacher education*

programmes, July 2004, Lifelong Learning UK/Further Education National Training Organisation.

3 *Including language, literacy and numeracy learning in all post-16 education: Guidance on curriculum and methodology for generic initial teacher education programmes,* March 2004, Further Education National Training Organisation/National Research and Development Centre for Adult Literacy and Numeracy.

Glossary of terms

Achievement data the number of learners who achieved their qualification, usually expressed as a percentage of those who completed

Context the setting in which learning occurs

Diagnostic assessment assessment occurring early in the learner journey to establish starting points or identify capability or skill level, particularly in relation to functional skills

Dyscalculia associated with difficulties in making sense of numbers and calculations

Dyslexia associated with a difficulty in reading and interpreting words and symbols

Embedded fixed firmly in the vocational context

Formula a mathematical rule

Functional skills basic skills of literacy and numeracy

ICT information and communication technology

ILP individual learning plan

Language written or spoken communication

Literacy the ability to read and write

LLUK Lifelong Learning (UK) Sector Skills Council

Minimum core standards of competence in language, literacy, numeracy and ICT

Numeracy the ability to use numbers

Retention the number of learners who complete their programme

Self-assessment an organisation's ability to monitor and quality assure its provision

Success rate the number of learners who complete and achieve their qualification, usually expressed as a percentage of those who commenced

SUMMARY

In this chapter we set out to achieve the following outcomes:

- To raise awareness of functional skills and the minimum core in the education and training sector.
- To identify opportunities to deliver functional skills and competences in language, literacy, numeracy and information communication technologies (ICT).
- To develop competence in language, literacy, numeracy and information communication technologies (ICT).
- To identify opportunities to develop your skills and understanding of literacy, language, numeracy and ICT.
- To demonstrate your progress through referencing teaching and learning activities and your personal development to the standards.

Your personal development

You have considered the history of functional skills and the minimum core and can apply each in the relevant context, i.e., functional skills for learners' development and minimum core for your personal development.

You have reviewed opportunities to embed functional skills into your delivery and teaching settings. You have looked at the overview of the Minimum Core standards and matched some of the jobs you do as a teacher to those standards. You have also had an opportunity to complete some exercises which meet the standards.

Finally, you will have created a system of recording your progress towards completion of the standards and presented these to your mentor or tutor for assessment and guidance.

Assessment of the minimum core is through self-assessment. Many of the activities, essays, presentations and discussions you have done in sessions will demonstrate and provide opportunities to collect evidence of competence. The sessions you have with learners and conversations with peers and managers will also provide evidence.

Note:
The numbering/coding system used in this chapter is unique to this publication and therefore may not be widely recognised.

Appendix: Top tips for successful teaching observations

First of all, don't worry…

Observations are your opportunity to showcase your expertise, but it is not about the teaching … the focus is on the learning.

- Are *all* of your learners learning?
- Is the session participative, exciting and interesting?
- Have *all* the learners made progress?

Don't assume your observer will come in at the beginning and stay until the end.

1 Be prepared and keep your lesson plan to hand. Remember though, it is a plan not a script – and it is OK to amend. Have a copy for your observer.

2 Lay out your desk with the resources you will use in the class, it saves time fumbling around for that board pen later!

3 Sit the observer out of your eye line, but where they can see what is going on. Give your observer plenty to read; whilst they are reading they are not watching!

4 Slow down, take deep breaths and try to overcome your nerves.

5 Check learning and progress frequently during the session, especially before moving on to another topic.

6 If you are nervous, don't hold a piece of paper in front of you, it wobbles as you tremble. Ensure board work is tidy and doesn't show a trembling hand.

7 Don't hide behind the desk, move around the room to check what's going on; remove the barrier. Be aware of what is going on in the room.

8 Have lots of activities that engage all of your learners: group work, gapped hand-outs, questioning, discussion groups and practical activities. The observer is looking for active learners who are developing their independence.

9 Welcome learners calmly into the room and seat according to your seating plan. Start the lesson promptly; have a starter activity to settle the group, focus the mind and introduce the topic whilst you take the register.

10 End the lesson with a means of assessing learning – quiz or nominated questions. Praise achievement of session outcomes and finally, indicate the connection to or preparation for the next lesson.

Theorists

NAME	TOPIC	RESEARCH
Argyris	Reflection	Action theories
Ausubel	Learning	Cognitivism, discovery learning
Bain	Reflection	Levels of reflection
Bandura	Motivation	Neo-behaviourism, self-efficacy
Belbin	Teaching	Group roles
Berlo	Communication	SMCR model
Berne	Communication	Transactional analysis
Biggs	Curriculum	Deep and surface learning
Black and Wiliam	Assessment	Assessment for learning

NAME	TOPIC	RESEARCH
Bloom	Curriculum	Taxonomy of learning
Boud	Curriculum	Process (problem solving) model
	Reflection	Reflective practice
Brewer	Learning	Cognitivism, conditioning & co-operation
Brookfield	Reflection	Critical Lenses
Brown	Assessment	Personal portfolios
Bruner	Curriculum	Process (problem solving) model
	Learning	Cognitivism, three stages of cognition, spirals
Coffield	Learning	Learning styles (alternative view)
Cooper	Learning	VAK learning preferences
Davis	Curriculum	Product/objectives model, verb use
DeBono	Teaching	Six thinking hats
Deming	Quality	Control processes
Dewey	Learning	Cognitivism, thinking and understanding leads to reflection
Eisner	Curriculum	Process/expressive model, personalisation
Freud	Learning	Behaviourism, group interaction, intuitive behaviours
Gagné	Learning	five levels of learning
Gardner	Learning	Multiple Intelligences

▶

NAME	TOPIC	RESEARCH
Goleman	Learning	Humanism, emotional intelligence
Grundy	Curriculum	Process/situational model
Hannaford	Learning	Cognitivism, brain gym concepts
Hattie	Assessment	Feedback
Herzberg	Motivation	Satisfaction theory
Hirst	Curriculum	Product/content model
Honey & Mumford	Learning	Learning preferences
Juran	Quality	Problem/cause analysis
Kennedy	Learning	Widening participation
Knowles	Teaching	Andragogy
Koffka	Learning	Gestaltism
Köhler	Learning	Gestaltism
Kolb	Learning	Learning cycle
Laird	Learning	Sensory learning
Lasswell	Communication	Linear transmission types
Lawton	Curriculum	Process/situational model
Lewin	Teaching	Group dynamics
Maslow	Motivation	Humanism, hierarchy of needs
McClelland	Motivation	Solution focussed learning

NAME	TOPIC	RESEARCH
McGregor	Motivation	Theory X and Theory Y
McLaughlin	Learning	Readability formula (SMOG)
Osgood & Schramm	Communication	Circular types
Pavlov	Learning	Behaviourism, classical conditioning
Petty	Motivation	Vicious and virtuous cycles
Piaget	Learning	Cognitivism, learning development (in children)
Race	Reflection	Ripples
Rogers	Learning	Humanism, experiential learning
Schön	Reflection	Reflective practice
Shannon & Weaver	Communication	Linear transmission types
Shewhart	Quality	Cycle of learning & improvement
Skilbeck	Curriculum	Process/situational model
Skinner	Learning	Neo-behaviourism, operant conditioning
Smith	Learning	Accelerated learning
Socrates	Teaching	Questioning style
Sperry	Learning	Cognitivism, split brain concepts
Stenhouse	Curriculum	Process model, learner responsive

NAME	TOPIC	RESEARCH
Thorndike	Learning	Behaviourism, law of effect
Tolman	Learning	Cognitivism, situational response
Tuckman	Teaching	Team development
Turner	Motivation	Praise and reward
Tyler	Curriculum	Product/objectives model, goal based
Watson	Learning	Behaviourism, trial and error in conditioning
Wertheimer	Learning	Gestaltism
Wessely	Reflection	Teaching squares
West-Burham	Curriculum	Profound learning
Weyers	Curriculum	Active learning

Abbreviations

AAIA	Association for Achievement and Improvement through Assessment
ACL	Adult and Community Learning
ADHD	Attention Deficit Hyperactivity Disorder
AI	Awarding Institution
ALI	Adult Learning Inspectorate
AO	Awarding Organisation
APEL	Accreditation of Prior Experiential Learning
APL	Accreditation of Prior Learning
ARG	Assessment Reform Group
ATLS	Associate Teacher Learning and Skills
AVCE	Advanced Vocational Certificate in Education
BIS	[Dept. for] Business, Innovation and Skills
BSA	Basic Skills Agency
BSL	Basic Sign Language
BTEC	Business and Technology Education Council
CADET©	Consistent, Accessible, Detailed, Earned, Transparent
CATS	Credit Accumulation and Transfer Scheme
CPD	Continuing Professional Development
CPPD	Continuing Personal and Professional Development
CTLLS	Certificate in Teaching in the Lifelong Learning Sector
CV	*curriculum vitae*
DCS	Direct Claims Status
DCSF	Department for Children, Schools and Families
DfES	Department for Education and Skills
DIUS	Department for Innovation, Universities and Skills

DTLLS	Diploma to Teach in the Lifelong Learning Sector
EFL	English as a Foreign Language
EM	External Moderator
EMA	Educational Maintenance Allowance
EQA	External Quality Assurer/Assurance
ESOL	English for Speakers of Other Languages
EV	External Verifier
F4E	Framework for Excellence
FE	Further Education
FHEQ	Framework for Higher Education Qualifications
FEnto	Further Education National Training Organisation
GCSE	General Certificate in Secondary Education
GFE	General Further Education
GLH	Guided Learning Hours
GNVQ	General National Vocational Qualifications
HE	Higher Education
HEI	Higher Education Institution
HND	Higher National Diploma
HR	Human Resources
IA	Initial Assessment
ICT	Information and Communication Technology
IfL	Institute for Learning
ILP	Individual Learning Plan
ILT	Information Learning Technology
IM	Internal Moderator
IQA	Internal Quality Assurer/Assurance
IT	Information Technology
ITE	Initial Teacher Education
ITT	Initial Teacher/trainer Training
IV	Internal Verification
iWB	Interactive White Board
JCQ	Joint Council for Qualifications

LCD	Liquid Crystal Display
LLUK	Lifelong Learning UK
LP	Learning/lesson Plan
LSC	Learning and Skills Council
LSIS	Learning and Skills Improvement Service
MCQ	Multiple Choice Questions
MIS	Management Information System
MTG	Minimum Target Grade
NCFE	Northern Council for Further Education
NOS	National Occupational Standards
NQF	National Qualifications Framework
NQT	Newly Qualified Teacher
NVQ	National Vocational Qualifications
OCN	Open Colleges Network
OTL	Observations of Teaching and Learning
PAT	Portable Appliance Testing
PDR (APR)	Performance Development Review; Annual Performance Review
PEST	Political, Economic, Social and Technological
PICA	Plan, Implement, Check, Act
PTLLS	[Award in] Preparing to Teach in the Lifelong Learning Sector
Q&A	Question and Answer
QA	Quality Assurance
QCA	Qualifications and Curriculum Authority
QCF	Qualification and Credit Framework
QTLS	Qualified Teacher Learning and Skills
RPL	Recognition of Prior Learning
SAR	Self-Assessment Report
SEN	Special Educational Needs
SENDA	Special Educational Needs and Disabilities Act (2001)
SMOG	Simple Measure of Gobbledegook

SOW	Scheme Of Work
SSC	Sector Skills Council
SWOT	Strengths, Weaknesses, Opportunities, Threats
TQM	Total Quality Management
UoA	Units of Assessment
URL	Universal Resource Locator
VAK/VARK	Visual, Auditory (Read/Write) Kinaesthetic learning preference
VLE	Virtual Learning Environment
WBL	Work Based Learning
WBT	Work Based training
YTS	Youth Training Scheme

Glossary

A

Academic relating to education, school or scholarships

Academic Standards agreed level of educational competence

Accelerated learning short, deep learning sessions

Accurate correct in all aspects

Achievement meeting learning goals

Achievement Gap expression used to focus on the way different groups in society perform against each other, e.g. boys and girls

Achievement data the number of students who achieved their qualification, usually expressed as a percentage of those who completed

Acronym an abbreviation or series of initial letters which together make another word

Ad hoc random, unplanned action

ADHD attention deficit hyperactivity disorder

Affective domain concerned with emotions and values

Affective concerned with emotions and values

Aim a broad statement of intent

Analysis a detailed examination

Andragogy how adults learn

Annotate to add notes to something to add explanation or context

Anti-discriminatory actions taken to prevent discrimination

APEL/APL accreditation of previous experience and/or learning

APL accreditation of prior learning

App software programme for Mobile applications and Smart phones

Appeal a request to reconsider a judgement made

Apprenticeship a framework or course to learn trade skills

Approval permission to deliver qualifications on behalf of an Awarding Organisation

APR Annual Performance Review

Aspiring one's hopes and ambitions

Assessment the checking of learning and demonstrating competence

Attainment reaching the goal or qualification aim

Audit an official inspection by an independent person

Authenticity to establish who wrote/owns the subject

Authoritative a self-confident or assertive method of teaching

Autocratic a domineering approach to teaching

Autonomous learner one who requires minimal guidance from the teacher

Autonomy independence in the ability to learn

Awarding Organisation a body approved by Ofqual to create and certificate qualifications (AO)

B

Behaviour the way someone conducts themselves

Behaviourist a school of thought associated with responses to stimuli

Benchmark a standard or point of reference to compare performance

Bibliography a complete list of everything investigated during the research, in alphabetical order

Blended (learning) a mixture of traditional and modern/computer-based learning technologies

Body language using conscious or unconscious gesture to express feelings

Boundaries the limits of the field of expertise

Brainstorm method of producing ideas
BTEC Business and Technology Education Council; a qualification title part of Edexcel; an Awarding Organisation
Buddy a peer, working companion or learning ally
Buzz group activities small groups interact with the teacher to gather answers

C

C&G City and Guilds; an Awarding Organisation
CADET© consistent, accessible, detailed, earned, transparent–principles of assessment
CATS Credit Accumulation and Transfer Scheme
Certificate a recognised outcome of a programme of study
Chalk and talk teaching by traditional methods with focus on a chalkboard
Chronological in date order
Closed (questioning) limited response type of questions
Cloze an activity in which words or phrases are deleted
Coaching encouraging learners to develop through problem solving techniques
Code of conduct a set of standards governing professional values
Cognitive domain concerned with thinking skills
Cognitivist a school of thought associated with thinking processes
Collaborate to work jointly with other peers
Collaboration work effectively with others on an activity or project
Collaborative work jointly with other peers
Communication a means of sending and receiving information to share or exchange ideas
Competence the knowledge of or ability to do something
Compliance to meet or agree recognised rules and standards
Comprehension understanding of an idea or concept
Concept an idea

Confidentiality secrecy of information
Conflict a disagreement or argument
Consistency unchanging, evenly applied
Constructive a term used to imply helpful feedback
Constructivism a learner-centred model of learning
Context the setting in which learning occurs
Context/Contextual describing the setting to aid understanding
Contingency plan planning for the unexpected occurence
Cooperative working jointly to shared goals, helping each other to learn
Copyright legal ownership of text or images
Counsellor an advisor or guide specialising in personal, social or psychological matters
CPD continuing professional development
CPPD the abbreviation for continuing personal and professional development
Criterion (pl: criteria) a standard of competence
Critical analysis a detailed examination resulting in an opinion or argument
Critical incidents events that have a significant effect
Critique detailed analysis
Cross reference linking evidence to more than one aspect of the qualification
Currency up to date, reflecting current practice
Curricula plural of curriculum
Curriculum a programme or model of study

D

Data facts and statistics used for analysis
Deep learning learning which is memorised and fully understood
Demand led prioritised funding
Democratic a style of teaching based on negotiation and shared values
Demographic the structure of the population
Demography a study of population trends
Develop advance or improve ability
Diagnostic assessment assessment occurring early in the learner journey to

establish starting points or identify capability or skill level, particularly in relation to functional skills

Didactic a style of teaching in which teacher projects morals or values

Differentiation catering for the needs of all learners to reduce barriers to learning

Direct assessment evidence of the learner's work

Direct (feedback/communication) clear and unambiguous link

Direct Claims Status a high level of confidence from an AO, resulting in the ability to claim certification without a visit from an EQA (DCS)

Disaffected learners no longer satisfied with the learning environment

Discipline a branch of knowledge

Discovery learning finding things out through research, investigation and discussion

Disengaged uninvolved with learning

Dispute a difference in opinion in an outcome

Distractor incorrect answer choices in MCQs

Diversity valuing and celebrating the differences in people

Domain an area or section of learning; a classification

Download copy data from one system to another

Due diligence proactive investigation to help prevent future incidents occurring

Dynamics the understandings, sensitivities and interactions within the group

Dyscalculia associated with difficulties in making sense of numbers and calculations

Dyslexia associated with a difficulty in reading and interpreting words and symbols

E

E-assessment electronic versions of assessment

Effective to produce the intended or desired result or outcome

Efficient productive working without waste

Ego self-importance or personal identity

E-learning learning using electronic systems or equipment

Eligibility satisfying entry conditions (of organisation, qualification or funding partner)

Embedded fixed firmly in the vocational context

Employability in a position or suitable to be employed

Empowered given responsibility for something

Engagement connecting with learning; being busy

Enrichment activities added to the curriculum or course to make a better learning experience

Equality the state of being equal or the same

Equality of opportunity legislation and focus on gender, age, culture, etc.

ESOL English for speakers of other languages

Ethics the acceptable rules or behaviours of research

Evaluation to form an idea about something by measuring its effectiveness

Evidence the output of an assessment activity; evidence of a learner's knowledge, understanding, skills or competence that can be used to make a judgement of their achievement against agreed standards/criteria

Evolution a gradual development

Excellence a grade one indicator meaning to be exceptionally good at teaching

Experiential learning learning by trial and error

Extended question a question that involves a long answer

Extrinsic motivation motivation derived from the outside of the person

F

Facilitate supporting or stimulating learning

Facilitator one who supports or stimulates learning

Fail an assessment decision; not at pass standard

Feedback verbal or written comments about the assessment intended to bring about improvement

Font a type or style of lettering in a printed document

Formative continuous assessment

Formative assessment interim or on going assessment

Formula a mathematical rule

Functional skills basic skills of literacy and numeracy

G

Generic referring to the whole or fundamental

Gestaltist a school of thought associated with the whole learning process

GFE General Further Education

Gifted and talented highly skilled or adept

Goals an aim or desired result

Grade a level or degree of competence

Grading the degree of competence, pass, merit, distinction

Grading Grids tables to determine the level of achievement

Graduates people who have a degree

Group learning collaborative learning techniques

H

Hierarchy ranking according to status or authority

High order most thorough level of learning

HND Higher National Diploma

Holistic the big picture; the whole qualification or curriculum

Hub the centre

Humanist a school of thought associated with meeting all human needs

Hyperlink an electronic link between documents

Hypothesis a supposition or belief

I

Ice-breaker an activity used to introduce learners to each other

ICT information communication technology

Identify to determine or recognise something

Idiosyncrasies a particular way of behaving

IfL Institute for Learning

ILP individual learning plan

ILT information learning technology

IM Internal Moderator

Imaginative a grade one indicator meaning creative or resourceful

Impact an effect; an influence

Inclusion finding opportunities to integrate all learners

Inclusive not excluding any individual or group of learners (adj.)

Independence free from the influence of others

Independent autonomous, working without supervision or dependence on another person

Indirect assessment evidence or opinion from others

Indirect (feedback/communication) a link via a secondary method

Induction a formal introduction to a programme/role

Inhibit to hinder, prevent or limit

Initial assessment assessment occurring very early in the learner journey to establish potential, aspirations, suitability or existing level of learning/experience

Inspectorate e.g. Ofsted, Ofqual

Inspirational a grade one indicator meaning one who encourages learners

Instructor direct or commanding delivery of information

Integrated the learning is comprised of a number of different learning methods and styles

Integrity having values and principles

interact to have an effect on

Intervention an interruption

Interactive have an effect on, engage with

Internal Quality Assurance (IQA) validating the integrity of the assessment

Intranet internal computer-based communications network

Intrinsic motivation from within the person; natural desire

Intuitive instinctive; apparently natural behaviour

Invigilation supervision of examination candidates

Ipsative self-assessment against standards of competence

IQA Internal Quality Assurer/Assurance

IT information technology

IV Internal Verifier

iWB Interactive White Board

J

Jargon language, words or expressions of a specialist occupation

JCQ Joint Council for Qualifications

Jigsaw group activities small groups discuss different themes within a topic, which are collated by the teacher at the end of the activity

Job description a list of duties typical of the job role

Journal a diary

Judgement a decision about an assessment

Justified text even distribution of words across the page within fixed margins

Justify explain and prove something

K

Key the correct answer in a MCQ

L

Laissez-faire a non-interference model of teaching; learner-devised; a laid-back approach

Laminate cover with a protective, usually plastic surface

Laminated covered with a protective, usually plastic surface

Language written or spoken communication

Leading (questioning) a question (with an indicated answer contained within the question)

Learner-centred the learner dominates the learning environment

Learner Involvement customer service initiative about listening to learner's opinions

Learner voice term given to processes which gather feedback from learners

Learning to gain knowledge or a skill; what the learners do during a session

Learning environment general term for where learning occurs

Learning goals what a learner sets out to do

Learning needs things which will help a learner to achieve their goal

Learning outcome the result of a learning session

Learning plan a written structure for a session

Learning preferences and educational needs the individual's favoured way of learning

Level 3 a position within the NQF indicating the value of a qualification

Linear (in communication) a message following a direct line

Linear (in curriculum) single dimensional

Literacy the ability to read and write

LLUK Lifelong Learning (UK) Sector Skills Council

Low order a superficial level of learning

LP abbreviation for lesson or session plan

LSIS Learning and Skills Improvement service (disbanded July 2013)

M

Malpractice improper or negligent actions

Mastery comprehensive ability

MCQ multiple choice question

Mentoring supporting development by working with more experienced people

Mind map a visual representation of ideas

Minimum core standards of competence in language, literacy, numeracy and ICT

MIS management information systems, computer-based data storage software

Model a description or example to represent an idea

Moderation to check marks and grades awarded by the assessment team

Modular a curriculum or programme made up from several modules or units

Motivation enthusiasm or interest

MTG Minimum Target Grade

N

National Occupational Standards (NOS) nationally set guidelines defining the level, size and subjects used in designing UoA

Negative reinforcement feedback that inhibits practice and lessens motivation

Negotiating agreement and compromise towards outcome

Neo-behaviourist a school of thought which believes learners are driven by goals

NQF National Qualifications Framework

NQT newly qualified teacher

Numeracy the ability to use numbers

Nurture development of characteristics, beliefs or attitudes

NVQ National Vocational Qualification

O

Objective a specific statement of intended outcome

Objectivism a teacher-centred model of learning

Objectivity without bias

Offline not connected to a network, Internet or similar

Ofqual Regulatory body, Office of the qualifications and examiners regulator

On-programme a term to describe a period of learning

Open (questioning) question designed to elicit a detailed response

Outcome the consequence or impact of the learning and assessment strategies

P

Paraphrasing rewording something with different (own) words

Participation to take part in

Pass assessment decision relating to satisfactory performance

Passion a grade one indicator meaning a strong desire to teach

Passive learning in which the learners accept teaching with little or no active response

Pastoral concerned with the well-being of learners

Pathway a route. Usually describing the combination of units to achieve the learner's goal

PDR abbreviation for performance development review; appraisal

Pedagogy the skill or ability of teaching

Peer someone of the same status

Perceptions to be aware of something through the senses

Performance criteria standards of required competence

Performance Management interventions and monitoring to maintain high standards

Person specification a list of characteristics required in the job role

Personalise to create for the individual

PEST an analysis tool to identify political, economic, social and technological influences

Philosopher someone who studies theories, attitudes or beliefs

PICA an acronym for remembering the parts of the Quality Cycle: plan, implement, check, act.

Plagiarism the passing off of someone else's work as your own without reference

Plenary a conclusion, ending or summary of a period of learning

Policy course of action by an organisation; a statement of intent

Portfolio a storage tool, used either paper-based or electronically to collect evidence

Positive reinforcement feedback that enhances practice and improves motivation

Post-compulsory education after the age of 16, not mandatory

Potential the opportunity to develop or impact on future success

Praxis practical skills as opposed to theoretical skills

Principle a set of values or beliefs promoted by the teacher; a rule or moral code

Proactive creating rather than reacting to a situation

Procedure a way of working

Process curriculum focuses on the delivery of learning

Product curriculum focuses on the outcome of learning

Professional working as an expert within the sector

Profile how information about a thing or person is recorded

Profiling identifying characteristic traits or skills/knowledge against a set of standards

Programme of study a structured list of sessions

Psyche the human mind or spirit

Psychology the study of the human mind or behaviour

Psychomotor concerned with physical, practical and co-ordination skills

Psychomotor domain concerned with practical skills

Q

Quality Assurance (QA) an official system to establish the quality of something such as an assessment

Q&A abbreviation for question and answer

QCF Qualification and Credit Framework

Qualification a set of specifications (UoA) leading to an award, certificate or diploma of achievement, a skill that makes someone suitable for a job

Qualitative data relating to opinions or thoughts

Quality Assurance a system of review to confirm that processes are in place and applied to guarantee the quality of the service or product; systematic checks to provide confidence

Quality Control checks the integrity of the process

Quality Improvement a process to improve the reliability of quality systems

Quality Management a statement of policy/cultural values in relation to quality

Quantitative data relating to statistics and number

Questioning queries inviting responses

R

Rapport a common understanding

Rationale the reasons for an action

Reactive responding to a stimulus rather than controlling it

Recreational learning a skill for pleasure

Reference a list of material cited in the research essay, in alphabetical order

Referencing a source of information

Referral to send to a specialist

Reflection a considered opinion expressed in speech or writing; thoughts or considerations, developing ideas or thoughts

Reflective practice thoughtful practice to develop skills

REfLECT™ Trade mark software recording system from IfL

Registration an official list of entrants on a qualification

Regulation a rule or directive made by an official organisation

Reliability a strategy to ensure that assessment decisions are consistent

Reliability (in research) the consistency of the measurement. Qualitative data is less reliable than quantitative data

Research an investigation

Resources a teaching aid to support learning

Restricted response limited choices in answers

Retention the number of students who complete their programme

Revision to repeat the content in order to refresh understanding

Risk-based a strategy of sampling used to minimise the danger of inexperience

Robust strong approach, highly confident, reliable

Role a person's position within a function or organisation

Rote teaching by repetition, e.g. learning multiplication tables

RPL Recognition of Prior Learning

Rules of combination an Ofqual term referring to how Units of Assessment can be put together to make a qualification

Rules validity/relevance; reliability; authenticity; currency/recency; sufficiency; power of discrimination; objectivity (rules of assessment)

S

Sample a representative of the whole to show trends

Sampling the probability or non-probability of the data

Sanction a penalty for disobeying rules

SAR self-assessment report

Scheme of work a document listing sessions within a programme

Screen shot a visual image from a software program reproduced into a document to support understanding

Second (or third) marking a marking process in which work is marked by two or more people to confirm a standardised approach

Self-assessment (an individual) a method of confirming own ability

Self-assessment an organisation's ability to monitor and quality assure its provision

Self-directed under one's own control

Self-financing generating sufficient income to cover costs and profit margins

Self-regulation the ability to check own performance without asking others

Sensory learning learning which relies on the five senses

Session a period of learning

Shallow learning learning which is retained for a short period

SMARTER specific, measurable, achievable, relevant, time-bounded, ethical and reviewed

SMOG a readability test

Snowball (pyramid) group activities pairs discuss then form gradually larger groups to gain a consensus of opinion on a topic or subject

SOW abbreviation for scheme of work

Specialism a particular focus within the broader meaning of teaching

Spider diagram a visual form of note-taking to collect thoughts

Spiky profile mixed levels of learning within topic

SSC Sector Skills Council: responsible for writing Units of Assessment

Stakeholder a person, either directly or indirectly, associated or interested in the learner or organisation

Standards an agreed level of competence

Standardisation a process to confirm decisions and create norms

Starter activity a short activity at the start of sessions to set scene, create learning ethos and engage learners quickly

Statute a written law passed by a legislative body

Stem the term given to a question in a MCQ

Stimulus to initiate a reaction; to motivate

Stimulating a grade one indicator meaning to excite or motivate

Strategy a systematic process

Stretch and challenge a series of activities to maximise potential

Subjective decisions influenced by other factors

Success recognition of achievement

Success rate the number of students who complete and achieve their qualification, usually expressed as a percentage of those who commenced

Sufficiency to check that there is enough evidence to cover the criteria

Summative assessment final or summary assessment

Surface learning shallow understanding of topic

Sustainable able to be maintained over a period of time

SWOT an analysis tool to identify strengths, weaknesses, opportunities and threats; used to assess current practice

Syllabus the structure of a qualification

T

Target an objective or focused path towards a specified outcome

Taxonomy a classification

Teacher-centred the teacher dominates the learning environment

Teaching to impart knowledge or a skill; what the teacher does during a session

Theorist someone who creates an idea or explanation of something

Theory an explanation or proof of an idea

TQM Total Quality Management

Tracking a method of recording progress

Transferable something learned in one context used and applied to another

Transmission type in communication, a message passing from one to another

Transparency overt, clear in meaning

Transparent overt, clear in meaning

Triangulate measuring by different perspectives

Triangulation/Triangulated the validation of one set of data against other sets.

Tutorial a one-to-one session to support learning

Tutoring one-to-one coaching and support for assigned individuals

U

Underpin support or form the basis of

Units of Assessment (UoA) statements of knowledge and/or competence which describe the learning and assessment outcomes of a unit, clustered to make a qualification

Upload to transfer data to a larger computer or network

V

VAK/VARK visual, auditory (read/write) and kinaesthetic learning preferences – different ways learners like to learn

Valid (in research) measured accurately to elicit reliable outcomes

Validity a strategy to ensure that judgements are made against criteria

Value something which is important

Value-Added relates to activities that enhance learning and achievement

Variables the analysis or acceptance that not everything will fit in the box

Verbal exposition teacher-talk

Verification to check assessment processes are reliable

Vision mental image of the desired future

VLE (virtual learning environment) – a modern teaching and learning style using computer technologies

Vocational relating to learning the skills of an occupation

VRQ vocationally related qualifications

W

WBL (work-based learning) learning that takes place predominantly in the workplace

Weighting adjustment to take account of special factors which may distort if not considered

Workshop an area of learning to promote practical skill acquisition or group study

Reference and bibliography

Books and publications:

Anderson, G. (1990) *Fundamentals of educational research*, Basingstoke: Falmer Press.

Anderson, L. W. and Krathwohl, D. R. (eds.) (2001). *A Taxonomy for Learning, Teaching, and Assessing: A Revision of Bloom's Taxonomy of Educational Objectives*. New York: Longman.

Argyris, C. and Schön, D. (1974) *Theory in Practice: increasing professional effectiveness*, San Francisco: Jossey Bass.

Argyris, C. and Schön, D. (1978) *Organizational learning: A theory of action perspective*, Reading, Mass: Addison Wesley.

Armitage, A. *et al*. (2003) *Teaching and Training in Post-Compulsory Education*, 2nd ed. Maidenhead: Open University Press, McGraw Hill.

Assessment Reform Group (1999) *Assessment For Learning: Beyond the Black Box*, University of Cambridge, School of Education.

Bain, D., Ballantyne, R., Packer, J. and Mills, W. (1999) 'Understanding journal writing to enhance student teachers' reflectivity during field experience placements', *Teachers and Teaching; theory and practice*, Vol 5, No 1, pp. 23–32.

Balancing Assessment of and for learning. Enhancement Themes – various researchers summarised on: http://www.enhancementthemes.ac.uk/themes/IntegrativeAssessment/IABalancingFeedforwardAss.asp (accessed May 2011)

Bandura, A. (1994) *Self-efficacy* in V.S. Ramachaudran (ed) (1998) *Encyclopedia of human behaviour* (Vol 4, pp. 71–81) New York: Academic Press.

Basic Skills Agency (2006) *Identifying and meeting needs*, London: DfES.

Belbin, M. (1993) 'Team Roles at Work' in Meredith, M. and Belbin, R. (1993) *Management Teams: why they succeed or fail*, Oxford: Butterworth: Heinemann.

Bell, J. (2005) *Doing your Research Project: A guide for first-time researchers in education, health and social science*, 4th ed. Maidenhead: Open University Press.

Berne, E. (1964) *Games people play*, New York: Grove Press.

Biggs, J. (1987) *Student approaches to learning and studying*, Melbourne: Australian Council for Education Research.

Biggs, J. (1999) *Teaching for quality learning at University*, Buckingham: Society for Research into Higher Education and Open University Press.

Biggs, J.B. (2003) *Teaching for quality learning*, 3rd ed. Buckingham: Society for Research into Higher Education and Open University Press.

Black, P. and Wiliam, D. (1998) *Inside the Black Box*, London: Kings College.

Bloom, B.S. (ed.) (1956) *Taxonomy of Educational Objectives: Handbook 1, Cognitive Domain*, London: Longman.

Bloom, B.S. (ed.) (1964) *Taxonomy of Educational Objectives: Handbook 2, Affective Domain*, London: Longman.

Boud, D. (1995) *Enhancing Learning Through Self-Assessment*, London: Kogan Page.

Boud, D. and Feletti, G. (eds.) (1991) *The Challenge of Problem-Based Learning*, London: Kogan Page.

Brewer, J. D. (2000) *Ethnography*, Buckingham: Open University Press.

Brookfield, S. (ed.) (1985) *Self-Directed Learning. From theory to practice*, San

Francisco: Jossey-Bass. http:// www
.infed.org/biblio/b-selfdr.htm.

Brown, R. A. (1992) *Portfolio development
and profiling for nurses*. Quay
Publishing Ltd, Lancaster.

Bruner, J. (1996) *The Culture of Education*,
Cambridge, MA: Harvard University
Press. http://tip.psychology.org/bruner
.html.

Budge, D. 'Tasting the Assessment Soup',
Times Educational Supplement,
18 February 2005.

Butcher, C., Davies, C. and Highton, M.
(2006) *Designing Learning: from module
outline to effective teaching*, Abingdon:
Routledge.

Child, D. (2004) *Psychology and the
teacher*, 7th ed. London: Continuum.

City and Guilds (2009) Level 2 Diploma in
Professional Food and Beverage
Service, 7103-02, Qualification
handbook, 500/7478/7. November
2009.

Coffield, F. (2008) *Just suppose teaching
and learning became the first priority*,
London: LSN.

Coffield, F., Moseley, D., Hall, E. and
Ecclestone, K. (2004) *Learning styles
and pedagogy in post-16 learning: a
systematic and critical review*, London:
LSRC.

Cohen, L., Manion. L. and Morrison, K.
(2000) *Research Methods in Education*,
5th ed. Abingdon: Routledge Falmer.

Cohen, L., Manion. L. and Morrison. K.
(2004) *A guide to Teaching Practice*,
Abingdon: Routledge.

Clutterbuck, D. and Hirst, S. (2003) *Talking
business: making communication work*,
Oxford: Butterworth Heinemann.

Cooper, R. (1996) 'Identifying real
differences in thinking and learning
styles', *National Journal of Vocational
Assessment: Assessment Matters*,
Issue 2, Spring: pp 3–5.

Cowley, S. (2003) *Getting the Buggers to
Behave*, 2nd ed. London: Continuum.

Curzon, L.B. (2004) *Teaching in Further
Education*, 6th ed. London: Continuum.

Dave, R.H. (1970) in Armstrong R. J. et al
(1975) *Developing and Writing
Behavioural Objectives*, Tuscon,

Arizona: Educational Innovators Press.
First reference at a Berlin conference in
1967.

Davies, I. K. (1976) *Objectives in
Curriculum Design*, New York: McGraw
Hill.

Davies, L. (2006) *Towards a new
professionalism in the further education
sector*, CPD Update, London: IfL.

Deming, W. (1996) *Out of the Crisis:
Quality, productivity and competitive
position*, Cambridge: Cambridge
University Press.

Denscombe, M. (2002) *Ground Rules for
Good Research*, Buckingham: Open
University Press.

Department for Education and
Employment (1999) *A Fresh Start –
Improving Literacy and Numeracy (The
Report of the working group chaired by
Sir Claus Moser)* London: DfEE.

Department for Education and Skills (2001)
*Adult Literacy: Core Curriculum
including spoken communication*,
London: DfES.

Department for Education and Skills (2001)
Adult Numeracy: Core Curriculum,
London: DfES.

Department for Education and Skills (2005)
*14–19 Education and Skills, (A response
to the Tomlinson Report, 2004)*, London:
DfES.

Devany, A. (2007) *Equality and Diversity*,
(unpublished) St George's Centre,
Birmingham.

Dewey, J. (1916) *Democracy and
Education*, New York: Macmillan.

Dewey, J. (1933) *How We Think. A
restatement of the relation of reflective
thinking to the educative process*
(Revised edn.), Boston: D. C. Heath.
http://www.infed.org/thinkers/
et-dewey.htm.

Dewey, J. (1938) *Experience and
Education*, London: Collier Macmillan
Publishers.

E-assessment: http://www.jiscinfonet.ac.
uk/InfoKits/effective-use-of-VLEs
/e-assessment

Ecclestone, K. (1996) *How to assess the
Vocational Curriculum*, London: Kogan
Page in Gray, D., C. Griffin and T. Nasta

(2005) *Training to Teach in Further and Adult Education*, 2nd ed. Cheltenham: Stanley Thornes.

Egan, J. (2002) *Accelerating Change*, Department for Trade and Industry.

Eisner, Elliot, W. (1985) *The art of educational evaluation: a personal view*, London: Falmer Press. http:// www .infed.org/thinkers/eisner.htm.

Fautley, M. and Savage, J. (2008) *Assessment for Learning and Teaching in Secondary Schools*. Exeter: Learning Matters.

Fawbert, F. (2003) *Teaching in Post-Compulsory Education: Learning, Skills and Standards*, London: Continuum.

Ento, F. (2004) *Including Language, literacy and Numeracy Learning in all Post-16 Education. Guidance on curriculum and methodology for generic initial teacher education programmes.* March 2004, Further Education National Training Organisation/National Research and Development Centre for adult literacy and numeracy.

Further Education Funding Council (1996) *Learning Works: The Kennedy Report*, Helena Kennedy QC.

Gagné, R.M. (1985) *The conditions of learning*, 4th ed. New York: Holt, Reinhart and Winston.

Gannon, A. (2012) *Great Teaching and Learning*. London: 157 Group.

Gardener, J. (ed) (2006) *Assessment and Learning*. London: Sage.

Gardner, H. (1983) *Frames of Mind, the theory of multiple intelligences*, New York: Basic Books.

Glaser, B. and Strauss, A. (1967) *The discovery of grounded theory*, Chicago: Aldine.

Gravells, A. (2009) *Principles and practice of Assessment in the Lifelong Learning Sector.* Exeter: Learning Matters.

Gray, D., Griffin, C. and Nasta, T. (2005) *Training to Teach in Further and Adult Education*, 2nd ed. Cheltenham: Stanley Thornes.

Grundy, S. (1987) *Curriculum: product or praxis?*, Lewes: Falmer Press.

Hillier, Y. (2005) *Reflective teaching in Further and Adult Education*, 2nd ed. London: Continuum.

Hirst, Paul H. (1974) *Knowledge and the Curriculum*, London: Routledge.

Honey, P. and Mumford, A. (1982/1992) *The Manual of Learning Styles*, Maidenhead: Peter Honey Publications.

Hopkins, D. (2002) *A teacher's guide to Classroom research*, 3rd ed. Maidenhead: Open University Press.

Huddleston, P. and Unwin. L. (2002) *Teaching and learning in Further Education*, 2nd ed. Abingdon: Routledge Falmer.

Institute of Assessors and Verifiers – an organisation funded by member's subscriptions – to support assessors and quality assurance staff and promote the sharing of best practice.http://www .ivalimited.co.uk

Jacques, D. (2000) *Learning in Groups: a handbook for improving group work*. 3rd ed. London: Kogan Page.

Kandola, R.S. and Fullerton, J. (1994) *Managing the Mosaic: Diversity in Action (Developing Strategies)*, Chartered Institute of Personnel and Development.

Kelly, A. (1983) *The Curriculum, Theory and Practice*, 4th ed. London: Paul Chapman.

Knowles, M. (1984) *The Adult Learner:a neglected species*, 3rd ed. Houston, Texas: Gulf Publishing.

Kolb, D. (1984) *Experiential Learning: experience as a source of learning and development*, Englewood Cliffs, NJ: Prentice-Hall.

Kyriacou, C. (2007) *Essential Teaching Skills*, 3rd ed. Cheltenham: Nelson Thornes.

Laird, D., Holton, E. and Naquin, S. (2003) *Approaches to Training and Development*, 3rd ed. US: Perseus Books.

Lawton, D. (1983) *Curriculum Studies and Educational Planning*, London: Hodder and Stoughton.

Likert Scales: http://psychology.about .com/od/lindex/g/likert-scale.htm (accessed May 2011)

Lightbody, B. (2008) *Ofsted Grade One Reports*, Training Handout modified from *Outstanding Teaching and Learning* (with permission). Update, Issue 2, April 2005, Batley: College Net.

Lightbody, B. (2009) *Outstanding Teaching and Learning 14–19* West Yorkshire: College Net.

LLUK (2004) *Addressing literacy, language, numeracy and ICT needs in education and training: defining the minimum core of teachers' knowledge, understanding and personal skills. A guide for teacher education programmes*, July 2004, Lifelong Learning UK/FEnto.

LLUK (2006) *New overarching professional standards for teachers, tutors and trainers in the Lifelong Learning Sector*, November 2006, Lifelong Learning UK.

LLUK (2007) *Addressing literacy, language, numeracy and ICT needs in education and training: defining the minimum core of teachers' knowledge, understanding and personal skills. A guide for teacher education programmes*, June 2007, The Sector Skills Council for Lifelong Learning.

Maslow, A.H. (1970) *Motivation and Personality*, 2nd ed. New York: Harper and Row.

McClelland, D. (1988) *Human Motivation*, Cambridge: Cambridge University Press.

McGregor, D. (1960) *The Human Side of Enterprise*, Columbus, Ohio: McGraw Hill.

McQuail, D. and Windahl, S. (1993) *Communication models: for the study of mass communications*, 2nd ed. NJ: Prentice Hall.

Moon, J. (1999) *Learning Journals: a handbook for academics, students and professional development*, London: Kogan Page.

Neary, M. (2002) *Curriculum Studies in Post Compulsory and Adult Education: A teacher's and student teacher's study guide*, Cheltenham: Nelson Thornes.

Opie, C. (2004) *Doing Educational Research*. London: Sage.

Pearsall, J. (ed.) (2001) *Oxford English Dictionary*, 10th ed. Oxford: Oxford University Press.

Peter, L.J. (1969) *Why things go wrong*, London: Bantam Books.

Petty, G. (2004) *Teaching Today: A practical guide*, 3rd ed. Cheltenham: Nelson Thornes.

Race, P. (2000) *500 Tips on Group Learning*. London: Kogan Page.

Race, P. (2005) *Making learning happen*, London: Sage.

Reece, I. and Walker, S. (2006) *Teaching, training and learning: A practical guide*, 6th ed. Sunderland: Business Education Publishers.

Riding, R. and Raynor, S. (1998) *Cognitive styles and Learning strategies: Understanding style differences in learning and behaviour*, London: David Fulton Publishers.

Rogers, A. (2002) *Teaching Adults*, 3rd ed. Maidenhead: Open University Press, McGraw-Hill Education.

Rogers, C. (1969) *Freedom to Learn*, Columbus, Ohio: Merrill.

Schön, D. (1983) *The Reflective Practitioner*, San Francisco: Jossey-Bass.

Shannon, C. and Weaver, W. (1949) *A mathematical theory of communication*, Urbana: University of Illinois Press.

Silberman, M. (1996) *Active Learning: 101 strategies to teach any subject*. Boston: Allyn and Bacon.

Skilbeck, M. and Reynolds, J. (1976) *Culture in the Classroom*, London: Open Books Publishing.

Skinner, B. (1984) *The Shame of American education*, American Psychologist, Issue 1984:11.

Smith, A. (1996) *Accelerated Learning in the Classroom*. Stafford, Network Educational Press.

Stenhouse, L. (1975) *An introduction to Curriculum Research and Development*, London: Heinemann.

Talbot, C. (2004) *Equality, Diversity and Inclusivity: Curriculum Matters*, Birmingham: Staff and Educational Development Association.

The Further Education Teachers' Continuing Professional Development and Registration (England) Regulations 2007 SI No, 2007/2116.

The Royal College of Speech and Language Therapists (2006), Communicating Quality 3, *RCSLT's guidance on best practice in service organization and provision*. London: The Royal College of Speech and Language Therapists.

Tuckman, Bruce W. (1965) 'Developmental sequence in small groups', *Psychological Bulletin*, 63, 384–399. Reprinted in *Group Facilitation: A Research and Applications Journal* - Number 3, Spring 2001. http://dennislearningcenter.osu.edu/references/GROUP%20DEV%20ARTICLE.doc. Accessed20th January 2013

Tummons, J. (2007) *Becoming a professional Tutor in the Lifelong Learning Sector*, Exeter: Learning Matters (1).

Tummons, J. (2007) *Assessing in the Lifelong Learning Sector*, 2nd ed. Exeter: Learning Matters (2).

Turner, C.H. (1990) *Corporate Culture: From vicious to virtuous circles*, London: Random House Business Books.

Tyler, R.W. (1949) *Basic Principles of Curriculum and Instruction*, Chicago: University of Chicago Press.

Walklin, L. (2000) *Teaching and Learning in Further and Adult Education*, Cheltenham: Nelson Thornes.

Wallace, S. (2007) *Teaching, tutoring and training in the Lifelong Learning Sector*, 3rd ed. Exeter: Learning Matters Ltd.

Watkins, C. (2011) Managing classroom behaviour. 3rd ed. London: Association of Teachers and Lecturers http://www.new2teaching.org.uk/tzone/images/managing-classroom-behaviour-july-2011_tcm7-26264.pdf

West-Burnham, J. and Coates, M. (2005) *Personalized Learning*, Stafford: Network Educational Press.

Weyers, M. (2006) *Teaching the FE curriculum*, London: Continuum.

Wilson, L. (2008) *Practical Teaching: A guide to PTLLS and CTLLS*, London: Cengage Learning.

Wilson, L. (2012) *Practical Teaching: A guide to Assessment and Quality Assurance*, Andover: Cengage Learning.

Wragg, E. C. (2002) 'Interviewing', in M.Coleman and A. R. J.Briggs (eds.), *Research Methods in Educational Leadership and Management*, Paul Chapman Publishing, pp. 143–148.

Web sourced references:

Assessment Reform Group. http://arg.educ.cam.uk/publications.html (accessed 29 09 07).

Atherton, J.S. (2005) *Learning and teaching: reflection and reflective practice*, On-line UK: http://www.learningandteaching.info/learning/reflecti.htm (accessed 01 04 08).

Barriers to Learning, http://www.open.ac.uk/inclusiveteaching/pages/inclusive-teaching/barriers-to-learning.php (accessed 30 12 06).

Baume, D. (2006) *Towards a meta-framework for European standards for teaching in higher education*, www.nettle.soton.ac.uk:8082/framweworks (accessed 01 08 08).

Behaviourism, http://simplypsychology.pwp.blueyonder.co.uk/behaviourism.html (accessed 01 03 08).

Berne, E. *Transactional Analysis*, http://www.businessballs.com/transact.htm (accessed 12 05 07).

Bloom's Taxonomy, www.businessball.com/bloomstaxonomyoflearningdomains.htm (accessed 22 03 08).

Brookfield, S. (2007) *Becoming a critically reflective teacher*, stephenbrookfield.com (accessed 26 03 08).

Conner, M. (2007) *Learning from Experience: Ageless Learner*, http://agelesslearner.com (accessed 19 02 08).

CPD: Teaching in Scotland, *An overview of the cpd framework and requirements for teachers in Scotland* (2003) www.scotland.gov.uk/Resources/Doc/47021/0023973.pdf (accessed 26 03 08).

Craig, J. and Fieschi, C. (2007) *DIY Professionalism: futures for teaching*, www.nationalschool.gov.uk/policyhub/. General Teaching Council (accessed 01 08 08).

Curriculum Design, http://www.ssdd.bcu.ac.uk/crumpton/curriculum-design/curriculum-design.htm (accessed 14 06 08).

Department for Education and Skills (2006) *Reducing Re-Offending through skills and employment – next steps*, London: DFES, Home Office, Department for Works and Pensions, http://www.dfes. gov.uk/publications/ offenderlearning/ (accessed 14 06 08).

Gannon, A. (2012) *Great Teaching and Learning: A report on the innovative conference involving managers, teachers and learners from across the diversity of further education and skills*, May 2012, ref 157G-105.London: Institute for Learning/157 Group (accessed 01 02 13).

Gillard, D. (2007) *Education in England: a brief history*, www.dg.dial.pipex. com/ history/ (accessed 04 07 08).

Guidelines on the procedure of Professional Review and Development for Teachers in Scotland (2004), www.scotland.gov.uk/ Resource/Doc/ 26487/0023803.pdf (accessed 26 03 08).

Hattie, J. (1999, 2003) http://www. education.auckland.ac.nz/uoa/fms/ default/education/staff/ Prof.%20John% 20Hattie/Documents/Presentations/ influences/Influences_on_student_ learning.pdf (accessed 01 02 13).

Inclusive Learning, http://www.open.ac .uk/inclusiveteaching/pages/inclusive-teaching/learning-environment.php (accessed 12 05 07).

Lasswell, H. (1976) *Power and Personality*, www.cultsock.ndirect.co.uk (accessed 08 03 08).

Lawrence, E., Heasman, H. and Smith, P. (circa 1995) *Equal Opportunities and the Curriculum*, Natfhe http://www.ucu. org.uk/media/pdf/s/4/EqualOpp Curriculum_1.pdf (accessed 20 07 08).

Learning Theories, http://tip.psychology. org/ (accessed 01 03 08).

McGregor D., www.businessballs.com/ mcgregor.htm, information about McGregor's Theory X and Theory Y motivation (accessed 08 03 08).

NATFHE, A guide to Language, http:// www.ucu.org.uk/media/docs/3/0/ eqlang_1.doc (accessed 20 07 08).

Ofsted, www.ofsted.gov.uk The handbook for the inspection of further education and skills. September 2012, reference no: 120061 (accessed Sept 2012).

QCA (2004) Levels of Competence, http:// www.qca.org.uk/14-19/qualifications/ index_nvqs.htm (accessed 20 07 08).

Qualifications and Initial Teacher Training, www.lifelonglearninguk.org (accessed 12 09 07).

Resources for FE from Lightbody, B., College Net Training. www.collegenet. co.uk (accessed 25 04 08, with permission).

Scottish Funding Council (2006) *Overcoming barriers; enabling learning. Planning, designing and delivering the full time FE curriculum in Scotland's Colleges,* HM Inspectors for Education and Scottish Funding Council (October 2006) http://www.sfc.ac.uk (accessed on 12 05 07).

Smith, M.K. (1996, 2000) *Curriculum theory and practice,* The encyclopedia of informal education, www.infed.org/ biblio/b-curric.htm (accessed 01 02 13).

Smith, M.K. (2002) *Jerome S Bruner and the process of education,* The encyclopaedia of informal education, http://www.infed.org/thinkers/bruner. htm (accessed 12 06 08).

SMOG McLaughlin, G.H. (1969) Readability Formula, www.readabilityformulas.com.

Staff Individualised Record (2005) www .lluk.ac.uk (accessed 14 04 08).

UCU and Equal Opportunities, http:// www .ucu.org.uk/media/pdf/s/4/EqualOpp Curriculum_1.pdf (accessed 10 06 08).

Quality agencies and systems:

www.dti.gov.uk/quality/tqm
www.qaa.ac.uk
www.qia.org.uk
www.centreforexcellence.org.uk
www.ofsted.gov.uk
www.estyn.gov.uk
www.hmie.gov.uk
www.deni.gov.uk
http://www.iso.org
http://www.ofsted.gov.uk/publications/2434
www.lsc.org.uk
http://ffe.lsc.gov.uk
http://www.investorsinpeople.co.uk

http://www.matrixstandard.com

www.ces-vol.org.uk

www.cabinetoffice.gov.uk

www.cbi.org.uk.

http://www.qcda.gov.uk/qualifications/60
.aspx (accessed Sep 2010)

http://www.paa-uk.org/Qualifications/
Regulated/Qualifications/QCF%20
Info/QCF%20 Support%20Pack/Rules
%20of%20Combination%20in%20
the%20QCF.pdf (accessed March
2011)

http://www.cilt.org.uk/home/research_and
_statistics/statistics/languages_in_the_
population/annual_school_census.aspx
(accessed March 2011)

www.homeoffice.gov.uk/crime/vetting-
barring-scheme/ (accessed March 2011)

http://www.hse.gov.uk/risk/fivesteps.htm
(accessed April 2011)

http://www.hse.gov.uk/pubns/indg36.pdf
(accessed April 2011)

http://www.equalities.gov.uk/
equality_act_2010.aspx and http://www.
smarta.com/advice/legal/employment-
law/the-equality-act-(october-1-2010)-
need-to-know-for-small-businesses?
gclid=CP7h7sy P76cCFcoa4Qod
Yhknaw

http://www.iebe.org.uk/index.php/code-of-
conduct-for-assessors

Index